ON ROMAN TIME

The Transformation of the Classical Heritage

Peter Brown, General Editor

MICHELE RENEE SALZMAN

ON ROMAN TIME
THE CODEX-CALENDAR OF 354 AND THE RHYTHMS OF URBAN LIFE IN LATE ANTIQUITY

UNIVERSITY OF CALIFORNIA PRESS
Berkeley • Los Angeles • Oxford

The publisher acknowledges
with gratitude the generous support
given this book from the

Art Book Fund

of the Associates of the
University of California Press,
which is supported by a major gift
from The Ahmanson Foundation

University of California Press
Berkeley and Los Angeles, California

University of California Press, Ltd.
Oxford, England

Library of Congress Cataloging-in-Publication Data

Salzman, Michele Renee.
  On Roman time.

  (The Transformation of the classical heritage ;
17)
  Includes index.
  1. Calendar, Roman.   2. Rome—Social life and
customs.   3. Rome—Religious life and customs.
I. Title. II. Series.
CE46.S25 1990 529'.3'0937   89–5116
ISBN 0–520–06566–2 (alk. paper)

Printed in the United States of America

1 2 3 4 5 6 7 8 9

The paper used in this publication meets the minimum requirements of
American National Standard for Information Sciences—Permanence of
Paper for Printed Library Materials, ANSI Z39.48–1984. ∞

TO MY PARENTS

CONTENTS

LIST OF ILLUSTRATIONS

following pages 26 and 73

LIST OF ABBREVIATIONS

PERIODICALS AND COLLECTIONS

AC	*L'antiquité classique*
AE	*L'année épigraphique*
AJA	*American Journal of Archaeology*
AJP	*American Journal of Philology*
Anth. Lat.	*Anthologia Latina*, vols. 1.1 and 1.2, ed. A. Riese (Leipzig, 1894–1906); vols. 2.1, 2.2, and 2.3, ed. F. Buecheler and E. Lommatzsch (Leipzig, 1897–1926)
ANRW	*Aufstieg und Niedergang der römischen Welt*, ed. H. Temporini and W. Haase (Berlin, 1972–)
AP	*Anthologia Palatina*, vol. 8 in *Anthologie grecque*, ed. P. Waltz and G. Soury (Paris, 1974)
Arch. Cl.	*Archeologia Classica*
BC	*Bollettino della Commissione Archeologica Communale di Roma*
Cabrol and Leclercq, *DACL*	F. Cabrol and H. Leclercq, *Dictionnaire d'archéologie chrétienne et de liturgie* (Paris, 1903–1952)
CCCA	*Corpus Cultus Cybelae Attidisque*, ed. M. J. Vermaseren, 7 vols. (Leiden, 1977–1986) = *EPRO* 50
CCL	*Corpus Christianorum Series Latina*
CIG	*Corpus Inscriptionum Graecarum*
CIL	*Corpus Inscriptionum Latinarum*. *See* Mommsen, *CIL* 1863, 1893
CIMRM	*Corpus inscriptionum et monumentorum religionis Mithriacae*, ed. M. J. Vermaseren, 2 vols. (The Hague, 1956–1960)

CJ	*Codex Justinianus*
Cohen, *Méd.*	H. Cohen, *Médailles impériales*, 2d ed., 8 vols. (Paris, 1880–1892)
CP	*Classical Philology*
CQ	*Classical Quarterly*
CR	*Classical Review*
CRAI	*Comptes rendus de l'Académie des Inscriptions et Belles-Lettres*
CSEL	*Corpus Scriptorum Ecclesiasticorum Latinorum*
C.Th.	*Codex Theodosianus*, ed. T. Mommsen and E. Meyer (Berlin, 1905)
Dar.-Sagl.	Ch. Daremberg and E. Saglio, *Dictionnaire des antiquités grecques et romaines*, 6 vols. (Paris 1881–1889)
Diehl, *ILCV*	E. Diehl, *Inscriptiones Latinae Christianae Veteres*, 3 vols. (Berlin, 1925–1928); supplement 1947
EPRO	*Etudes préliminaires aux religions orientales dans l'Empire Romain*
FHG	*Fragmenta Historicorum Graecorum*, 4 vols., ed. C. Müller (Paris, 1841–1870)
HSCP	*Harvard Studies in Classical Philology*
HTR	*Harvard Theological Review*
ICUR	*Inscriptiones Christianae urbis Romae Septimo Saeculo antiquiores*, ed. G. B. De Rossi, 2 vols. (Rome, 1857–1861, 1886); supplement to vol. 1 by J. Gatti (1915)
ICUR, n.s.	A. Silvagni and A. Ferrua, *Inscriptiones Christianae urbis Romae*, n.s., 9 vols. to date (1922–1964)
IG	*Inscriptiones Graecae* (Berlin, 1873ff.)
IGR	*Inscriptiones Graecae ad Res Romanas Pertinentes*, ed. R. Cagnat, 4 vols. (Paris, 1911–1927)
ILS	*Inscriptiones Latinae Selectae*, ed. H. Dessau, 5 vols. (Berlin, 1892–1916)
JAC	*Jahrbuch für Antike und Christentum*
JRS	*Journal of Roman Studies*
Lewis and Short, *Lat. Dict.*	C. T. Lewis and C. Short, *A Latin Dictionary* (Oxford, [1879] 1975)
MAAR	*Memoirs of the American Academy in Rome*
MAL	*Memorie di Accademia dei Lincei*

MDAIR	*Mitteilungen des deutschen archäologischen Instituts. Römische Abteilung*
MEFR	*Mélanges d'archéologie et d'histoire de l'Ecole française de Rome*
Mem. Pont. Acc.	*Atti della Pontificia Accademia Romana di Archeologia. Memorie*
MGH	*Monumenta Germaniae Historica.* 15 vols. 1877–1919, repr. 1961. *See* Mommsen, *MGH* 1892
Mus. Helv.	*Museum Helveticum*
PBSR	*Papers of the British School at Rome*
PG	*Patrologia Graeca,* ed. J. P. Migne (Paris, 1857–1936)
PL	*Patrologia Latina,* ed. J. P. Migne (Paris, 1844–1900); supplement 1958–1974
Platner-Ashby, *Topo. Dict.*	S. B. Platner and T. Ashby, *A Topographical Dictionary of Ancient Rome,* 2d ed. (Rome, 1965)
PLRE 1	A. H. M. Jones, J. R. Martindale, and J. Morris, *The Prosopography of the Later Roman Empire,* vol. 1: A.D. 260–395 (Cambridge, 1971)
PLRE 2	J. Martindale, *The Prosopography of the Later Roman Empire,* vol. 2: A.D. 395–527 (Cambridge, 1980)
RA	*Revue archéologique*
RAC	*Reallexikon für Antike und Christentum*
RE	A. Pauly, G. Wissowa, and W. Kroll, *Real-Encyclopädie der klassischen Altertumswissenschaft,* 1893–
REA	*Revue des études anciennes*
REG	*Revue des études grecques*
REL	*Revue des études latines*
Rend. Pont. Accad.	*Rendiconti della Pontificia Accademia Romana de Archeologia,* 1921–
RIC	*The Roman Imperial Coinage,* vols. 1–7, 9, ed. H. Mattingly, E. A. Sydenham, C. H. V. Sutherland, and R. A. G. Carson (London, 1923–1967); vol. 8, ed. J. P. C. Kent (London, 1981)
Roscher, *Lex.*	W. H. Roscher, *Ausführliches Lexikon der griechischen und römischen Mythologie,* 6 vols. (Leipzig, 1884–1937)
SC	*Sources chrétiennes*
Schanz-Hosius, *GRL*	M. Schanz and C. Hosius, *Geschichte der römischen Literatur,* 4 vols. (Munich, 1927–1935)

H. A.   *Historia Augusta*

SIG   *Sylloge Inscriptionum Graecarum*, 3d ed., ed. G. Dittenberger, 4 vols. (Leipzig, 1915–1924)

SIRIS   *Sylloge inscriptionum religionis Isiacae et Sarapiacae*, ed. L. Vidman (Berlin, 1969)

TAPA   *Transactions of the American Philological Association*

TLL   *Thesaurus Linguae Latinae*

ZPE   *Zeitschrift für Papyrologie und Epigraphik*

FREQUENTLY CITED MAJOR WORKS

The following list sets out the major modern works that are cited regularly in an abbreviated form in this volume.

Akerström-Hougen 1974 = G. Akerström-Hougen, *The Calendar and Hunting Mosaics of the Villa of the Falconer in Argos*, Skrifter Utgivna av Svenska Institutet i Athen, vol. 23, pt. 4 (Stockholm, 1974)

Alföldi 1943 = A. Alföldi, *Die Kontorniaten: Ein verkanntes Propagandamittel der stadtrömischen heidnischen Aristokratie in ihrem Kampfe gegen das christliche Kaisertum* (Budapest, 1943)

Alföldi 1976 = A. Alföldi and E. Alföldi, with C. L. Clay, *Die Kontorniat-Medaillons*, part 1, catalogue, 2 vols. (Rome, 1976) [Deutsches Archäologisches Institut. Antike Münzen und geschnittene Steine, vol. 6, pt. 1]

Baehrens 1882 = E. Baehrens, *Poetae Latini Minores* (Leipzig, 1882)

Chastagnol 1960 = A. Chastagnol, *La préfecture urbaine à Rome sous le bas-empire* (Paris, 1960)

Courtney 1988 = E. Courtney, "The Roman Months in Art and Literature," *Museum Helveticum* 45 (1988): 33–57

Degrassi 1963 = A. Degrassi, *Inscriptiones Italiae*, vol. 13: *Fasti et elogia*, fasc. 2: *Fasti Anni Numani et Iuliani* (Rome, 1963)

Eastwood 1983 = B. S. Eastwood, "Origins and Contents of the Leiden Planetary Configuration (Ms. Voss. Q. 79, fol. 93v): An Artistic Astronomical Schema of the Early Middle Ages," *Viator* 14 (1983): 1–40

Ferrua 1939 = A. Ferrua, "Filocalo. L'amante della bella lettera," *La Civiltà cattolica* 1, quad. 2125 (1939): 35–47

Ferrua 1942 = A. Ferrua, *Epigrammata Damasiana* (Vatican City, Rome, 1942) [= Sussidi allo studio delle antichità cristiane, vol. 2]

Fink, Hoey, and Snyder 1940 = R. Fink, A.D. Hoey, and P. Snyder, "The Feriale Duranum," *Yale Classical Studies* 7 (1940): 1–222

Geffcken 1978 = J. Geffcken, *The Last Days of Greco-Roman Paganism*, trans. and with updated notes by S. MacCormack (Amsterdam, 1978); originally published as *Der Ausgang des griechisch-römischen Heidentums* (Heidelberg, [1920] 1929)

Latte 1960 = K. Latte, *Römische Religionsgeschichte* (Munich, 1960)

Levi 1941 = D. Levi, "The Allegories of the Months in Classical Art," *Art Bulletin* 23 (1941): 251–291

Magi 1972 = F. Magi, *Il calendario dipinto sotto Santa Maria Maggiore* (Rome, 1972) [= Atti della Pontificia Accademia Romana di Archeologia, Memorie 11.1]

Michels 1967 = A. K. Michels, *The Calendar of the Roman Republic* (Princeton, N.J., 1967)

Mommsen 1850a = T. Mommsen, "Über den Chronographen vom Jahre 354," *Abhandlungen der sächsischen Gesellschaft der Wissenschaften* 1 (1850): 549; cited pages refer to reprint in Mommsen, *Gesammelte Schriften*, vol. 7 (Berlin, 1909), pp. 536–579

Mommsen 1850b = T. Mommsen, "Epigraphische Analekten no. 8," *Berichte über die Verhandlungen der sächsischen Gesellschaft der Wissenschaften* 2 (1850): 62–72; cited pages refer to reprint in Mommsen, *Gesammelte Schriften*, vol. 8 (Berlin, 1913), pp. 14–24

Mommsen, *MGH* 1892 = T. Mommsen, "Chronographus Anni CCCLIIII," *Monumenta Germaniae Historica. Auctorum Antiquissimorum*, pt. 9: *Chronica Minora Saec. IV–VII*, vol. 1 ([Berlin, 1892]; Munich, 1981), pp. 13–148

Mommsen, *CIL* 1863 = T. Mommsen, *Corpus Inscriptionum Latinarum*, vol. 1 (Berlin, 1863)

Mommsen, *CIL* 1893 = T. Mommsen, *Corpus Inscriptionum Latinarum*, vol. 1, 2d ed. (Berlin, 1893)

Nordenfalk 1936 = C. O. Nordenfalk, "Der Kalendar vom Jahre 354 und die lateinische Buchmalerei des IV. Jahrhunderts," *Göteborgs Kungl. Vetenskap- och Viterhets-Samhaelles Handlingar*, fol. 5, ser. A, pt. 5, no. 2 (1936): 5–36

Nordh 1936 = A. Nordh, *Prologomena till den Romerska Regionskatalog* (Göteborg, 1936)

Nordh 1949 = A. Nordh, *Libellus de Regionibus Urbis Romae*, Skrifter Utgivna av Svenska Institutet i Rom, 2d ser. 8.0, vol. 3 (Göteborg, 1949)

Parrish 1984 = D. Parrish, *Season Mosaics of North Africa* (Rome, 1984)

Pietri 1976 = C. Pietri, *Roma Christiana. Recherches sur l'église de Rome, son organisation, sa politique et son idéologie de Miltiade à Sixte III (311–440)*, Bibliothèque des Ecoles françaises d'Athènes et de Rome, no. 224 (Rome, 1976)

Salzman 1981 = M. R. Salzman, "New Evidence for the Dating of the Calendar at Santa Maria Maggiore in Rome," *TAPA* 111 (1981): 215–227

Scullard 1981 = H. H. Scullard, *Festivals and Ceremonies of the Roman Republic* (Ithaca, N.Y., 1981)

Stern 1953 = H. Stern, *Le Calendrier de 354. Etude sur son texte et ses illustrations* (Paris, 1953)

Stern 1981 = H. Stern, "Les calendriers romains illustrés," *Aufstieg und Niedergang der römischen Welt* 2.12.2 (1981): 431–475

Strzygowski 1888 = J. Strzygowski, *Die Calenderbilder des Chronographen vom Jahre 354* (Berlin, 1888) [= Jahrbuch des kaiserlichen deutschen archäologischen Instituts, Ergänzungsheft I]

Valentini and Zucchetti I, 1940 = R. Valentini and G. Zucchetti, *Codice topographico della città di Roma*, vol. 1 (Rome, 1940)

Valentini and Zucchetti II, 1942 = R. Valentini and G. Zucchetti, *Codice topographico della città di Roma*, vol. 2 (Rome, 1942)

Webster 1938 = J. C. Webster, *The Labors of the Months in Antique and Mediaeval Art to the End of the Twelfth Century* (Princeton, N.J., 1938)

Wissowa 1912 = G. Wissowa, *Religion und Kultus der Römer*, 2d ed. (Munich, 1912)

PREFACE

By modern standards, Roman methods of counting time were extremely imprecise. Yet the Romans retained their awkward system of calculating time by Kalends, Nones, and Ides for centuries. Clearly, what the Romans required in a calendar was not mere efficiency. What functions, then, did a Roman calendar serve? How does the Roman calendar reflect the society that used it? These questions intrigued me as I wrote this book. In order to answer them, however, it seemed best to focus on a particular document, in a specific time and place. The choice was simple—only one calendar has survived in its entirety from the time of the Roman Empire: the Codex-Calendar of A.D. 354. This document represents the culmination of centuries of tradition and change in Roman calendars. It also reflects the society that produced it; written in Rome, it leads us down the streets of that late-antique city, allowing us to see aspects of daily life and institutions otherwise closed to view.

In a graduate seminar, Professor Agnes K. L. Michels first opened my eyes to the possibilities calendars offered for understanding Roman religion and society. From that seminar, I proceeded to undertake dissertation research; this book grew out of that work. Thus, above all, I would like to thank my teachers at Bryn Mawr College, Agnes K. L. Michels and Russell T. Scott, the supervisor of my dissertation, for sharing with me their wisdom, for giving me the tools necessary to pursue such research, and for their support through the years. I am indebted to many other teachers as well; in particular, I should like to thank Arlene Fromchuck-Feili, Julia Gaisser, and Myra Uhlfelder.

My greatest debts are to Alan Cameron and Peter Brown. As a friend and colleague, Alan Cameron has made me see the world of late antiquity in a new light. I have benefited greatly from discussions with him over the years, and from his comments on early drafts of this book. As series editor, Peter Brown's reading and criticism of the preliminary manuscript have helped enormously. His own writings first guided me in my study of late antiquity, and they have continued to inspire me. Following Peter's lead, I have written this book in such a way that its technical discussions may, I hope, be accessible to the general reader as well as to the specialist.

Many people have helped me in the completion of this book. Revised versions of chapters were read and significantly improved by the following friends and colleagues: Martin Ostwald, Ron Mellor, David Parrish, J. Arce, Steven Muhlberger, Florentine Mütterich, Marcia Kupfer, Sandra Joshel, Elizabeth Clark, and Kathleen Shelton. Richard Tarrant lent his considerable expertise by reading and commenting on the text and translations of the poetry in Chapter 3 and in Appendix 4. Thomas Gelzer very generously procured a photocopy of a book critical for this study and not available in this country. My colleagues at Boston University have lent their support and advice, among whom I would like to thank in particular Meyer Reinhold, J. Rufus Fears, Donald Carne-Ross, Jim Wiseman, Steve Scully, Emily Albu-Hanawalt, Ann Vasaly, and David Ulansey. While I give my warmest thanks to the many who have helped, I acknowledge that any remaining errors or infelicities are my own.

It would not have been possible to finish this book without the resources and refuge offered by the American Academy in Rome; its library and staff have been invaluable. I would like to thank the American Council of Learned Societies for supporting my work in its beginning stages. I am especially grateful to the Mellon Foundation for a year-long Fellowship in Classical Studies at the American Academy in Rome, which gave me the time essential to complete this study.

I would like to thank Boston University for grants that enabled me to pursue summer research and to procure help in readying the final manuscript. Michele Ronnick was invaluable in tracking down illustrations, and Barbara Feinberg aided me greatly in manuscript preparation. Dan Caner worked with great patience on the index. The book has gained much from the editorial and production staff of the University of California Press; I would like to thank them, and especially Doris Kretschmer, Mary Lamprech, Anne Canright, and Richard Holway, for making the process such a pleasant one.

Finally, I would like to thank my family, especially my parents, Aron and Sylvia, and my brother Kelvin, for their support. My gratitude to my husband, Steven Brint, for his encouragement and critical reading of this work cannot be encompassed in mere words.

Boston, Mass., February 1989

· PART I ·

THE BOOK: THE CODEX-CALENDAR OF 354

· I ·

INTRODUCTION: ANTECEDENTS AND INTERPRETATIONS OF THE CODEX-CALENDAR OF 354

A wealthy Christian aristocrat by the name of Valentinus received an illustrated codex containing a calendar for the year A.D. 354. Valentinus must have been pleased by the gift. The calligraphy was of exceptional quality, being the work of the most famous calligrapher of the century, Furius Dionysius Filocalus; Filocalus, himself a Christian, had inscribed his own name alongside the wishes for Valentinus's well-being which adorned the opening page of the codex (Fig. 1).[1] The attractive illustrations that accompanied the text were also somewhat unusual; these, the earliest full-page illustrations in a codex in the history of Western art, may have also been the handiwork of Filocalus.

Aside from its handsome physical apearance, the codex was of great utility for an aristocrat living in Rome. The illustrated Calendar of 354 marked the important events celebrated in the city in that year, including pagan holidays, imperial anniversaries, historical commemorations, and astrological phenomena. It was the public calendar of Rome. Thus, the notations and illustrations conceived for the Calendar provide an invaluable source of information about public pagan religion and ritual in fourth-century Rome.

Yet the Calendar was only the nucleus of a much larger manuscript, compiled as a single codex for Valentinus. For his own information, several unillustrated lists were added to the Calendar proper, containing a wide range of chronological and historical material, such as the names of the Roman consuls and prefects of the city of Rome and those of the

1. For a discussion of Filocalus and Valentinus, see Chapter 5.

bishops of the Catholic church in Rome. There were various other illustrated sections as well, including representations of the astrological signs
of the planets and depictions of the eponymous consuls. Given the diverse nature of its contents, a more accurate title for the original codex
would be the Illustrated Almanac of 354. But "Calendar" is the traditional
title, and I will use it. Hereafter, then, I shall refer to the entire book as
the Codex or Codex-Calendar of 354; the calendar section alone I shall
call simply the Calendar or the Calendar of 354.

The transmission of the Codex-Calendar of 354 suggests that it continued to be a valued object long after Valentinus used it in Rome in 354.
Almost a century later, Polemius Silvius probably consulted it in preparing his own annotated calendar for the year 449.[2] A sixth-century
copyist apparently used the illustrations of the Codex-Calendar of 354
in preparing a planisphere.[3] And we find possible traces of the Codex-
Calendar in the seventh century: Columbanus of Luxeuil in 602 may have
copied its Paschal Cycle, and an Anglo-Saxon text of 689 may refer to
this work.[4] The next secure indication of the survival of the fourth-
century original occurs in the Carolingian period, when, owing to its
associations with the age of Constantine, an illustrated copy of the
Codex-Calendar of 354 (the Luxemburgensis) was made.[5] After the ninth
century, the original manuscript disappears from view. The discovery of
the Carolingian copy, however, aroused great excitement in the Renaissance, inspiring several sixteenth- and seventeenth-century copies; the
best of these (Romanus), executed under the careful supervision of the
great scholar Nicholas-Claude Fabri de Peiresc, is now in the Vatican
Library.[6] Unfortunately, the Luxemburgensis was damaged and several
pages were lost prior to the production of the Renaissance copies. Today
the Codex-Calendar of 354 survives only in fragments and only in copies
made either from the original codex or from the Carolingian copy. Even
the Carolingian version is lost; happily, Peiresc's detailed description of
that important copy survives.[7]

2. Stern 1953, p. 35; and see Chapter 6 below.
3. A planisphere for 579; see Eastwood 1983, p. 39.
4. Stern 1953, p. 35.
5. Another Carolingian copy, the unillustrated Sangallensis (= ms. 878, St. Gallen,
Bibliothèque du Convent), may have been copied from either the fourth-century original
or a later intermediary. See Appendix 1 for discussion.
6. The Vatican Library has Romanus 1 = Barb. lat. 2154 and Romanus 2 = Vat. Lat.
9135. The German manuscripts S. and T., derived probably from L., date to the fifteenth
century. For a fuller discussion, see Chapter 3 and Appendix 1.
7. Peiresc's description in a letter of 1620 is printed in part by Mommsen, *MGH* 1892,
pp. 17–29; printed in full by Strzygowski 1888, pp. 7–20. For discussion of the transmission
of the manuscripts, see Chapter 3 and Appendix 1.

The history of the Codex-Calendar of 354 suggests the difficulties inherent in an attempt to reconstruct the contents and format of the original codex. Yet it is a task worth undertaking. The small number of surviving late-antique manuscripts—fewer than twenty—partly justifies studying copies of a copy.[8] Moreover, no other fourth-century codex-calendar has come down to us; thus, analysis of the contents and formal aspects of this work provides invaluable information about fourth-century Rome. Prior to this study, though, such an analysis was difficult because no modern work provided a complete edition of the text and illustrations of the Codex-Calendar of 354. The interested reader had to turn to several different publications to gain a sense of its original nature. This study attempts to address that difficulty.

Although the Codex-Calendar of 354 is a unique document, certainly numerous other calendars were circulating in Rome that year, in all sorts of media. Hence our Calendar, albeit unique to us, cannot be interpreted without an understanding of its antecedents, of the traditions of Roman calendars and their coded language.

The Codex-Calendar of 354 allows us the rare opportunity of entering into the world that produced it, of seeing the daily round of social and religious events—the urban rhythms—in the life of a fourth-century resident of Rome. This, to my mind, is the most significant aspect of this study. The unique yet traditional Codex-Calendar provides access to the year 354 in Rome in a way that no other artifact, literary or archaeological, can. Moreover, the year and place—A.D. 354 in Rome—are important. As the Codex-Calendar will show, this was a critical point in the transition from paganism to Christianity among the aristocracy of Rome. In this period, as the Calendar reflects, the forces for accommodation and assimilation facilitated the Christianization of Rome and the continuation of aristocratic culture into the Christian present.

THE ROMAN CALENDAR

The Romans recognized early in their history the need to regulate their activities, in which task the construction of a calendar was an obvious first step. Roman writers of the Augustan Age attributed the earliest calendar either to King Romulus, the legendary founder of Rome,

---

8. See E. A. Lowe, *Codices Latini Antiquiores* (Oxford, 1934), vol. 1, codex nos. I, IV, XIV–XV.

or to King Numa, the alleged author of Roman religion.[9] These origins are purely conjecture, being as obscure to the Romans of the Augustan Age as they are to us today. Nevertheless, this attribution suggests a fundamental truth about the importance of the calendar in Roman society: the calendar was considered the product of one of Rome's most honored founders and was granted an antique pedigree because it enjoyed status as a Roman institution deserving of appreciation in its own right.

Although establishment of the Roman calendar by Romulus or Numa made mythical sense, the most likely historical origin is the 450 B.C. publication (on wood?) by the Decemvirate of a calendar of named days—holidays, the days on which legal actions could not proceed—as part of the Twelve Tables.[10] According to Livy, Cicero, and other Roman sources, it was the curule aedile, Flavius, who in 304 B.C. posted in the Roman Forum a calendar of the year designating the legal days for conducting business, recorded in inscriptions on white tablets.[11] This calendar probably also listed the legitimate dates for the meetings of the assemblies (*comitia*) and holidays.

The public posting of a calendar in the Forum is explained by Livy as a patrician response to the plebeian demand for access to this vital information, which until that time the aristocratic priests and magistrates had jealously guarded. As Rome had grown, the complexities of daily life had only increased the value of this information. The denial of free access to the calendar was one of many battles that the plebeians fought in order to gain greater political and economic freedom. A compromise was reached; the senatorial aristocracy—the priests and magistrates—established and promulgated the civic calendar in the republic, an activity that in the empire was assumed by the imperial government.

In 189 B.C., the consul M. Fulvius Nobilior compiled the first commentary on a Roman calendar (*fasti*). This he deposited in the temple of Hercules and the Muses, which he had just built.[12] We do not know whether Fulvius's calendar was a roll or an inscription or, if an inscription, whether it was incised or painted on the wall of the temple; generally, though, it is assumed to have been painted on a temple wall for

9. Plutarch *Numa* 18–19; M. York, *The Roman Festival Calendar of Numa Pompilius* (New York, 1986); Michels 1967; and E. Liénard, "Calendrier de Romulus: Les débuts du calendrier romain," *AC* 50 (1981): 469–482.

10. Michels 1967, p. 129, observes that "in antiquity a strong tradition [existed] that a code of laws should contain a calendar." The Twelve Tables are the earliest written laws of Rome, traditionally dated to 450 B.C.

11. See Michels 1967, pp. 108–109, for full citations; Cicero *Att.* 6.1.8 and *Pro Murena* 25; Livy 9.46.5.

12. Michels 1967, pp. 124–125; Macrobius *Sat.* 1.12.16.

decoration, like the only surviving pre-Julian calendar, the *Fasti Antiates Maiores*. Fulvius's calendar may have inspired Verrius Flaccus, whose commentary on the days of the year, it is almost certain, was added to the calendar inscribed on marble that has come to light in Palestrina.[13]

Verrius Flaccus's calendar and his personal prestige, along with Augustus's support for such antiquarian undertakings, made fashionable the practice of inscribing calendars on stone to decorate the walls of public and private buildings. This custom reached the height of its popularity (to judge by extant carved wall calendars) in the years beginning with Augustus and continuing into the reigns of Tiberius and Claudius. Out of a total of forty-eight extant calendars from the Italian peninsula from Roman times, some forty-four are from this period.[14] The red-painted highlighting of lettering against a white background, whether inscribed in stone or painted in fresco, would have made these calendars highly desirable wall decorations, as well as useful. Indeed, the bright letters gave rise to their name: *fasti picti,* or painted calendars.[15]

Until the discovery of the frescoed wall calendar from S. Maria Maggiore in Rome in 1966, the practice of decorating walls with calendars was believed to have disappeared after the Julio-Claudian period. This calendar, dated to the late second or early third century A.D.,[16] demonstrates that this presumption was not true; even the fashion of inscribing calendars on stone walls probably continued, although it was less popular. While no calendars in stone exist from after the first century A.D., we do have shorter lists of holidays inscribed in stone or written in manuscripts—*ferialia,* meant for "specific states, regions, sacred precincts, private associations or for the army."[17] One such *feriale* from Rome is dated to A.D. 362 and was inscribed in stone for a wall decoration.[18] The continued custom of inscribing *ferialia* on walls for ornamental purposes suggests that wall calendars may have been similarly intended.

13. Michels 1967, p. 6.
14. See Degrassi 1963, pp. xxiiff. All the *fasti* that can be dated belong to the times of Augustus and Tiberius, but some contain additional notes added during the reign of Claudius.
15. Ovid *Fasti* 1.11; and see the commentary by F. Bömer, *P. Ovidius Naso. Die Fasten* (Heidelberg, 1957).
16. Salzman 1981, pp. 215–227.
17. Degrassi 1963, pp. 277ff.: "spectant et ad civitates regionesve et ad fana et ad collegia et ad exercitus."
18. Degrassi 1963, pp. 277–283, notes all *ferialia* on stone: (1) *Feriale Cumanum* (A.D. 4–14), pp. 278–280; (2) *Feriale Amerinum* (Augustan Age or a little later), p. 281; and (3) *Feriale Campanum* (A.D. 387), pp. 282–293. There are also *ferialia* on papyrus: (1) *Feriale Tebtunense* (A.D. 169–176, in Greek); see S. Eitrem and L. Amundsen, *Papyri Osloenses,* 3 (Oslo, 1936), no. 77, pp. 45–55; (2) *Feriale Duranum* (A.D. 225–235, in Latin); see Fink, Hoey,

Forty-six of the forty-eight extant calendars from Italy are fragmen-tary[19] and were either painted or inscribed on the walls of houses or temples. The two complete surviving ancient Roman calendars are in the form of a book or codex. This study is about one of those calendars: the Codex-Calendar of 354, the only Roman calendar that can be securely dated to the fourth century A.D.[20]

Private Calendars and *Ferialia*

The production of a calendar for a private individual in the year 354 was not unusual. Texts from antiquity provide other examples. Petronius describes one such private calendar in the dining room of the nouveau riche Trimalchio:

> Under this inscription a double lamp hung from the ceiling, and two calendars were fixed on either doorpost, one having this entry, if I re-member right: "Our master C. goes out to supper on December 30th and 31st," the other painted with the moon in her course, and the like-nesses of seven stars. Lucky and unlucky days were marked too with distinctive knobs.[21]

---

and Snyder 1940; and Degrassi 1963, p. 277, for further bibliography; (3) *Feriale di Spello* (A.D. 14–A.D. 37?); see S. Priuli, "Osservazioni sul Feriale di Spello," *Tituli* 2 (1980): 47–80; and (4) one disputed *feriale, Feriale Rusticum Volsiniense, MEFR* 84 (1972): 623–638. Degrassi (1963, p. 277) considers three Latin epigraphic documents similar enough to be considered *ferialia*: *CIL* 14.2112 = *ILS* 7212; *CIL* 6.10234 = *ILS* 7213; *CIL* 6.33885 = *ILS* 7214. A fourth epigraphic document can be added, *CIL* 6.31075 (A.D. 362): "Descriptio fer[iarum———] / quae in cohorte [———vig(ilum)———]." These *ferialia* provide important information about the development of the Roman calendar year in the post–Julio-Claudian period.

19. Degrassi 1963, pp. 29–277, published forty-four calendars or *fasti* from Italy. The *Fasti Tauromentani* were published as an addendum at the end of fascicle 2; they were also published by G. Manganaro, *Arch. Cl.* 15 (1963): 13ff. Since this calendar is not from Italy, it lies outside our total number. Three new *fasti* have been found in Italy and published: Magi 1972 published the *Fasti* from S. Maria Maggiore in Rome; and S. Panciera published two very fragmentary calendars, "Due nuovi frammenti di calendario romano," *Arch. Cl.* 25–26 (1973–1974): 481–90. New fragments of the already known *Fasti Cuprenses* have also come to light and been published by G. Paci, "A proposito di un nuovo frammento del calendario romano di Cupra Maritima," *Annali Macerata* 13 (1980): 279–295. The forty-eighth calendar came to light in excavations of the *Horologium Augusti* in Rome, published by E. Büchner, "Solarium Augusti und Ara Pacis," *MDAIR* 83 (1976): 319–365; and "Hor-ologium Solarium Augusti," *MDAIR* 87 (1980): 355–372; reprinted in E. Büchner, *Die Son-nenuhr des Augustus* (Mainz am Rhein, 1982).

20. The other calendar is that of Polemius Silvius, dated to A.D. 449, printed by Mommsen, *MGH* 1892, pp. 511–552; text only in Degrassi 1963, pp. 263–276. It provides an invaluable comparandum. See my discussion in Chapter 6.

21. Petronius *Sat.* 30, trans. M. Haseltine (London, 1975): "Sub eodem titulo et lu-cerna bilychnis de camera pendebat, et duae tabulae in utroque poste defixae, quarum

The tablets (*tabulae*) with distinctive knobs (*distinguente bulla*) suggest the type of calendar known as a *parapegma*, a limited list of festivals written or inscribed on wood or clay plaques, with holes and pegs to mark special days not noted in the civil calendar—the ancient equivalent of the modern agenda. One such *parapegma*, dating to the Constantinian period, was found in the Baths of Trajan on the Caelian Hill in Rome; it indicates the continuing popularity of such private, small-scale, practical calendars into the fourth century.[22]

These unofficial *parapegmata* and the abbreviated agricultural calendars, or *menologia rustica*, were regularly illustrated. Most often, they depicted the astrological signs. The *parapegma* from the Baths of Trajan, for example, included an astrological circle as well as illustrations of the seven planetary gods.[23] The first-century *Menologium Rusticum Colotianum* depicts, at the head of a column of festivals and agricultural activities for each month, the appropriate astrological sign: thus January is illustrated by the sign of Capricorn, February by that of Aquarius, and so on.[24]

These illustrations, not to mention the contents of the *parapegmata* and *menologia rustica*, indicate the growing tendency to include astrological information in Roman calendars made for private individuals as early as the first century A.D. Scattered literary references support this conjunction of astrology and calendars, as in the passage from Petronius's *Satiricon* cited above. Another instance is provided by Juvenal, who satirizes popular belief in astrology when he describes a calendar with astrological information carried by a Roman lady of somewhat dubious character.[25] Pliny also remarks on the use of astrological texts by individuals, though not in conjunction with a calendar.[26]

Extant specimens provide the best evidence for the conjunction of astrological and chronological information in the official Roman calendar. Perhaps the most spectacular example is the monumental calendar and *horologium* (ancient clock), decorated with monumental bronze letters, recently excavated in the Campus Martius in Rome.[27] A monumental

altera, si bene memini, hoc habebat inscriptum: 'III. et pridie kalendas Ianuarias C. noster foras cenat,' altera lunae cursum stellarumque septem imagines pictas et qui dies boni quique incommodi essent, distinguente bulla notabantur."

22. Degrassi 1963, pp. 308–309; D. Manicoli, "Un calendario astrologico al Museo della Civiltà Romana," *Bollettino dei Musei Comunali di Roma* 28–30 (1981–1983): 18–22.

23. Degrassi 1963, pp. 308–309.

24. Ibid., pp. 286–290.

25. Juvenal *Sat.* 6.569–575.

26. Pliny *N. H.* 29.9.

27. Büchner, "Solarium Augusti und Ara Pacis," pp. 319–365.

horologium and solar calendar was constructed by Augustus; later in the first century (the excavator dates it to the Domitianic period),[28] the *horologium* was reconstructed and a zodiacal calendar parallel to a calendar of the Julian months was added. Hence, the astrological notations in the calendar from S. Maria Maggiore and in the Calendar of 354 follow traditional, indeed imperial, precedents.

Most other references to private calendars are to portable ones in the form of papyrus rolls. Only Ovid's *Fasti* (1.657–658) provides a clear-cut reference to a Roman calendar in a papyrus roll, however. Other passages mentioning calendars or papyrus rolls are ambiguous because they can refer either to calendars or to consular lists, both of which were called *fasti*. Moreover, since consular lists were often added to calendars, reference to one might well include the other.[29]

If calendars in rolls followed the patterns of other secular books, it would seem likely that the papyrus roll remained the norm for calendars until the third century A.D. While no such calendars survive, we do have *ferialia* in this form, one of which dates from the third century A.D. (though no papyrus-roll *feriale* exists from the fourth century).[30] Based on surviving examples and textual references, we cannot be certain if these papyrus-roll *ferialia* were illustrated; in any case, their restricted purposes may explain the lack of illustration.

Codex-Calendars

The codex became popular for illustrated secular texts only in the late third or early fourth century. Previously, the papyrus roll was most often used.[31] We can thus date the production of codex-calendars, like the illustrated Codex-Calendar of 354, to, at the earliest, the late third century. Consequently, the designer of the Codex-Calendar of 354 may well have had to work out certain problems of design without the aid of codex prototypes. Nor can we assume that there were illustrated calendars in papyrus rolls to serve as a guide; none are extant, and their importance, if any, has yet to be shown.[32] The likelihood that a codex-

28. Ibid., pp. 359ff.

29. Stern 1953, pp. 302–303; Michels 1967, p. 98.

30. The *Feriale Duranum* is dated to the first quarter of the third century; see Fink, Hoey, and Snyder 1940; Degrassi 1963, p. 277.

31. See C. H. Roberts and T. C. Skeat, *The Birth of the Codex* (Oxford, 1983), pp. 24–37, 67–76.

32. The connection between illustrated papyrus rolls and the illustrated codex remains the essence of the theory advanced by K. Weitzmann; see his *Illustrations in Roll and Codex: A Study of the Origin and Method of Text Illustration*, 2d ed. (Princeton, 1970), passim,

calendar was a fourth-century innovation receives further support from the illustrations found in the Codex-Calendar of 354. Not only are these the earliest known full-page illustrations for a codex in Western art, but the extensive number of motifs pictorializing each month also coincides with fourth-century artistic trends in other media.

The novelty of an illustrated codex-calendar in the fourth century must remain a hypothesis, but analysis of the formal aspects of the Codex-Calendar of 354 does indicate the transference of certain characteristics of inscribed Roman wall calendars to the codex medium. The 1966 discovery of the wall calendar from S. Maria Maggiore in Rome is significant in this regard. This calendar, dated to the late second or early third century, indicates the vitality of inscribed Roman wall calendar traditions well past the Julio-Claudian period, when (or so scholars believed) they were last attested.[33] The traditions for inscribing Roman calendars on walls provide a fruitful and underappreciated source of inspiration for the design and illustration of the Calendar of 354.

Although the Codex-Calendar of 354 is the only fourth-century calendar we have, its unique survival and the silence in our sources concerning codex-calendars in general are surely accidental. Four illustrated consular annals dated to the late fourth and early fifth centuries are relevant as comparanda; so too are the illustrated World Chronicles, one of which even contains a calendar, or at least illustrations of the months of the year.[34] Such illustrated chronographic works and calendars in codices were no doubt numerous; unfortunately, we do not know how numerous or when they became so.

Contents of a Roman Calendar

The organization of information remained generally the same for the six centuries of the Roman calendar's recorded usage. Each month occupies a column, with the name of the month at the top and the days of the month listed vertically below (see Figs. 24, 25). Most calendars con-

---

esp. pp. 83–84, 106; and *Ancient Book Illumination* (Cambridge, 1959), passim, esp. pp. 59–60; see also K. Weitzmann, *Studies in Classical and Byzantine Illumination*, ed. H. L. Kessler (Chicago, 1971), pp. 96ff.

33. See Magi 1972, pp. 1ff.; Salzman 1981, pp. 215–227.

34. See Weitzmann 1971, pp. 121–124; and my discussion of illustrated consular lists and World Chronicles in Chapter 2, notes 31–32 and 82. A World Chronicle was a very abbreviated history of civilization, beginning with Adam and continuing in a year-by-year summary to contemporary times.

tain at least three columns of information for each month. At the extreme left is a column of letters, A through H, which repeats throughout the year; these letters, the so-called *nundinals*, record the traditional Roman market week, which followed an eight-day cycle. Next is a column recording the name of the day—either the festival name, written in full or abbreviated, or the Kalends, Nones, and Ides. In the Calendar of 354, and in approximately half of extant Roman calendars, the Kalends, Nones, and Ides, located immediately to the right of the nundinals, are included to allow calculation of the day of the month; the festival name is written directly to the right of this column.

After the name of the day is often a column of letters designating the specific nature of the day: for instance, "F" for *dies fasti*, days on which legal business could be transacted; "N" for *dies nefasti*, days on which legal business could not be transacted; or "C" for *dies comitiales*, days on which the *comitia* (in the republican period and early empire) could meet. On unnamed days, these designations appear directly after the nundinals. The Calendar of 354 omits these letters, as do certain other calendars, notably that from S. Maria Maggiore in Rome.[35] The disappearance of these letters from late Roman calendars reflects the decline of the institutions for which the notations were devised. Conversely, the contemporary importance of the Senate in Rome probably explains why the Calendar of 354, unlike those of the early empire, records the meeting days of this body.[36]

In some calendars another column of letters, the *hebdomadales*, running A through G, indicates a seven-day weekly cycle.[37] This column appears in the Calendar of 354 to the left of the nundinals and to the right of the named days. The Calendar of 354, moreover, is unique in including, to the left of the hebdomals, one other sequence of letters, A through K, which were used to calculate the days of the full and new moon.[38] The inclusion of the lunar and solar weekly cycles underscores the influence of astrology, both in the Calendar and as attested elsewhere in the Codex as well.[39]

---

35. This discussion of named and unnamed days is a simplification and distillation of a rather complex and controversial topic. For the ancient evidence concerning these designations, see Degrassi 1963, pp. 331–337; and Michels 1967, the most lucid modern discussion of these letters and their significance.

36. Degrassi 1963, p. 569.

37. Ibid., p. 326.

38. Ibid.; Stern 1953, pp. 55–57; T. Mommsen, *Die römische Chronologie bis auf Caesar,* 2d ed. (Berlin, 1859), pp. 309ff.

39. See my discussion of the astrological sections of the Codex-Calendar in Chapter 2.

Following the columns of weekly cycles are entered the names of the festivals and holidays in honor of the pagan gods and goddesses or the emperor and the imperial cult, or in commemoration of some event in Roman history or for contemporary life. Roman calendars often included information about individual days, ranging from brief notations of games (*ludi*) or circus races (*circenses*) to quite lengthy commentary on historical events or religious activities. The best-known annotated calendar is the *Fasti Praenestini*, generally attributed to Verrius Flaccus.[40] Consider, for example, what this calendar says about the festival to honor the Magna Mater on 4 April:

> F, on the day before the Ides, c[*omitialis*]. The Games to the Idaean Great Mother of the Gods. These are called *Megalensia* because that goddess is called *Megale*. Mutual exchanges of dinner invitations are frequently and customarily made by the nobles, because the Great Mother who had been summoned in accord with the Sibylline books changed her locale from Phrygia to Rome.[41]

Unlike the *Fasti Praenestini*, the Calendar of 354 includes only brief notices for the holidays and activities on each day. Although reference to cult ritual and sacrifice is generally omitted, the Calendar does include some such information. For example, on 13 February is entered "Virgo Vesta[lis] parentat," signifying that the Vestal Virgin holds a memorial service on this Roman holiday in honor of dead parents or relatives, a day that in earlier calendars is referred to as the *Parentalia*. As we shall see, because of its recorded holidays, the Calendar of 354 is a rich source of information about late Roman paganism. The Christian holidays noted in the other sections of the Codex were as yet not of civic significance in Rome and thus were omitted from the Calendar. Furthermore, the inclusion of a seven-day hebdomadal cycle in the Calendar of 354 does not have any peculiarly Christian meaning; seven-day weekly cycles came to Rome via an interest in astrology as early as the first century B.C.[42] Thus, the Calendar of 354 follows its calendrical antecedents in recording a seven-day week and in including astrological information in the text; not only is the position of Sol in the astrological firmament noted every month, but the unlucky days (*dies aegyptiaci*) are also recorded.[43]

---

40. Degrassi 1963, pp. 107–145; Suetonius *De Grammaticis et Rhetoribus* 17, ed. G. Brugnoli (Leipzig, 1963).

41. Degrassi 1963, p. 127: "[F] pr.(idie), c(omitialis). Ludi M(atri) D(eum) M(agnae) I(daeae). Megalensia vocantur, quod [e]a dea Megale appellatur. Nobilium mutitationes cenarum solitae sunt frequenter fieri, quod Mater Magna ex libris Sibyllinis arcessita locum mutavit ex Phrygia Romam."

42. Michels 1967, p. 89 n. 6.

43. Degrassi 1963, p. 569.

Using a Roman Calendar

To its fourth-century Roman recipient, the Codex-Calendar of 354 was not just an object of visual delight and a handy reference work; it was also, in itself, the embodiment of a venerable tradition. Centuries of writers, grammarians, historians, and specialists had devoted themselves to the study of the Roman calendar and the rites it recorded. Varro, Ovid, Censorinus, and later Ausonius, Macrobius, and Dracontius, to name but a few of the outstanding writers on the subject, had deemed the Roman calendar a topic worthy of poetry, praise, and scholarly investigation.[44] For centuries Roman children learned about the calendar and its rites as part of their schooling in the Roman past. The didactic function of the calendar continued into the Christian times of the fifth and sixth centuries, as the fifth-century calendar of Polemius Silvius and the writings of Macrobius attest:

> This then is what I would have this present work be: a repository of much to teach and much to guide you, examples drawn from many ages but informed by a single spirit, wherein—if you refrain from rejecting what you already know and from shunning what you do not—you will find much that it would be a pleasure to read, an education to have read, and of use to remember; [11] for, to the best of my belief, the work [the *Saturnalia*] contains nothing that is either useless to know or difficult to comprehend, but everything in it is calculated to quicken your understanding, to strengthen your memory, to give more dexterity to your discourse, and to make your speech more correct.[45]

The prologue to Macrobius's *Saturnalia*, a long dialogue devoted in large part to explaining the intricacies of the Roman calendar and the religion it records, underscores the value of the Calendar of 354. The setting is the house of the Roman aristocrat Agorius Praetextatus, who lived in the second half of the fourth century. During the festival of the *Saturnalia*, he and several of his fellow aristocrats meet and discuss aspects of Roman paganism, including the calendar and its holidays as well as the greatest Latin author, Virgil. Information about the Roman calendar and Roman paganism was considered by Macrobius essential

44. For a bibliography of the Roman calendar, see ibid., pp. 314–316.
45. Macrobius *Sat.* 1 praef. 10–11, trans. P. Davies (New York, 1969): "Tale hoc praesens opus volo: multae in illo artes, multa praecepta sint, multarum aetatium exempla, sed in unum conspirata: in quibus si neque ea quae iam tibi sunt cognita asperneris, nec quae ignota sunt vites, invenies plurima quae sit aut voluptati legere aut cultui legisse aut usui meminisse. nihil enim huic operi insertum puto aut cognitu inutile aut difficile perceptu, sed omnia quibus sit ingenium tuum vegetius, memoria adminiculatior, oratio sollertior, sermo incorruptior."

to his son's education, for whom this work is ostensibly written. Nor was Macrobius's son unusual. There is good evidence that from the earliest times of the Roman Republic and continuing well into the fifth century, schoolchildren memorized the list of named holidays (as well as, probably, the more daunting list of consuls), disseminated via papyrus rolls, tablets, or verbal transmission.[46] Although Macrobius emphasizes the didactic function of such knowledge, the renowned speakers in his dialogue indicate that this learning was what distinguished a Roman aristocrat. In a letter by the eminent Roman noble Symmachus, the man's pride in having acquired this knowledge is evident: "You perform the duty of a good brother, but stop reminding me. We are knowledgeable concerning the ceremonies of the gods and the festivities of the divinity that have been commanded."[47]

These two elements—didactic function and aristocratic distinction—were the result of the special development of the Roman calendar, in both its use and its role within Roman society and education. To the fourth-century recipient of the Calendar of 354, traditional formal aspects as well as content were appropriate reflections of the venerability of this item and served only to increase its value. Indeed, it should be emphasized that the traditional appearance and content of the Calendar of 354 reflect the very ideals of the society that produced it, for in this society an object or idea was all the more revered if it was antique: "Love of custom is great."[48]

By the time of Macrobius, much of the information he was explaining to his son must have referred to holidays that were no longer celebrated. Nevertheless, knowledge of these festivals and their rites—and of how to use the Roman calendar—was still valued in the Christian fifth century, for it was useful for the study of classical history and literature. To know, for example, that the Roman holiday of the *Regifugium* commemorated the expulsion of the kings and the beginning of the republic was to have a basic understanding of some of the most fundamental institutions and facts of the history of early Rome. Certainly, to understand allusions to the deities and their rites is essential for appreciating much of Latin literature, as even a glance at any contemporary college text amply indicates. The didactic impulse also lay behind the creation of the

---

46. Michels 1967, p. 136.
47. Symmachus *Ep.* 2.53, ed. O. Seeck (Berlin, 1883), *MGH* 1883, 6.1, before A.D. 395: "Fungeris boni fratris officio, sed desine memorem commonere. Notae nobis sunt caerimoniae deorum et festa divinitatis imperata."
48. Symmachus *Ep.* 3.7: "Consuetudinis amor magnus est."

fasti of Polemius Silvius.[49] One could even learn elementary math through calculation of dates in the Roman calendar.

The educational function of the Roman calendar probably began in the period of the republic and continued through the six centuries of the calendar's attested usage, if not longer.[50] Hence, it was to a large degree true that knowledge of the Roman calendar and its contents was the earmark of a learned aristocrat, as Symmachus implied. And the inclusion of such a calendar in the Codex-Calendar of 354 fits well within the aristocratic milieu in which this work belongs. Yet the many antecedents of the Codex-Calendar of 354 should not obscure its essentially functional nature. Unlike the calendar of Polemius Silvius from 449, we can be certain that the Calendar of 354 was intended for practical use, for its notations accurately record the contemporary holidays and festivals actually celebrated in mid-fourth-century Rome.

INTERPRETATIONS OF THE PAGANISM IN THE CALENDAR OF 354

Because the antecedents of the Calendar of 354 and the peculiar but stock elements of a Roman calendar were not fully understood, some nineteenth- and some twentieth-century scholars mistakenly argued that the Calendar of 354 was merely a piece of antiquarianism. The omission of the letters specifying the nature of individual days (*F, N, C,* and so on) and of lengthy descriptions of cultic acts, coupled with the changed nomenclature for certain holidays in this fourth-century calendar as compared with those of the first century, led Mommsen, for one, to suggest that the holidays recorded in the Calendar of 354 were no longer celebrated with cultic acts in the Christian fourth century.[51] Comparison with earlier Roman calendars, however, has shown this view to be untenable. Descriptions of cultic acts were not always included in Roman calendars; the pre-Caesarian *Fasti Antiates Maiores* contains none, nor do

---

49. See Mommsen, *MGH* 1892, p. 518, the prologue to that calendar. Elizabeth Dulabahn has argued convincingly that the calendar of Polemius Silvius was created for a didactic function and that calendars were used in the Roman school setting; see her "The Laterculus of Polemius Silvius," Ph.D. diss., Bryn Mawr College, 1986.

50. Michels 1967, p. 136, suggests: "I would guess that the memorization of the list [of named days] would be a part of a Roman's education, just as he must have had to face the appalling task of memorizing the list of consuls." The use of school calendars and their didactic function probably explains the lists of holidays known as *hermeneumata* as well. See Dulabahn, "The Laterculus of Polemius Silvius."

51. Mommsen, *MGH* 1892, p. 28.

other first-century calendars, such as *Fasti Maffeiani* (A.D. 8), one of the most complete calendars extant.[52] The letters *F, N, C,* moreover, probably disappeared from the Roman calendar during the second century A.D. in connection with the calendar reforms of Marcus Aurelius and the waning importance of the republican institutions to which they referred;[53] they are missing by the late second or early third century, when the calendar from S. Maria Maggiore was painted.[54]

Knowledge of the antecedents of the Calendar of 354 has disproved Mommsen's denial of the contemporary reality behind the text. Corroborating evidence from archaeological, literary, artistic, and epigraphic remains likewise argues convincingly against such an assessment of the text and illustrations of the Calendar of 354.

Because it was the calendar of the city of Rome, the Calendar of 354 provides accurate and unique information about late Roman paganism. But there is one noteworthy limitation to any study of paganism that is based—as the present study is—on the Roman calendar, a limitation that results from the particular role and development of the calendar itself. Roman calendars recorded only public, officially recognized events and festivals, and not private festivals or ceremonies; that is, Roman calendars noted only those aspects of pagan cult that were significant to the state and its officially recognized cults. Hence, this examination of the Calendar of 354 and the religion it records will, owing to the very nature of the Roman calendar, focus on public cult.

The concentration on public cult should not, however, be seen negatively. Too often, to a modern mind brought up in the Judeo-Christian tradition, personal religion and individual feelings of spirituality are considered to be the only truly valid religious impulses. Yet in fourth-century Rome, as we shall see, public cult and its official manifestations in urban life were the true mainstays of late Roman paganism. Indeed, it is in the public pagan cults, so intimately woven into the fabric of the urban daily life of the Roman aristocracy and so closely tied to the emperor and the Roman state, that we will gain insight into the appeal of late Roman paganism.

Recognition of the vitality of Roman calendric traditions and of late Roman paganism in a post-Constantinian calendar is a relatively recent scholarly achievement. The problem of how to interpret the Codex-Calendar of 354—above all, the nature of the paganism recorded in the text and illustrations of the Calendar of 354—was first recognized by the

---

52. Degrassi 1963, pp. 1–28, 70–84.; Stern 1953, pp. 96–99.
53. *H.A. Marc. Ant.* 10.10; Stern 1953, pp. 97–98.
54. Salzman 1981, pp. 215–227.

Renaissance scholar Peiresc.[55] Peiresc was aware that this pagan calendar belonged to the reigns of mid-fourth-century Christian emperors. To Peiresc, its pagan contents were compiled at a time that was at odds with its date, some thirty years after the Emperor Constantine had converted to Christianity. Moreover, as Peiresc knew, laws prior to 354 had outlawed pagan sacrifice.[56] How, then, if its date was correct, to explain the pagan religion it recorded? Peiresc believed that by this time paganism was actually almost extinct. The Calendar was compiled and celebrations allowed because Constantine's son, Constantius, not wanting to destroy all of paganism, had retained certain of the games in the circus because of their historic significance for the Roman people.[57]

Mommsen, the first modern scholar to clarify the manuscript tradition of the Codex-Calendar of 354 and to analyze its text, interpreted the original as a piece of fourth-century nostalgia, written after pagan rites had ceased to have any real religious significance in a Christian empire. In Mommsen's view, the festivals noted in the Calendar were essentially neutral ceremonies, celebrated without offensive pagan sacrifice or attendance at pagan temples.[58] These religious celebrations, allotted originally for the cults of the pagan gods, were merely formal holidays, or *dies feriati*; only the games (*ludi*) were allowed to remain intact.[59] Mommsen supported this view by pointing to the evidence within the Calendar, whose format and text included no description of cultic acts or religious indications of days (*dies fasti* and *nefasti*), as he believed earlier Roman calendars had.[60] Yet the lists of Christian information and the dedication of the codex with a Christian formula indicated that the Calendar was written in Christian times.[61]

Subsequent studies of the Calendar in the late nineteenth century and in the first half of the twentieth focused on isolated issues without challenging Mommsen's basic premise concerning the paganism attested in the Calendar of 354. Strzygowski focused on the illustrations of the months in the Calendar, which he deemed a nostalgic reproduction of an earlier calendric cycle, devoid of any real religious content.[62] The

55. Mommsen, *MGH* 1892, p. 28, records Peiresc's remarks, as does Strzygowski 1888, pp. 1ff.

56. Mommsen, *MGH* 1892, p. 28, prints Peiresc's statements.

57. Ibid.

58. Mommsen 1850b, pp. 63–74.

59. Mommsen, 1850a, p.570.

60. Ibid.; Mommsen, *MGH* 1892, p. 48.

61. Mommsen, *MGH* 1892, pp. 38, 70–71.

62. Strzygowski 1888, pp. 82ff. Nordenfalk and Byvanck studied the art historical significance of the images for illustrations in books; see Nordenfalk 1936; A. W. Byvanck, "Antike Buchmalerei III. Der Kalender vom Jahre 354 und die Notitia Dignitatum," *Mnemosyne*, 3d ser., 8 (1939–1940): 186ff.

attempt by Volgraff to redate the Calendar to the pagan revival under Julian is noteworthy, for it indicates the degree to which certain scholars had found the dating of the Calendar at odds with their interpretation of the religious and social climate that produced it.[63]

Although Mommsen's views dominated studies on the Calendar per se, general studies of paganism began slowly to undermine his position. Wissowa, in his monumental study of Roman religion, observed that Mommsen had failed to appreciate the essential paganism of the Calendar; he took another view, explaining the document's existence as the result of the unique situation of pagan cult in Rome in the middle of the fourth century.[64] Wissowa did not expand on these remarks, however, and when Geffcken later developed Wissowa's views on the vitality of late Roman paganism, he did not apply them to the Calendar of 354.[65] Finally, in one specific instance, A. Alföldi demonstrated how the Calendar of 354 represented real cultic practice.[66]

Only in 1953, with the work of H. Stern, was the Calendar considered in its entirety and interpreted as a compendium of pagan festivals and imperial anniversaries that reflected the living reality of late Roman paganism. Stern studied the text of the Calendar to elucidate the real practices of pagan cult in Rome, which in turn would enable him to analyze more accurately the illustrations in the Codex-Calendar, the focus of his study.[67] Stern viewed the text of the Calendar as "le dernier témoin de la pratique intégrale du culte païen à Rome" and its illustrations as "une somme de l'art que pratiquaient les milieux qui conservaient ce culte."[68] Stern's work reflected the shift of scholarly attention to the survival of pagan rites in post-Constantinian Rome—the starting point for my own studies of the Codex-Calendar.

PRINCIPAL CONSIDERATIONS OF THIS STUDY

Building on the work of earlier scholars, I have been guided throughout by four principal considerations. First, by placing the iconography and text of the Calendar within the context of archaeological and literary evidence, I argue that it is possible to extend and emend previous inter-

63. G. Volgraff, "De Figura Mensis Ianuarii e Codice Luxemburgensi Deperdito Exscripta", *Mnemosyne* 59 (1931): 401.

64. Wissowa 1912, p. 97

65. Geffcken 1978, pp. 115–222.

66. A. Alföldi, *A Festival of Isis in Rome Under the Christian Emperors of the Fourth Century* (Budapest, 1937), pp. 32ff.

67. See Stern 1953, p. 10.

68. Ibid., p. 11.

pretations and so arrive at a more accurate idea of pagan ritual and religion in fourth-century Rome. In the years since Stern's publication, much new evidence—archaeological, literary, epigraphic, and scholarly—has come to light to clarify these interpretations. In addition, new calendars must be taken into account, the number of calendar inscriptions having almost doubled since 1892 when Mommsen published all then known Roman calendars. Stern, in 1953, was not able to utilize Atilio Degrassi's magnificent edition of the complete corpus of Roman calendars with its exhaustive commentaries and indices, published in *Inscriptiones Italiae* 13.2 in 1963.[69] And new inscriptions of calendars have come to light since Degrassi's publication as well,[70] perhaps the most spectacular of these being the painted calendar from S. Maria Maggiore in Rome.[71] With all this new material and new scholarly tools, the time seemed right to undertake a new study of the Codex-Calendar of 354.

The second consideration is methodological. Unlike Stern, who seeks far and wide for visual and textual evidence throughout the empire and beyond, I believe that the proper context for explication of the document can be found in the city of Rome itself. This approach can be justified because (1) we know from the Calendar that it was produced in Rome for use in the year 354 and (2) we know that Roman paganism was essentially a localized phenomenon, flourishing, expressing itself, and finally vanishing locality by locality.[72] Thus the Calendar, intended for use in Rome in 354, must reflect—by definition—the paganism of its immediate milieu. As far as possible, therefore, I have restricted my focus in discussing the Calendar to Rome and to local Roman practices.

Third, I hold that a close reading of the text in conjunction with in-depth historical research allows for a determination of the dominant cults in the fourth-century city and a deeper understanding of the particular appeal and vitality of Roman paganism in late antiquity. In short, I have extended my discussion beyond analysis of the particulars of pagan cultic rites and practices to include a synthetic analysis of the nature of paganism as practiced in Rome in the mid fourth century.

Fourth, I believe that by decoding the information contained in the Calendar, we can bring the world that produced it into sharper focus. Indeed, it is a world and a period of critical importance in understanding

69. Degrassi 1963.

70. See Chapters 1, 3, and 4, and my forthcoming article on the Roman *fasti* in *ANRW*.

71. Magi 1972, pp. 1ff.

72. For the production of the Calendar, see Chapters 2, 3, 4, and 5; and Stern 1953, pp. 42–47. For Roman paganism as a localized phenomenon, see, for example, R. MacMullen, *Paganism in the Roman Empire* (New Haven, Conn., 1981), pp. 1–17, 41ff.; and A. Wardman, *Religion and Statecraft in Rome* (Baltimore, 1982), pp. 1ff.

the transformation and conversion of pagan Rome into a Christian city. Surprisingly, this period has received little scholarly attention. The conversion of Constantine to Christianity and his subsequent establishment of his new religion (313–337), as well as the pagan revivals associated with the Emperor Julian (361–363), with the return of the Altar of Victory to the Roman Senate (382–384), and with the usurpation of Eugenius (391–394), have been the subject of much modern scholarship. The valleys of relative quiet between these dramatic historical moments are less often considered, but they are perhaps of even greater importance if we are fully to comprehend the nature of Roman society and religion in the fourth century: during these times of relative calm fundamental changes in thought and belief took hold, and in such a way as to preserve rather than eradicate the pagan past.

Personal artifacts like the pagan Calendar of 354 written for a Christian aristocrat or the silver casket of the Christian bride Proiecta decorated with the image of the pagan goddess Venus take on much significance, for they reflect the mundane reality that lay behind large-scale social and religious change.[73] Indeed, precisely this level of daily reality is so often lost when we try to comprehend the ancient world. Through the inclusion of pagan and Christian information in a single, ornate edition, the Codex-Calendar of 354 makes clear what the abstract terms *pagan* and *Christian* actually meant to a person living in the mid fourth century. It may also indicate the areas and ways in which pagans and Christians accommodated themselves to coexistence, enabling them, with time, to share a common cultural heritage. To be sure, the assimilation of pagan culture into a Christian framework was well under way in 354, and would ultimately end in the conversion of Roman society and its aristocracy to Christianity—yet along with the preservation of much of (traditionally pagan) Roman culture.[74] The Codex-Calendar of 354 can illuminate this complicated and lengthy process for us, as can the identity of its recipient, Valentinus, who, as I will demonstrate, was probably a Christian member of one of the most staunchly pagan aristocratic families in Rome. (See Chapter 5.)

Examples of the light that the Codex-Calendar can shed on Roman

---

73. For discussion of the Proiecta casket, see K. Shelton, *The Esquiline Treasury* (London, 1981), pp. 1–11 and passim. For the controversy over the dating of this object and the Treasure, see Chapter 5, note 94.

74. One of the best studies of this process is still C. N. Cochrane, *Christianity and Classical Culture: A Study of Thought and Action from Augustus to Augustine* (Oxford, 1940); and see the sound remarks of P. Brown, "Aspects of the Christianization of the Roman Aristocracy," *JRS* 51 (1961): 1–11; reprinted in *Religion and Society in the Age of St. Augustine* (London, 1972), pp. 161–182.

society abound. Not only do we gain insight into how Romans thought about the dominant institutions of the city, but through similarities in the unillustrated lists of pagan and Christian information included in the text we can also see how Christian religious institutions were assimilated to preexisting secular models of political life. Likewise, the Chronicle of Rome (section XVI in the Codex) reveals fourth-century attitudes toward the Roman emperor and his role in Roman urban life. (See Chapter 2.)

The Rome that emerges from the pages of the Codex-Calendar of 354 is best characterized as a city dominated by the processes of accommodation and assimilation, as the inclusion of two separate but equivalent lists of holidays, one pagan and one Christian, emblematizes. Discussion of contemporary historical evidence will corroborate this view. (See Chapter 5.) By the beginning of the fifth century, the tide had turned; the forces for accommodation and assimilation had made possible the gradual and relatively peaceful Christianization of Rome and its aristocracy, the impact of which can be seen in the fifth-century calendar of Polemius Silvius. (See Chapter 6.)

In sum, the Codex-Calendar of 354 is a specific historical document, a deluxe codex produced by the famous fourth-century calligrapher Furius Dionysius Filocalus for a wealthy Christian, Valentinus, for use in Rome in A.D. 354. Yet this edition has wider significance—for the study of late Roman religion and society, for the study of late Roman paganism, for analysis of relations between pagans and Christians, and for understanding the assimilation of classical culture into a Christian framework.

· II ·

DESCRIPTION OF THE CONTENTS
OF THE CODEX-CALENDAR OF 354

To create the Codex-Calendar of 354,[1] more than a dozen diverse texts were brought together and united into one codex. These texts were already in circulation and readily available in Rome when work began on this deluxe edition in A.D. 353.[2] Each text, therefore, has an independent existence, can be located within its own tradition, and is of interest in its own right; indeed, the background and sources for these diverse texts have been much discussed. Little analyzed or appreciated, however, is the fact that each of these texts was chosen for this particular codex. Consequently, the process by which these texts were joined together to form a coherent whole, as well as the inherent logic and organization of the codex, which would have been apparent to its fourth-century reader, remains to be explored. The purpose of this chapter is therefore three-fold: first, to describe the discrete texts, or sections, of the original fourth-century Codex-Calendar of 354; second, to analyze the organizing impulse or logic behind the compilation of the Codex-Calendar, a logic seen in the choice of the texts for inclusion, in the editing of certain texts, and in the interrelationship of the texts; and third, to discuss how the Codex-Calendar opens out into Roman society of the mid fourth century in its

1. As noted in Chapter 1, the designation of the entire book as the Codex-Calendar of 354 is intended to distinguish it from the section of the Codex that is the Calendar for Rome for A.D. 354; this section (VI in the list pp. 24–25) is hereafter referred to simply as the Calendar or the Calendar of 354.

2. For a detailed discussion of the dating of the original Codex-Calendar of 354, see Appendix 5.

highlighting of the three dominant institutions in Rome—the imperial government, the urban bureaucracy (with its close links to the senatorial aristocracy), and the Christian church.

The material in the Codex-Calendar concerning these institutions was in part useful, indicating, for example, who was bishop, urban prefect, or emperor, and when. Yet utility was not the only criterion for inclusion. Taken as a whole, the sections reveal the growth and contemporary significance of these three most important institutions of the fourth-century city, each of which seems to make parallel claims to status. Indeed, the Christian church is represented here, for perhaps the first time in the century, as a respectable Roman institution with traditions and a past venerable enough to appeal to any aristocratic Roman. Nevertheless, the centerpiece of the Codex-Calendar of 354 was its illustrated Calendar, a section based entirely on pagan and secular imagery and recording only pagan festivals and imperial anniversaries. Thus, in 354 these pagan festivals and traditions, associated with the Roman senatorial aristocracy and the imperial government, and not the rites and traditions of the church, were accorded the greatest communal support.

The sections at issue are as follows:[3]

Section I	Dedication to Valentinus
Section II	Representations of the Public Fortune (Tyche) of Four Cities
Section III	Imperial Dedication
	List of *Natales Caesarum*
Section IV	The Planets and Their Legends
Section V	*Effectus XII Signorum*. Text and Signs of the Zodiac[4]

3. Those sections in brackets and starred were probably not included in the original Codex-Calendar of 354. The numbering of the sections is conventional; see Stern 1953, pp. 14–16; and Mommsen, *MGH* 1892, pp. 13–148.

Mommsen, *MGH* 1892, p. 37, includes as section XVII the Vienna Annals. These are made up of the *Fasti Vindobonenses priores*, a set of consular annals covering the periods 44 B.C.–A.D. 403 and 455–493, and the *Fasti Vindobonenses posteriores*, consular annals for 44 B.C.–A.D. 387, 439–455, and 495–539. Both are found in the Vindobonensis ms., MS. 3416 (fols. 15–24, 47–53), together with the Codex-Calendar of 354. Fuller entries of the Vienna Annals for the years 390–473 appear in the Sangallensis ms., MS. 878 (fol. 303), again together with the Codex-Calendar of 354. Yet because these *fasti* were definitely not included in the original Codex, they are not included here. For discussion and text, see Mommsen, *MGH* 1892, pp. 31–32, 37ff., and 263ff.

4. Stern 1953, p. 16, n. 16, and pp. 60ff., questions the inclusion of the text (that survives only in the unillustrated Sangallensis ms., MS. 878) in the fourth-century manuscript. I do not, however, see any valid reason to doubt the inclusion of the text in the

Section VI	Calendar Text and Illustrations
	Distichs of the Months[5]
	[*Tetrastichs of the Months]
Section VII	Portraits of the Consuls
Section VIII	List of Consuls
Section IX	Easter Cycle
Section X	List of Urban Prefects of Rome
Section XI	Depositions of the Bishops of Rome
Section XII	Depositions of Martyrs
Section XIII	List of Bishops of Rome
[*Section XIV	Regions of the City of Rome (*Notitia*)]
[*Section XV	*World Chronicle (Liber Generationis)*]
Section XVI	*Chronicle of the City of Rome (Chronica Urbis Romae)*

The Codex-Calendar of 354 can be divided into two parts. The first part (sections I–VII) is illustrated and contains texts with information about the imperial, astrological, pagan religious, or urban/civic realms. The second part (sections VIII–XVI) is not illustrated and includes texts on the imperial, urban/civic, or Christian realms. While Christian themes are omitted from the first part, pagan religion per se is missing from the second, although historical and legendary information is included.

To understand the relationship between the illustrated and unillustrated sections and to gain perspective on the unity of the original Codex, I shall describe the sections and their contents as they appeared in the original Codex-Calendar, based on a collation of the various Renaissance manuscripts. (See Appendix 1.) This sequential analysis will, in the conclusion to this chapter, enable us to analyze the intended effect of the Codex.

THE ILLUSTRATED SECTIONS OF THE CODEX-CALENDAR OF 354

Dedication (Section I)

The Codex-Calendar, like all ancient codices, begins with a dedication page (Fig. 1), which in this case supplies information about the circumstances of the Codex's production. The dedicatory wish, that Val-

---

original and have thus included text and illustrations in this section. See my discussion of section V below.

5. These verses may have been part of the original Codex-Calendar, though they were created earlier; see Chapter 3.

entinus flourish in God (*Floreas in Deo*)—that is, with God's assistance—
is inscribed on both sides of an elaborate monogram reiterating that same
wish. Two putti hold up a rectangular box, also inscribed with wishes
that Valentinus live, flourish, and enjoy (*Vivas, Floreas, Gaudeas*). On either
side of this box, in smaller lettering, is the name of the artist, Furius
Dionysius Filocalus, and the latin verb *titulavit*, indicating, literally, that
Filocalus "wrote the title for" this work.

This title page is our only clue to the identity of the recipient. Since
this dedication uses a Christian formula and since the Codex includes
Christian information, we may assume that Valentinus was a Christian.[6]
The title page and the personalized nature of this highly decorated Codex
indicate that its recipient probably belonged to the uppermost stratum
of Roman society. Most likely he was a wealthy Roman, probably an
aristocrat or one of the new men who, in a position of power, had to
mingle with the old aristocracy still in Rome. (See Chapter 5.)

The title page also identifies the creator of the manuscript, *Furius
Dionysius Filocalus titulavit*, an artist who, in the opinion of his most recent biographer, was "one of the greatest Roman calligraphers of all
time."[7] He has been credited with the creation of the monumental majuscule alphabet used in inscriptions.[8] Indeed, the term *titulavit* is the
common term for engraving found in stone and marble inscriptions. The
Codex-Calendar is the only instance of the term on vellum, where presumably it refers to the layout and execution of the lettering, not just on
the title page but throughout the book. Moreover, the location of Filocalus's name on the first page in the position where ancient Greek and
Roman books conventionally present the author's name or portrait suggests that Filocalus was responsible not only for the lettering and illustrations, but perhaps for the content of the Codex as well.

The inclusion of the name of the calligrapher or artist in a codex is
unusual, and it implies that Filocalus was no mere calligrapher. Either
he was already an artist of some renown at the time the Codex-Calendar
was executed or he was a man of the same social standing as Valentinus.
His later epigraphic work for Pope Damasus reinforces this view of Filocalus's status in Roman society and indicates that he, like Valentinus,
was probably a Christian. Whatever Filocalus's situation in A.D. 354, the
inclusion of his name underscores the special nature of this edition.

6. R. Von Haehling, *Die Religionszugehörigkeit der hohen Amtsträger des Römischen Reiches
seit Constantins I. Alleinherrschaft bis zum Ende der Theodosianischen Dynastie (324–450 bzw. 455
n. Chr.)* (Bonn, 1978) (= *Antiquitas*, 3d ser., 23), pp. 19ff., establishes criteria for religious
affiliation.

7. Ferrua 1939, pp. 42ff.

8. Ferrua 1942, pp. 21–35.

Fig. 1. Dedication to Valentinus, Romanus 1 ms., Barb. lat. 2154, fol. 1. Biblioteca Vaticana, Rome.

Fig. 2. The city of Rome, Romanus 1 ms., Barb. lat. 2154, fol. 2. Biblioteca
Vaticana, Rome.

Fig. 3. The city of Alexandria, Romanus 1 ms., Barb. lat. 2154, fol. 3. Biblioteca Vaticana, Rome.

Fig. 4. The city of Constantinople, Romanus 1 ms., Barb. lat. 2154, fol. 4.
Biblioteca Vaticana, Rome.

Fig. 5. The city of Trier, Romanus 1 ms., Barb. lat. 2154, fol. 5. Biblioteca
Vaticana, Rome.

Fig. 6. Imperial dedication, Romanus 1 ms., Barb. lat. 2154, fol. 6. Biblioteca
Vaticana, Rome.

Fig. 7. The *Natales Caesarum*, Romanus 1 ms., Barb. lat. 2154, fol. 7. Biblioteca Vaticana, Rome.

Fig. 8. The planet Saturn, Romanus 1 ms., Barb. lat. 2154, fol. 8, Biblioteca
Vaticana, Rome.

Fig. 9. The planet Mars, Romanus 1 ms., Barb. lat. 2154, fol. 9. Biblioteca Vaticana, Rome.

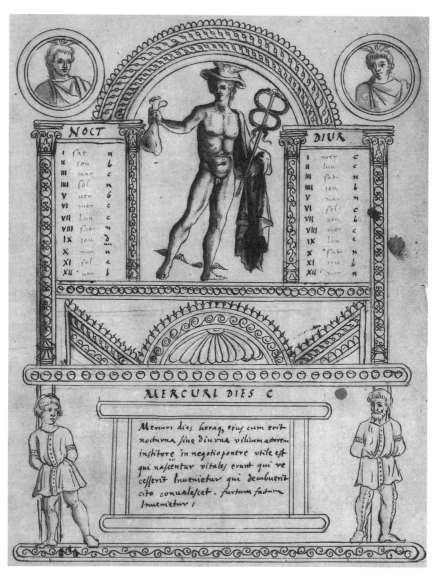

Fig. 10. The planet Mercury, Romanus 1 ms., Barb. lat. 2154, fol. 10. Biblioteca Vaticana, Rome.

Fig. 11. The planet Sol, Romanus 1 ms., Barb. lat. 2154, fol. 11. Biblioteca Vaticana, Rome.

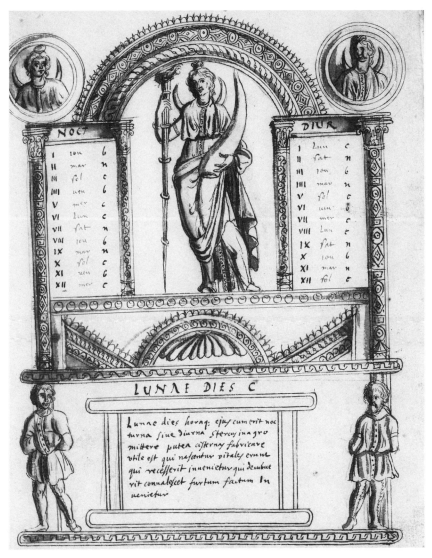

Fig. 12. The planet Luna, Romanus 1 ms., Barb. lat. 2154, fol. 12. Biblioteca Vaticana, Rome.

Fig. 13. Portrait of the Consul of the Year (the Emperor Constantius II),
Romanus 1 ms., Barb. lat. 2154, fol. 13. Biblioteca Vaticana, Rome.

Fig. 14. Portrait of the Consul of the Year (the Caesar Gallus), Romanus 1 ms.,
Barb. lat. 2154, fol. 14. Biblioteca Vaticana, Rome.

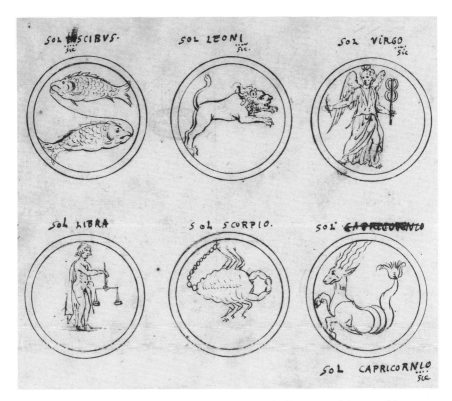

SOL PISCIBVS. *sic*

SOL LEONI *sic*

SOL VIRGO *sic*

SOL LIBRA

SOL SCORPIO.

SOL CAPRICORNLO

SOL CAPRICORNLO *sic*

Fig. 15. Signs of the zodiac, Romanus 1 ms., Barb. lat. 2154, fol. 15. Biblioteca
    Vaticana, Rome.

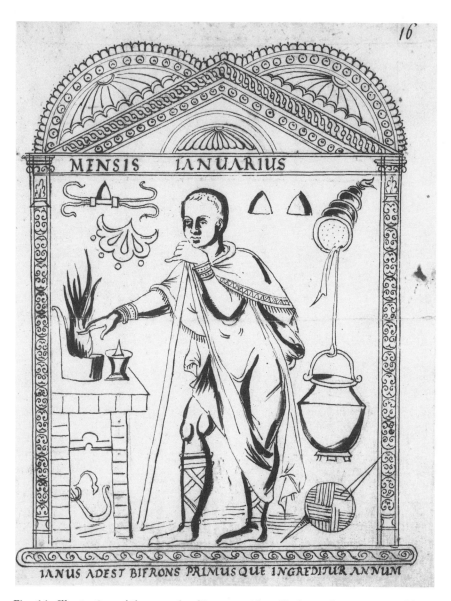

Fig. 16. Illustration of the month of January, identified as a forgery created by Jean Gobille, Romanus 1 ms., Barb. lat. 2154, fol. 16. Biblioteca Vaticana, Rome.

Fig. 17. Illustration of the month of February, Romanus 1 ms., Barb. lat. 2154, fol. 17. Biblioteca Vaticana, Rome.

Fig. 18. Illustration of the month of March, Romanus 1 ms., Barb. lat. 2154, fol. 18. Biblioteca Vaticana, Rome.

Fig. 19. Illustration of the month of August, Romanus 1 ms., Barb. lat. 2154, fol. 19. Biblioteca Vaticana, Rome.

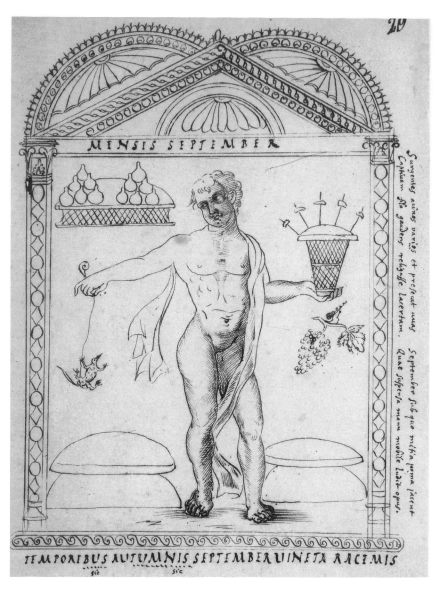

Fig. 20. Illustration of the month of September, Romanus 1 ms., Barb. lat. 2154, fol. 20. Biblioteca Vaticana, Rome.

Fig. 21. Illustration of the month of October, Romanus 1 ms., Barb. lat. 2154, fol. 21. Biblioteca Vaticana, Rome.

Fig. 22. Illustration of the month of November, Romanus 1 ms., Barb. lat. 2154, fol. 22. Biblioteca Vaticana, Rome.

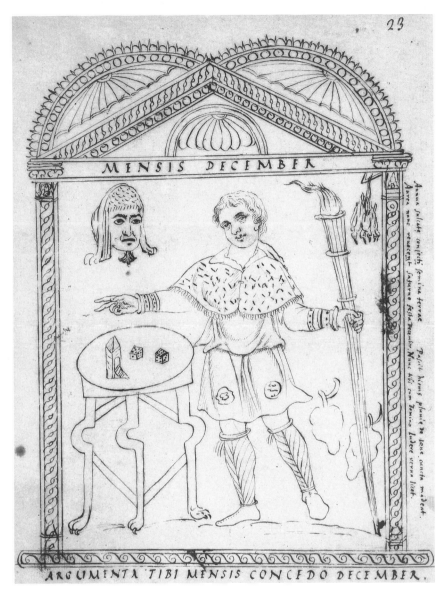

Fig. 23. Illustration of the month of December, Romanus 1 ms., Barb. lat. 2154, fol. 23. Biblioteca Vaticana, Rome.

DIES · X·X·X·I·

a	a	a	Kal	ian	senatus legitimus
	b	b	IIII	Non	dies aegyptiacus
	c	c	III	ludi	uotorum numcupatio
b	d	d	pr	ludi	
	e	e	non	ludi	
	f	f	VIII	idus	dies aegyptiacus
c	g	g	VII	iano	patri · c̄m̄ · xx IIII.
	a	h	VI		
	b	a	v	senatus legitimus	
d	c	b	IIII		
	d	c	III	dies carmentariorum	
	e	d	PR		
e	f	e	idib·	soui statori · c̄m̄ · xx IIII	
	g	f	XIX	kal feb.	
	a	g	XVIII	carmentalia	
f	b	h	XVII	dies aegyptiacus	
	c	a	XVI	ludi palatini	
	d	b	XV	ludi ·	
g	e	c	XIIII	ludi	
	f	d	XIII	N̄· gordiani · c̄m̄ · xx IIII.	
	g	e	XII	ludij	
h	a	f	XI	ludi	
	b	g	X	senatus legitimus	
	c	h	IX	N̄· D̄· hadriani · c̄m̄· xx IIII.	
i	d	a	VIII	N̄· chartis	
	e	b	VII		
	f	c	VI		
k	g	d	V		
	a	e	IIII		
	b	f	III		
a	c	g	PR		

sol Aquario

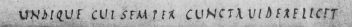

UNDIQUE CUI SEMPER CUNCTA UIDERELICET

Fig. 24. Text of the month of January, Romanus 2 ms., Vat. lat. 9135, fol. 232. Biblioteca Vaticana, Rome.

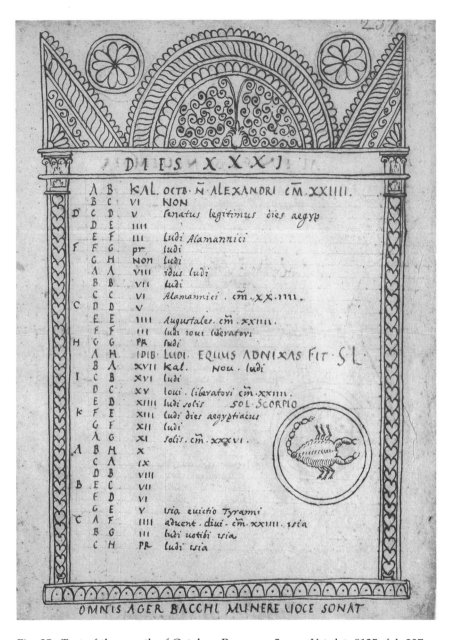

DIES · X X X I

A	B	KAL.	OCTB · Ñ · ALEXANDRI · CM · XXIIII.
B	C	VI	NON
D C	D	V	senatus legitimus dies aegyp
D	E	IIII	
E	F	III	ludi Alamannici
F F	G	pr	ludi
G	H	Non	ludi
A	A	VIII	idus ludi
B	B	VII	ludi
C	C	VI	Alamannici · cm · XX · IIII.
C D	D	V	
E	E	IIII	Augustales · cm · XXIIII.
F	F	III	ludi ioui liberatori
H G	G	PR	ludi
A	H	IDIB	LUDI · EQUUS ADNIXAS FIT · SL ·
B	A	XVII	kal. Nou · ludi
I C	B	XVI	ludi
D	C	XV	ioui · liberatori cm · XXIIII.
E	D	XIIII	ludi solis SOL · SCORPIO
k F	E	XIII	ludi dies aegyptiacus
G	F	XII	ludi
A	G	XI	solis · cm · XXXVI ·
A B	H	X	
C	A	IX	
D	B	VIII	
B E	C	VII	
F	D	VI	
G	E	V	isia euictio Tyranni
C A	F	IIII	aduent · diui · cm · XXIIII · isia
B	G	III	ludi uotibi isia
C	H	PR	ludi isia

OMNIS AGER BACCHI MUNERE UOCE SONAT

Fig. 25. Text of the month of October, Romanus 2 ms., Vat. lat. 9135, fol. 237.
Biblioteca Vaticana, Rome.

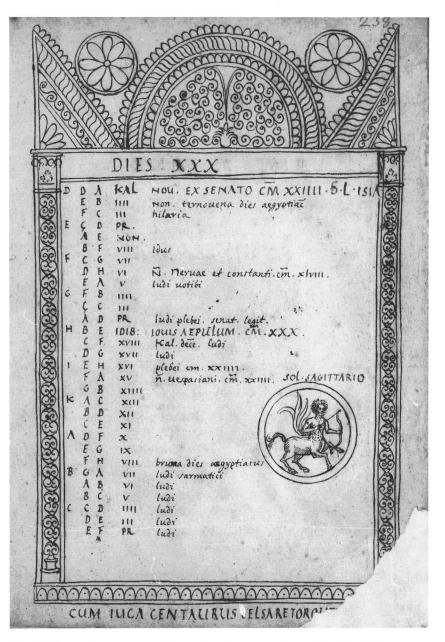

Fig. 26. Text of the month of November, Romanus 2 ms., Vat. lat. 9135, fol. 238. Biblioteca Vaticana, Rome.

Fig. 27. Dedication to Valentinus, Romanus 2 ms., Vat. lat. 9135, fol. 218.
Biblioteca Vaticana, Rome.

Fig. 28. Illustration of the month of November, Berlinensis ms., Ms. lat. 61, fol. 236r. Staatsbibliothek Preussischer Kulturbesitz, Berlin.

Fig. 29. Dedication to Valentinus, Vindobonensis ms., MS. 3416, fol. 1. Österreichische Nationalbibliothek, Vienna.

Fig. 30. Illustration of the month of January, Vindobonensis ms., MS. 3416, fol. 2v. Österreichische Nationalbibliothek, Vienna.

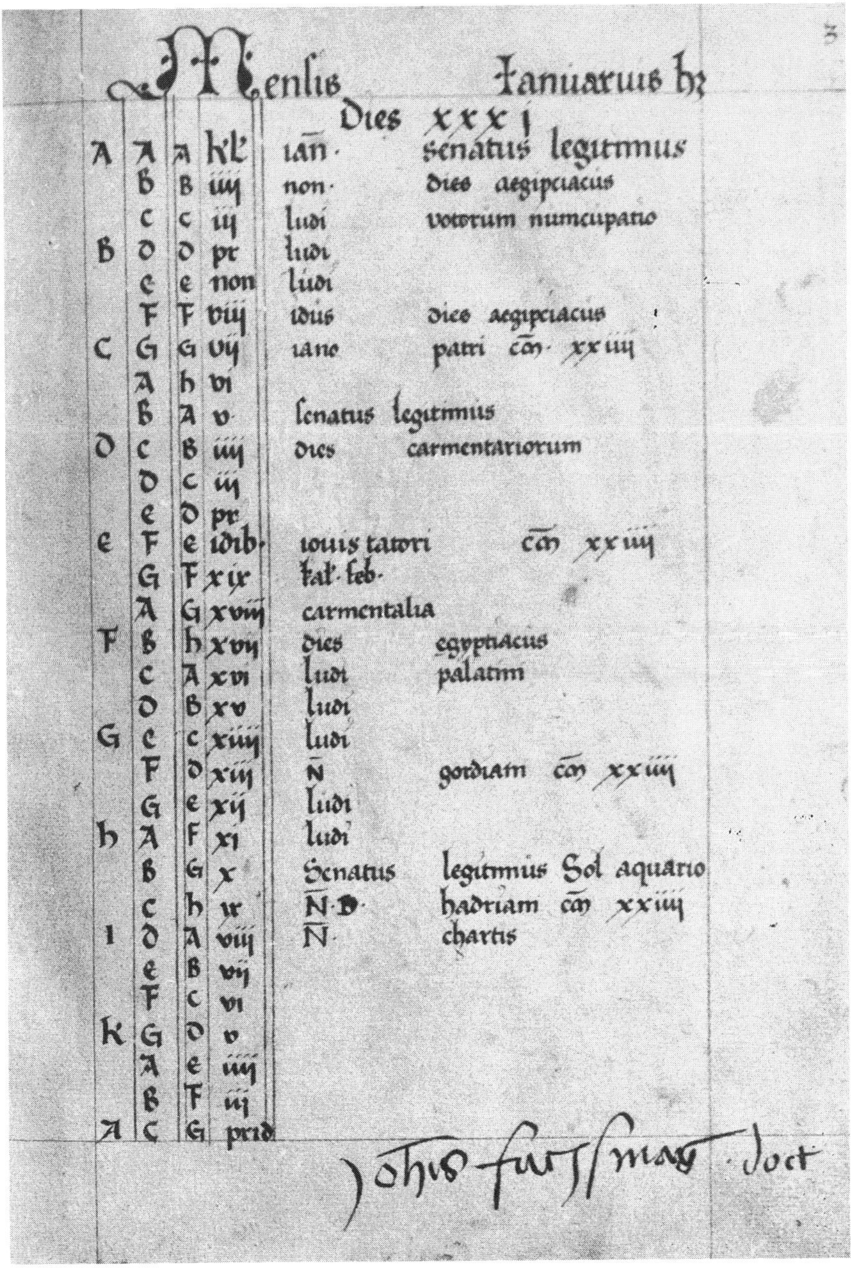

Fig. 31. Text of the month of January, Vindobonensis ms., MS. 3416, fol. 3r. Österreichische Nationalbibliothek, Vienna.

Fig. 32. Illustration of the month of February, Vindobonensis ms., MS. 3416, fol. 3v. Österreichische Nationalbibliothek, Vienna.

Fig. 33. Illustration of the month of March, Vindobonensis ms., MS. 3416, fol. 4v. Österreichische Nationalbibliothek, Vienna.

Fig. 34. Illustration of the month of April, Vindobonensis ms., MS. 3416, fol. 5v. Österreichische Nationalbibliothek, Vienna.

Fig. 35. Illustration of the month of May, Vindobonensis ms., MS. 3416, fol. 6v. Österreichische Nationalbibliothek, Vienna.

Fig. 36. Roman mosaic, 4th century A.D. Palatine Antiquarium, Rome. Photo: Deutsches Archäologisches Institut, Rome.

Fig. 37. Illustration of the month of June, Vindobonensis ms., MS. 3416, fol. 7v. Österreichische Nationalbibliothek, Vienna.

Fig. 38. Illustration of the month of July, Vindobonensis ms., MS. 3416, fol. 8v. Österreichische Nationalbibliothek, Vienna.

Fig. 39. Illustration of the month of August, Vindobonensis ms., MS. 3416, fol. 9v. Österreichische Nationalbibliothek, Vienna.

Fig. 40. Illustration of the month of September, Vindobonensis ms., MS. 3416, fol. 10v. Österreichische Nationalbibliothek, Vienna.

Fig. 41. Illustration of the month of October, Vindobonensis ms., MS. 3416, fol. 11v. Österreichische Nationalbibliothek, Vienna.

Fig. 42. Illustration of the month of November, Vindobonensis ms., MS. 3416, fol. 12v. Österreichische Nationalbibliothek, Vienna.

Fig. 43. Illustration of the month of December, Vindobonensis ms., MS. 3416, fol. 13v. Österreichische Nationalbibliothek, Vienna.

Fig. 44. Dedication to Valentinus, Bruxellensis ms., MS. 7543–7549, fol. 197. Bibliothèque Royale, Brussels.

Fig. 45. Illustration of the month of February, Bruxellensis ms., MS. 7543–7549, fol. 201. Bibliothèque Royale, Brussels.

Fig. 46. Illustration of the month of March, Bruxellensis ms., MS. 7543–7549, fol. 201. Bibliothèque Royale, Brussels.

Fig. 47. Illustration of the month of August, Bruxellensis ms., MS. 7543–7549,
fol. 201. Bibliothèque Royale, Brussels.

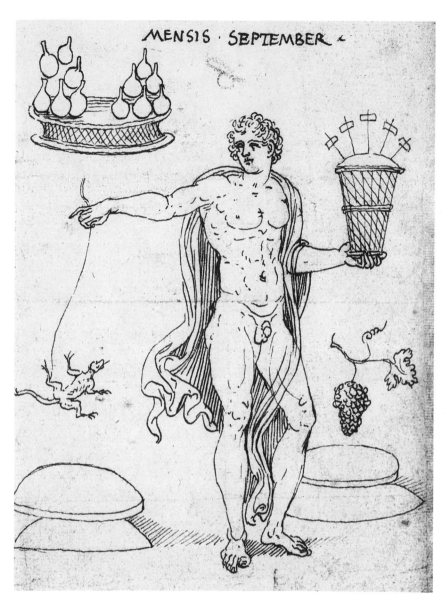

Fig. 48. Illustration of the month of September, Bruxellensis ms., MS. 7543–7549, fol. 201. Bibliothèque Royale, Brussels.

Fig. 49. Illustration of the months of February, March, August, and September, Bruxellensis ms., MS. 7543–7549, fol. 201. Bibliothèque Royale, Brussels.

Fig. 50. Illustration of the month of October, Bruxellensis
ms., MS. 7543–7549, fol. 202. Bibliothèque Royale,
Brussels.

Fig. 51. Illustration of the month of November, Bruxellensis
ms., MS. 7543–7549, fol. 202. Bibliothèque Royale,
Brussels.

Fig. 52. Illustration of the month of December,
Bruxellensis ms., MS. 7543–7549, fol. 202.
Bibliothèque Royale, Brussels.

The Four City Tyches (Section II)

Following the dedicatory page is the illustrated section II, comprising the representations of the city goddesses or divine Fortunes (Tyches) of four major cities of the late Roman empire.[9] Rome (Fig. 2), depicted on the first page, takes pride of place as the preeminent capital of the empire; she alone is seated, a further indication of her dominance. In her right hand she holds a globe, on top of which stands a winged Victory; in her left hand she holds a spear. Beside her throne on the floor to her left is a bag of money with a monetary value of MCCCC: 1,400 coins, presumably silver or bronze, which a putto distributes in the traditional act of *sparsio*. This wealth is yet another mark of Rome's preeminence, since the only other city goddess depicted with a sack of coins, Constantinople, has only M, or 1,000, coins; moreover, no putto distributes her wealth.

On successive pages, the city Tyches of Alexandria, Constantinople, and Trier (Figs. 3–5) are depicted, each with symbols of their contributions to the empire. Alexandria holds a staff of grain in her right hand and a pomegranate in her left; she is flanked by two ships, indicating her role in grain production; and two putti holding candlesticks stand on either side of her. Constantinople is also flanked by putti bearing candles, while two other putti crown her; a sack of coins rests at her feet. Trier concludes the group, pictorialized as a warrior guarding a prisoner and surrounded by deluxe vessels. All four illustrations allude to the gifts of nature and products of human activity that these cities contribute to the empire, as seen in the coins available for distribution as *sparsio* and even in the putti bearing candles—generic signifiers, perhaps, of the celebrations traditionally held in honor of these city Tyches as benefactors of the cities themselves and of the empire as a whole.

The representation of city goddesses enjoyed a long tradition in Greek and Roman art. For centuries, however, Rome was depicted alone. The inclusion of Rome in a group of Tyches appears to be a late-antique (third–sixth-century A.D.) development, as is the tendency to equate the imperial cities of Rome and Constantinople, first attested on the *vota* coinage of Constantius II in A.D. 343.[10] Both of these iconographic innovations appear in the Codex-Calendar. A conscious parallelism is evident in the placement of the two pairs of city Tyches: Rome and Alexandria

9. For further discussion of imperial *tyches,* see Stern 1953, pp. 124–144; and K. Shelton, "Imperial Tyches," *Gesta* 18 (1979): 27–38. For Tyche or *fortuna* in general, see Dar.-Sagl., s.v. "Fortuna," J. A. Hild.

10. See J. M. C. Toynbee, "Roma and Constantinopolis," *JRS* 37 (1947): 135–144; Shelton, "Imperial Tyches."

balance Constantinople and Trier. Even the iconography is carefully orchestrated: the helmeted Rome alternates with the crowned Alexandria, balanced by the crowned Constantinople and the helmeted Trier; a curtain appears behind Rome, who begins the group, and behind Trier, who concludes it. The iconography of Rome and Constantinople is given particular attention: a helmeted Rome, seated on a throne, holds a spear, while a crowned Constantinople, standing, holds a scepter; both are shown with sacks of coins. Thus the symbolic significance of these parallel capitals, the old Rome and the new Rome, Constantinople, now intended to be viewed together as the dominant capitals of a united empire, is reinforced. Moreover, the four Tyches depicted in the Codex-Calendar are not the standard ones;[11] this arrangement, together with the unusual combination of iconographic traits and the deliberate parallelism in the depiction and placement of the two city pairs, suggests the conscious choice of the creator of the Codex, perhaps Filocalus.

This section is relevant to our understanding of the Codex-Calendar in one more way. Because comparable late-antique monuments that include groups of city Tyches and represent Rome and Constantinople as equals are associated primarily with public office or imperial works,[12] the imagery of section II can be read within the context of official or imperial art. It therefore serves well to introduce section III, whose two illustrations similarly share an official or imperial iconographic source. This association and the imperial dedication also reinforce the impression that Valentinus was a man of some standing in Rome, probably a holder of public office.

Imperial Dedication: *Natales Caesarum* (Section III)

The first page of section III (Fig. 6) is illustrated by a female winged Victory who inscribes a shield with the wish that "under safe Augusti, Valentinus may prosper" (*Salvis Augustis, Felix Valentinus*). This dedication effectively joins the well-being of Valentinus to that of the emperor and his ruling house, for the plural address "Augusti" must refer to the Emperor Constantius II and his ruling Caesar. (see Appendix 5.) The illustration on the facing page (Fig. 7) is intimately associated with this imperial dedication. A portrait of the emperor, identified as Constantius II, is depicted with the attributes of Sol Invictus—the raised right hand, nimbus, and phoenix—attributes that are part of imperial iconography

---

11. Stern 1953, pp. 124–144. The standard group included six cities; here, Antioch and Carthage are omitted.

12. These comparable works are cited by Shelton, "Imperial Tyches."

as well. Even the "hand of god" shown here can be derived from imperial iconography. This portrait of Constantius heads a list of *Natales Caesarum,* the "Anniversaries of the Caesars," whose birthdays were celebrated as official holidays. The emphasis on imperial concerns is thus conveyed pictorially by the portrait of the emperor and the winged Victory, and in writing by the wish itself and the listing of *Natales.*

This list of *Natales Caesarum* raises several questions. It begins with January and continues month by month, recording first the name of the caesar in the genitive case, then the date of the anniversary in the ablative. The contents are thought to be derived from official documents, for the birthdays of the consecrated emperors were public celebrations associated with the imperial cult. Yet the list is selective; starting at the time of Augustus, it proceeds to the reign of Probus, then resumes with members of the Constantinian house.[13] The caesars recorded here, moreover, coincide with the emperors considered "good" in the *Scriptores Historiae Augustae,* with one exception: Lucius Aelius Caesar, whose brief rule as caesar (A.D. 136–138) left him honored but not deified.[14] Consequently, he is the only caesar included in this list who was not a consecrated emperor and who is not noted in the text of the Calendar with an anniversary, which suggests that his *Natalis* was not an official public celebration. His inclusion here may owe to his significance for the dynastic concerns of the Emperor Constantius II and so be a pointed political reference to the Caesar Gallus, whose elevation and adoption resembled Lucius Aelius's.[15]

Aside from Lucius Aelius's inclusion, this listing of the *Natales Caesarum* reflects the contemporary imperial concern with the dynastic claim of Constantius II and emphasizes the ruling family, however fictive this family lineage may be. Herein may lie the major reason for the presence

13. There is an apparent error in the transmission of the text: the *natalis* of *Divi Claudi* is omitted. Stern 1953, p. 93, observed that this list of names does not correspond to any as yet identified official occasion or list, such as the magistrate's oath of office or the prayers of the Arval Brethren.

14. Pertinax and Gordian were *divi* and so appear in the list of *Natales,* although neither was a "good emperor." H. Stern, *Date et destinaire de "L'histoire Auguste"* (Paris, 1953), p. 55, rightly distinguishes between *divi principes* and *optimi electi.*

15. For further discussion of this list and of Lucius Aelius Caesar, see ibid., pp. 52–61. Stern used the evidence of the *H.A. Ael.* 2.2 to argue for the dynastic importance of L. Aelius Caesar; the passage discusses the designation of Maximian (identified either as Maximian Hercules or Maximian Galerius) and Constantius (identified as Constantius Chlorus) as caesars, "as if they were the true sons and heirs of the majesty of Augustus." The political reference to Gallus would be obvious. Yet Stern's further argument (pp. 60–61), that this situation is repeated only once in the fourth century—and then under Constantius and Julian—and that consequently the *H.A.* should be dated to the reign of Constantius, is not convincing.

of this list: its selection of emperors represents the contemporary official view of the imperial past and of Constantius's family history, both of which support the positions of the emperor and his caesar.

The Planets (Section IV)
and the *Effectus XII Signorum* (Section V)

The next sections are devoted to astrology, whose widespread appeal in the fourth century, even among Roman aristocrats, pagan and Christian alike, has been well documented. In A.D. 334, for example, Firmicus Maternus, then a pagan, wrote a handbook on astrology which he dedicated to the wealthy pagan aristocrat Mavortius. After his conversion to Christianity made Firmicus a hostile opponent of paganism (as demonstrated by his virulent polemical tract, *The Error of the Pagan Religions*), he nevertheless neither recanted his views on nor attacked astrology. Firmicus Maternus's work has numerous parallels in the art and personal artifacts from this period, which only emphasize the importance of astrology, even at the highest levels of Roman society where the recipient of the Codex-Calendar of 354 was situated. The appeal of this science in general terms, and its obvious affinity with the other chronographic material in the Codex, explains its inclusion; but the actual extent of astrological information (these two sections plus the astrological notations in the Calendar text itself) may reflect the personal interests of the recipient.[16]

Section IV originally contained illustrations of the seven planets, as then conceived, ordered according to the seven days of the astrological week, which they controlled. Traditionally, Saturnus is at the beginning, followed by Sol, Luna, Mars, and Mercury (Figs. 8–12); Jupiter and Venus, the last two planets, although certainly included in the fourth-century original, are unfortunately missing from all extant manuscripts. This section of the Codex-Calendar was mutilated sometime before 1560, when it was last seen and copied in its entirety in Vienna (which copy alone includes the entire series of illustrations of the months)—a loss that accounts for the differing order of the planets in certain manuscripts.[17] The original must have begun with Saturnus, as can be reconstructed by a

16. See I. Hadot, *Arts libéraux et philosophie dans la pensée antique* (Paris, 1984) (= *Etudes augustiniennes*), pp. 242–246, for astrology's appeal.

17. The dislocation of this section of the manuscript in the Romanus copy led Mommsen to reconstruct the order of the planets somewhat differently than is suggested here; see Mommsen 1850a, pp. 538–543; Mommsen, *MGH* 1892, pp. 42–46. But, as Stern 1953, p. 50, rightly points out, the placement of Saturnus on the reverse of the page of the *Natales Caesarum* would indicate the correct ordering of the planets in the archetype.

collation of manuscripts and by the fact that this planet's illustration is included on the reverse of the page of the *Natales Caesarum* (Romanus 1 ms., Barb. lat. 2154, fol. 4r).

Because the Codex-Calendar reproduces the traditional pagan astrological week beginning with Saturn and does not follow the week made popular by the Christians, Mithraists, and Sol worshipers, all of whom displaced Saturn's day and made Sunday the first day of the week, we can be certain that this section of the manuscript derived from an astrological source.

The seven-day astrological week, generally considered to have come to Rome from Egypt,[18] is determined by the planetary hours; each day was divided into twenty-four hours, with twelve hours of night preceding twelve hours of day.[19] The hours are listed in two columns alongside the illustration of each sign: at the top to the left is the title *noct[urnae horae]*; to the right, *diur[nae horae]*. Each hour is recorded with its specific properties, considered either good (*bona*), bad (*noxia*), or indifferent (*communis*). Next to the hour is the name of the planet that presides over that hour; the planets are recorded in red ink, ordered according to their periodic times (Saturn is farthest from the earth and takes the longest time to complete the round of the heavens, followed by Jupiter, Mars, Sol, Venus, Mercury, and, last, Luna, the moon). The day was designated by the planet presiding over its first hour, and is so illustrated. Below each image, inscribed in a pedestal, is a description of the effects (or powers) of that planet. In essence, this is a series of generalized predictions for those born under the sign of each planet, much like the horoscopes in a modern newspaper.

To complete the astrological section of the Codex-Calendar (and to be able to cast a complete horoscope), one would need only a zodiac circle of the months—thus the rationale for the next section, the Effects of the Twelve Signs (section V), in which are indicated, very generally, the appropriate activities for mortals when the moon is in each of the astrological signs.[20] For example, when the moon is in Aries, Cancer, Libra, or Capricorn, it is auspicious to make a will, wash wool, or castrate one's herd. Accompanying this text (itself divided into three groups of

18. C. Pietri, "Le temps de la semaine à Rome et dans l'Italie chrétienne (IV–VI s.)," *Le temps chrétien de la fin de l'antiquité au Moyen-Age (III–XIII s.) (Actes du Colloque, 9–12 Mars, 1981, Paris)* (Paris, 1984), pp. 63–98.

19. This sequence begins with the setting of the sun, following the astrological day; the civil day ran from midnight to midnight. See Stern 1953, p. 53. This is also the Jewish habit adopted by the church; see C. Pietri, "Le temps de la semaine à Rome."

20. Mommsen, *MGH* 1892, p. 47, incorrectly prints "*Effigies XII Signorum*" instead of the correct "*Effectus XII Signorum*." See note 4 above.

four signs), the signs of the zodiac would likely have been depicted, as the text itself suggests. Unfortunately, these illustrations have not survived, for this section is preserved in only one manuscript (Sangallensis, MS. 878, ninth century), which is not illustrated.[21] But since illustrations of the zodiac were fairly standardized, those accompanying this page of text were probably similar to the astrological signs depicted, each within a circular design, on the monthly pages of the Calendar text and also, in my view, on folio 15 of the Romanus copy (Fig. 15).

The Calendar (Section VI)

To avoid confusion, I should begin by noting that the page depicting the six signs of the zodiac preserved in the Romanus copy of the Calendar (fol. 15, Fig. 15) was apparently drawn from the zodiacal signs included in the Calendar text and not from the *Effectus XII Signorum* (section V); these six illustrations were executed as an example for Peiresc's correspondent in Rome.[22] Peiresc's copy had lost two folios, containing the illustrations of Jove and Venus (fols. 7r and 7v) and the signs of the zodiac and their effects (fol. 8r).

On the back of *Effectus XII Signorum* in Peiresc's copy would have been the representation of the month of January (fol. 8v)—marking the beginning of the Calendar (section VI). (The image of January that survives in Peiresc's copy [Fig. 16] is a forgery that is not based on the Luxemburgensis.) Reconstruction of the Calendar's beginning is hypothetical because the Luxemburgensis, the lost Carolingian copy of the archetype, was mutilated sometime before the Renaissance copies of the

21. Mommsen, *MGH* 1892, pp. 25–26; and see Appendix 1 for a fuller discussion of the Sangallensis MS. 878.

22. All the evidence indicates that Peiresc's copy of the manuscript did not include the page with the *Effectus XII Signorum* (section V) and that the page with the six illustrations of the zodiac (fol. 15; Fig. 15) is derived from the illustrations included in the text of the Calendar. These illustrations may well have coincided with those of the lost archetype, but their inclusion and location in the Romanus manuscript reflects only Peiresc's desire to fulfill the request of his correspondent in Rome, Aleandro, for copies of the zodiac. The evidence against this page being part of the original is compelling. First, the illustrations in the Romanus copy (Fig. 15) are not followed by the text of the Effects of the XII Signs, as found in the Sangallensis manuscript. If the text was in the Carolingian copy and Peiresc failed to copy it in the Romanus, this would be a unique instance of his including illustrations without text. Moreover, Peiresc makes no mention of the text or of its illustrations in his careful description of the Carolingian copy. Second, the astrological signs described by Peiresc coincide with the iconography of the signs included in the text of the Calendar (see, for example, Peiresc's description of Aquarius with the Phrygian cap, which coincides with the illustration in Romanus's January). For further details, see Mommsen, *MGH* 1892, pp. 25–26, n. 3.

Calendar were executed.[23] Nevertheless, since only one illustration of the months appears to have been lost, it seems likely that the Calendar, the central section of the Codex, has no title page.

The illustration of each month (Figs. 17–23)—a single figure depicted in an activity and accompanied by two sets of verses, tetrastichs and distichs, describing attributes appropriate to that month—faces the text of holidays for that month (Figs. 24–26). The tetrastichs (*Anth. Lat.* 395, ed. Riese) were added sometime after the completion of the original Codex but before the Carolingian copy was executed; thus, they were probably not part of the original Codex. While the distichs (*Anth. Lat.* 665, ed. Riese), written across two pages below the illustration and the text of each month, may have been included in the original, they are not a fourth-century creation and I personally doubt their incorporation at that time. (See Chapter 3.)

Because this is the only securely dated fourth-century Roman calendar to have survived, problems of interpretation of the images and text understandably persist. In my view, three of the months represent seasonal activities, five show a combination of seasonal and popular motifs, and the remaining four illustrate pagan religious festivals. Moreover, since this is the only cycle of illustrations of the months surviving in codex form (albeit known today only by its Renaissance copies) and the earliest codex with full-page illustrations in Western art, the Calendar illustrations provide a unique opportunity for studying the development of late-antique book illumination.

The text of the Calendar is equally noteworthy. Each month is organized into five columns, set within an ornate architectural frame (Figs. 24–26, 31). Column one records the letters A–K, to indicate the phases of the moon; column two records the letters A–G, for the seven days of the astrological week; column three records the letters A–H, the traditional Roman eight-day market week; column four records the days of the month by the typical Roman system of time reckoning, using Kalends, Nones, and Ides; and column five records what is to happen on any given day—that is, the pagan festivals, imperial anniversaries, historic events, and senatorial meetings that were celebrated in the fourth-century city. Also in this last column are notations of "unlucky days" (*dies aegyptiaci*) and the entrance of the sun into a new sign, accompanied by a zodiacal illustration.

The text indicates that this was the official civil calendar of Rome; as contemporary evidence corroborates, it includes the imperial anniver-

---

23. See ibid., pp. 19ff; and Appendix 1 below.

saries and pagan holidays actually celebrated in Rome in 354. Neither
Christian religious events nor ecclesiastical functions are entered, even
though the Calendar dates to some twenty years after Constantine's bap-
tism as a Christian. Christian holidays are recorded in two separate sections, the Depositions of Bishops and of Martyrs (sections XI and XII),
which in themselves constitute a veritable Christian calendar.[24] Although Christian holidays were beginning to take on a wider public import, the Calendar indicates that this had not yet occurred in Rome in
354.[25]

Portraits of the Consuls (Section VII)

The illustrated part of the Codex-Calendar concludes with the portraits of the two eponymous consuls, identified as the Emperor Constantius II (Fig. 13) and the Caesar Gallus (Fig. 14). Once more, as in the
illustration of Rome, the preeminence of the emperor is stated visually.
Although both consuls are dressed in elaborately ornamented togas and
hold scepters in their left hands, only the emperor is shown seated,
wearing a diadem and a bejeweled toga as he dispenses coins from his
right hand in the act of *sparsio*.[26] To indicate the lower rank of the caesar,
Gallus is depicted standing, in less ornate attire (his toga lacks jewels
but is decorated with pictures), and without a diadem; he holds a Victory
in his right hand, and a bag of coins rests on the ground at his feet. This
consular imagery is strikingly similar to contemporary consular diptychs,
those ivory plaques whose carvings often show the consul opening the
January New Year games by throwing down the *mappa* and distributing
coins. Like the diptychs, the Calendar also conveys to the recipient the
wish for happiness and success, that is, for all the good things that the
consul can give. This imagery invokes the same ideas as did the imperial
Tyches and imperial dedication: all allude to the good fortune associated

24. Mommsen, *MGH* 1892, pp. 70–71, prints section XII under the heading *Feriale
Ecclesiae Romanae*, following De Rossi. The two sections seem to me worthy of the appel-
lation a "veritable Christian calendar."

25. See Pietri 1976, pp. 126–129, 159ff., and 617–624, for Christian celebrations; for
the civic status of Christian holidays, see my discussion of the legislation pertaining to
Christian holidays in the Epilogue, Chapter 6 below.

26. The iconography of the scepter is problematic. A miniaturized head of a man,
depicted with beard and helmet, is shown on top of a round shieldlike object. Usually, the
nonimperial consul holds such a scepter with the bust of the ruling Augustus. Here it is
Constantius, as emperor, who holds such an image. This head has been tentatively identified as either an ancestor of Constantius or Roma; see Stern 1953, p. 165.

with the leading cities, the consuls, and the emperor that should be granted to Valentinus.[27]

THE UNILLUSTRATED SECTIONS
OF THE CODEX-CALENDAR OF 354

The List of Consuls (Section VIII)

The illustrations of the eponymous consuls are appropriately placed before the first of the unillustrated sections, the List of Consuls. The functional difference between the Calendar and the List of Consuls is, generally, the same difference noted between the first part (sections I–VII) and the second part (sections VII–XVI) of the Codex-Calendar. Most of the first part marks recurring time patterns or events in A.D. 354, be they recurring astrological phenomena (sections IV and V), imperial events (sections III and V), or events in the calendar year (section VI), whereas the second part appears not so much to identify cycles (though sections IX, XI, and XII do that as well) as to provide historical or chronographic information to mark past time in relation to the fourth-century present. (This is true for sections VII, X, XIII, and XVI [and XV, if it was included in the original] and to a lesser extent for sections IX, XI, and XII; section XIV does not fit this pattern—another reason why it was probably not in the original [see below].) In a way, then, the unillustrated sections in part two of the Codex-Calendar supplement the function and content of the Calendar proper (section VI). What is so interesting in these sections is the different "pasts" that are represented: the imperial past, the urban past of Rome and its empire, and the Christian past. Subsequent chapters will elucidate the first two "pasts," which are most relevant to the Calendar. For the moment, however, let us focus on the lists in part two of the Codex.

The inclusion of an unillustrated list of consuls to accompany a calendar has a long Roman tradition. Originally, as Cicero tells us, every year the Pontifex Maximus wrote the names of consuls and other magistrates alongside the holidays *(dies fasti)* and noted other significant items on a whitened board *(tabula dealbata pontificum)* set up in the Regia in the Roman Forum.[28] When these were made public is unknown, but

---

27. Ibid. pp. 153ff.

28. Cicero *De Orat.* 2.12.52: "res omnis singulorum annorum mandabat litteris pontifex maximus efferebatque in album et proponebat tabulam domi." Cf. Servius "Auctus," who preserves Verrius Flaccus *Ad Aen.* 1.373: "tabulam dealbatam quotannis pontifex maximus habuit in qua praescriptis consulum nominibus et aliorum magistratuum digna me-

by the first century B.C., as the fragmentary remains of the *Fasti Antiates Maiores* (84–55 B.C.) record, lists of consuls and censors were displayed publicly and inscribed on walls alongside Roman calendars, a conjunction that continued into the early empire.[29] The addition of such a consular listing to the Calendar would be of clear utility, since by the fourth century Roman dating by consular year was universal; in section IX, for example, it was used to compute the days of the Easter cycle, and in section X it was used to establish the terms of office of the city prefects.

The List of Consuls in the Codex-Calendar is the most complete and reliable record of Roman consuls to survive.[30] Beginning with the consuls under the kings of Rome, it extends to the consuls for A.D. 354. In four columns are (1) the year, numbered according to the traditional Varronian date used to calculate the foundation of Rome; (2) the *cognomina* of the two consuls for the year (for every fourth year, reproducing here the nomenclature of the *Fasti Capitolini*, the eponymous consular name is preceded by the standardized notation *b*, for *bisextus*, to indicate the leap year); (3) the day of the week; and (4) the lunar phase of the first day of the year, on which date the consul entered office. These last two columns are unique among consular lists and were evidently included here for calculating the *Supputatio Romana*, an eighty-four-year cycle, constructed originally by astrologers, later used for tax purposes by the Roman bureaucracy under Diocletian, and then taken up by Christian chronographers to determine the dates for Easter (as in section IX).

This impersonal, anonymous, and uniform consular listing is punctuated by only a few historical notes. Like the list itself, the annotations are formulaic. The election or omission of dictators, for example, is always recorded beginning with a reference to the year (*Hoc anno*) and followed by the statement that there were or were not dictators, with the nominative of the noun, *dictatores*, and the verb *fuerunt* invariably used. These are the only secular annotations to this section; the rest, albeit similarly formulaic, refer to events relating to Christianity or to the church at Rome, such as the birth and passion of Christ, the entry into Rome of Peter and Paul, and their martyrdom. Each note begins with an indication of time, *Hoc cons.* or *His cons.*, followed by a reference to a

---

moratu notare consueverat domi militiaeque, terra marique gesta per singulos dies." For further discussion, see B. Freier, *Libri Annales Pontificum Maximorum: The Origins of the Annalistic Tradition, MAAR* 27 (L'Aquila, Italy, 1979): 83–105, 171ff.

29. See A. Degrassi, *Inscriptiones Italiae*, vol. 13, pt. 1 (Rome, 1947); and Degrassi 1963, pp. xixff.

30. The only noteworthy correction is the omission of consuls for 461; for the text, see Mommsen, *MGH* 1892, pp. 50–61.

single event, generally through use of a passive verb. Given the inclusion and careful spacing of these Christian notations in all extant manuscript copies, it is likely that they were not later additions but were in the original 354 compilation.

The inclusion of Christian entries in the List of Consuls indicates the concern of contemporary Christians not only to commemorate significant events in Christian history but also to calibrate these moments with the Roman past. This concern is perhaps best exemplified by the vogue for universal histories, one of which may have been included in the 354 Codex (section XV). Moreover, the inclusion of Christian information underscores the personalized nature of this Codex, for it indubitably reflects the Christianity of the recipient, Valentinus.

The List of Consuls is not like other, later, extant fourth- and fifth-century consular lists or annals,[31] which contain, along with the consuls' names, a contemporary record of events, with material about the emperors and their dynasties, the Roman state, ecclesiastical literature and history, natural disasters, and so forth. These later consular annals were generally extremely meticulous in the information they recorded, giving, for example, hours as well as dates for events (in this they are more similar to section XV). In addition, there is now enough fragmentary evidence to indicate that several of these consular annals were illustrated.[32] In contrast, the unillustrated List of Consuls from the Codex-Calendar of 354 has no such precise details and contains no record of contemporary events; the most recent event noted is the martyrdom of Peter and Paul.

It would appear that consular annals developed into a subliterary

---

31. Mommsen, *MGH* 1892, pp. 251–339, groups seven of these texts, calling them *Consularia Italica* as opposed to the *Consularia Constantinopolitana.* See R. Bagnall, A. Cameron, S. Schwartz, and K. Worp, *Consuls of the Later Roman Empire* (Atlanta, 1987), pp. 47–57.

32. The illustrated consular annals to which I refer appear in the following publications: (1) A. Bauer and J. Strzygowski, *Eine Alexandrinische Weltchronik. Text und Miniaturen eines griechischen Papyrus der Sammlung W. Golenischev,* Denkschrift der Kaiserlichen Akademie der Wissenschaften zu Wien, Philosophisch-Historische Klasse, no. 51 (1906) [Alexandrian consular list and World Chronicle of the early fifth century]; (2) H. Lietzmann, "Ein Blatt aus einer antiken Weltchronik," *Quantulacumque: Studies Presented to Kirsopp Lake* (London, 1937), pp. 339–348 (= *Kleine Schriften I* [Berlin, 1958], p. 419–429) [ca. A.D. 400 for the Berlin papyrus fragment]; (3) *Excerpta Barbari,* edition of "Scaliger's Barbarian," which has no extant illustrations but left room for them; complete editions by A. Schoene, *Eusebii Chronicorum liber prior* (Berlin, 1875), pp. 177–239; and C. Frick, *Chronica Minora,* vol. 1 (Leipzig, 1892), pp. 183–371 [a late Latin translation of a Greek chronicle to A.D. 387]; and (4) B. Bischoff and W. Koehler, "Un' edizione illustrata degli Annali Ravennati del basso impero," *Studi Romagnoli* 3 (1952): 1–17 [early-fifth-century Latin chronicle].

genre for recording contemporary history somewhat later in the fourth century. If the Codex-Calendar is any indication, the West was, in A.D. 354, not yet familiar with this type of consular annal; the four extant illustrated *exempla* of the genre are all from the late fourth or fifth century and of Greek origin.[33] It seems likely, therefore, that this particular use of consular annals was transmitted by the Greek East to the West, probably in the last two decades of the fourth century.[34] Indeed, the fact that the List of Consuls in the Codex-Calendar was not continued past 354 and never became the basis for a later annal may reflect this transition. When a later user wanted to update the Codex-Calendar, he was forced to remedy its lack of historical information by adding the *Fasti Vindobonenses,* a consular list that began recording contemporary events in A.D. 378.[35]

The List of Consuls in the Codex-Calendar of 354 provides important information on the dates and sources of the original compilation. Obviously, since this list concludes with the two consuls for 354, the Codex-Calendar was compiled and intended for use in that year. What has not been remarked, however, is the deletion of the usurpers Magnentius and Gaiso (Western consuls, 351), Decentius and Paulus (Western consuls, 352), and Magnentius and Decentius (consuls in Gaul, 353); these were replaced by the notations *post Sergio et Nigriniano* (351); *Constancio V* and *Constantio iun.[ior]* (352), and *Constancio VI et Constantio II* (353). The usurpers were defeated in July 353, Magnentius and Decentius committed suicide in August 353, and Constantius passed his law of amnesty on 6 September 353; thus, the corrected List of Consuls could not be earlier than the *damnatio memoriae* suffered by Magnentius and his followers, that is, before September 353. The creator of the Codex-Calendar of 354, then, was still at work—at least on this section—in the fall of 353. The deletion of the names of the usurpers may also suggest an official source for this list, from either the imperial or urban archives.[36] An of-

33. This conclusion assumes that Mommsen's hypothesis that the Chronicle of Ravenna is a continuation of the Alexandrian Chronicle, as was "Scaliger's Barbarian," is correct. Indeed, Mommsen's ideas were confirmed by the Ravenna Chronicle; see Bagnall, Cameron, Schwartz, and Worp, *Consuls,* pp. 49–51.

34. For an excellent discussion of the tradition of consular annals, see S. Muhlberger, "Prosper, Hydatius, and the Chronicle of 452: Three Chroniclers and Their Significance for Fifth-Century Historiography," Ph.D. diss., University of Toronto, 1981, pp. 1–61, and his forthcoming book, *The Fifth Century Chronicles: Prosper, Hydatius, and the Gallic Chronicler of 452.*

35. Muhlberger, "Prosper, Hydatius, and the Chronicle of 452," pp. 50–61.

36. These observations are not meant to suggest that the List of Consuls was copied directly from an official document. Although the late consular annals are useful comparanda, it is worth noting that they are no longer believed to be official in origin but were

ficial source would explain why this list has been corrected while certain others, notably that of the urban prefects (section X), were not.[37]

The Easter Cycle (Section IX)

The List of Consuls was used to compute the date of Easter in Rome, based on an eighty-four-year lunar cycle derived from an earlier table by the Roman bishop Hippolytus (A.D. 170–235/236).[38] The calculated dates are recorded chronologically by consular year in section IX, the Easter Cycle, from 312 to 354; after 354 and up to 411 the projected date is given.[39] The inclusion of an Easter Cycle underscores the growth of the Christian community in Rome. The list begins in 312 presumably because in that year Constantine issued his famous edict of religious toleration; certainly 312 is a turning point in the history of Christianity, for it signals imperial acceptance of the religion.[40] This initial date for the Easter Cycle may allude as well to controversies within the church concerning the proper time and methods for calculating the celebration of Easter, the significance of which for early Christians was so great that "in the latter half of the second century, the controversy about the time of keeping Easter nearly split the Church in twain."[41]

---

probably created by private booksellers in Constantinople; see O. Seeck, "Idatius und die Chronik von Constantinopel," *Neue Jahrbücher für Philologie und Paedagogik* 139 (1889): 603–632; and the excellent discussion by Muhlberger, "Prosper, Hydatius, and the Chronicle of 452," pp. 38–46. The List of Consuls from the Codex-Calendar of 354 may similarly have been circulated by private booksellers who had access to some official source. For a fuller discussion of the dating and sources of the Codex-Calendar of 354, see Appendices 5 and 6.

37. The only other explanation is that since these other lists were already complete, the creator of the Codex was unwilling to tamper with them by deleting names. This explanation will not, however, account for the List of Urban Prefects, which was still being worked on in December 353. See Appendix 6.

38. Hippolytus's cycle was only partly successful: his sixteen-year Easter cycle had to be corrected as early as A.D. 243; see M. Richard, "Comput et chronographie chez Saint Hippolyte," *Mélanges de science religieuse* 8 (1951): 32ff. But he did influence Christian chronographical writings, especially in Rome, as his importance for sections XIII and XV indicates.

39. Owing to a scribal error, the consuls of 368 are placed beside the Easter Day of 359; this error continues for the remaining computations of Easter.

40. Mommsen, *MGH* 1892, p. 62, posited this reason. Mommsen 1850a, pp. 572ff., suggested a second reason for the initial date of 312: it was the first year of an indiction cycle, the eighty-four-year tax cycle by then in use throughout the empire. See B. Krusch, *Der 84-jährige Ostercyclus und seine Quellen* (Leipzig, 1880).

41. *New Catholic Encyclopedia* (New York, 1967), s.v. "Easter Controversy," p. 159.

In 325, the Council of Nicaea largely adopted the Roman practice in an attempt to see Easter celebrated on the same date in the East and the West.[42] The consensus did not last.[43] At the councils of 342–343, the rift between the two churches was symbolized by the adoption of different dates for Easter.[44] The calculation in the West continued to be made according to the eighty-four-year lunar cycle (as the Codex-Calendar of 354 attests), whereas in the East either the Alexandrian nineteen-year cycle was used or, especially in Antioch, the old custom of observing Easter on the Sunday after the Jewish Passover was retained. By choosing to follow their own traditions, the Eastern bishops were stating their independence from the Western church and from the authority of the bishop of Rome, an authority stated elsewhere in the Serdican Canons of 342.[45] Although the legal confirmation of the Roman bishop's primacy was not yet forthcoming, this council marks the beginning of the struggle between the churches of East and West.

The fourth century saw no uniformity in the adoption of Easter cycles, and so the issue remained divisive.[46] The religious conflict inherent in the celebration of Easter suggests why the Roman see kept careful records of these dates. Thus, in addition to its utility for the recipient of the Codex-Calendar (whose Christianity has already been established by the dedication and by the inclusion of Christian elements in the List of Consuls), this section states the orthodox Roman view of the preeminence of the bishop of Rome, the successor of Peter, in internal Church polity. It therefore seems likely that the church records at Rome were the basis of this Easter Cycle; the inclusion of the dates of past celebrations of Easter, for forty years prior to 354, suggests an ecclesiological and commemorative purpose to the listing. Indeed, in this regard the Easter Cycle is comparable to the inscription of the ten-year paschal cycle on a monumental statue of Hippolytus found in Rome and now in the Vatican Library; like the Easter Cycle, this inscription commemorates not

42. The Council of Nicaea apparently approved the practice of celebrating Easter on the Sunday after both the fourteenth of Nisan and the vernal equinox, thereby neglecting both Quartodeciman and Jewish calendars (Eusebius *Vita Constantini* 3.17–20); see *New Catholic Encyclopedia*, s.v. "Easter Controversy," p. 159.

43. See Pietri 1976, p. 181.

44. H. Chadwick, *The Early Church* (London, 1967), p. 139.

45. See H. Leitzmann, *From Constantine to Julian: A History of the Early Church*, vol. 3, trans. B. Woolf (New York, 1950), p. 121. Lietzmann notes (p. 205) that an agreement on Easter was reached between Rome and Alexandria at the Council of Serdica.

46. See L. Duchesne, *Origines du culte chrétien*, 3d ed. (Paris, 1903), p. 251; and V. Gumel, "Le problème de la date pascal aux IIIe et IVe siècles," *Revue des études byzantines* 18 (1960): 163–178.

only Hippolytus, the originator of the Roman Easter cycle, but also the traditions of the Christian church in Rome.

The List of Urban Prefects of Rome (Section X)

The List of Urban Prefects of Rome is recorded by consular year from A.D. 254 to 354. Its contents suggest that the compiler of this section has used not official or imperial sources but rather unofficial sources that sometime earlier may have been derived from the archives of the urban prefect; this unoffical source may have been compiled with the aid of a church archive, because both this section and the next, the Depositions of Roman Bishops, cover the same period, A.D. 255–352. (See Appendix 6.) Whatever the source, the accuracy of the List of Urban Prefects is well documented. Moreover, its value as a historical record is incomparable, for it is the sole complete listing of urban prefects from Rome that has come down to us.[47]

Following a strict chronological sequence, the list records for each year (1) the names of the Western consuls for that year, (2) the name of the urban prefect for that year, and (3) his title, *praefectus urbis*. For some years starting in 288, and almost every year from 302 on, the day and month of the prefect's entry into office are added before his name as well; and in certain years (e.g., 307, 308, and 318) additional remarks cite special circumstances affecting the date on which he took office. The List of Urban Prefects therefore provides invaluable evidence for dating the original Codex-Calendar. Because the section was updated to include the prefect designated for the year 354—Vitrasius Orfitus, who entered office on 8 December 353—evidently the book was still being completed on that date, perhaps for presentation on 1 January 354.[48]

Analysis of the list's function points to the aristocratic milieu of the Codex-Calendar. Since the names of the urban prefects were not used to date the year, as the List of Consuls was, the inclusion of such a list was clearly not for chronographic purposes. And although the detailed notations may suggest an official or ceremonial use, we simply do not know what that was, if indeed there was one. What appears most relevant for explaining the inclusion of a List of Urban Prefects is the increased status of this office in fourth-century Rome. Since the office of

47. See esp. Chastagnol 1960, p. 2.
48. Stern 1953, p. 45, conjectures—plausibly, though it cannot be demonstrated—that the Codex-Calendar of 354 was presented on New Year's Day.

consul was effectively closed to them, Western aristocrats habitually filled the position of urban prefect. This political privilege was one important indicator of social prestige, which was, increasingly in the fourth century, demonstrated by contributing money for the traditional games and circuses at Rome.[49] Presumably the recipient of this Codex-Calendar was one of these Roman aristocrats or someone with official ties; one can imagine the pleasure he felt as he recognized in this section the names of friends and relatives. In addition, the list provided useful historical information to one interested in the urban aristocracy and its familial connections.

Interestingly, the inspiration for including such a list in a Codex-Calendar may lie in Christian chronographic works and universal histories, both of which recorded secular lists of kings and local rulers alongside church leaders, prophets, and so on. Such Christian works, like the third-century *Chronographies* by Hippolytus, may have set the precedent for this joining of the names of local secular officials with the listing of Christian bishops that follows (section XIII).[50] The unofficial nature of the contents of this list supports this hypothesis as well.

The Depositions of Bishops (Section XI) and of Martyrs (Section XII)

The next two sections are extremely important documents for the history of the church in Rome: they are the earliest record of the dates of death of the Roman bishops from the period 255–352 and of the Roman martyrs officially commemorated by the church in Rome in the fourth century.[51] The celebration of these dates unified the Christian community and instilled in it a sense of its own history, it being "the perpetual responsibility [of the Catholic church] to maintain the memory of its heroes and leaders."[52] The commemoration of the deaths of bishops and martyrs increasingly became, over the course of the fourth century, the responsibility of the bishops of Rome, a listing of whom (section XIII) quite logically follows.

49. Chastagnol 1960, p. 451.
50. See note 38 above.
51. As befits their significance, the bibliography on each of these two lists is vast. Specific relevant works will be cited below. For additional bibliography on these lists, see Pietri 1976, pp. 365–387, 603–624 (incl. p. 365, n. 3); Stern 1953, pp. 113ff.; and C. Pietri, "Le temps de la semaine," 63–98; H. Lietzmann, *Petrus und Paulus in Rom* (Berlin, 1927), pp. 1–29; and, more generally, J. P. Kirsch, *Der stadtrömische christliche Festkalender im Altertum* (Münster, 1924).
52. P. Brown, *The Cult of the Saints* (London, 1981), p. 31.

The Depositions of Bishops begins in 255 and is composed in two parts: the names of bishops honored during each month of the year for 255–335 and, at the end of the list and out of the monthly sequence, two additional names of bishops who died in 336 and 352—providing important confirmation of the two recensions of this list and for the dating of the codex. The coincidence of the initial date for the depositions—255—with that of the List of Urban Prefects (starting in 254) has prompted several scholars to attribute all three sections (X–XII) as well as the List of the Bishops of Rome (section XIII) to the same source, be it the archives of the pretorian prefect or of the church at Rome. Scholars have suggested that all these lists began in 254 because the pertinent information was available and in order only from that year on; that is, only from the middle of the third century was it necessary for Roman bishops to register with urban authorities.[53] Whether this conjecture holds or not, the third century saw the beginning of the church's internal organization at Rome and so is a likely time for the origins of an ecclesiastical historical record-keeping attempt. The *Liber Pontificalis* notes that it was Pope Fabian (236–250) who "appointed seven subdeacons who directed seven clerks to faithfully gather the deeds of the martyrs in their entirety."[54] Although this pope may have used the prefectural archives to reconstruct the acts of martyrs, it is not necessarily the case that his successors, who continued his work, did.[55] Regardless of the sources, however, these sections of the Codex-Calendar reflect the attempts of the Christian church, in the middle of the third century, to organize internally and to construct an official, uniform view of its past.

Constantine's establishment of Christianity was the turning point in the development of the cult of martyrs, for only then could such worship be manifested in legal, public communal celebrations. In 354—and certainly not in 336, when these two lists were originally drawn up—the commemorations of the martyrs were not yet the equal of the pagan festivals and imperial holidays; the Christian holidays were not noted in the civil calendar of Rome (section VI), whereas the pagan and imperial ones were. Rather, as sections XI and XII show, Christians developed a separate calendar for the commemoration of the celebrations of the cult of martyrs. In Rome, it was not until the second half of the fourth century

53. G. B. De Rossi, *La Roma sotterranea cristiana*, vol. 1 (Rome, 1864), pp. 117ff.

54. Valentini and Zucchetti II, 1942, p. 225: "fecit VII subdiaconos, qui VII notariis imminerent, ut gestas martyrum in integro fideliter colligerent."

55. The utilization of official sources may also have continued; note the consistent omission of the usurpers' names from the Christian lists (sections IX, XI, and XII), which apparently utilized the official consular lists. The inclusion of some usurpers in section XIII, however, makes this hypothesis uncertain. For further discussion, see Appendix 6.

that the bishops developed the ceremonial and public commemorative aspects of the cult of martyrs.[56] The efforts of Pope Damasus and his willingness to honor the tombs of martyrs with appropriate monumental buildings began some ten years later than the Codex-Calendar of 354; nevertheless, his name is of particular interest, for he employed the same artist for the monumental inscriptions at the tombs as created this codex—Furius Dionysius Filocalus.

The placement of the Depositions of Martyrs and of Bishops on facing pages reflects the close link between the two sections, as the veneration of martyrs at their place of burial in the suburban cemeteries expanded to include veneration of the martyr's confessor: "Before very long, the names of confessors also began to find a place in the lists [of saints], for confessors and bishops were already written in the diptychs, and in those days the line between praying to a departed servant of God and praying for him was by no means so clearly defined as it is with us now."[57] Indeed, the Depositions suggest that by the time the list was compiled in 336, a recently deceased bishop was customarily paid the highest honors of the church and given a liturgical place equal or similar to that of a martyr. The commemoration of the deposition of Pope Sixtus (257–258), for example, is recorded only once: under the Depositions of the Roman Martyrs.

As if to reflect their functional similarity, both lists of depositions use the same formula for their notations, recording in columns and in chronological sequence, following the months of the year, first the date (according to the Roman system of Kalends, Nones, and Ides), then the name of the bishop or martyr to be commemorated (whose name is declined in the genitive case after the word *Depositio*), and finally the official location of the celebration, generally the suburban cemeteries of Rome. For example, the little-known Saints Parthenius and Calocerus, martyred under Diocletian and Maximianus in 304, are recorded with their date and place of celebration, the cemetery of Callistus; and the martyrdoms of Abdos and Semnes were commemorated in the cemetery of Ponti-

56. Brown, *Cult of the Saints*, has argued that the conflict between the bishops and the aristocracy was over control of the cult of the martyrs. This thesis is criticized—and correctly—by C. Pietri, "Les origines du Culte des Martyrs (d'après un ouvrage recent)," *Rivista di Archeologia Cristiana* 3, no. 4 (1984): 293–315. Nevertheless, the bishops in Rome were, along with the emperor, the dominant figures in developing cult ceremonial in the later fourth century and in building appropriate shrines for these martyrs in Rome; see Pietri 1976, pp. 603–624.

57. *New Catholic Encyclopedia*, s.v. "Confessor," p. 161; H. Lietzmann, *From Constantine to Julian* 3:324.

anus, with the direction added "ad ursum piliatum." It is interesting that the formula for the Depositions of Bishops and of Martyrs repeats that used in the *Natales Caesarum* (section III): all three sections record the transition of the individual—caesar, bishop, or martyr—into a new, sacred state of existence; the similarity in formula highlights a similarity in function.

Together, the Depositions of Bishops and of Martyrs provide a virtual abbreviated calendar, or *feriale*, of the most important dates observed by the church at Rome. Yet in the Codex-Calendar of 354 they are recorded in two separate sections—an indicator of the early stage of development of the Christian calendar in Rome. (By the time of Julian [A.D. 361–363], at least in the East, the depositions of martyrs and bishops were combined into one listing.)[58] In fact, such inventories can be considered the earliest attested calendar of saints' days in the West, an accurate reflection of the early stage of development of the cult of martyrs in the fourth-century city and a telling predictor of the cult's subsequent growth in public importance.

The Depositions of Martyrs (section XII) is perhaps the most famous section of the Codex-Calendar: it is the earliest attested Christian martyrology for the church in the West. The church year begins with the nativity of Christ, celebrated in Rome on 25 December. The anniversaries of the martyrs follow chronologically, according to the months of the year. Every month except April has at least one or two martyrs' festivals—an easily understandable lacuna given the activity and strictures surrounding the celebration of Easter. Most of these festivals occur from July to September, the months traditionally filled with pagan ceremonies and when it was easiest to visit the suburban cemeteries.[59]

The majority of martyrs belong to the third and early fourth centuries and are of local Roman significance. But three popular African martyrs, Saints Cyprian, Perpetua, and Felicitas, were also recorded, along with their African origin, because they were honored in areas of Rome. These annotations underscore the practical value of this section for inhabitant of Rome and pilgrim alike.

The Depositions of both Bishops and Martyrs have been the subject

58. The Syriac martyrology, derived from a Greek calendar composed in Nicomedia under Julian, attests this combination. H. Lietzmann, *Kleine Texte*, vol. 2 (Leipzig, 1908), pp. 7–15, sees this mansucript, written in Edessa in Syriac in A.D. 411, as recording the festivals of the church in the East. He dates the original to approximately the reign of Julian.

59. For further discussion of the Christian calendar year, see Pietri 1976, pp. 365–401, 617–623; and his "Le temps de la semaine."

of much scholarly discussion. Notable debates concern (1) the omission of Pope Sixtus from the former and his inclusion in the latter and (2) the entry of the deposition of Pope Marcellinus on the date of that of Pope Marcellus, presumably an error of the scribe, who confused Marcellus with Marcellinus.[60]

Perhaps the most famous crux is the notation for 29 June in the Depositions of the Martyrs: "Petri in Catacumbas et Pauli Ostense, Tusco et Basso Cons A.D. 258."[61] This, the earliest record of the veneration of the two saints Peter and Paul in Rome, omits any mention of the Shrine of the Apostles on the Vatican Hill, a notation that one would expect given Constantine's building of the Basilica of St. Peter. Although archaeological excavations have not clarified this textual problem, many solutions have nonetheless been proposed. Some have seen the notation as an accidental corruption of an original entry in the manuscript identical with the entry for 29 June in the sixth-century *Martyrologium Hieronymianum,* which reads: "Peter at the Vatican, Paul on the Road to Ostia, both at Catacumbas."[62] Pietri, the eminent historian of early Christianity, has proposed that the Depositions text is indeed accurate and reflects the mid-fourth-century reality of suburban veneration of these apostles, who were worshiped at Rome since A.D. 258. According to Pietri, the notation in the Codex-Calendar would indicate that the Constantinian basilica was not yet fully available for the official celebration of these martyrs even in 354. Pietri's argument is convincing, for it coincides with the contemporary attempt on the part of the church at

60. Mommsen, *MGH* 1892, pp. 70–74; Stern 1953, pp. 44, 113ff.

61. See Valentini and Zucchetti II, 1942, p. 19, n. 1, for the history of the scholarship on this famous crux.

62. H. Chadwick, *Boethius: The Consolations of Music, Logic, Theology, and Philosophy* (Oxford, 1981), pp. 35–36, has argued that the extraordinary silence about the Vatican shrine in the Codex-Calendar can be explained if the Carolingian manuscripts depended on a model written in the Laurentian camp, ca. A.D. 502–506—a time when the faithful were not encouraged to include the Vatican in their lengthy processions on the city's patronal festival. "During this period of 4 years the opponents of Symmachus could celebrate St. Peter only at the Basilica of the Apostles on the Via Appia by the place Catacumbas which gave its name to the catacombs" (p. 36). Chadwick goes on to point out the appeal this text had for the senatorial circle supporting Laurentius, who would have carefully preserved it, though with some alterations. Chadwick's suggestion is clever, but not convincing. While the omission does occur in three manuscripts of the Codex, all three derive from the same copy. Thus, accidental corruption is as plausible as intentional change. Moreover, the designation of the year of celebration—A.D. 258—and the fact that the other martyrs are recorded in their suburban cemeteries perhaps suggest that the calendars record only the year in which the pope ordered the celebration of the feast on the Via Appia (see Franchi de' Cavalieri, "S. Bassilla," *Note Agiografiche,* pt. 5 [Rome, 1915], pp. 124–125 [= *Studi e Testi* 27]); that is, only the historical feast and locale are commemorated in this earliest record of the cult of martyrs.

Rome to venerate and legitimate the apostolic cult, celebrated there for at least a century.[63]

The apostolic cult is recorded in this list of martyrs a second time, by the Festival of St. Peter's Chair on 22 February, a holiday commonly understood to commemorate the day on which the Apostle Peter took up office as first bishop of Rome.[64] But why include this Christian holiday in a martyrology? The most likely answer raises an issue of particular interest for this study, namely, the relationship between pagan and Christian holidays. The Christian holiday St. Peter's Chair falls on the same date as the pagan festival of the *Caristia*, a familial banquet held at the grave of a dead relative.[65] It has been suggested that Christians maintained the pagan custom of such a banquet by keeping a chair (*cathedra*) for the dead relative at a memorial meal, and hence the Christian festival for the dead came to be called the festival of the *cathedra*. In worship, however, the Roman congregation gave thanks more specifically for the establishment of the *cathedra* of the Apostle Peter, founder of the Roman bishopric (section XIII).[66] This explanation is convincing; not only does it account for the inclusion of this Christian holiday in a martyrology, but it also elucidates the transformation of pagan cult and funerary practices into the calendar and liturgy of the Christian church.

The List of Bishops of Rome (Section XIII)

Since the bishop orchestrated the ceremonies in honor of the martyrs, the inclusion of the List of Bishops of Rome after the Depositions is appropriate from an ecclesiastical point of view. This section is of critical importance for historians of the Catholic church: not only is it the earliest known source for the famous *Liber Pontificalis* (also composed in the fourth century), but, more important, it is also the most ancient surviving episcopal list to follow a rigid chronology. Although earlier episcopal lists are known to have existed (Irenaeus [ca. 140/160–ca. 202] is the first known redactor of such a list), these apparently lacked the chronological precision seen in this section.[67] Only Hippolytus, in his

63. See Pietri 1976, pp. 366–380.

64. See Kirsch, *Der stadtrömische christliche Festkalender*, pp. 18ff.; and his "Le feste degli apostoli S. Pietro e S. Paolo," *RAC* 2 (1925): 62–79; cf. Pietri 1976, p. 381, n. 1, for bibliographic material.

65. Degrassi 1963, p. 414.

66. The theory and relevant bibliography are set forth in Pietri 1976, pp. 381–389.

67. For the *Liber Pontificalis*, see L. Duchesne, *Le Liber Pontificalis*, vol. 1 (Paris, 1886); rev. ed. and text by C. Vogel (Paris, 1957), pp. viff.; and for the Codex's list of bishops, see Mommsen, 1850a, pp. 549–668; and Mommsen, *MGH* 1892, pp. 73–76. For discussion

third-century *World Chronicle,* is generally credited with having added to his episcopal list the length of rule of each bishop.[68] His synthesis of this information was apparently continued by Pope Pontianus in 235, and thereafter the church maintained a careful listing of its bishops. Even though episcopal succession may appear to be no more than a listing of facts, the systematization adopted here is of particular significance, for it does not merely list the bishops of Rome, attaching each one to a historically accurate consular date; rather, its contents reveal a specifically Rome-oriented ecclesiology.

This section begins with the notation that under the rule of Tiberius Christ was crucified and after his ascension Peter became the first bishop of Rome.[69] It then continues, in chronological sequence, to record each bishop by name, along with the length of his rule in years and days, the name of the contemporary emperor, and the consular dates of the bishop's rule. For some bishops, the date and place of death are also recorded, along with brief historical notes concerning notable building projects in Rome (e.g., basilicas or tombs), miraculous events (e.g., the visitation on Pope Pius [146–161] of an angel), or historical events (e.g., the deportation of Pope Hippolytus to Sardinia in 235). An example of one such notation is that for the Bishop Lucius: "Lucius ruled for three years, eight months, ten days. He lived during the consulship of Valerianus and Gallus until that of Valerianus (for the third time) and Gallienus (for the second time). He was in exile and afterward, with the nod of God, he was returned unharmed to the church. Three days before the Nones of March, [he died]."[70] This list ends with Liberius's entrance into office (352), hence its alternative name as the Catalogue of Liberius. The inclusion of this last bishop, with the notation that Gallus was caesar, provides further evidence for the dating of the Codex-Calendar.

After 235 the information in this section is quite reliable. But if we compare this section with other lists of bishops for the period prior to 235, significant variations appear. Two differences are worthy of com-

---

and bibliography, see Pietri 1976, p. 389, n. 2; E. Caspar, "Die älteste römische Bischofsliste," in *Königsberger Gelehrten Gesellschaft,* vol. 2, pt. 4 (Berlin, 1926); and L. Koep, in *RAC* 2 (1925), s.v. "Bischofsliste," pp. 407–415.

68. See Caspar, "Die älteste römische Bischofsliste," pp. 384ff., 424. There is no longer doubt that Hippolytus's *World Chronicle* contained a list of bishops, as H. Lietzmann and A. Bauer once suggested; see H. Lietzmann, in *RE,* vol. 8, pt. 2 (1913), s.v. "Hippolytus," col. 1877. See my discussion of section XV, pp. 50ff. below.

69. For the text of this list, see Mommsen, *MGH* 1892, p. 73.

70. Text and emendation from Mommsen, *MGH* 1892, p. 75: "Lucius ann. III m. VIII d.X. fuit temporibus Galli et Volusiani usque Valeriano III et Gallieno II [255]. hic exul fuit et postea nutu dei incolumis ad ecclesiam reversus est. . . . III non. Mar. cons. s̄s̄."

ment. The first is the inclusion of the bishop Clemens after Linus and before Anacletus; the recording of Clemens before Anacletus in this list and not in others has been attributed to Western Christian traditions. The renown of Clemens in the West explains his displacement in section XIII, a citation that lent greater prestige to this episcopal list.[71]

A more obvious indicator of the originality and viewpoint of this list is found at the beginning, where the Apostle Peter is entered as the first bishop of Rome.[72] This position contrasts with the chronology and ecclesiology of Eusebius, who, in his *Church History*, places Linus at the head of the series of bishops; further, he states that the episcopal hierarchy in Rome established itself some twenty years after that of Jerusalem (founded by James) and also some years after that of Alexandria (founded by Mark), but around the same time as that at Antioch (held by Euodius); in effect, Eusebius distinguishes the period of the apostolic mission from that of the episcopate—something the List of Bishops of Rome does not do.[73] In the Roman list, Peter appears after the ascension as the initiator of the hierarchy of Roman bishops; the foundation of the church and the Roman hierarchy is dated to A.D. 30, and the martyrdom of the apostle Peter to 55. This chronology and view of Peter, then, supports the claim of the church at Rome to preeminence and anteriority based on its association with Peter.

The arbitrary nature of the information in the List of Bishops of Rome, especially prior to 235, is masked by the format, which gives the inventory an air of precision and historical accuracy. Bishop follows bishop, without gaps, according to consular year. The making of a single bishop into two—Cletus and Anacletus, Marcellinus and Marcellus—may pose historical problems, but it gives this list a continuity that fits with the consular notations. While some effort has gone into making the dates consistent with the fixed-date anniversaries of the previous section (XII), absolute consistency is lacking.[74] The opportunity remains for interpretation and for the insertion of a point of view concerning the origins of the bishopric.

The implicit message of the List of Bishops is similar to that of the

71. Pietri 1976, pp. 392–393. Section XIII records two separate bishops, Cletus and Anacletus. This is probably a doubling of one man, Anacletus.

72. Apparently Hippolytus did not include Peter as bishop. See Caspar, "Die älteste römische Bischofsliste," p. 424.

73. The originality of the List of Bishops in section XIII was underlined in ibid., p. 195; Linus is the first bishop in Eusebius *H. E.* 3.2, 5.6.1–3. Eusebius cites James as first bishop for Jerusalem (*H.E.* 2.1), Mark for Alexandria (2.16), and Euodius for Antioch (3.22). For further discussion, see Pietri 1976, pp. 393–396.

74. For example, the length of the pontificate of Callistus in section XIII is not made to coincide with his *natalis*, recorded in section XII on 14 October; see Pietri 1976, p. 395.

Lists of Consuls and Urban Prefects, insofar as all three lists claim a venerable antiquity in Rome. This similarity highlights the three major sources for and institutions recorded in this second portion of the Codex-Calendar: the imperial bureaucracy, the municipal or urban structures, and the Christian church. All three institutions are of particular importance for the recipient of the Codex-Calendar—hence the need to record dates and events important for each. Most striking in this regard is the fact that the three institutions are chronicled according to the succession of the authorities who exercised control over them—that is, Roman consul, urban prefect, and Roman bishop. This may reflect the traditions of Roman society at large, but it may also reflect, as I will argue, the class of the Codex's recipient, namely, the Roman aristocracy.

Regions of the City of Rome (*Notitia*); World Chronicle (*Liber Generationis*); Chronicle of the City of Rome (*Chronica Urbis Romae*) (Sections XIV–XVI)

We cannot be certain that sections XIV and XV were included in the Codex-Calendar of 354, though they are, without doubt, products of fourth-century Rome, a shared provenance that ultimately led to their collocation with the Calendar. These sections are nonetheless invaluable, for they, along with section XVI, not only indicate contemporary chronographic and literary trends but also constitute a rich and reliable source of information about the fourth-century city.

Section XIV is the famous *Notitia*, or catalogue of buildings, monuments, and noteworthy sights in the fourteen regions of the city.[75] Section XV is the *Liber Generationis* or *World Chronicle* (one of two Latin translations of the Greek original by Hippolytus, composed in A.D. 230–234);[76] this epitome of universal history begins with the biblical origin of man, Adam, and proceeds in strict chronological fashion, extending past Hippolytus's third-century work down into the consulates of Paulus and Optatus in 334, synchronizing Christian historical events with profane mythical/historical events in the Greco-Roman past. Section XVI is the *Origo Gentis Romanorum ex quo primum in Italia regnare coeperunt*—

---

75. Nordh 1936, pp. 131–132; and Nordh 1949, pp. 24–25, 64.

76. The *World Chronicle* of Hippolytus survives in the abridged Latin translations in the Codex-Calendar and in the seventh-century *Fredegar Chronicle*; for discussion, see Mommsen, *MGH* 1892, pp. 78–153. For an opposing view of the origin of the *World Chronicle*, see K. Frick, *Chronica Minora* (Leipzig, 1892), pp. v–lxvii. Mommsen, as well as Stern 1953, pp. 14–17, 44, 113–115, thought the *Chronicle* was extended until A.D. 334 for inclusion in the Codex-Calendar

or, as it is better known, the *Chronica Urbis Romae* or *Chronicle of Rome*[77]—which records the rulers of Rome from the mythical reign of Picus until the death of the Emperor Licinius in A.D. 324.

Some consider these last three lists either as part of the original Codex-Calendar of 354 or as remnants of an earlier edition that was reused for the Codex. The latter argument centers on their temporal closeness to the 354 collocation: section XIV dates to the years 334–357, section XV to 334, and section XVI to 324–337.[78] Yet such an argument, based only on a possible range of dates, does not stand up to scrutiny; nor does it begin to justify inclusion of these sections in the original Codex-Calendar of 354. Indeed, there is good evidence against the inclusion of sections XIV and XV in the original.

The manuscript tradition indicates that the *Notitia* (section XIV) and the *World Chronicle* (section XV) survive in only one version of the Codex-Calendar of 354. This weak tradition for the *Notitia* becomes suspect if we take into account its general popularity, for we find it today in some twenty-seven codices.[79] There is, moreover, no literary precedent for the inclusion of a regional catalogue in a codex devoted to chronological information.[80]

The inclusion of the *World Chronicle*, too, with its universal and biblical focus, runs against the marked local character of the Codex. Nor does a precedent exist for the conjunction of a Christian World Chronicle with a calendar-almanac.[81] Only one extant illustrated Greek World Chronicle

77. Mommsen 1850a, pp. 549–693; and H. Peter, "Die Schrift *Origo gentis Romanae*," *Berichte sächs. Gesell.* 64 (1912): 103–114.

78. Mommsen, *MGH* 1892, p. 37, argued that these last three sections were so intimately linked to one another and to the Codex-Calendar in time and place that they could not be considered extraneous to it. He suggested that these sections were created for a collection made in 334, the same year to which he dated the *Notitia* and the *Chronicle of the City of Rome*. Stern 1953, pp. 14–17, 44, 113–115, followed Mommsen in including these last three sections in the original Codex-Calendar of 354; he observed, though, that since several other sections (XI, XII, and XIII) indicate a third date of compilation—in 336—there were in fact three recensions behind the Codex-Calendar.

79. Valentini and Zucchetti I, 1940, pp. 77–88, questioned the inclusion of the *Notitia* in the Codex-Calendar of 354 because of this manuscript tradition; see also Nordh 1936, pp. 131–132; and Nordh 1949, pp. 24–25, 64.

80. The *Chronicle* of Hippolytus does not provide a precedent. The *Stadiasmos*, a measurement in *stadia* of the distance from Alexandria to Spain, with a description of the harbors, dock facilities, and shores of the Mediterranean as a guide to navigation is not comparable to the regionary catalogue in the Codex-Calendar. Nor is Hippolytus's ethnographic catalogue *Diamerismos*, which showed how the world was divided among Noah's progeny, comparable. See J. Quasten, *Patrology*, vol. 2 (Westminster, Md., 1953), pp. 163–174. Polemius Silvius's list of *Quae sint Romae* (Mommsen, *MGH* 1892, p. 545) is comparable to the regionary catalogue, but it is later.

81. Neither Eusebius's *Chronicle* nor Jerome's continuation of it included a calendar.

includes representations of the months and thus possibly a calendar, but this work was certainly later than the Codex-Calendar of 354 and should be associated with the flowering of chronicles in the Greek East, probably evolving at Constantinople in the last decades of the century.[82]

In contrast to sections XIV and XV, the manuscript tradition and the contents of section XVI, the *Chronicle of Rome,* allow it to be placed with confidence in the Codex-Calendar of 354. The *Chronicle* provides an abbreviated history of the city of Rome, recording, in succinct chronological order, the rulers of Rome, beginning with a catalogue of the Latin, Alban, and Roman kings; the length of each man's rule; and any noteworthy mythical or historical actions that he performed or that occurred during his reign. Romulus's rule is exemplary of the notations for the kings:

> Romulus, the son of Mars and Ilia, ruled for thirty-eight years. He founded the city, Rome, on 21 April, which day is called the Parilia. He established ten months in the year, starting from March through December. He chose one thousand young men from the Roman plebs, whom he called soldiers, and one hundred of the elders, whom he called senators. He gave as a donation a Roman measure of wine [to be shared] among twelve men. When he was swimming toward the Goat Pond, he suddenly disappeared. After he was taken up among the number of the gods, he was called the god Quirinus.

> Romulus Martis et Iliae filius regnavit annos XXXVIII. Urbem Romam condidit XI kal. Mai., qui dies appellatur Parilia. Hic X menses in annum constituit a Martio in Decembrem. Mille iuvenes de plebe Romana legit, quos milites appellavit, et centum seniores, quos senatores dixit. Congiarium dedit congium vini inter homines XII. Hic cum natat ad paludem Caprae, subito nusquam conparuit. In numerum deorum relatus deus Quirinus appellatus est.[83]

See A. Mosshamer, *The Chronicle of Eusebius and the Greek Chronographic Tradition* (Lewisburg, Pa., 1979), pp. 15–83. Jerome's continuation may have included a martyrology, but since it dates after the Codex-Calendar of 354, it does not supply a precedent; see A. Schoene, *Die Weltchronik des Eusebius in ihrer Bearbeitung durch Hieronymus* (Berlin, 1900). Jerome decided to translate Eusebius's *Canons* in ca. 380.

82. Hippolytus's *Chronicle* has been seen as a source for the illustrated Alexandrian *World Chronicle* and as the Greek source for "Scaliger's Barbarian" (see n. 32 above). For discussion, see Bauer and Strzygowski, *Eine Alexandrinische Weltchronik*, pp. 90–92. The Alexandrian *World Chronicle*, illustrated in papyrus-roll style, is dated to the fifth century by Bauer and Strzygowski; it is certainly no earlier than 392. Its very fragmentary illustrations of the months may have accompanied a calendar. Bagnall, Cameron, Schwartz, and Worp, *Consuls*, pp. 48, 54–55, suggest that the illustrated consular annals originated at Constantinople in the 360s, beginning with the *Fasti Hydatiani.*

83. Text according to Mommsen, *MGH* 1892, p. 144. This version of Romulus's disappearance—i.e., swimming in the Goat Pond in the Campus Martius—is contrary to the normal version in which he is haranguing his troops. (See my discussion of the illustration for March in Chapter 3.) Yet this is probably a variant version and not a mistaken gloss,

Following the kings is a catalogue of Roman dictators from the years of the republic. The *Chronicle* ends with a list of the Roman emperors, the *Imperia Caesarum*, which records their length of rule, donations of money and games (*congiaria*), place and cause of death, and, for some, building projects or notable events of a somewhat sensational sort, such as a great famine (under Maxentius), a mule that ate a man (under Gordianus), or the appearance of a *polyfagus*, a performer who entertained by eating everything from wooden baskets to napkins.[84] The entry for Alexander Severus described this charming spectacle:

> Alexander ruled for thirteen years, eight months, and nine days. He gave a donation of 1,600 *denarii*. During his reign there was a performing glutton, Italian by birth, who ate several things: a wooden box, lettuce, a small vase of sardines[?], ten sprats, seventy melons, boughs from a palm branch, four napkins, four loaves of bread of the military size[?], a wooden box, thistles and their spines. He drank a large quantity of Greek wine, and he came to the temple of Dea Syria and drank a full vessel [of wine?] and still he seemed to be desirous of more. Also, the Alexandrian baths were dedicated. Alexander was killed at Mainz.

> Alexander imper. ann. XIII. m. VIII d. IX cong. dedit X DC. Hoc imp.[erante] fuit polyfagus natione Italus qui manducavit [non] pauca: cistam, lactucas, vascellum sardinarium, sardas X, melopepones LXX, t[h]allos de scopa palmea, mappas IIII, panes castrenses IIII, cistam, cardos cum suas sibi spinas, et ebibit vini graecanicum plenum et venit ad templum Iasurae et ebibit labrum plenum et adhuc esuriens esse videbatur. Et thermae Alexandrinae dedicatae sunt. Alexander occisus Mogontiaco.[85]

Each entry follows the same formula. In this regard, and in the impersonal nature of the information presented, this section is similar to the later fourth- and fifth-century consular annals.[86]

The sources for the *Chronicle of Rome* are much disputed. Mommsen

---

as Valentini and Zucchetti I, 1940, p. 270, have argued. See G. Traina, *Paludi e bonifiche del mondo antico* (Rome, 1988). The donation of wine among twelve men is not otherwise attested but may be a confused allusion to the more common version of Romulus's augury of twelve birds; see, for example, Livy 1.3ff.

84. See B. Baldwin, "Polyphagus: Glutton or Crocodile," *AJP* 98 (1977): 406–409.

85. Text from Mommsen, *MGH* 1892, p. 147, with changes or clarifications as follow. A *vascellum sardinarium* is defined by A. Souter, *Glossary of Later Latin* (Oxford, 1949), as a vase full of sardines; *tallos* = *thallos*, as suggested by Valentini and Zucchetti I, 1940, p. 277; I take *panes castrenses* to refer to a size and type of loaf common to soldiers' camps; Mommsen suggests reading *vini graecanicum* as *Graecanici cadum*; *Iasurae* = *Deae Syriae*; and Platner-Ashby, *Top. Dict.*, p. 531 identify *thermae Alexandrinae* with the *thermae Neronianae*.

86. See notes 31–34 above.

saw this section as a continuation of the *World Chronicle* because it covered the same time period and answered one of that work's chapter headings: *imperatorum Romanorum nomina a Gaio Iulio Caesare et consulibus.*[87] The evidence for this view, however, is weak. First, the list of imperial names begins from "Gaio Caesare et dictatoribus," not from "consulibus." Second, although the *World Chronicle* of Hippolytus did include a list of emperors, it indicated only the name and length of rule and none of the specifically Roman and sensational information included here. Finally, arguments for dating these two sections to the same year are not convincing. Although the *World Chronicle*, which ended with the consuls of A.D. 334, may be more or less contemporary with the *Chronicle of Rome* (324–337), no precise correlation is possible.

The contents of the *Chronicle of Rome* argue against any association with the *World Chronicle* as well. In sharp contrast with the *World Chronicle*, which advocates a particularly Christian point of view, the *Chronicle of Rome* makes no reference to Christianity; the information is strictly secular and historical. Rather than connect these two chronicles, therefore, I would suggest that they emerge from two different historiographic traditions, one Christian, one secular.

Determining the historiographic origins of the *Chronicle of Rome* is difficult, for it evidently drew on a variety of sources. Some collection of *mirabilia* was clearly used, but the primary source of information on the lives of the emperors is still open to question. Mommsen posited that the imperial information derived from some augmented edition of Suetonius, a lost *Kaisergeschichte* presumably of the fourth century (hereafter *KG*); Barnes, however, has argued against such a source. Whatever the derivation—and some imperial history must have been used, if not the augmented Suetonius—the *Chronicle of Rome* often preserves a "purer historical tradition" and more accurate information than do contemporary historians dependent on the *KG*.[88]

Regardless of its sources, the contents of the *Chronicle of Rome*, with attention on the rulers of Rome and their activities in the city, fit comfortably with the rest of this Rome-focused codex, suggesting the interests of the Codex-Calendar's fourth-century reader. Yet the omissions, too, provide insights into contemporary concerns and the intended effect of this codex. For example, it is of some interest that the *Chronicle* does not list the names of the republican consuls; rather, this period is re-

87. Mommsen, *MGH* 1892, p. 145.
88. T. D. Barnes, "The Lost *Kaisergeschichte* and the Latin Historical Tradition," *Antiquitas*, 4th ser., *Beiträge zur Historia Augusta Forschung*, vol. 7 (Bonn, 1970), p. 24.

corded only by its dictators.[89] If, as is possible, the *Chronicle* was edited to avoid repeating information already given in the List of Consuls (section VIII), we have another telling indication of the careful attention with which this codex was compiled. Yet the omission of a consular list may be due to generic considerations: the *Origo Gentis Romanae*, a tripartite work of unknown authorship that is similar in composition to the *Chronicle of Rome*, has no list of consuls either. If such an omission was a common feature of chronicles of Rome as a genre, we may be seeing the beginnings of the attitude evidenced by Byzantine chroniclers, who tended to "forget" the Roman Republic as a period too distant and with a form of government too different from their own.[90]

The historical data and succinct form of the *Chronicle of Rome* were appealing to a fourth-century reader. Such works were part of the contemporary zeal for keeping knowledge of the Roman past alive, an especially important task in a world where Christian and barbarian influences were threatening traditional learning. Concise encyclopedic and scholarly reference works—epitomes, chronicles, and *breviaria*—were

> especially popular after the crisis of the third century; a new leading class had emerged which clearly had difficulty in keeping straight the simple facts of Roman history. These works served well the need of these new men, who, coming from the provincial armies or from Germany and having acquired wealth and power, wanted knowledge of Rome, its past history and its antiquities, in order to mix with the senatorial aristocracy.[91]

Thus, the *Chronicle of Rome*, a pagan recapitulation of Roman history, would be complimentary to its recipient if he were a senatorial aristocrat from an old Roman family, and useful if he were a new man intent on mixing with that class.

The *Chronicle of Rome* provides a satisfactory end note to the unillustrated part of the Codex-Calendar; concluding with a list of emperors, it strikes an imperial chord reminiscent of the consular images of the Emperor Constantius and the Caesar Gallus that closed the illustrated part. The parallel placement of these sections (VII and XVI) devoted to infor-

89. Mommsen, *MGH* 1892, p. 143.

90. E. Jeffries, "The Attitudes of Byzantine Chroniclers Toward Ancient History," *Byzantion* 49 (1979): 199–238.

91. A. Momigliano, "Pagan and Christian Historiography in the Fourth Century," in *The Conflict Between Paganism and Christianity in the Fourth Century*, ed. A. Momigliano (Oxford, 1963), pp. 79–99.

mation about imperial rulers appears to the reader as an intentional jux-
taposition and an effective means of unifying the Codex.

The *Chronicle of Rome* is also a fitting conclusion to the book as a
whole, for it effectively summarizes the Codex-Calendar and its concerns. The final list of emperors with historical notations turns us to the
imperial presence in Rome, a dominant influence and one reflected in
this codex. The formulas and, to a degree, the contents of the *Chronicle*
remind one of those for the List of Bishops of Rome (section XIII)—
which, in my reconstruction, directly precedes this section. The formula
used to record the rule of each emperor in the *Chronicle of Rome* is the
same: name, length of office, expenditures for games, donatives (*congiaria*), building projects and notable events of some sensationalism, and
place and cause of death. The bishops in section XIII are recorded by a
similar formula: name, time in office according to consular dating, noteworthy activities in Rome (e.g., building projects), and somewhat sensational events, albeit Christian (e.g., martyrs, angels, persecutions,
internal political developments). The bishop's place of burial—the only
information missing from this formula—is recorded separately in section
XI. The lists of bishops and of emperors may have shared sources, but
that does not deny the implicit comparison of emperor and bishop created by the collocation of these sections and by their essentially similar
content. Both sections highlight the public ceremonial aspects of leadership, to which is added a penchant for the sensational or miraculous.
Hence the *Chronicle* ties in, albeit indirectly, with the Christian church
in Rome, an important influence reflected in the pages of the Codex.

WHY PRODUCE THIS CODEX-CALENDAR?

If we look past the specifics of these sections, we can discern more
general implications about fourth-century Roman society, its attitudes,
and its dominant institutions. It might seem overambitious to search for
purpose in a work like the Codex-Calendar of 354, made up as it is of
diverse preexisting texts and anonymous, annotated chronological lists
of facts and dates. Nevertheless, decisions concerning what material was
worth including and excluding must inevitably reflect the prejudices and
world view of the creator and his audience, as well as the traditions
within which he worked. Thus, however great the debt to his sources,
the creator of the Codex-Calendar of 354 has, even if only through the
act of selection and organization, imposed his own attitudes on his bor-
rowings. He has also taken into account the attitudes of the society that

will use the work and of the recipient in particular. Even the choice of genre—a calendar with chronological lists—may be significant.

As noted above, the formulas used in sections XIII and XVI highlight the similarity in perceived function of emperor and bishop in the city. Public and traditional demonstrations of their preeminence are recorded in terms of *congiaria*, building projects, and ceremonies to commemorate the birth and death of leaders. (These activities are found if we compare the lists of the Depositions of Bishops and of Martyrs [XI–XII] with the *Natales Caesarum* [III] and the list of emperors in the *Chronicle of Rome* [XVI].) Fulfilling the same function in Rome were the circus games and holiday festivals recorded in the pagan secular Calendar (section VI) and, to a lesser public extent at this point, the Christian celebrations at the tombs of martyrs and bishops. All these activities—alms giving, feast giving, holiday celebrating, monument building—were conspicuously public demonstrations of power intended to impress the populace—the same means of expressing authority that the urban prefect and Roman consul had at their disposal.

The logic behind many of the sections is now evident. Four sections (VIII, X, XIII, and XVI) record positions—consul, urban prefect, bishop, and, at the top of this structured social pyramid, emperor—where the holder could and did demonstrate his power in the city by performing traditional acts of largesse against the proper ceremonial background. Three other sections (III, VI, and VII) can be similarly, if less directly, explained. Even the dating formula used in the *Natales Caesarum* (III) is comparable to that in the Depositions of Bishops and of Martyrs (XI and XII), for all three lists record the transition of the individual into an elevated, sacred position.[92]

The positions recorded in these sections consistently refer the reader to the three institutions dominant in the fourth-century city: the lists of Roman consuls (VIII) and of emperors (XVI) reflect a concern for the imperial bureaucracy; those of urban prefects (X) and consuls (VIII) reflect a concern for the urban government, which in the fourth century still had strong ties to the senatorial aristocracy; and that of bishops of Rome (XIII) reflects a concern for the Christian church. Some knowledge of these dominant institutions would be of daily utility for the recipient of the Codex-Calendar. Yet the selection of information on these dominant institutions cannot be understood only in terms of the "daily needs" and everyday life of a fourth-century resident. What, after all, is the need on the Ides of April in A.D. 354 to know who was pope in 258 or consul

92. Texts in Mommsen, *MGH* 1892, pp. 13–148.

in 259? Or, to put it another way, who, in A.D. 354 in Rome, would want
to have such information?

The consistent concern with leadership and its public ceremonial
manifestation that the Codex-Calendar displays leads us to that very
class we have already, owing to the sumptuous nature of this edition,
identified as worthy of our attention: namely, the fourth-century Roman
aristocracy. In Rome, it was still the *officium* of the senatorial class to hold
prestigious public positions. Since social prestige was largely dependent
on wealth, conspicuous displays of magnanimity while in public office
were obligatory. Hence, the sections of the Codex focusing on positions
of authority and the public display of largesse would naturally appeal to
one belonging—or wanting to belong—to such an aristocratic milieu.
The inclusion of antiquarian and historical information about Rome, its
past history and institutions, also points to that class, for such knowledge
was the mark of a privileged education. (See Chapter 1.)

A similar concern for leadership and for the public ceremonial by
which that leadership was manifested is reflected in the Christian sections in the Codex-Calendar (especially sections IX and XI–XIII)—for
example, in the "official" view of the Roman church, which establishes
the legitimacy and antiquity of the bishop of Rome by claiming the Apostle Peter as first bishop of the city (section XIII). In its presentation of
Christian leadership, and in the kind of information recorded, the
Codex-Calendar attempts (perhaps for the first time in the fourth century) to place the church as an institution on a par with the dominant
secular institutions. Like these secular institutions, the church emerges
from the pages of the Codex-Calendar in possession of a venerable past,
with leaders and heroes of greatness and traditions and festivals of specifically Roman import. This view of the Christian church at Rome and
its leadership was conveyed by the form, content, and organization of
the Codex: the unillustrated Christian sections are similar in format to
the unillustrated secular sections; all the anonymous, unillustrated lists
record events impersonally in a language of uniformly simple syntax.
The interweaving of Christian and pagan sections in the unillustrated
portion of the Codex, moreover, reinforces the impression of parity. As
a result, Christianity appears to be neither alien nor repugnant to the
cultural forms and institutions of Rome; on the contrary, it seems strikingly familiar and respectable, a quality that would only facilitate its acceptance by conservative aristocratic Romans.

I am not suggesting that the fourth-century recipient and creator of
the Codex-Calendar perceived the Christian church, the urban government with its close ties to the senatorial aristocracy, and the imperial

bureaucracy as "the same," for striking differences certainly existed among them. These are highlighted by the Codex itself, the most obvious difference being the separation of the veritable Christian calendar (sections XI and XII) from the civil-pagan one (section VI), a separation accentuated by the lack of illustration in the Christian sections.[93] Nevertheless, the similarity of the unillustrated sections in terms of format—anonymous, formulaic, simple sentence structures, repetitive actions—and content indicate that the Codex-Calendar was intended to impress its fourth-century recipient with the parallels between the Christian, imperial, and urban institutions of Rome.

In A.D. 354, however, pagan holidays and imperial anniversaries still dominated Roman life. Hence, the centerpiece of the Codex-Calendar of 354, the official Calendar of Rome for that year (section VI), includes no Christian holidays but only pagan or secular seasonal imagery, festivals, and anniversaries—which, after all, remained the most important communal moments in the public life of the Roman aristocracy.

The Codex-Calendar of 354 is the product of a fourth-century Roman concerned with providing information about the dominant contemporary institutions in the imperial capital. While the work reflects in part the daily needs of a fourth-century resident of that city, the edition has been personalized to address the interests of its recipient. The Christian sections, and probably the astrological sections as well, reinforce the personal note first sounded by the dedicatory inscription (section I). Moreover, the information included goes beyond meeting daily needs: several sections convey information about Rome's past and the past of its institutions; sections III, VIII–XI, XIII, and XVI (and XIV and XV, if we include them) attest strongly to historiographic interests, in addition to serving a chronographic function. In essence, these lists commemorate specifically Roman institutions and, by so doing, lend them venerability and respectability.

The information reported reflects a consistent perspective, generally the "official view" of the dominant institutions of Rome.[94] One can see in this emphasis on "accepted" institutional history, on positions of au-

93. Although Christian holidays were not yet as important, the division into two separate lists cannot be explained simply in terms of popularity. It would have been easy enough to incorporate the information into one calendar; the Calendar of Polemius Silvius, for example, written for a Christian bishop in Lyons in the middle of the fifth century, included pagan and Christian celebrations. For further discussion of Polemius Silvius's Calendar, see Chapter 6.

94. The one exception to the "official view" is the preservation of the names of failed usurpers in the List of Urban Prefects (section X).

thority, and on the public demonstration of authority the attitude of the creator and his society: the public and powerful are what are noteworthy. In addition, an aristocratic view of fourth-century society is discernible—a milieu that will become more evident as we consider the illustrations and the identity of the recipient. (See Chapters 3 and 5.)

The creation of the Codex-Calendar of 354 represents the joining—but not the fusing—of secular-pagan and Christian chronographic information in one illustrated, encyclopedic edition. If we consider the future of the codex in general, we note that such a conjunction is attested in greater number at the end of the century,[95] as the spread of Christianity made coordination of these two pasts even more critical.

In sum, the Codex-Calendar of 354 seems a somewhat unusual, even experimental work, a view that its contents reinforce: the consular lists contain no illustrations, in contrast with later fourth- and fifth-century annotated consular lists; the Depositions of Bishops and of Martyrs are listed separately, while in an edition from the time of Julian, less than ten years later, these are combined. The work's innovativeness may also explain why no Christian illustrations are included, for there might not yet have been a full repertoire of Christian imagery applicable to such a codex. The joining of a pagan-civic calendar with Christian and secular celebrations and anniversaries in one codex is not earlier attested. These unique aspects, not to mention the decorative calligraphy of Filocalus, contributed greatly to the edition's value. Certainly this carefully planned, illustrated, and edited work was more than a handy reference guide; it was intended as well to impress and compliment its Christian recipient, Valentinus.

Although Valentinus's Christian interests are reflected in the Codex-Calendar of 354 and Christianity emerges as one of the three dominant Roman institutions, Christian themes were not yet incorporated into the civic Calendar of Rome (section VI). In this centerpiece of the Codex, rather, the pagan festivals and imperial anniversaries still represented the most significant communal moments in the public life of Rome and its aristocracy. Accordingly, as I turn to the Calendar in more detail, I will focus on the two institutions that this section so vividly documents: late Roman paganism, with its ties to the Roman aristocracy, and the imperial cult, linked to the emperor.

95. See pp. 37–38 and pp. 51–52.

· PART II ·

THE CALENDAR: A ROMAN CALENDAR FOR A.D. 354

· III ·

THE ILLUSTRATIONS OF THE
MONTHS IN THE CALENDAR OF 354

Although the illustrations of the months in the Calendar (section VI)
have been much studied, they continue to be misinterpreted. According
to one view, the illustrations of the months were merely decorative,
added to the Calendar for nostalgic effect; a second interpretation suggests that they were created for a completely different object and were
simply reused for the Calendar of 354. Both of these views and the con-
sequent identification of iconographic features of the individual months
are untenable. Unlike other pictorial cycles of the months, the illustrations in the Calendar of 354 were designed for their context: for a calendar, for a codex, for a Christian patron in Rome in the year 354.

Each month is allotted two facing pages: the illustration of the month,
represented by a single figure depicted in some activity and accompanied by attributes appropriate to that month, on one page and the text
of holidays for that month on the opposite page (see Figs. 21 and 25, 22
and 26). By taking into account not only the visual comparanda but also
the literary traditions of Roman calendars, and by reading each illustration with its text, we can discern three dominant pictorial themes: pagan
rites, popular holidays, and seasonal activities. As I will show, the illustrations (as much as the text) of the Calendar have a firm basis in the
artistic, religious, civic, and daily life of mid-fourth-century Rome; perhaps most striking is the way they underscore the vitality of late Roman
paganism. At the same time, however, the illustrations of the months
indicate the beginnings of accommodation to the growth of Christianity.

The many iconographic variations preserved in the manuscript tradition frequently make identification of individual illustrations difficult.

But the critical approaches adopted to interpret these illustrations have obscured their meaning even more. Although some scholars have looked for the sources of the illustrations of the months in contemporary visual comparanda, the literary traditions of the Roman calendar have been noticeably overlooked. I will therefore begin by reviewing the scholarly approaches to the illustrations and assessing the instruments of transmission, the manuscript copies of the Codex-Calendar. I will then show how each of the illustrations of the months was inspired by the world in which the Calendar was produced and used.

To facilitate discussion, I have grouped the months according to the subject depicted. Four months—December, November, January, and April—represent pagan holidays or festivals noted in the text of the Calendar.[1] I argue that the illustration for April, rather than, as is commonly argued, being an illustration of the *Veneralia* festival celebrated on 1 April, actually depicts another well-known Roman festival, the *Megalesia* or *Megalensia*, celebrated in the city from 4 to 10 April. January can be reidentified as portraying the New Year celebration, which incorporated traditional aspects of the *ludi Compitales*. November is associated with the festival of Isis, celebrated (in the fourth century) from 28 October through 3 November. December depicts the rites of the *Saturnalia*, celebrated on 17 December. I have placed together the purely seasonal illustrations, representing the four months of June, August, February, and October.[2] The final grouping—May, July, September, and March (I have reidentified July and March)—includes "mixed illustrations," combining seasonal imagery, popular beliefs, and elements of contemporary festivals recorded in the Calendar text.[3]

CRITICAL APPROACHES TO THE ILLUSTRATIONS

In his influential study *Ancient Book Illumination*, published in 1959, K. Weitzmann described the illustrations of the months in the Calendar of 354 as follows:

1. The categories adopted here for analysis of the illustrations are those established by Stern in his 1953 study, *Le Calendrier de 354*. Stern also includes the four months—December, November, January, and April—in the religious festival category, but identifies two with different holidays. An excellent review article is Stern 1981 (but written in 1977), "Les calendriers romains illustrés."

2. Of these four months, Stern 1953, pp. 234–248, identifies only February and October as purely seasonal.

3. Stern, ibid., pp. 248–265, identifies the illustrations of May, August, and September as combining popular beliefs and seasonal motifs. No reference is made to popular festivals, an omission that disassociates the illustrations from the text and is noteworthy.

A picture set of the Labors of the Months surely must have existed in manuscripts even before the well-known Filocalus calendar of the year 354 with its splendid full-page miniatures which have survived only in seventeenth-century drawings. But also this picture set is less firmly anchored in the text compared with the scientific, didactic, and literary illustrations discussed in this study, in which the pictures were made for the text. In the calendar manuscripts, vice versa, the picture existed first and the explanatory lines of writing were made *ad hoc* for the pictures.[4]

In describing these illustrations as a "picture set" used in earlier illustrated calendar manuscripts and merely reused for this particular codex, Weitzmann posited an earlier lost archetype. Although no earlier illustrated calendars in codices or papyrus rolls have survived to support this view, Weitzmann and his followers could point to numerous cycles of the months extant in floor mosaics or fresco cycles in both the Greek East and Latin West that show iconographic ties to the cycle found in the Calendar of 354.[5] Thus, Weitzmann's approach inspired subsequent scholars to study the illustrations of the months in the 354 Calendar in order to define further ties to comparable cycles.

This comparative approach has been useful for placing the Calendar's iconography of the months within a specific artistic tradition. For example, the depiction of a single figure for each month occurs in the Calendar of 354 and numerous earlier cycles,[6] as well as in medieval and Byzantine calendars. The subject matter of the Calendar of 354 can also be related to other cycles of months. The earliest cycles were probably illustrated by representations of religious festivals; in addition, seasonal activities, generally related to the annual agricultural cycle, were depicted[7]—a readily comprehensible development, since so many early religious festivals were tied to the agricultural seasons. Themes from astronomy, folklore, urban cults, and popular practices enriched festival and seasonal imagery. Yet it is noteworthy that, compared to these other cycles, the illustrations in the Calendar of 354 represent a most complex instance of thematic interweaving.

Given the broad spectrum of iconographic sources for the months in the Calendar of 354, as well as the tendency for iconography to travel

4. K. Weitzmann, *Ancient Book Illumination* (Cambridge, 1959), p. 129.

5. See, for example, Levi 1941; Strzygowski 1888; Webster 1938. For comparable cycles of the months from the Latin West, see Appendix 2.

6. See, for example, the first-century altar from Gabii (see App. 2, no. 1) and the second–third-century mosaic from Hellín, Spain (App. 2, no. 4; Figs. 102–106).

7. For example, the third-century mosaic calendar from El-Djem (App. 2, no. 9; Figs. 59–70) includes representations of agricultural activities along with illustrations of religious festivals.

across media in the empire, identification of this section's iconography has been advanced by studies of comparable pictorial and textual cycles of the months from antiquity. But this comparative approach leaves many questions unanswered. Moreover, it ignores the most fundamental distinguishing feature of the Calendar illustrations. In contrast to comparable cycles of the months, which were painted on walls in fresco, paved in mosaic floors, or occasionally sculpted in relief—all generally without a full text—the illustrations in the Calendar of 354 were designed for a specific book and accompanied a text detailing pagan religious holidays, popular festivals, civic events, and seasonal notations. In short, this cycle, unlike so many others, illustrated its text.

What we know about the circumstances of production of the Codex-Calendar reinforces my view that the illustrations of the months were thoughtfully considered and were executed to accompany the text. For one thing, the Calendar in which they appear was the very centerpiece of the Codex, which in turn was conceived, organized, and produced with utmost care. A similar degree of concern is therefore to be expected in the illustrations of the months as well. Second, because the codex format had become the norm for secular texts only after 300, the pictorialization of such texts was a recent phenomenon; it bears repeating that these are the earliest extant full-page illustrations in a codex in the history of Western art. To create the Codex-Calendar, the designer of these images may well have had to solve problems of design—most notably for this cycle of months—never before encountered.

The illustrations of the months in the Calendar of 354 were intended to be read in context, in relation to the text of the Roman calendar facing it. The very form of the work as a whole—a codex—indicates a literary tradition, not just a visual one. Indeed, the Roman calendar was itself the subject of learned study and a quasi-literary subject.[8] Thus, the circumstances of the Calendar's production and the codex format indicate that we take a closer look at the text associated with the illustrations; and by examining the contemporary world as recorded in that text, we may better analyze the iconography of the months.

The unwillingness of some scholars to see the most obvious source for the illustrations—the text of the Calendar itself—as their inspiration led to Weitzmann's surprisingly erroneous argument and has clouded interpretation of the images since. This reluctance can be explained in several ways. The search for comparanda in extant cycles of the months is one contributing factor, as discussed above. Another is the view found

8. See Degrassi 1963, pp. 314–316; and my discussion in Chapter 1.

in the early-twentieth-century scholarship on the Calendar: that the Calendar illustrations and text were a piece of fourth-century nostalgia, written after pagan rites had ceased to influence a Christian empire.[9] The art historian J. Strzygowski, for example, following T. Mommsen, termed the pagan imagery in the Calendar a sentimental reproduction of an earlier calendar cycle, devoid of any contemporary meaning.[10] J. C. Webster and D. Levy, in pursuit of comparable cycles, did not challenge this view.[11] Only after A. Alföldi published his 1937 study of the Isis festivals in Rome, in which he identified the iconography of November as depicting a specific fourth-century celebration of the goddess, was the Calendar imagery entirely reconsidered.[12]

H. Stern's 1953 study of the Calendar—a work that indicates the attention scholars had begun to pay to the survival of pagan rites in the post-Constantinian period—viewed the illustrations as a fourth-century creation reflective of the contemporary world. I agree with Stern's premises insofar as I too believe that these images are directly related to the text of the Calendar and that they depict rites actually practiced in Rome in the mid fourth century. Unlike Stern, though, who relied on visual and textual evidence from the entire empire and beyond, I shall in this study attempt to place the Calendar illustrations within their proper context: the city of Rome itself. However many comparable calendar cycles from all over the empire one may adduce to help decipher the iconography of the Calendar, the local nature and context of this Calendar are of far greater weight.

The contemporary context is especially significant for interpretation of the illustrations of pagan festivals and holidays. Roman ritual practice is specifically depicted in several images. But appreciating the contemporary context is important for deciphering the other months as well. Seasonal themes, popular beliefs, astrological notations, and urban associations reflect mid-fourth-century Rome as much as pagan practice did.[13] Moreover, this cycle of the months mirrors local beliefs not only

9. Mommsen, *MGH* 1892, pp. 13–38.

10. Strzygowski 1888, pp. 82ff.

11. Webster 1938, pp. 13–20; Levi 1941, pp. 241–291.

12. A. Alföldi, *A Festival of Isis in Rome Under the Christian Emperors of the Fourth Century* (Budapest, 1937).

13. In this regard, the ancient illustrators are comparable to the medieval illustrators of cycles of the months, as Webster 1938, p. 1, remarks: "Since the scenes [of the labors of the months] had an immediate and contemporary relationship to the artist who carved or painted them, their content was not so rigidly set as in the case of sacred representations, the subject matter of which was recorded in the scriptural narratives. . . . Thus, although the sacred scenes differed in details of iconography or costume, the labors of the months,

in its choice of subject matter but also in the iconographic variation evident here as compared to other cycles—either earlier than or contemporary to the Calendar of 354.

Another reason for scholarly reluctance in seeing the text as a source of inspiration for the illustrations, and a contributing factor to misinterpretation of the images in general, lies in the confusion over how the illustrations relate to the verses that accompany each month.[14] Two sets of verses are paired with each illustration. The tetrastichs (*Anth. Lat.* 395, ed. Riese), written vertically in the margin to the right of the architectural pilaster that frames each monthly drawing and lacking any calligraphic effect or design, were certainly not part of the original Codex-Calendar of 354. Rather, they were added to that work, although at some time prior to the ninth-century manuscript copy, the lost Luxemburgensis.[15] Indeed, it has been argued that these verses may have been a fifth-century creation.[16]

The distichs (*Anth. Lat.* 665, ed. Riese), in contrast, may have been part of the original codex, since they fit the page in terms of both calligraphy and location: the hexameter below the illustration and the pentameter below the text of each month.[17] While the distichs cannot be securely dated (they provide only a secure *terminus post quem* of the mid first century A.D.),[18] nevertheless, the independent manuscript tradition provides strong evidence against their creation specifically for the Calendar; most likely these verses predate the Calendar and existed independently.

Although the distichs may have been included in the fourth-century Codex-Calendar, they do not describe the illustrations of the months which they accompany; too many discrepancies preclude this as a possibility. That, however, is not the case with the tetrastichs. Although

---

in their very subject-matter, could react more freely to the influence of contemporary life and reflect with more variety the customs of different localities."

14. See, for example, Weitzmann, *Ancient Book Illumination*, p. 129, quoted on p. 65 above.

15. The verses must have been included in the lost Luxemburgensis because several of L.'s copies have them. It seems most likely that these verses were added to the Codex-Calendar of 354. See Appendix 1.

16. Courtney 1988, pp. 33–57. See Appendix 3.

17. For the text of these verses, see Appendix 4; for their manuscript transmission, see Appendix 1.

18. A. E. Housman, "Disticha de Mensibus," *CQ* 26 (1932): 129–136. See also Appendix 4.

these verses were not part of the original Calendar, they have been especially valued because certain lines describe activities similar to those depicted in the illustrations.[19] Indeed, some scholars have privileged the tetrastichs as a virtual gloss on the illustrations. This view, however, is not justified. For one thing, the textual evidence indicates a date for these verses in the fifth century. Moreover, such numerous and significant iconographic differences separate the tetrastichs and the illustrations that it is not possible to accept this poetry as a priori more valid than other contemporary sources. The tetrastichs neither were the source for the illustrations nor were they contemporary with them. If, therefore, we were to distrust any information in our manuscript, it would be the tetrastichs and not the images. To put it another way, it would be much safer to relate the images to the contemporary text of the Calendar than to use the tetrastichs to interpret the images.

Research on iconographic motifs supports this approach to the imagery, for a fourth-century creation is indicated. Certain seasonal motifs appear for the first time on Roman sarcophagi from A.D. 330–360, and the bulk of comparative visual evidence confirms these dates.[20] All the monthly cycles most similar to that in the Calendar of 354 date to the later decades of the fourth and fifth centuries, and all derive from the Latin West.[21] However, iconographic similarities between the 354 Calendar and these later cycles do not necessitate a specific, common archetype. Certain motifs for the months were shared by artists working in a variety of media, including codices, mosaics, and wall frescoes, and these motifs traveled all over the empire. After all, shared motifs indicate a shared world. What is noteworthy about these motifs is not the number that were shared, but rather the local variation in both iconography and

19. For example, see Stern 1953, pp. 293ff., who focuses on certain iconographic details (notably the knot in the dress of the figure representing February and the nude male in July) that he noted in the tetrastichs and observed in the Calendar illustrations; these details are, in his opinion, so similar that the tetrastichs had to be a fourth-century creation, and he posits a common source for them in a now lost mosaic or fresco cycle, such as from the Constantinian Baths in Rome or Constantinople.

20. Stern 1953, pp. 258–266, 291–294. Stern's analysis of August, a nude male drinking from a glass bowl, and of September, a male holding a lizard on a string over a wine jar, quite specifically traces these seasonal motifs to Roman monuments from A.D. 330–360. Stern's view is opposed to that of Levi 1941, pp. 241–291, who posits an earlier prototype in classical art that was simply copied into the Codex-Calendar of 354.

21. See Stern 1981, pp. 455ff., who lists the calendars "derived" from the Calendar of 354 as a mosaic from Ostia; a mosaic from Catania (Sicily); two mosaics from Carthage, one lost and one at the British Museum; and the Acton mosaic in Florence (see App. 2, nos. 14–18).

subject matter—yet another indicator of the fourth-century creation of the Calendar of 354.

To sum up, the provenance of the Calendar's iconography in fourth-century art, the tangential relationship of the tetrastichs and distichs to the illustrations, and the increasing amount of evidence for the survival of late Roman paganism in fourth-century Rome suggest that we seek the sources of the iconography of the months in the most obvious and most neglected place: the text of the Calendar proper.

THE INSTRUMENTS OF TRANSMISSION: THE MANUSCRIPT COPIES

In order to interpret the illustrations of the months, we must consider the instruments of transmission, the manuscript copies of the Codex-Calendar of 354. Since the original codex is lost, careful assessment of these copies for accuracy and general stylistic tendencies is important. The following discussion, then, distills and offers a set of judgments concerning the various mansucript copies that have allowed me to unravel some of the fourth-century reality behind the illustrations of the months.[22] I include here only those manuscripts of import for the illustrations of the months, the focus of this chapter.

Mommsen, the first modern scholar to deal with the Calendar as a whole, clarified the tradition of its manuscripts.[23] He derived all surviving Calendar manuscripts from a lost Carolingian copy, the Luxemburgensis (hereafter cited as L.),[24] which was last described in a letter of 18 December 1620 by one of the most erudite seventeenth-century scholars and collectors of antiquities, Nicholas-Claude Fabri de Peiresc (1580–1637).[25] Although L. is now lost, several sixteenth- and seventeenth-century copies of it survive. The best of these is considered to be the

---

22. For fuller discussion of the manuscripts, see Appendix 1.

23. The only edition of the Calendar that escaped Mommsen's notice was *Furii Philocali calendarius sub annum CCCLII* [sic], scriptum a Fr. Xysto Schier (Graz, 1781), noted by Stern 1953, p. 7, n. 5.

24. Mommsen 1850a, pp. 549–668; partial reprint in *Gesammelte Schriften*, vol. 7 (Berlin, 1909), pp. 536–579. He published the Calendar without illustrations in *CIL*, 1863, and revised his discussion for the second edition, 1893.

25. Peiresc's letter is published by Mommsen, *MGH* 1892, pp. 19–28; and by Strzygowski 1888, pp. 7–20. The bibliography on Peiresc is extensive; see, for example, F. Gravit, *The Peiresc Papers*, Contributions in Modern Philology, no. 14 (Ann Arbor, 1950), pp. 1–57; and C. Rizzi, *Peiresc e l'Italia* (Turin, 1965).

Romanus (hereafter cited as R.), executed under Peiresc's care and now in the Vatican Library.

There are only two other manuscript traditions for the Calendar of 354. One is represented by a ninth-century manuscript, unillustrated, now at St. Gallen (Sangallensis MS. 878, hereafter cited as S. G.).[26] The only other manuscript tradition that can be posited with certainty is that via the miniatures of the Vossianus manuscript (Vossianus lat. q. 79, fol. 93v, hereafter cited as Voss.).

Peiresc's excitement over the discovery of L. was shared by his Renaissance contemporaries, as the sheer number of sixteenth- and seventeenth-century copies attests. The partial listing below includes only those with illustrations of the months; these are ordered according to their importance for this chapter.

1. L. = Luxemburgensis. Ninth-century manuscript copy from fourth-century original. Illustrated but now lost.

2. R. = Romanus, Rome, Bibliotheca Apostolica Vaticana. R1 = Barb. lat. 2154; R2 = Vat. lat. 9135. R1 was copied from L. in 1620; R2 was copied from R1 at the same time. Both illustrated. (Figs. 1–23 from R1; Figs. 24–27 from R2.) R. (= R1 + R2) is the best copy we have, for it faithfully preserves the iconographic detail and, arguably, even the style of L.[27] Unfortunately, R. was copied from L. after L. had lost several folios;[28] consequently, R. contains only the illustrations of seven of the original twelve months—February, March, and August–December.

3. B. = Bruxellensis, Brussels, Bibliothèque Royale. MS. 7543–7549. B. was copied from L. circa 1560 and no later than 1571.[29] Illustrated. (Figs. 44–52.) Although the images are placed four to a page in B. instead of on separate pages as they were in L., a comparison of R. and B. reveals that the latter does faithfully reproduce the general iconography and the specific attributes for each month. Differences between these two manuscripts are noticeable in style, but not in content or iconography. Thus, B. provides another reliable copy of L. and corroborates R.

4. V. = Vindobonensis, Vienna, Österreichische Nationalbibli-

---

26. Stern 1953, pp. 14, 17–21.

27. For the fidelity of R., see Appendix 1.

28. See Strzygowski 1888, pp. 7–20; and Stern 1953, pp. 14ff. The loss of folios can be dated to sometime after V., 1500–1510, and before B., 1560–1571. See Appendix 1.

29. Mommsen, *MGH* 1892, p. 29; C. Gaspar and F. Lyna, *Les principaux manuscrits à peintures de la Bibliothèque Royale de Belgique*, vol. 1 (Paris, 1937), pp. 1–7, pls. 1, 2. See Appendix 1.

othek. MS. 3416. V. was copied from L. ca. 1500–1510.[30] Illustrated. (Figs. 29–43.) V. is extremely important for study of the illustrations of the Calendar of 354 because it was copied from L. before L. lost several folios.[31] Thus, V. and Voss. are the only two manuscript copies to contain the illustrations of all twelve months of the Calendar. Although stylistic and formal (e.g., spatial) alterations appear in V., as compared with R. and B., which must be taken into account, nevertheless it is a trustworthy copy of L. as regards the iconography and text of the months. V. includes no details or attributes not attested in the other manuscript copies for the seven surviving months (see R. above), and comparison with Voss. for the remaining five months (January, April–July) confirms the overall veracity of these as well. Corroborative evidence from these other copies and from contemporary fourth-century art and archaeology, then, allows us to use V. with confidence.

    5.   Voss. = Vossianus, Leiden, Bibliothek der Rijksuniversiteit. Ms. Voss. lat. q. 79, fol. 93v. Illustrated. (Fig. 53.) This manuscript, created in the last quarter of the sixth century, derives its illustrations of the months from either the original Codex-Calendar of 354 or an intermediary copy, dated after 354 but prior to 579.[32] The page discussed here includes miniature illustrations of the months and planets set within a planisphere.[33] Voss. is very important for this study: not only do the twelve illustrated months in Voss. reproduce the general iconography, movement, gestures, and attire of their monthly counterparts in the R., V., and B. manuscript copies, but the depictions of January, April, May, June, and July in particular are of critical value in corroborating the parallel depictions in the only other manuscript that preserves these months, V. Unfortunately, Voss. omits—and at times alters—many of the accompanying attributes of the images of the months. Although these discrepancies are explicable given its miniature size and transmission, nevertheless, unlike the manuscript copies cited above, Voss. should not be considered a completely trustworthy reproduction of the illustrations of the months in the original Calendar unless corroborated by other manuscript or archaeological evidence.

    30. Mommsen, *MGH* 1892, p. 31; J. H. Hermann, *Die illustrierten Handschriften und Inkunabel in Wien. Die frühmittelalterlichen Handschriften des Abendlandes,* vol. 1 (Leipzig, 1923), pp. 1–5; Stern 1953, p. 15.

    31. See notes 28 and 29 above.

    32. For the arguments linking Voss. to the Calendar of 354 and the dating of Voss., see Appendix 1.

    33. Stern 1953, pp. 27–41; G. Thiele, *Antike Himmelsbilder* (Berlin, 1898), pp. 138–141; W. Köhler and F. Mütherich, *Die karolingischen Miniaturen,* vol. 4: *Die Hofschule Kaiser Lothars* (Berlin, 1971).

6. Berl. = Berlinensis, Berlin, Staatsbibliothek Preussischer Kulturbesitz. Ms. lat. 2061B1, fols. 231r–237r (new pagination). Berl. was copied from L. before 1604.[34] Illustrated. (Fig. 28.) Berl. reproduces the iconography of R. but not its style.

Most important for study of the months in the Calendar of 354 is the ability to assess the accuracy and fidelity of the Renaissance copies of the lost Carolingian copy of the lost fourth-century original. The skill of Carolingian scribes in faithfully reproducing classical models is generally accepted by scholars.[35] While patience is required to contend with the difficulties inherent in studying copies of a copy, only by establishing a chain of emendation can we accurately project the original image. Thus, by isolating and comparing specific examples of fourth-century iconography (preserved in the Renaissance copies of the Calendar) with extant Roman works of art and archaeological artifacts and by utilizing comparable illustrations of the months (preserved mostly in Roman mosaic cycles and wall paintings) we may demonstrate that the Renaissance copies of the Calendar have indeed faithfully preserved the iconographic content of the Carolingian copy and that the Carolingian copy, in turn, has preserved the iconography (and perhaps even the style) of the fourth-century archetype.[36]

In fact, the similarities between the Romanus copy and extant fourth-century art have led some art historians to argue that the Luxemburgensis (the source for the Romanus copy) was not a Carolingian copy at all, but the fourth-century original.[37] That seems unlikely for a variety of reasons, not the least of which is the inclusion of Carolingian elements of handwriting and design in the Romanus copy.[38] Still, the argument is interesting, for it indicates the fidelity of the Renaissance instruments of transmission to possible fourth-century sources—an idea that receives further support from my research on the iconography of the months.[39]

In the discussion of the Calendar that follows, I include the distich and tetrastich texts for easy reference, and also because so much scholarly interpretation of these images uses these verses, though in my opinion incorrectly.[40]

34. Stern 1953, p. 1A, erratum; Mommsen, *MGH* 1892, pp. 30ff.
35. Stern 1953, pp. 14ff., 32ff., 341–359; see also my discussion in Appendix 1.
36. M. Schapiro, "The Carolingian Copy of the Calendar of 354 A.D.," *The Art Bulletin* 23 (1940): 270–272.
37. See, for example, Nordenfalk 1936, pp. 7–8.
38. Schapiro, "The Carolingian Copy," pp. 270–272.
39. Stern 1953, esp. pp. 341–359; and see Appendix 1.
40. For a fuller discussion of the often very corrupt text of the distichs, see Appen-

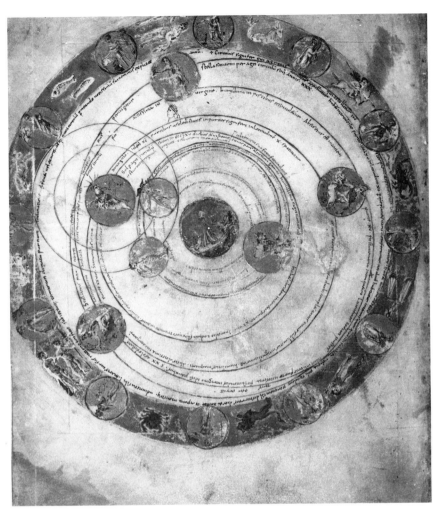

Fig. 53. Planisphere, Vossianus lat. q. 79, fol. 93v, 9th century. Bibliothek der Rijksuniversiteit, Leiden.

Fig. 54. The planets Mercury and Venus (detail), Manuscript S, Vat. Pal. lat. 1370, fol. 98v, 15th century. Biblioteca Vaticana, Rome.

Fig. 55. The planets Saturn, Jupiter, and Luna (detail), Manuscript T, MS.
Md2, fol. 320v, 15th century. Universitätbibliothek, Tübingen.

Fig. 56. The planets Mars, Sol, Mercury, and Venus, Manuscript T, MS. Md2, fol. 321r, 15th century. Universitätbibliothek, Tübingen.

Fig. 57. Planisphere (detail of January, February, and March), Bol. MS. 188, fol. 30r, 10th century. Bibliothèque Municipale, Boulogne-sur-Mer.

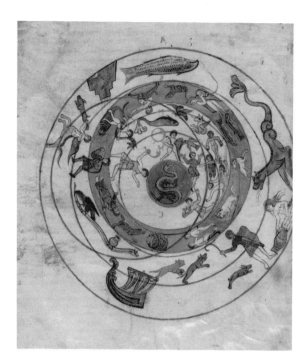

Fig. 58. Planisphere, Bernensis MS. 88, fol. 11v,
10th century. Bibliothèque Muncipale, Bern.

Fig. 59. January (detail), El-Djem Mosaic, 3d
century. Musée Archéologique, El-Djem,
Tunisia. Photo: Deutsches Archäologisches
Institut, Rome.

Fig. 60. February (detail), El-Djem Mosaic, 3d
century. Musée Archéologique, El-Djem,
Tunisia. Photo: Deutsches Archäologisches
Institut, Rome.

Fig. 61. March (detail), El-Djem Mosaic, 3d century.
Musée Archéologique, El-Djem, Tunisia.
Photo: Deutsches Archäologisches Institut,
Rome.

Fig. 62. April (detail), El-Djem Mosaic, 3d century.
Musée Archéologique, El-Djem, Tunisia.
Photo: Deutsches Archäologisches
Institut, Rome.

Fig. 63. May (detail), El-Djem Mosaic, 3d century.
Musée Archéologique, El-Djem, Tunisia.
Photo: Deutsches Archäologisches Institut,
Rome.

Fig. 64. June (detail), El-Djem Mosaic, 3d century.
Musée Archéologique, El-Djem, Tunisia.
Photo: Deutsches Archäologisches Institut,
Rome.

Fig. 65. July (detail), El-Djem Mosaic, 3d century. Musée Archéologique, El-Djem, Tunisia. Photo: Deutsches Archäologisches Institut, Rome.

Fig. 66. August (detail), El-Djem Mosaic, 3d century. Musée Archéologique, El-Djem, Tunisia. Photo: Deutsches Archäologisches Institut, Rome.

Fig. 67. September (detail), El-Djem Mosaic, 3d
century. Musée Archéologique, El-Djem,
Tunisia. Photo: Deutsches Archäologisches
Institut, Rome.

Fig. 68. October (detail), El-Djem Mosaic, 3d
century. Musée Archéologique, El-Djem,
Tunisia. Photo: Deutsches Archäologisches
Institut, Rome.

Fig. 69. November (detail), El-Djem Mosaic, 3d century. Musée Archéologique, El-Djem, Tunisia. Photo: Deutsches Archäologisches Institut, Rome.

Fig. 70. December (detail), El-Djem Mosaic, 3d century. Musée Archéologique, El-Djem, Tunisia. Photo: Deutsches Archäologisches Institut, Rome.

Fig. 71. March (detail), Carthage Mosaic, 4th century. British Museum, London.

Fig. 72. April (detail), Carthage Mosaic, 4th century. British Museum, London.

Fig. 73. July (detail), Carthage Mosaic, 4th century. British Museum,
London.

Fig. 74. November (detail), Carthage Mosaic, 4th century.
British Museum, London.

Fig. 75. March (detail), Ostia Mosaic, 4th century.
Archeological Park, Ostia, Italy. Photo:
Deutsches Archäologisches Institut, Rome.

Fig. 76. April (detail), Ostia Mosaic, 4th century. Archeological
Park, Ostia, Italy. Photo: Author.

Fig. 77. Roman relief, Attis *pudens,* Centre Archéologique, Hôtel
de Sade, Glanum, France. Photo: from M. J. Vermaseren,
The Myth of Attis in Greek and Roman Art (Leiden, 1966),
pl. 21.2.

Fig. 78. Contorniate reverse: Attis, 4th century.
Staatliche Museen, Berlin. Photo: from Alföldi
1976.

Fig. 79. Contorniate obverse: Theatrical masks, 4th
century. Staatliche Museen, Berlin. Photo:
from Alföldi 1976.

Fig. 80. Attis, terracotta figurine, from P. Romanelli's excavations in Palatine temple area, Rome. Photo: Soprintendenza Archeologica di Roma.

Fig. 81. Attis(?), terracotta figurine,
hermaphrodite, from P. Pensabene's
excavations in Palatine temple area. Photo:
P. Pensabene.

Fig. 82. Bronze statuette, dancing
Attis, from Banasa, North
Africa. Musée
Archéologique, Rabat,
Morocco.

Fig. 83. Dominus Julius Mosaic, Carthage, 4th century. Bardo Museum, Tunis.
Photo: Deutsches Archäologisches Institut, Rome.

Fig. 84. *Notitia Dignitatum,* Insignia of the *Comes Sacrarum Largitionum,*
Ms. Canon. Misc. 378, fol. 142v, Bodleian Library, Oxford.

Fig. 85. Mosaic of Bacchus holding a lizard on a string, El-Djem, Tunisia, 4th century. Bardo Museum, Tunis. Photo: Deutsches Archäologisches Institut, Rome.

Fig. 86. Sarcophagus of the Seasons, no. 181 in the Lateran Collection, Vatican Museum, Rome. Photo: Deutsches Archäologisches Institut, Rome.

KALENDARIVM ROMANVM VETVS.
Sub CONSTANTIO Imperatore , Conſtantini Magni
filio, vt apparet, editum, circa annumCHRISTI vulga-
rem 354. & VALENTINO cuidam inſcriptum.

Mm 2   NA-

Fig. 87. Dedicatory page of the *De Doctrina Temporum*
Commentarius in Victorium Aquitanum, ed. A. Bouchier
(= A. Bucherius), Anvers, 1634. Biblioteca Vaticana,
Rome.

Fig. 88. Drawing of lost Carthage Mosaic, late 4th–early 5th century. Drawing: Cagnat. Photo: from Cagnat.

Fig. 89. January–February (detail), Argos Mosaic, 6th century. Photo: G. Akerström-Hougen.

Fig. 90. March–April (detail), Argos Mosaic, 6th century. Photo: G. Akerström-Hougen.

Fig. 91. November–December (detail), Argos Mosaic, 6th century. Photo:
G. Akerström-Hougen.

Fig. 92. Women worshiping Attis, possibly for April (detail), Carthage Mosaic, 4th century. Photo: from G. C. Picard, *La Carthage de Saint Augustin* (Paris, 1956), p. 126.

Fig. 93. September (detail), Trier Mosaic, 2d–3d century. Rheinisches Landesmuseum, Trier.

Fig. 94. October (detail), Trier Mosaic, 2d–3d century. Rheinisches Landesmuseum, Trier.

Fig. 97. July (detail), Trier Mosaic, 2d–3d century.
Rheinisches Landesmuseum, Trier.

Fig. 95. November (detail), Trier Mosaic, 2d–3d
century. Rheinisches Landesmuseum,
Trier.

Fig. 96. June (detail), Trier Mosaic, 2d–3d century.
Rheinisches Landesmuseum, Trier.

Fig. 98. May (detail), the Acton Mosaic, 4th century. Private
collection of Sir Harold Acton, Villa La Pietra, Florence.
Photo: Author.

Fig. 99. June (detail), the Acton Mosaic, 4th century. Private
collection of Sir Harold Acton, Villa La Pietra, Florence.
Photo: Author.

Fig. 100. September (detail), the Acton Mosaic, 4th century. Private
collection of Sir Harold Acton, Villa La Pietra, Florence.
Photo: Author.

Fig. 101. January, March, May, July, and June(?),
Catania Mosaic, 4th century. Museo Civico del
Castello Ursino, Catania, Italy. Photo: from
Stern 1981, ill. 36, no. 96.

Fig. 102. April (detail), Hellín Mosaic, 2d–3d century. Museo Arqueológico Nacional, Madrid, Spain.

Fig. 103. May (detail), Hellín Mosaic, 2d–3d century. Museo Arqueológico Nacional, Madrid, Spain.

Fig. 104. August (detail), Hellín Mosaic, 2d–3d century. Museo Arqueológico
Nacional, Madrid, Spain.

Fig. 105. October (detail), Hellín Mosaic, 2d–3d century. Museo Arqueológico
Nacional, Madrid, Spain.

Fig. 106. November (detail), Hellín Mosaic, 2d–3d century. Museo
Arqueológico Nacional, Madrid, Spain.

Fig. 107. Planisphere (detail with April), Vossianus lat. q. 79, fol. 93v, 9th
century. Bibliothek der Rijksuniversiteit, Leiden.

ILLUSTRATIONS OF PAGAN RELIGIOUS FESTIVALS

December[41]

665.23–24[42]

Argumenta tibi mensis concedo *Decembris*
    †quae sis quam vis. . . . . . . †[43]

I grant the subjects of the month December to you,
    †. . . . . . . you are as you wish. . . . . . . †

395.45–48

Annua sulcatae coniecta en semina terrae
    pascit hiems; pluvio de Iove cuncta madent.
Aurea nunc revocet Saturno festa December.
    Nunc tibi cum domino ludere, verna, licet.[44]

Behold! Winter nourishes the seed thrown each year into the plowed earth; all is wet with rain sent from Jove. Now let December call once more the golden festival for Saturn. Now you, slave, are allowed to play [dice games] with your master.

December survives in the R., V., and B. manuscripts (Figs. 23, 43, 52). The central figure is a young man with short hair. He is dressed in a short tunic that extends to his thighs and has over it a fur collar; the tunic is ornamented with circular accessories (*galliculae* or *calliculae*) and with decorations on the sleeves. In his left hand he holds a torch; his right hand is half closed, with two fingers pointing straight out and held over a table before him. Apparently he has just thrown the dice, shown on the tabletop next to a small tower with stairs (*pyrgos*), part of the game of dice. In the background at the upper left is a face mask; in the upper right corner birds are depicted hanging on a hook; in the lower right are heart-shaped objects, too vaguely drawn to be identifiable.

---

dix 4. Emendations of the tetrastichs, which are somewhat better preserved, may be found in the footnotes. However, both the tetrastichs and the distichs present grave difficulties for the translator owing to ambiguities as well as corruptions in the text. I have based my text of the tetrastichs on that of Stern 1953; he, in turn, relied heavily on those of *Anth. Lat.*, 1.2 and Baehrens 1882. D. R. Shackleton Bailey's *Anthologia Latina* (Stuttgart, 1982) does not, in my view, offer an improved text; Courtney 1988, however, makes some helpful suggestions. Comparable cycles of the months in Latin poetry are listed in Appendix 3.

41. Comparable pictorial cycles of the months from the Latin West have been collected in Appendix 2.

42. Identifying numbers with poetry texts refer to *Anth. Lat.*, listed in Appendix 3.

43. This line (24) was lost from S.G. Conjectures in the later manuscripts and by scholars cannot make sense of this line. See Appendix 4.

44. Line 45: *coniecta en* Heinsius: *connectens* Baehrens: *coniecti* all the manuscripts. See Appendix 4 for key to scholars and method used to note poetry variations for *Anth. Lat.* 665 and 395.

December illustrates the popular holiday of the *Saturnalia*, noted in the Calendar text on 17 December. This Roman holiday included sacrifices at the temple of Saturn in the Forum and a public banquet, and continued for several days with entertainment and revelry in private homes.[45] The dice player suggests the games and gambling that were allowed in public only during the *Saturnalia*. The torch represents the nocturnal celebrations held during this holiday.[46] The mask illustrates the entertainments at this festive time of year.[47] And the birds are appropriate gifts for the holiday season.[48] Only the status of the central figure is in question.

A distinctive feature of the *Saturnalia* is the Roman custom by which slaves were given the liberty to play games with their masters on equal footing on this day.[49] Because of this practice and the accompanying tetrastich, the central figure has been interpreted as a slave.[50] Yet no visual evidence supports this conclusion. On the contrary, his attire, specifically the short fringed wool cloak and heavy leggings, represents that of a hunter in late Roman art. Although this attire is also appropriate to the season, it indicates—along with the birds—the figure's rustic provenance.[51] I therefore see the man as a rustic hunter in winter attire celebrating the popular festival of the *Saturnalia*.

The omission of any iconography to indicate a servile status for the central figure is noteworthy. First, it shows creative license on the part of the fourth-century artist, for the iconography used here differs from that found in an earlier extant illustration of this festival.[52] Moreover,

45. The festival is noted on only one day in the Calendar of 354, but was probably celebrated until 23 December. See Degrassi 1963, pp. 539–541.

46. An exact parallel to the torch depicted here exists in a mosaic, dated to the first half of the fourth century, from Cherchel (Caesarea), Algeria, published by Parrish 1984, no. 18.

47. Stern 1953, pp. 283–284. There is no evidence for theatrical activities at this festival, however.

48. Some birds are shown as autumn gifts in the mosaic of Dominus Julius (App. 2, no. 21; Fig. 83).

49. This aspect of the holiday is noted by Polemius Silvius, who records for this day *Feriae Servorum*. Testimony provided by Degrassi 1963, pp. 539–541; Seneca *Ep*. 47.14 provides the fullest description.

50. Stern 1953, pp. 283–285, cites *Anth. Lat*. 117, lines 23–24, to support his view.

51. Akerström-Hougen 1974 p. 26, n. 25, notes the short cape of the hunter in the Argos image for December (Fig. 91) as an important indication of popular images making their way into Roman art at the time of Constantine.

52. The late-second–early-third-century mosaic from El-Djem (App. 2, no. 9; Fig. 70) also alludes to the *Saturnalia*, but it depicts three slaves, clearly identified as such by their attire (notably, the *subligacula*), facing one another. Two of the figures stretch out their hands as if to entreat the third one, who holds a *cereus* (wax candle), a traditional gift at the *Saturnalia*. See L. Foucher, "Découvertes archéologiques à Thysdrus en 1961," *Notes et*

this omission means that the Calendar does not agree with the verses, which note a home-born slave, or *verna* (*Anth. Lat.* 395, ed. Riese, v. 48)—the first of several instances in which the verses and imagery of the Calendar do not agree. This disjuncture does not suggest, however, that the illustration is not a product of the fourth century; although no comparable contemporary illustration of December survives from the Latin West, the iconography fits comfortably with other fourth-century works.[53]

November

665.21–22

Frondibus amissis repetunt sua frigora mensem,
  cum iuga Centaurus celsa retorquet eques.

After the leaves have fallen, its accustomed wintry frosts fall upon this month once more, when the equestrian Centaur [Sagittarius] turns back the Great Plough.[54]

395.41–44

Carbaseos post hunc artus indutus amictus
  Memphidos antiquae sacra deamque colit.
A quo vix avidus sistro compescitur anser,
  devotusque tuis incola, Memphi, deis.[55]

After this [month], he [November], clothing his limbs in fine linen, reveres the sacred rites and goddess of ancient Memphis [i.e., Isis]. And by him [November], the greedy goose is scarcely restrained with the *sistrum*, as is the inhabitant [of your temple?] who is devoted to your deities, Memphis.[56]

---

documents de l'Université de Tunis (Institut National d'Archéologiques et des Arts) 5 (1961): 46; H. Stern, "Un calendrier romain illustré de Thysdrus," *Tardo antico e alto medioevo. La forma artistica nel passaggio dall'antichità al medioevo*, Quaderno dell'Accademia Nazionale dei Lincei, no. 105 (Rome, 1968), p. 194.

53. We can note as authentic and accurate details of fourth-century life the game of dice with the small tower (*pyrgus*) and the attire worn by the central male figure, including the circular accessories (*galliculae* or *calliculae*), which appear only at the end of the third century; the fur collar, short tunic, and the bulky leggings are attested in this period as appropriate winter attire. See Stern 1953, pp. 283–286; Akerström-Hougen 1974, p. 26.

54. According to A. E. Housman, "Disticha de Mensibus," Sagittarius makes the Northerly Plough rise again.

55. Line 41: *carbaseos post hunc artus* Riese: *postquam* mss.: *post calvus atrox* Baehrens. Line 44: *tuis* Shackleton Bailey: *satis* mss.: *Memphidos* Baehrens, Riese: *Memfidus* or *Memphidus* mss.: *Memfideis* Stern: *Memphi* Courtney.

56. Courtney 1988, p. 55, would identify the *incola*, or inhabitant, as connected with the temple, perhaps the serpent. In this he follows G. Binder, *Der Kalender des Filocalus oder*

November survives in the R., V., and B. copies (Figs. 22, 42, 51). Depicted is a male figure wearing a long tunic that extends to his ankles. In R. and B. he is bald and wearing sandals. In his right hand he holds a *sistrum*, a rattle; in his left hand he holds a plate, on which are depicted a snake, several leaves, broken branches, and (probably) some olives. A goose is shown in the lower left corner. To his right is a bust or mask of the Egyptian god Anubis, placed on a high stone base. Pomegranates— five in R.—are shown in the background.

This illustration is inspired by the cult of Isis, whose festivals were recorded in the Calendar from 28 October to 3 November. The fourth-century importance of this goddess and her cult at Rome is so well known that each attribute depicted here is easily identified.[57] The *sistrum* is an instrument carried by priestesses and priests of Isis; the goose is sacred to the goddess; and the Anubis head indicates either the god Anubis, worshiped alongside Isis, or the Anubophors, priests of Isis who paraded in these masks at Isis festivals.[58] The plate with the serpent, leaves, broken branches, and olives alludes explicitly to a particular rite of the Isis festivals, described in the fourth-century *Carmen contra Paganos*; after a period of mourning for the lost Osiris (the goddess's consort), his joyful return is celebrated by devotees who carry the broken olive branch at the festival day called the *Hilaria*, (noted in the Calendar on 3 November).[59] Finally, pomegranates, symbols of fertility, are frequently depicted with Isis.

Notably, the depiction of certain iconographic elements in this illustration is relatively rare, such as the goose and the male—not female—

der Chronograph vom Jahre 354 (Meisenheim/Glan, 1970–1971), pp. 8–9. This line is difficult to understand.

57. See Stern 1953, pp. 279–283; A. Alföldi, *A Festival of Isis*, pp. 44ff. M. Malaise, *Les conditions de pénétration et de diffusion des cultes égyptiens en Italie* (Leiden, 1972), pp. 450–455. For the importance of Isis and Sarapis for imperial *vota*, see A. Alföldi, "Die Alexandr. Götter und die Vota Publica am Jahresbeginn," *JAC* 8–9 (1965–1966): 53–87.

58. Apuleius *Met.* 11.11; M. Malaise, *Inventaire préliminaire des documents égyptiens découverts en Italie* (Leiden, 1972), pls. 1ff.

59. *Carmen contra Paganos*, v. 102, *Anth. Lat.* 1.1, pp. 20–25. The identification of the pagan addressee is disputed. L. Cracco Ruggini, *Il paganesimo romano tra religione e politica (384–394 d.c.). Per una reinterpretazione del Carmen Contra Paganos*, Atti della Accademia Nazionale dei Lincei. Memorie, classe di scienze, morali, storiche e filologiche, ser. 7, vol. 23, fasc. 1 (Rome, 1979), would identify the addressee as Praetextatus, urban prefect in 384, instead of the more conventional person, Nicomachus Flavianus, urban prefect in 394. For the date of the *Hilaria*, which fluctuated in Roman calendars between 1 and 3 November, see H. Stern, "La date de la fête d'Isis du mois de Novembre à Rome," *Comptes rendus de l'Académie des Inscriptions* (1968): 43–50.

priest of Isis holding a plate. To my knowledge, moreover, no extant examples from the extensive body of Isis imagery show the same combination of attributes as appear here.[60] These factors reinforce the view that November in the Calendar was not a mere reproduction of traditional iconography, used here for decorative purposes; rather, November is a virtual encyclopedia of Isis imagery drawn from fourth-century cultic practice.

Contemporary literary evidence supports this view. The fourth-century *Poem to a Senator* describes a noble consul who was portrayed in a wall painting in his home as a priest of Isis bearing an Anubis mask and rattle.[61] *The Augustan History: Life of Commodus* represents that emperor similarly: Commodus is said to have shaved his head and to have worn the Anubis mask in the service of Isis.[62] In the fourth century, too, the Roman nobility were dominant in the priesthood of the Anubophors.[63] Hence, by so depicting a male priest, November fits well with attested Roman aristocratic practices of the cult of Isis.[64]

The contemporary, and particularly local (i.e., Roman), influences observed in the Calendar, as well as the artistic independence of the illustrator, are underscored if we compare this depiction with those in mosaic cycles from the third- and fourth-century Latin West. Each of the three surviving illustrations for November that represent the festival of Isis use iconography different from that shown in the Calendar of 354,[65] a variation explained by local custom and diachronic change in festival practice.[66]

60. Stern 1953, pp. 279–283; M. Malaise, *Inventaire préliminaire*, pp. 1–316; Malaise cites the evidence for Rome, pp. 112–246, including 471 items.

61. Pseudo-Cyprian (attrib.), *Carmen ad senatorem ex Christiana religione ad idolorum servitutem conversum*, vv. 30–31, ed. W. Hartel, *CSEL* vol. 3, pt. 3 (1871), pp. 302–305, and then ed. R. Peiper, *CSEL*, vol. 23, pt. 1 (1881), pp. 227ff.; dated to the fourth century by L. Cracco Ruggini, *Il paganesimo romano*, p. 32; and by Stern 1953, pp. 279–283.

62. *H.A. Comm.* 6.9; although the precise date of the *H.A.* is disputed, it belongs in the fourth century. For bibliography, see R. Syme, *Historia Augusta Papers* (Oxford, 1983), pp. 224–229.

63. Alföldi, *A Festival of Isis*, pp. 44ff.; Prudentius *Contra Symm.* 2.354ff.

64. R. Hari, "Une image du culte égyptien à Rome en 354," *Mus. Helv.* 33 (1976): 114–118, argues that this imagery often includes Isis herself but very rarely a priest of Isis. He argues further that in exporting Isis mythology into the Roman world, the priests of Isis had integrated attributes belonging to other, lesser known Egyptian divinities.

65. See (1) the third-century mosaic from Trier (App. 2, no. 3; Fig. 95), which represents November as a female priest of Isis holding a *situla*; (2) the El-Djem Mosaic (App. 2, no. 9; Fig. 69), which represents November with three men dressed in animal costumes who are identified as *Anubiacii*, priests of Anubis in the service of Isis, taking part in the *Hilaria*, celebrated on 1 or 3 November; and (3) the mosaic from Hellín (App. 2, no. 4; Fig. 106), which, though somewhat damaged, preserve a female priestess of Isis, identifiable by her Isis knot.

66. Compare, for example, the male Isis priest from the Calendar of 354 with the

January

665.1–2
Primus, Iane, tibi sacratur †ut omnia†[67] *mensis*
  undique cui semper cuncta videre licet.

The first month of the year †and all things† is dedicated to you, Janus,
  who is permitted to see always all things on all sides.

395.1–4
Hic Iani mensis sacer est, en aspice ut aris
  tura micent, sumant ut pia tura Lares,
annorum saeclique caput, natalis honorum,
  purpureis fastis qui numerat proceres.[68]

This is the sacred month of Janus. Lo, look how the incense flashes on
the altars, how the Lares receive the pious incense! January—the beginning of years and of seasons—is the month for celebrating honors
and for recording noble men in its purple *fasti*.[69]

January survives in only one full-page illustration, preserved in V.
(Fig. 30).[70] Fortunately, the miniatures of Voss. (Fig. 53) preserve this
month as well. Voss. is therefore most important, for it allows us to verify
the central figures and activities, if not the attributes and iconographic
details, of the month. Because of the manuscript tradition of the Calendar, contemporary mosaics are especially useful for January (as for
April), for they not only serve as comparanda but also help to verify the
fourth-century provenance of the Calendar image.

January is represented by a man dressed in a long tunic; a heavy
toga is draped on top of the tunic, over his left arm and shoulder.[71] The
borders of the toga are ornamented with gems. On his head is a fur cap,
out of which flows a long veil. He wears shoes or slippers. He is in the
act of sacrifice, throwing incense on or pointing to flames that rise with
much smoke into the air before him. The flames are in a burner at the
figure's right; behind the burner is a rooster. The male holds a trefoil-

---

female priestess of Isis holding a *situla*, in a mosaic from Carthage (App. 2, no. 16; Fig.
74).

67. For alternative readings, see Appendix 4.
68. Line 4: *purpureis, -us, -um* var. mss.: *purpureos* Scaliger.
69. The *fasti* probably refer to the consular annals, called "purple" after the purple
clothing of the consuls; cf. Sidonius *Ep.* 8.8. The emendation *purpureos* would indicate only
the noble men's attire.
70. January in R1 (Fig. 16) is a forgery. See Appendix 1.
71. See R. Delbrück, *Die Consulardiptychen und verwandte Denkmäler 1–2*, Studien zur
spätantiken Kunstgeschichte, no. 2 (Berlin and Leipzig, 1929), pp. 46–47, for this draped
toga.

flower or leaf in his left hand. To the left of the man is a covered jar or urn on a large base. The miniatures in Voss. verify the depiction of January in the Calendar as a man dressed in a toga that covered his head and motioning toward a flaming object. Unfortunately, the cap is missing, as are details of clothing and all accessories.[72]

This image has been interpreted in two contradictory ways. Some scholars see January as a *vicomagister* who sacrifices with incense to the Lares at the *ludi Compitales*, the games recorded in the Calendar for 3–5 January.[73] Others interpret the figure as a consul who, after sacrificing at the Capitolium, made his formal announcement of vows on behalf of the well-being of the state (*votorum nuncupatio pro salute rei publicae*) on 1 January.[74] Despite these conflicting interpretations, the activity depicted is really not problematic. By the fourth century—and probably as early as the second—the celebration of the Kalends of January and the *ludi Compitales* had become so intertwined as to be virtually indistinguishable. Similarities in ritual and meaning certainly facilitated this synthesis. The *ludi Compitales* was originally a Roman domestic and agricultural festival to close the old year and pray for good things and protection in the new from the Lares and later from the *genius Augusti*; in time the New Year ceremonies included, in addition to domestic and agricultural rites, the vows of the consul who took office on 1 January and his wishes to Jupiter Optimus Maximus and Janus on behalf of the *salus*, or well-being, of the city and the emperor. January in the Calendar of 354 depicts this synthesis of ritual activities associated with the Kalends and *ludi Compitales* as practiced in Rome,[75] as, in fact, do comparable mosaic cycles from the Latin West and Greek East.[76]

72. A copy of the Voss., the Boulogne-sur-Mer manuscript (Fig. 57), also depicts January with a veiled head.

73. For instance, G. Volgraff, "De Figura Mensis Januarii e Codice Luxemburgensi Deperdito Exscripta," *Mnemosyne* 59 (1931): 394–402. He identified the cloak, with its ornamental bands, as the *toga praetexta* and the cap as the *pileus* worn by *vicomagistri* at these *ludi*, though represented here in a sixteenth-century stylization. The urn would either be a cinerary urn or a container for the incense used in the sacrifice; the cock would be the domestic animal associated with the Lares; and the trefoil would be a magic wand of Mercury, used as protection against the Lares.

74. For instance, Stern 1981, p. 457. The cock, alluded to by Libanius *Or.* 9.53, ed. R. Foerster (Leipzig 1903–1921), p. 395, would indicate the morning of the New Year; the trefoil would be a good-luck charm. The *votorum nuncupatio* is noted on 1 January by Degrassi 1963, p. 389.

75. M. Meslin, *La fête des kalendes de janvier dans l'Empire Romain*, Collection Latomus, *REL*, no. 115 (Brussels, 1970), pp. 52ff., collected the evidence for this celebration and schematically describes the rituals on the first days of January. On the eve of the first there were collective vigils, ritual dances, and banquets, including the rite of the *tabula fortuna*, the setting up of a table filled with good things for the year. On the morning of the first,

January in the Calendar of 354 provides a virtual encyclopedia of contemporary Roman rites and symbols for the first days of January. The cock represents the early rising of celebrants on 1 January and is the harbinger of the New Year; the trefoil leaf, probably an evergreen, signifies good luck;[77] and the urn pictorializes either the ritual offering of incense—as, for example, in January in the mosaic from St.-Romain-en-Gaul[78]—or the cinerary urn of the Lares (both interpretations would be appropriate for the New Year). Only the identity of the central figure involved in the ritual offering of incense is disputed.

Because of the gems on his toga, I would say that this man is a consul performing a sacrifice to Jupiter Optimus Maximus at the Capitolium as part of his vows *pro salute rei publicae*, the act with which the consul traditionally opened the New Year on 1 January.[79] Although no law

---

at the first crowing of the rooster, Romans rose to decorate their homes with laurel. After dressing in festival attire and taking private auspices for the year, they attended civic ceremonies. A procession followed, led by the new consuls for the year to the temple of Jupiter Optimus Maximus, with the consuls performing a sacrifice, offering *vota pro salute rei publicae*, and taking auspices prior to the meeting at the Senate; then, after a distribution of *sparsiones* by the consul and the offering of official *strenae* both to and from the emperor, came the exchange of *vota* and *strenae* among friends. A night of banquets and dancing on the first of January was followed by a day of rest and domestic celebration on the second. Then on the third were the great public and civic celebrations, noted in the text of the Calendar as *votorum nuncupatio*, with the giving of circus games by the consul and distributions of coins and gifts to the crowd. One sees in this description the remnants of the earlier *Compitalia*: in the ritual exchange of the *strenae*, in the sacrifices to the domestic Lares and to the *genius Augusti*, and in the taking of auspices.

76. Several comparands present themselves: (1) a second–third-century mosaic from St.-Romain-en-Gaul (App. 2, no. 5), where January is depicted by a male in a long toga who sacrifices incense in front of a large house identified as the home of the Lares; (2) a second–third-century mosaic from El-Djem in which two men in festival attire (long white tunics with *angusticlavii*) embrace and apparently exchange New Year's wishes (App. 2, no. 9; Fig. 59); to their left is a table with a base sculpted in the form of a statuette, suggestive of a Lar; the tabletop is filled with small cakes, laurel branches, and perhaps a doll, all appropriate New Year gifts (*strenae*); (3) a late-fourth–early-fifth-century mosaic from Carthage, extant only in notes and a drawing (App. 2, no. 17; Fig. 88), with January described as a male, flanked by a rooster, who holds a forked object in one hand and a basket of breads in the other; this mosaic has been read as a private individual taking auspices at the crowing of the rooster on 1 January or as representing a rite of augury (Akerström-Hougen 1974, p. 124); (4) a fourth-century mosaic from Catania (App. 2, no. 18; Fig. 101), in which the rooster alone is adequate attestation for January.

77. See Meslin, *La fête des kalendes*, p. 74, n. 1, for the cock and references to the laurel or evergreen as traditional good-luck foliage.

78. See App. 2, no. 5.

79. On 1 January was the *votorum nuncupatio pro salute rei publicae* to Jupiter Optimus Maximus, celebrated without games; see Degrassi 1963, p. 389. The *votorum nuncupatio pro salute imperatorum*, on 3 January, was, according to the text of the Calendar of 354, cele-

stated specifically that only a consul could wear gems on his toga on this day, references to the *trabea* heavy with gold and to the consul's ornate *toga picta* at this ceremony are frequent.[80] A diptych shows a consul at the games in an apparently gemmed toga similar to the one depicted here.[81] Traditional and contemporary associations of January vows with the consul, attested in late Latin and Greek poetry of the months, further support my identification of the central figure as a consul.[82]

The iconography for January—the consul involved in an act of sacrifice with incense—derives from traditional scenes of incense burning in honor of the Lares at the *ludi Compitales*[83] or, in Rome, by the consul in honor of Jupiter Optimus Maximus.[84] Whether in a private or public ambience, then, January in the Calendar illustrates the festival and rituals associated with the New Year in Rome in the mid fourth century. The choice of incense burning to depict the New Year, however, is meaningful only in the Latin West, where it recalls the rites and iconography of the *ludi Compitales* specifically.[85] In the Greek East, comparable pictorial cycles illustrate January with a consul opening the games for the New

---

brated with *ludi*. Stern 1981, p. 463, correctly observes that the drapery and combination of tunic and toga are similar to other representations of consular attire; these items of clothing are not, however, so significantly different from the attire of any magistrate or, for that matter, of a well-dressed aristocratic Roman to justify his interpretation of the central image as consul. Although by the fourth century the toga was increasingly reserved for magistrates in their official capacities (Delbrück, *Die Consulardiptychen* 1:44), only the *toga picta* distinguished the consul; see note 80 below. This point indicates the importance of the gems on the toga in January, a fact that Stern does not discuss.

80. Ausonius *Gratiarum Actio* 9.52–54, ed. S. Prete (Leipzig, 1978); Claudian *De cons. Stilichonis* 2.339; Claudian *Pan. dictus Olybrio et Probrino cons.* 205; and Claudian *Pan. dictus Honorio Augusto IV cons.* 585ff. The earliest use of such gemmed togas in official attire may be the result of innovations under Diocletian; see A. Alföldi, "Insignien und Tracht der römischen Kaiser," *MDAIR* 50 (1935): 3–154, esp. p. 154; reprint in *Die monarchische Repräsentation im römischen Kaiserreiche* (Darmstadt, 1970). For *toga picta* distinguishing the consul, see ibid., pp. 25–43. Although Alföldi (p. 36) also states that the privilege of a gemmed toga was reserved for the emperor, this does not seem to have been the case in fact; see note 81 below for a counterexample.

81. W. F. Volbach, *Elfenbeinarbeiten der Spätantike und des frühen Mittelalters*, 3d ed. (Mainz, 1976), no. 3, Asturius, Gaul (?), A.D. 449.

82. Note the appearance of this figure in the poems in *Anth. Lat.*, 117.1–2, 395.1–4, 874A.1–2; and *AP* 9.383.5, 9.580.1, 9.384.1–2.

83. See, for example, the figure sacrificing incense to the Lares represented in the mosaic from St.-Romain-en-Gaul (App. 2, no. 5).

84. Even the trefoil can be explained within a consular context; see Alföldi 1976, Petronius Maximus Contorniate, no. 461.

85. One extant diptych of Italian origin, dated to ca. 400, represents a consul opening the games with a libation; it provides a comparand and support for my interpretation of the illustration of January in the Calendar of 354; see Volbach, *Elfenbeinarbeiten*, no. 59.

Year by throwing down a flag (*mappa*).[86] In other words, he is shown—as he is on numerous fourth- and fifth-century consular diptychs[87]—in his most significant role: as giver of games.

April

665.7–8

Caesareae Veneris *mensis*, quo floribus arva
    prompta virent, avibus *quo* sonat omne nemus.[88]

This is the month of Caesarean Venus, when the open fields bloom with flowers, when every wood resounds with [the songs of] birds.[89]

395.13–16

Contectam myrto Venerem veneratur Aprilis.
    Lumen veris habet quo nitet alma Thetis.
Cereus et dextra flammas diffundit odoras;
    Balsama nec desunt, queis redolet Paphie.[90]

April honors Venus covered in myrtle. This month possesses the radiance of spring with which nurturing Thetis[91] glistens. And the candle to his [April's] right pours forth scented flames; nor is balsam lacking, with which the Paphian Venus is scented.

The illustration of April survives only in V. and in Voss. (Figs. 34, 53, 107).[92] The central image of April is of a man wearing a short tunic ornamented with a round patch (*orbiculus*) on each shoulder.[93] He performs a dance with long castanets (*krotaloi*) before a cult statue.[94] The physical traits of the dancer, who is beardless and bald (or shaven?) with

86. This took place on 2 or 3 January; see Degrassi 1963, pp. 388–391; Akerström-Hougen 1974, pp. 75–76.

87. For diptychs, see Volbach, *Elfenbeinarbeiten*, nos. 8–11, 16–18, 20–21, 36. On the role of consul, see Chastagnol 1960, pp. 10, 31, 138 and passim; Mamertinus *Pan. Lat.* 11(3).2, ed. E. Galletier (Paris, 1949–1955), in 362 noted: "in consulatu honos sine labore suscipitur."

88. See Appendix 4; line 7 does not scan.

89. Translation of line 7 follows Schenkl's proposed reading, *Caesareae*; see Appendix 4. "Caesarean Venus" suggested a first-century date for this poem to Housman, "Disticha de Mensibus," p. 132.

90. Line 14: *lumen veris . . . Thetis* mss.: *Lumen turis . . . Ceres* Strzygowski 1888, p. 65 (on the erroneous assumption that the verses describe the image): *Ceres* in certain mss. Line 15: *odoras* Riese: *odores* mss.

91. Binder, *Der Kalender des Filocalus*, pp. 9–10, interprets "Thetis" as meaning sea and suggests a reference to the beginning of the navigation period.

92. The argument for this identification of April was presented in large part in my article, "The Representation of April in the Calendar of 354," *AJA* 88 (1984): 43–50.

93. The *orbiculus* is typical of late-antique dress; see G. Fabre, "Recherches sur l'origine des ornements vestimentaires du bas-empire," *Karthago* 16 (1971–1972): 109–128.

94. The *krotaloi* are true to antique examples; see Stern 1953, pls. 47.2, 41.1.

heavily drawn facial lines and bulging chins, have been interpreted as those of an elderly man. In the background to the dancer's left stands a statue of a male deity, flanked by two leafy branches and placed on an eight-pointed, star-shaped pedestal; the pedestal rests on a high rectangular plinth decorated with what appears to be two large jewels. The features of the cult statue are not clearly depicted, but his right arm is bent over his breast and his left hand is placed across his groin. In front of the plinth and the statue is a large candle in an elaborate candlestick. In the lower right corner of the illustration is an object on which the dancer rests his right foot. The object has been identified as a Renaissance version of an ancient percussion instrument, a *scabellum*, which was played with the foot by krotalist dancers and pantomimists and is frequently depicted in theatrical contexts.[95]

The illustration of April in the Calendar of 354 has aroused much controversy. While its survival in only V. (Fig. 34) and Voss. (Figs. 53 and 107) certainly contributes to the problem of interpretation, this is not the main reason for the ongoing dispute. Rather, the problem with April is that virtually all explanations of its imagery have been based on the accompanying verses: it is seen as the worship of a cult statue of Venus by an elderly male dancer who performs an unidentified rite with castanets. The cult statue should resemble a Venus *pudica*, but is was mistakenly interpreted as a male god by the sixteenth-century copyist;[96] the candle allegedly represents the nocturnal celebration of such rites, and the leafy boughs the myrtle huts built for the worship of Venus.[97] According to this interpretation, April depicts a little-known festival in honor of Venus, the *Veneralia*, recorded on 1 April in the Calendar of 354.

Yet interpretation of the image as depicting the worship of Venus mentioned in the epigram raises numerous problems. If the worship of Venus is intended, would any copyist confuse so basic a fact as the sex of the cult statue being adored? The copyist has not preserved the Venus

95. Ibid., p. 270.

96. Strzygowski 1888, p. 65; Webster 1938, p. 14; Levi 1941, p. 239; Stern 1953, p. 268; and Stern 1981, p. 458.

97. Stern 1953, pp. 272–274. Stern cites as evidence the monthly verses and the *Pervigilium Veneris*, ed. R. Schilling (Paris, 1944), vv. 5ff., 42ff. But the date of this poem, the religious festival it describes, and its connection to the *Veneralia* are open to debate. See Stern 1953, p. 272; R. Schilling, "La place de la Sicile dans la religion romaine," *Kokalos* 10–11 (1964–1965): 279–282; P. Boyancé, "Le *Pervigilium Veneris* et les *Veneralia*," in *Mélanges d'archéologie et d'histoire offerts à A. Piganiol* (Paris, 1966), p. 1548; and L. Catlow, *Pervigilium Veneris* (Brussels, 1981), pp. 26–35.

pudica pose, since the left hand of our cult statue exposes rather than hides the lower body. The two leafy branches that frame the cult statue are not particular to the cult of Venus: other scenes of sacrifice include very similar representations.[98] Moreover, if the illustration is a reference to the rites of Venus, why is the dancer portrayed as an elderly male? The distinctive rite in honor of Venus on 1 April is the ritual bathing of the female worshipers and of the cult statue of Venus. After the bath, goddess and worshipers are covered with myrtle, the plant sacred to Venus.[99] Although the relevant literary sources (which span the imperial period) are in accord concerning this rite on 1 April, no allusion is ever made to a ritual dance with castanets or to male participation in the celebration of Venus on this day.[100]

Unfortunately, comparison of April in the Calendar of 354 with like representations in Roman mosaic cycles does not solve these problems. A third-century mosaic from El-Djem (Fig. 62; App. 2, no. 9) portrays two women dressed in long robes; each carries a castanet and a torch as they move from left to right before a cult statuette in a pose of the Venus *anadyomene* type (with two arms raised to hold out long, streaming hair). The statue in its temple, though, is so small and so crudely executed that it is indistinct; hence, it is of only marginal value for deciphering the sex of the cult figure in the Calendar image.[101] A fourth-century mosaic from Carthage (Fig. 72; App. 2, no. 16) depicts a female in an elaborately ornamented long robe performing a ritual dance with castanets before a statue; in this case, however, the cult figure is damaged and again of

98. Cf. the sacrifice to Diana in the mosaic of the small hunt in G. V. Gentili, *The Imperial Villa of Piazza Amerina* (Rome, 1970), pl. 14.

99. Lydus *Mens.* 4.65; Plutarch *Numa* 19.2; Ovid *Fasti* 4.133–139. Ovid's description of the rites to Venus on 1 April is complicated by the addition of rites associated with Venus Verticordia (i.e., drinking a potion, *Fasti* 4.151–156), and with *Fortuna Virilis* (women offering incense to insure fertility, *Fasti* 4.145–152). The late sources do not include these other rites as part of the festivities on 1 April; hence, they presumably fell out of use by the fourth century. See Roscher, *Lex.*, s.v. "Venus," pp. 49–192; and J. W. Halporn, "Saint Augustine Sermon 104 and the *Epulae Veneris*," *JAC* 19 (1976): 82–108.

100. Neither Stern 1953, pp. 276–277, nor Halporn, "Saint Augustine," pp. 88–92, convincingly explains the silence in our sources concerning this rite.

101. L. Foucher, "Découvertes archéologiques à Thysdrus," pp. 35–37. Although Foucher expressed reservations about this identification with the *Veneralia*, he called the deity Venus *anadyomene* on the basis of Stern's identification of the cult status in the image of April in the Calendar of 354 as Venus *pudica*. Photographs of this mosaic (App. 2, no. 9) support Foucher's description of the stance and the long hair of the statuette, but they do not suggest its gender. Differences between this cult statue and the image in the Calendar of 354 should also be noted: the statuette is not flanked by two leafy branches but is depicted instead within a small *aedicula* and appears to have a raised right leg, which does not coincide with the Venus *pudica* pose in the Calendar.

little assistance in establishing the gender of the statuette represented in the Calendar illustration.[102] In a fourth-century mosaic from Ostia (Fig. 76; App. 2, no. 15), the image of the cult statue survives, but the dancer with castanets does not. Nevertheless, the mosaic has so suffered from reworking that although the *pudicus* stance of the statuette can be discerned, its gender cannot.[103]

While none of this comparative visual evidence precisely parallels the Calendar iconography, it does indicate that the image of April in the Calendar—a dancer with castanets before a cult statuette—is consistent with late-antique iconography in both subject matter and design. I would argue, however, that the traditional interpretation of April as a rite of Venus is highly tenuous, relying as it does on the Latin verses that accompany the image in certain manuscripts—verses that, as we have seen, were actually independent, later additions to the Calendar.[104] In fact, numerous examples of dancers with castanets are to be found in texts and monuments from antiquity.[105] The pose of the dancer in the Calendar shows one phase of the krotalist dance; the presence of the cult statue in a niche and the burning candle suggests a ritual dance with religious significance. The majority of male krotalist figures recorded in a religious context in literature and art depict Galli, the priests of Cybele, who, like the whirling dervishes in Turkey, danced themselves into a frenzy.[106] Catullus, for one (*Carmina* 63), describes the dancing of the Galli with their *citatis tripudiis*—fast, leaping steps—to the sound of cymbals, pipes, and drums.

The Galli ritually reenacted the myth of Cybele, the mother goddess of Anatolia, and her young male consort, Attis. Cybele had instructed Attis in the art of dance, and he is said to have danced to please her (Fig. 82).[107] Yet Attis was unfaithful to the goddess; she retaliated by driving

102. See N. Davis, "On Recent Excavations at Carthage," *Archaeologia* 38 (1860): 227–230 and pl. 11; Stern, "Un calendrier romain illustré de Thysdrus," pp. 176–200. Stern claims that on the base of the cult statue in the Carthage mosaic is the discarded cloak of a Venus statuette, but not enough remains of either the statuette or the cloak to make this identification certain. Most interesting is the dancer, who is here identifiable with African priestesses of Dea Syria-Atargatis; see Apuleius *Met.* 8.27. Her attire suggests that illustrations of the month were reinterpreted according to local custom.

103. G. Becatti, *Mosaici e pavimenti marmorei, Scavi di Ostia*, vol. 1 (Rome, 1961), pp. 235–241, no. 438.

104. Stern 1953, pp. 232–298; also see my discussion, pp. 68–69 above, and Appendix 1.

105. Dar.-Sagl., s.v. "Crotalum," pp. 1571–1572.

106. M. J. Vermaseren, *The Myth of Attis in Greek and Roman Art* (Leiden, 1966), pp. 41–43.

107. Julian *Orat.* 5.165c, ed. W. Wright (Cambridge, 1913–1923); cf. Arnobius *Adv. Nat.* 4.35: "saltatur et Magna sacris compta cum infulis Mater."

him mad, and in his frenzied state Attis castrated himself.[108] (Hence the frequent allusions to his sexuality, the source of his torment, and the hermaphroditic qualities of his representations.[109] The Galli, who reenacted this myth, even practiced ritual castration.)[110] Although Attis's castration resulted in his death, Cybele's grief was so great that Attis was returned to life. As the god who conquered death and was reborn in the spring, Attis was joyfully honored in annual festivals at the end of March.[111]

The ritual dancing of the Galli was a distinctive feature of all festivals in honor of the goddess and her consort, as we know from literary descriptions of the great festival of Cybele (or the Magna Mater, as Romans called her), celebrated in Rome in April.[112] Originally, this festival commemorated Cybele's official entry into Rome in 204 B.C., when she was welcomed as the goddess who would defeat Hannibal.[113] After the Roman success, the festival in honor of the Magna Mater—called the *Megalesia* or *Megalensia*, allegedly after her title[114]—was celebrated annually on 4 April. A second celebration, on 10 April, was held each year to commemorate the dedication of her temple on the Palatine Hill in Rome, the remains of which are visible today.[115]

By the first century B.C., the festivities of the *Megalesia* were so popular that they expanded to fill the days from the fourth to the tenth of April,[116] exactly when they are listed in the Calendar of 354 and when, according to our sources, the priests of Cybele, the Galli, as well as a society of dancers (*sodales ballatores Cybelae; CIL* 6.2265) and an association

---

108. In the myth, Attis is unfaithful to Cybele and falls in love with a nymph; see Julian *Orat.* 5.165c; Ovid *Fasti* 4.229ff.; Lactantius *Div. Inst.* 1.17.7. Concerning the *iactatio fanatica*, see Arnobius *Adv. Nat.* 5.13; Catullus 63.5; Ovid *Fasti* 4.230ff. The dances of the Galli, their self-flagellation, and their self-castration imitate the *delirium* and *iactatio fanatica* of Attis; see Ovid *Fasti* 4.243–244; Augustine *De civ. Dei* 7.24ff.

109. The young Attis is most frequently depicted with oriental trousers (*anaxyrides*) or with a tunic blown open, in a stance that clearly emphasizes his sexuality; see Vermaseren, *Myth of Attis*, pls. 33.1, 33.3, 33.4. Vermaseren further identifies an Attis *pudens* type (pl. 21.2; Fig. 77 this volume) in which the god shields his lower body with his hand. For allusions to the hermaphroditic nature of Attis in literature and sculpture, see ibid., pp. 31–38, pl. 21.3, and pp. 33–34 with texts, esp. Catullus 63.4–74.

110. H. Graillot, *Le culte de Cybèle, mère des dieux à Rome et dans l'Empire Romain* (Paris, 1912), p. 75, n. 2; cf. *CIL* 13.510, which records a Eutyches who "sacrificed his masculinity" in A.D. 239.

111. For further discussion of this cult and its festivals, see Chapter 4.

112. Ovid *Fasti* 4.179–187, 4.346ff.

113. Livy 29.14.5–14.

114. Varro *De ling. lat.* 6.15.

115. Livy 36.36.3.

116. See Degrassi 1963, p. 435, on this expansion, attested by the Roman calendars.

of reciters of hymns (*hymnologoi Cybelae*; CIL 6.32444), performed. The festivities included the traditional Roman rites, consisting of sacrifices, a procession, games, and plays in circus and theater;[117] as early as 194 B.C., moreover, theatrical performances were incorporated into the *Megalesia*,[118] which Cicero values as traditional, held at a temporary theater erected annually in front of the temple of the Magna Mater on the Palatine Hill.[119]

Theatrical performances at the *Megalesia* and, specifically, the ritual reenactment of the myth of Attis and Cybele in the theater by the Palatine temple were part of the long-standing Roman celebration of the April holiday. The continuation of these performances into the fourth century is well attested. Certain of the bronze pseudomedallions, the contorniates, struck at Rome beginning in the mid fourth century depict the god Attis on the obverse and theatrical masks on the reverse (Figs. 78, 79).[120] Textual evidence further testifies to the continuing popularity of mimes and pantomimes at Roman festivals; the writings of the Christian fathers, particularly Arnobius and Augustine, are quite pointed in condemning these performances, and at the very time when the Calendar was composed.[121]

The central image of April—the elderly male who performs a ritual dance with castanets—can therefore be identified either as a Gallus, a eunuch priest of the Magna Mater whose traditionally fleshly appearance would be indicated by his bulging chin,[122] or as a theatrical performer participating in the *Megalesia*. The pose of the dancer in the Calendar, with one arm raised over his head and the opposite foot advanced, is similar to conventional representations of Attis dancing and of his priests, the Galli (Fig. 82).[123]

That the dancer is shown as an elderly man can be explained by a variant fourth-century account of a legendary celebration of the *Megalesia*, which Servius poses as the origin of the proverb "All things are

117. Ovid *Fasti* 4.179–187, 4.346ff.; circus games appear in calendars from the first century B.C., as Degrassi 1963, p. 435, notes.

118. Livy 34.54.3, 36.36.3.

119. Cicero *Har. Resp.* 12.20–29 condemns, on religious grounds, the disruption of these performances in 56 B.C.

120. Alföldi 1976, pp. 194–195, reverse nos. 23–29.

121. Arnobius *Adv. Nat.* 4.35, 7.33; Augustine *De civ. Dei* 2.4, 4.26, 6.9, 7.26.

122. See Macrobius *Sat.* 7.10.14 on fleshly eunuchs; and for their soft bodies, Ovid *Fasti* 4.243–244; Augustine *De civ. Dei* 7.26.

123. See Vermaseren, *Myth of Attis*, pp. 47–56, for a catalogue of statues of the dancing Attis type. Numerous bronze figurines survive from Italy, Germany, North Africa, France, and Egypt. Vermaseren notes the difficulty of distinguishing the statue of the god from that of his dancing priests.

favorable if the old man dances" (*Omnia secunda, saltat senex*): "The Romans were suffering afflictions caused by the anger of the Mother of the Gods, and were unable to placate her with sacrifices at the public games; a certain old man danced at the circus games which had been established in her honor. This was the sole means of placating the goddess."[124] Several other explanations of this proverb exist, and there is no reason to suppose that Servius's had a stronger claim on the truth than the rest. What is important, however, is that a late-fourth-century writer associated an elderly mime with the festival of the Magna Mater.

The male cult statue venerated in the illustration represents the god Attis as the young consort of the goddess. The image depicted—a hermaphroditic youth with arms over chest and groin—reflects the myths associated with him, as does the Attis *pudens* type identified by Vermaseren (Fig. 77).[125] Admittedly, the Calendar representation of the cult statuette is unusual because lacking are the well-attested Phrygian cap and trousers attributed to Attis. There are two possible explanations for the omission of these features: either the copyist, confronted with the image of Attis, misconstrued the details of his model or simplified it to be more easily understood;[126] or else this particular way of depicting Attis reflects a peculiarly Roman style, in which the attributes most often associated with Attis, namely the Phrygian cap and trousers, are omitted and Attis—often shown as a young man or hermaphrodite—is depicted bareheaded or with a sort of flat cap and wearing, if anything, a mantle (Figs. 80–81).[127] The Calendar, then, may reflect the peculiarly Roman version of Attis, attested at the Palatine sanctuary by hermaphroditic, nude figurines, whose pose and arm placement make reference to the castration of the god and his worshipers (Fig. 81).[128]

124. Servius *Ad Aen.* 3.279: sciendum sane moris fuisse ut piaculo commisso ludi celebrarentur; nam cum Romani iracundia matris deum laborarent et eam nec sacrificiis nec ludis placare possent, quidam senex statutis ludis circensibus saltavit, quae sola fuit causa placationis—unde et natum proverbium est *omnia secunda, saltat senex*. For further discussion of this passage, see Appendix 7.

125. Vermaseren, *Myth of Attis*, pp. 31–37; see also note 109 above.

126. Such simplification is consistent with the work of the Vienna copy; it thus appears more likely than the "sex change" required by the identification as Venus, proposed, for example, by Stern 1953, p. 267.

127. *CCCA* 3 (1977), nos. 2–199. The excavations at the Palatine temple of the Magna Mater have uncovered numerous terracotta figurines of Attis depicted as a child, as a young man (or young hermaphrodite), and as an old man. For representations of Attis with a flat cap, see *CCCA* 3, nos. 13, 36, 59; for Attis with mantle and flat cap, see nos. 35, 37, 56. Noteworthy comparanda for the Calendar image are nos. 43 and 63; both are bare-headed, and no. 63 is described as "having a special tuft of hair on the top of his head," which may be reflected in the hairstyle of the Calendar statuette; similar to no. 63 are nos. 64 and 65.

128. For Attis with a pose similar to the Calendar statuette and for hermaphroditic

The framing of the cult statue in the Calendar by two leafy branches before which a candle burns is a generic representation of a religious rite.[129] The elaborate candlestick, too, is typical of late-antique cultic paraphernalia.[130] The octagonal base on which the statuette stands has no exact late-antique parallel; it is, apparently, the work of the Viennese copyist.[131] The list of April holidays reported in the Calendar text supports the proposed new identification of this image. The festival of the Magna Mater is included,[132] beginning on the fourth and continuing through the tenth, when twenty-four circus races conclude the holiday (yet another indication of the popularity of this festival).[133]

April in the Calendar of 354 thus represents the popular festival of the Magna Mater, with imagery appropriate to its fourth-century Roman context. Comparable pictorial illustrations of April may be reinterpreted

---

representations of the god, see the examples cited above in note 109. See Vermaseren, *Myth of Attis*, pl. 33.3. If I am correct in identifying the cult statuette in the Calendar as an Attis, then the statuette in the Thysdrus mosaic can be so interpreted as well. For an Attis with arms raised in the same position as the statuette in the Thysdrus mosaic, see *CCCA* 4 (1978), pl. 1, no. 3. Attis is often depicted with long hair in a feminine style, as, for example, in *CCCA* 3, pl. 140, no. 249; and pl. 37, no. 36. Attis's long hair was a symbol of his eternal life; see Arnobius *Adv. Nat.* 5.7, who relates that although Attis died, his hair would grow forever. To imitate the god and to mark their sorrow for his death, the Galli grew their hair long; cf. Ovid *Fasti* 4.244–248; Firmicus Maternus *De Err. Prof. Rel.* 4; Servius *Ad Aen.* 10.220.

129. See, for example, the mosaic of the small hunt at Piazza Amerina, in Gentili, *Imperial Villa*, pl. 14.

130. See P. Romanelli, "Tomba Romana con affreschi del IV secolo dopo Cristo nella regione di Gagáresh (Tripoli)," in *In Africa e a Roma* (Rome, 1981), pp. 405–427, figs. 8–9; and Stern 1953, pl. 283, for the fifth-century mosaic. The candlestick has no precise late-antique parallel, for its late Gothic form and the snails at its base are, no doubt, the embellishments of the sixteenth-century Viennese copyist (see Appendix 1).

131. The snail motif (for the feet of the furniture) and a six-pointed-star-shaped statue base are found in the Sebaldus tomb monument, which was executed by Peter Vischer the Elder and his son, Peter Vischer the Younger. J. H. Hermann, *Die illustrierten Handschriften und Inkunabeln in Wien. Die frühmittelalterlichen Handschriften des Abendlandes 1* (Leipzig, 1923), pp. 1–5, attributes the Viennese copy to Vischer, noting the telltale snails at the candlestick base, but not the star-shaped base, as evidence. Thus Hermann's identification of the Viennese copyist as belonging to that group of sixteenth-century Nuremberg artists, if not the Vischers themselves, is given further support; see A. Feulner and T. Müller, *Geschichte der deutschen Plastik. Deutsche Kunstgeschichte 2* (Munich, 1958), pp. 377–379, fig. 310, for the statuette of St. Sebaldus.

132. The Calendar calls the festival the *ludi Megalesiaci*; this changed nomenclature does not reflect any change in substance. See Chapter 4.

133. By contrast, the *Veneralia*, noted on only one day in April, was not celebrated by circus games or by *ludi*; the *ludi* recorded in the Calendar on 1 April are identified with the anniversary of Constantius Chlorus. See Degrassi 1963, pp. 433–434.

as representing the festival of the Magna Mater as well, but with iconography appropriate to local cultic practice. A fourth-century mosaic from Carthage depicts a female priest identified with the cult of Dea Syria-Atargatis (Fig. 72; App. 2, no. 16), and not a Gallus or male castanet dancer of the Magna Mater. This discrepancy is explicable if we recall the close ties between the two cults; the followers of Dea Syria-Atargatis were described, at least in North Africa, as followers of the Magna Mater.[134] Local practice may account for the female worshipers of the El-Djem mosaic (Fig. 62; App. 2, no. 9) and of another mosaic, dated to the first half of the fourth century: in the latter representation, two women carry objects of great value as an act of worship before a statuette of Attis; Attis is depicted in a shrine of garlands, framed much as in the Calendar of 354 (Fig. 92; App. 2, no. 22). Because the archaeological context of this mosaic is missing, we cannot definitively identify it as part of a cycle of the months, as certain scholars have suggested;[135] nevertheless, it shows a comparable illustration of the worship of Attis, whose statuette is clearly depicted.

ILLUSTRATIONS OF SEASONAL THEMES

June

665.11–12
Iunius ipse sui causam tibi nominis edit
    praegravida attollens fertilitate sata.

June himself proclaims the reason of his name to you,
    bringing forth very heavy[136] crops in abundance.

395.21–24
Nudus membra dehinc solares respicit horas
    Iunius ac Phoebum flectere monstrat iter.
Lampas maturas Cereris designat aristas
    floralisque fugas lilia fusa docent.[137]

Next June, with naked limbs, looks back at the sundial and shows that Phoebus changes his route. The torch indicates that the wheat of Ceres

---

134. Apuleius, *Met.* 8.27, 9.10; Dar.-Sagl., s.v. "Syria," esp. p. 1593, n. 20.

135. See Appendix 2, no. 22, for bibliography.

136. *Praegravidus* means very heavy or ponderous, weighty—i.e., weighing down the branch or stalk.

137. Line 21: *nudus* Riese; *nuda* mss. Line 23: *lampas* mss.: *iam falx* Baehrens, Shackleton Bailey. Since *lampas* makes sense in context, no emendation is needed.

is ripe, and the scattered lilies show that the time of blooming flowers passes quickly.[138]

June in V. (Fig. 37) is depicted by a nude male turned away from the viewer, his right hand pointing to a sundial placed atop a column capital. In his left hand he holds a large torch; a mantle or loose cloth is draped over his left arm. In the lower left of the page is a fruit-filled basket (apples?), with a sickle shown above it. In the background to the central figure's right is a flowering plant. Voss. (Fig. 53), which has the only other copy of this illustration, verifies the pose of the man holding the torch and pointing to some tall object of vague outline. In lieu of the basket with fruit is an amphora.[139]

The central image of a nude male with torch and sundial has been interpreted as an allegory of the summer solstice—noted in the Calendar text as *solstitium* on 24 June,[140] a day that was called *dies lampadarum*, the "day of torches," perhaps in reference to the heat of the summer sun.[141] Since the *solstitium* traditionally marks the beginning of the harvest season, moreover, the harvest is the central theme for the month; it is represented by the sickle, the fruit in the basket, and the plant (which I would identify as a bean plant harvested at this time of year:[142] the text of the Calendar notes for 1 June *ludi Fabarici,* the popularly celebrated "Beans Kalends" commemorating the first fruits of summer).[143]

Although the iconography for this month can be explained, there are conflicting views about the meaning of the term *dies lampadarum* and the nature of the celebration that occurred on this day, the *solstitium.* Despite attempts to interpret the term *dies lampadarum* as a reference to Ceres' search for her lost daughter Persephone with torches—a search that was recreated by reaping corn by torchlight, an allusion to the sum-

---

138. Although the *TLL* attests *floralis* as specifically associated with Flora and the *Floralia* were celebrated in late April or early May, I follow Binder's more general temporal interpretation of this term in *Der Kalender des Filocalus*, pp. 9–10.

139. Stern 1953, p. 29. Perhaps this amphora has mistakenly been copied from August, where it belongs but is missing from Voss.

140. Stern 1953, pp. 252–258; Stern 1981, p. 459, esp. n. 111, repeats this identification for the central image and the attributes.

141. This name appears in a late Latin homily, dated to between the end of the fourth to the sixth century and probably from North Africa; see Stern 1953, p. 253.

142. See, for example, the plant depicted in the fourth-century mosaics for June from Catania (App. 2, no. 18; Fig. 101) and from Aquileia (App. 2, no. 14; Fig. 99). Stern 1953, p. 253, would identify it as a lily signaling the beginning of the harvest season, as noted in the tetrastichs.

143. Macrobius *Sat.* 1.12.33; Varro *De vita pop. Rom. apud Nonium*, 1. 539, ed. W. M. Lindsay (Oxford, 1901); Latte 1960, pp. 70–71.

mer sun's heat—I see no reason to explain this day as hosting, in fourth-century Rome, a popular, semireligious festival in honor of Ceres.[144] Moreover, no known festival or rite to Ceres is noted in any Roman calendar for this month. Unlike the popular winter celebration of the equinox, the *Bruma*, the *solstitium* is not otherwise attested as a communal festival or quasi-religious rite.[145] The torch depicted in the Calendar of 354 is an easily understood symbol for summer heat, hence the popular designation *dies lampadarum.*

August

665.15–16

Tu quoque, Sextilis, venerabilis omnibus annis,
   Numinis Augusti nomen †in anno venis†.

You too, Sextilis,[146] venerable in every year,
   †Come, you who bear† the name of the godly Augustus.[147]

395.29–32

Fontanos latices et lucida pocula vitro
   cerne, ut demerso torridus ore bibat.
Aeterno regni signatus nomine mensis
   Latona genitam quo perhibet Hecaten.[148]

Look how he [August], parched, plunges his mouth [in the water] and drinks the spring water from the bright glass cups. This month, designated by the eternal name of rule [i.e., Augustus], is the one in which Latona says her daughter Hecate was born.

144. Although the name *dies lampadarum* is attested in a late Latin homily, the primary evidence for interpreting this as a festival is Fulgentius's *Mytholographia* 1.11, ed. R. Helm (Leipzig, 1898), pp. 22ff. Writing in sixth-century North Africa, Fulgentius explained this day in relation to Ceres: "for it was also said that her mother [Ceres] searched for her [Persephone] when she was stolen away, with torches, whence the day of torches has been dedicated to Ceres, clearly for the reason that at that time crops are joyfully sought for reaping with torches, that is, with the sun's heat." Fulgentius's allegorizing remarks and their fourth-century Roman application are suspect; for his statement of method, see the prologue to the *Mytholographia*; for his allegorizing tendencies when explaining such iconographic attributes (e.g., Saturn's scythe and Pluto's watchdog), see L. G. Whitbread, *Fulgentius, the Mythographer* (Columbus, Ohio, 1971), pp. 14–27. Degrassi 1963, p. 473, denies the festival nature of the *solstitium*; Stern 1953, pp. 107ff., supports it.

145. Stern 1953, pp. 107ff.

146. Sextilis is the sixth month in the old Roman calendar year, which began in March.

147. Line 16: the phrase in daggers conveys the sense of R. Tarrant's emendation. See Appendix 4.

148. Line 30: *demerso* Riese: *dimerso* mss.: *demisso* Courtney. Line 32: *Hecaten* Riese: *Echaten* several mss. This is an error: Hecate is mistakenly inserted because of her association with Diana; the *Natalis Dianae* fell on 13 August.

August (Figs. 19, 39, 47) survives in R., V., and B. The month pictorializes the summer season[149] with a nude male drinking (water?) out of a large glass bowl[150]—iconography representing the thirst created by the summer heat. To the upper right of the central figure is a jacket, thrown off in the heat;[151] below it is an amphora, closed with a flower to preserve the fresh water.[152] On the amphora, the Carolingian copyist has poorly copied the Latin transcription *ZHCHC* = *ZESES* (from the Greek, meaning "to your health"), mistakenly replacing it with *ZLS*. In the upper left corner of the page is illustrated a peacock fan above three melons. All these motifs would be readily comprehensible to a fourth-century Roman as depicting the heat of the summer season.[153]

October

665.19–20
Octobri laetus portat vindemitor uvas,
    omnis ager Bacchi munere, voce sonat.

The cheerful vintager carries the grapes for October;
    every field resounds with the gift of Bacchus, and with his voice.

395.37–40
Dat prensum leporem cumque ipso palmite foetus
    October; pingues dat tibi ruris aves.
Iam bromios spumare lacus et musta sonare
    apparet: vino vas calet ecce novo.[154]

October brings the captured rabbit and the produce together with the young vine-sprout; it brings fat birds of the countryside to you. Now it is clear that the Bromian [Bacchic] vats [of wine] are foaming and the must resounding. Look! the vessel grows hot with new wine.

149. Stern 1953, pp. 258–263 classifies this image as a mixed illustration that incorporates popular beliefs and seasonal themes. My category of mixed illustrations includes festival iconography with seasonal themes, and so I have categorized this image as only seasonal.

150. The miniatures in Voss., V., and B. confirm this image. In Voss. the secondary attribute of the amphora is also shown.

151. Pseudo-Paulinus (attrib.), *Carmen ad Antonium,* v. 139 (*Carmen* 32, ed. W. Hartel, *CSEL,* vol. 30 [Leipzig 1894], pp. 329ff.), mentions the credulous crowd hanging their jackets up for the sun at the festival of the *Volcanalia,* which celebration appears in the Calendar text on 23 August as *ludi Vulcanalici.* Perhaps the discarded jacket was an allusion to this festival?

152. See Stern 1981, p. 459, n. 114, for comparandum for the flower.

153. The central figure with the glass bowl to represent summer heat can be traced to monuments from the second quarter of the fourth century, appearing on Roman seasonal sarcophagi from 330–360; see Stern 1953, p. 260.

154. Line 39: *bromios* Riese: *Bromios* Courtney: *Bromio* Baehrens: *Ambromius* R.

Like August, October (Figs. 21, 41, 50) survives in R., V., and B. The central figure is a male, depicted as a hunter with a mantle draped over his left shoulder.[155] Around him are illustrations of various sorts of hunting. Bird catching is shown in the upper left corner by lime sticks, cloth, and a decoy bird; hare hunting is enacted by the central figure, who holds in one hand a hare, caught in an elongated basket-trap with a cover on a line; and hunting for acorns (?) is illustrated by the baskets in the upper and lower registers of the page.[156] Compared with illustrations of hunting in other pictorial cycles,[157] this October provides the most extensive collection of hunting motifs and demonstrates the illustrator's inclination to assemble as many iconographic elements as possible to pictorialize a theme. This encyclopedic tendency, typical of other works of fourth-century literature and art, will be discussed at length in the conclusion to this chapter.

February

665.3–4
Umbrarum est alter, quo mense putatur honore
   pervia terra dato Manibus esse vagis.

The second [month] belongs to the shades, in which month
   it is thought the earth is made passable for the wandering Manes after
   honor has been given to them.

395.5–8
At quem caeruleus nodo constringit amictus
   quique paludicolam prendere gaudet avem,
Daedala quem iactu pluvio circumvenit Iris
   Romuleo ritu februa mensis habet.

But the month which is bound in a blue knotted cloak and which rejoices at seizing the swamp-inhabiting bird [i.e., a duck], and which the Daedalean [i.e., brightly colored] Iris overtakes with a downpour, this month has the festival of purification which is celebrated according to Romulean rite.

In February (Figs. 17, 32, 45) is depicted the only female in the Calendar. R. (Fig. 17) represents February as a woman, dressed in a long

---

155. The miniatures in Voss. (Fig. 53) verify this month as depicting a hunter, but he is wearing a short tunic, not a flowing mantle; all accompanying attributes are missing in Voss.

156. Stern 1953, p. 245, identifies the fruits in the basket as grapes; in Stern 1981, p. 460, he identifies them as mushrooms. They seem more likely, however, to be acorns, gathered for fattening pigs, a recurrent motif in medieval cycles; see Webster 1938, pp. 15ff.

157. Stern 1953, pp. 245–248.

robe with a hood knotted on her head, holding a goose or duck (?) in both hands.[158] Surrounding the central figure are illustrated aquatic animals—a virtual encyclopedia of marine life—including a large fish, three seashells, two octopi, and a squid (?), as well as a stork (?) and an overturned urn out of which water pours.

Although some have read this woman as a Vestal Virgin sacrificing at the *Parentalia* on 13 February,[159] nothing in the image indicates a sacrifice or any other religious act. A duck or goose is not the appropriate sacrifice to the dead for the *Parentalia*. Rather, the seasonal image represented by February here is well attested,[160] with the rainy winter season indicated by the attire of the central female figure, the aquatic animals, and the overturned urn.

ILLUSTRATIONS COMBINING SEASONAL AND FESTIVAL THEMES

May

665.9–10
Hos sequitur *laetus* toto iam corpore Maius,
    Mercurio et Maia quem tribuisse *Iovem*.

May follows these [months], delighting now in his whole body, the
    month which [it is said] was born from Maia and which Jove gave
    to Mercury.[161]

395.17–20
Cunctas veris opes et picta rosaria gemmis
    liniger in calathis, aspice, Maius habet.
Mensis Atlantigenae dictus cognomine Maiae,
    quem merito multum diligit Uranie.

Look! May is dressed in linen and stands amidst the the wicker baskets;
    he has all the wealth of spring and its rose gardens, colored with buds.

158. The miniatures in Voss. (Fig. 53) attest to the stance and attire of the central image, but they do not depict any of the secondary attributes. Stern 1953, pp. 234–239, identifies February as a male, but he changes his identification, correctly in my opinion, in Stern 1981, p. 457. The Argos mosaic (App. 2, no. 28; Fig. 89) depicts February as a woman with a knotted cloak.

159. Strzygowski 1888, p. 60, was influenced by the tetrastichs and the fact that this was the only month illustrated by a woman; Levi 1941, p. 254, follows his interpretation.

160. Stern 1953, pp. 234–239; Stern 1981, p. 457, n. 104.

161. The translation of line 10 is very tentatively based on the outlines of Housman's proposed emendation. The omission of a verb of saying/thinking with *tribuisse* is problematic, but not impossible. See Appendix 4.

This month was named after Maia, daughter of Atlas, the one whom Urania [the Muse of Astronomy] deservedly loves much.

May survives only in V. (Fig. 35) and in the miniatures in Voss. (Fig. 53). In V., May is depicted as a young male in a long, flowing robe—a *dalmatica*, distinguished by its long sleeves.[162] In his left arm he holds a basket with roses. With his right hand he raises a flower to his nose. His hair is long and appears to be blown by the wind.[163] In the background is a large flowering plant, identified as an antirrhinum or snapdragon;[164] in the foreground is a peacock. Voss. verifies a central image as in V., holding a basket of flowers and sniffing blossoms.[165] The various attributes are, characteristically, missing from Voss.

Although spring is pictorialized on some seasonal sarcophagi by a young male carrying a basket of fruit and flowers accompanied by a peacock, the addition of certain details to the Calendar illustration has been interpreted as adding a particular festival association to the image.[166] May can be read as depicting the Festival of the Roses—noted in the Calendar on 23 May as *Macellus rosas sumat*[167]—given the basket of roses and flowers and the ornate *dalmatica*, a festival robe, which indicates some sort of ceremonial role for the central figure. The young male has been identified as the "king" of this festival, head of a fictive army in the war between winter and summer.[168] Comparable mosaics for May include iconography identifiable with this festival, such as sacrificial fillets, floral crowns, and wine amphorae.[169]

162. Dar.-Sagl., s.v. "Dalmatica."

163. Despite the length and effeminate qualities of the figure, the Voss. (Fig. 53), the Boulogne-sur-Mer manuscript (Fig. 57), and the Bern copy (Fig. 58) indicate conclusively that he is male.

164. Stern 1981, p. 458.

165. The only noticeable iconographic difference is that in V. (Fig. 35) the *dalmatica* appears to be slipping off the central figure's shoulders; that detail is missing in Voss. (Fig. 53).

166. The image of a young man carrying baskets filled with fruit or flowers and accompanied by a peacock occurs on several seasonal sarcophagi of the fourth century, such as the one at the Villa Albani in Rome; see Stern 1953, pl. 40.1 and p. 250, n. 1. He categorizes this illustration as mixed in Stern 1953, pp. 249–251, but changes it to seasonal in Stern 1981, p. 458, n. 108.

167. I adopt the reading by A. D. Hoey, "Rosalia Signorum," *HTR* 30 (1937): 15–35. For a contrary reading, see Degrassi 1963, pp. 460–461.

168. As suggested by Stern 1953, p. 251, though the evidence is Byzantine. Cf. W. Tomaschek, "Über Brumalia und Rosalia," *Sitzungsberichte der Kaiserlichen Akademie der Wissenschaften in Wien* 11 (1868): 375–377.

169. See, for example, a fourth-century mosaic of May (App. 2, no. 19; Fig. 36), which depicts a young male in a white tunic standing next to a basket with what may be identified as *vittae* or sacrificial ribbons and a wine amphora, indications of a banquet. In another fourth-century mosaic, a young male wears a floral crown (App. 2, no. 14; Fig. 98).

The Calendar's use of the popular Rose Festival to illustrate May reflects the contemporary import of this celebration, which by the fourth century had eclipsed the festival of Mercury, the source of inspiration for May in earlier iconographic and literary cycles of the months.[170] The Rose Festival was celebrated as a large public holiday, with games (*ludi*) and theatrical performances in the amphitheater.[171] Although the actual date of the festival varied locally according to regional harvest schedules, it was celebrated in most of the Roman world in May; the Calendar indicates its official date.

The social and economic reality underlying the Rose Festival in the fourth century may further elucidate its thematic inclusion in the Calendar of 354. Roses were gathered in spring for pleasure and perhaps also for making perfume. The combined agricultural and commercial importance of the rose harvest for the owners of large estates in North Africa allegedly transformed traditional spring imagery to reflect seasonal customs of the local African nobility. The iconography for spring on two late Roman mosaics from North Africa, for example, derives from the Rose Festival as it was celebrated on the large estates of the African nobility.[172] One of these mosaics—using imagery similar to that in the Calendar—depicts a woman in a richly embroidered tunic, holding a basket of roses and wearing a rose fillet, who places a flower in her hair.[173] The second mosaic, however (the Dominus Julius Mosaic, Fig. 83; App. 2, no. 21), pictorializes North African festival customs in a manner quite different from that of the Calendar of 354, with the mistress of the estate receiving as gifts from servants a necklace and a basket of roses.[174] The close social and economic ties between the North African aristocracy and that at Rome suggest why this same festival would appeal as the subject both for May in the Calendar and for spring in these late Roman mosaics.

170. Earlier cycles allude generally to the god Mercury, whose holiday in the fourth century continued to be commemorated on the fifteenth of the month. See the calendars from the second and third centuries, from Hellín (App. 2, no. 4; Fig. 103) and El-Djem (App. 2, no. 9; Fig. 63) and the tetrastichs and distichs, *Anth. Lat.* 117.9–10, 395.17–20, 665.9–10; Ausonius *Ecl.* 9.5, 10.9–10, ed. S. Prete (Leipzig, 1978). See Appendix 3 for these poems and bibliography.

171. The *Feriale Capuanum* (A.D. 387) notes on *III id. mai(as) Rosaria Amphitheatri*; see Degrassi 1963, pp. 281–293.

172. See D. Parrish, "Two Mosaics from Roman Tunisia: An African Variation of the Season Theme," *AJA* 83 (1979): 279–285.

173. The pavement from Jebel Oust, illustrated in ibid., pl. 40, fig. 2, is dated to the late fourth or early fifth century.

174. Ibid., p. 279. The Dominus Julius Mosaic is dated to the late fourth or early fifth century.

Finally, the economic reality behind the Rose Festival can perhaps clarify its otherwise unattested nomenclature in the Calendar of 354. *Macellus rosas sumat* may be translated as "The marketplace receives roses."[175] If this is a reference to a celebration of the arrival of perfume or roses from North Africa at the marketplace in Rome—like that of the arrival of papyrus from Egypt, which was also noted in the Calendar— then the term is indeed appropriate.

July

665.13–14
Quam bene, Quintilis, *mutastis* nomen! *honori*
   Caesareo, Iuli, te pia causa dedit.

How well, Quintilis,[176] you have changed your name! A pious
   cause gave you, July, as an honor for Caesar.

395.25–28
Ecce coloratos ostentat Iulius artus,
   crines cui rutilos spicea serta ligat.
Morus sanguineos praebet gravidata racemos,
   quae medio Cancri sidere laeta viret.[177]

Look! July shows his bronzed limbs; his red hair is tied back by a garland
   of corn. The full mulberry tree offers its blood-red clusters of fruit, which
   blooms abundantly at the time of the middle of the sign of Cancer.

July in V. (Fig. 38) depicts a nude male standing in an exaggerated *contrapposto*. With his right hand he grasps a sack, which is closed with long drawstrings. On the ground below is a heap of coins in an open sack. In his left hand, above two covered containers, he holds a shallow basket containing three plants. Only one alteration marks the Voss. (Fig. 53) miniatures as compared with V.: the sack in the man's right hand has become a long curved object, identified alternatively as a shepherd's crook, a sickle, or a plant.[178]

The central figure, a nude male, represents warm weather (June and August are similarly illustrated by a nude male); the accompanying at-

175. Neither Stern 1953, 1981; nor Mommsen, *MGH* 1892; nor Degrassi 1963 notes this as a possible interpretation.
176. *Quintilis* is the fifth month in the old Roman calendar year.
177. Line 26: *ligat* Riese: *legat* mss.
178. Stern 1953, p. 29, compares this object to a caduceus of Mercury in a tenth-century manuscript. This is not visually convincing. More likely, Voss. has borrowed the stick or sickle, which appears in other representations of July depicting the harvest, as, for example, in Ms. Vat. Gr. 1291, a manuscript of Ptolemy's works in the Vatican, dated to the ninth century as a copy of a third- or fourth-century version.

tributes pictorialize the bounty of the summer harvest.[179] The sack that the figure holds often appears in fourth-century art as a symbol of abundance and wealth;[180] the two covered containers illustrate the same ideas (similar containers represent wealth in the fourth-century *Notitia Dignitatum* as well; see Fig. 84). The basket with plants alludes to the harvest and can be read in association with the central image.

In July, certainly, these motifs signify the bounty of the summer harvest, which the Romans believed resulted from Apollo's beneficence, for he is the god of light.[181] This association with summer and the harvest explains why traditionally each season was placed under the special protection of a god—Apollo or Ceres being the deity of the summer season.[182] The Neoplatonists of the third and fourth centuries popularized this seasonal association, placing summer under Apollo or his equivalent, Sol or Helios.[183] Consequently, in July, the critical harvest month of summer cereals, Apollo had to be placated to insure the well-being of crops and men. This practice is considered the origin of the games of Apollo, noted in the text of the Calendar for 5–13 July and celebrated with circus races.[184] Indeed, Sol/Apollo's association with the circus and the popularity of circus races in the fourth century are so well documented as to require no further comment here.[185]

The heap of coins (or *stips*—"a gift or donation . . . given in small coin")[186] in the open sack probably represents the games of Apollo, where such giving was a distinctive custom; it was, moreover, continued by the Christian festival of the *Collectes*, celebrated on the same days as the games of Apollo in fifth-century Rome.[187] The plants in the basket

179. Stern 1953, p. 459, identifies July as only a reference to the rewards of the harvest season; the wheat that is reaped gives the peasant the hope of recovering his expenditures.

180. See, for example, the sack in the hands of summer as depicted on a late bronze vessel; G. Hanfmann, *The Season Sarcophagus in Dumbarton Oaks*, 2 vols. (Cambridge, 1951–1952), 2:167, no. 363; Dar.-Sagl., s.v. "Marsupium."

181. J. Gagé, *Apollon Romain* (Paris, 1955).

182. *Anth. Lat.* 1.2, esp. no. 568, for Apollo associated with summer; and cf. nos. 567, 570, 573, 575; Macrobius *Sat.* 1.16.44ff. for summer and Ceres. Nonnus *Dionysiaca* 11.485 and *Anth. Lat.* 1.1, no. 389, express the traditional link between Apollo/Helios and the seasons, a view that dates to the Hellenistic period according to Hanfmann, *The Season Sarcophagus* 1:153–156. For further discussion of Apollo associated with the summer season, see ibid., 1:96ff., 152–157, 254ff.

183. Macrobius *Sat.* 1.18.19, after Cornelius Labeo, *De oraculo Apollinis Clarii*; see further E. Peterson, *Eis Theos* (Göttingen, 1926), pp. 241ff., who, along with Hanfmann, *The Season Sarcophagus* 1:156, observes that according to Porphyry the highest god was the sun.

184. Livy 25.12.8, 26.23.27, 27.23.5; Macrobius *Sat.* 1.17.25ff.

185. Hanfmann, *The Season Sarcophagus* 1:161ff., with comprehensive bibliography.

186. Lewis and Short, *Lat. Dict.*, s.v. "Stips."

187. St. Leo the Great, *Sermo VI. De Collectis. Admonitio in Sequentes Sermones*, ed.

may represent the fruit of the noble laurel, Apollo's tree, which produces flowers and succulent berries in axillary clusters.[188] Even the basket may have ritual associations, for its shape resembles the *liknon*, the basket used for carrying sacred objects.

We must wonder why July alludes to the *ludi Apollinares* with this particular combination of attributes. While the sack, the coins, the covered containers, and the basket with the plants certainly symbolize the abundance of harvesttime, they do not appear in other comparable representations of this theme.[189] More commonly in late Roman cycles, July is illustrated as someone eating berries.[190]

But sacks, coins, and containers were more than mere symbols of wealth: they were all actually present at consular games, where they were given as gifts[191]—as several diptychs show.[192] Corippus, for one, testifies to officials hauling sacks and boxes of coins and other objects for distribution to the happy populace at a consular inauguration in Constantinople on 1 January A.D. 566.[193] In the fourth century, however, the

---

J. P. Migne, *PL*, vol. 54 (Paris, 1881), cols. 155–158. See also Dom Morin, "L'origine des quatre temps," *Revue Benedictine* 14 (1897): 337–346 and 30 (1913): 231–234.

188. Perhaps the central figure, which has been suggested to derive from an ancient statue, was derived from statues of the well-known Apollo Lykeios type? See M. Bieber, *The Sculpture of the Hellenistic Age* (New York, 1954), fig. 17. Can the vestiges of a topknot be seen on the figure's forehead?

189. Comparable mosaic representations of July that allude to the harvest show a man carrying sticks, as at El-Djem (App. 2, no. 9; Fig. 65); a second–third-century mosaic from Zliten shows a harvester beating wheat (App. 2, no. 10); and a fourth-century mosaic from Carthage shows a harvester (App. 2, no. 17; Fig. 88).

190. Stern 1953, pp. 287ff., originally identified the illustration in the Calendar of 354 as a composite Mercury-Cancer with mulberry trimmings, based on the following comparable mosaics: a late-fourth–early-fifth-century mosaic from Carthage illustrates July with a feminine figure actively picking berries from a bowl with a skewer (App. 2, no. 16; Fig. 73); a fourth-century mosaic from Aquileia shows a man picking large fruit from a basket, but as a representation for June, not July (App. 2, no. 14; Fig. 99); and one reference to eating berries as part of a summer lunch, again in June, not July, appears in an anonymous sixth-century poem, *Anth. Lat.* 117. Stern 1981, p. 459, dropped this identification and merely called July a seasonal image.

191. A third-century mosaic from North Africa depicts the sacks of money that a certain Magerius paid for the day's games, and the accompanying inscription records the demands of the crowd that the sacks be carried into the arena; M. Azedine Beschaouch, "La mosaïque de chasse à l'amphithéâtre découverte à Smirat en Tunisie," *Comptes rendus de l'Académie des Inscriptions* (1966): 134–157.

192. Volbach, *Elfenbeinarbeiten*, no. 15, Clementinus diptych, consul, Constantinople, A.D. 513; no. 31, Orestes diptych, consul, Rome, A.D. 530; no. 33, Justinus diptych, consul, Constantinople, A.D. 540. (Dates according to Volbach.)

193. Corippus *In laudem Justini* (A.D. 567) 4.90–205, ed. A. Cameron (London, 1976). Ample testimony to this practice at consular games is collected and discussed by R. Del-

office of consul was effectively closed to members of the Western senatorial aristocracy, and the consular games were often held, with great
expenditure, where the emperor resided; with the consul and emperor
(who was often also consul) absent from Rome, the urban prefect probably filled in for the consul at the 1 January games in the city.[194] Roman
senators instead ostentatiously displayed their wealth at their own praetorian games, which, in the fourth century, were held in July, at the time
of the *ludi Apollinares.*[195] Hence, July pictorializes simultaneously the
wealth of Apollo apparent in the abundance of the summer season and
the distribution of gifts at the games in his honor—or, more precisely,
the magnanimity (*liberalitas*) of the praetor traditionally in charge of these
games.[196]

One principal way that the Roman aristocrat demonstrated, and
thereby maintained, his social and economic position was by providing
games and gifts at Roman festivals. Although real enough, games and
gifts were symbols of the power the Roman aristocrat, as patron, had at

---

brück, *Die Consulardiptychen und verwandte Denkmäler 1–2.* Studien zur spätantiken Kunstgeschichte 2 (Berlin and Leipzig, 1929), pp. xxxivff., 68ff. See the *sparsio* of Constantius II (Fig.
13) in the Codex-Calendar of 354.

194. Chastagnol 1960, p. 138.

195. Symmachus *Opera*, ed O. Seeck (Berlin, 1883), p. clxvi, and *Ep.* 164.5, 165.22;
Olympiodorus *Frag.* 44, in *FHG*; and J. A. McGeachy, "Quintus Aurelius Symmachus and
the Senatorial Aristocracy of the West" (Ph.D. diss., University of Chicago, 1942), pp. 103ff.
Constantine's reorganization of the praetorship required those officials to deposit large
sums of money for distribution at the games; see *C.Th.* 6.4.2 (A.D. 327). Constantius instituted praetorian games at Constantinople, but there they lasted only seven days, versus
the nine-day celebration in Rome: *C.Th.* 6.45 (A.D. 340); and Olympiodorus *Frag.* 44.

196. In a paper delivered at the Byzantine Studies Conference in 1982, I argued that
the coins depicted in the open sacks in the illustration for July might represent contorniates,
those bronze pseudomedallions identifiable by their raised outer edges. The coins in the
July image all have uniform concentric furrows or grooves around the edges that would
be otherwise problematic. No other depictions of coins occur in V., but the coins in the
sparsio of the Emperor Constantius (Fig. 13) in R. lack this double edge, as do the coins in
the fourth-century *Notitia Dignitatum* (Fig. 84). There are few fourth-century illustrations
of coins to which we may turn for comparanda: the coins in the distribution of money
depicted on the Arch of Constantine are one example, but these lack the uniform furrow
illustrated in July; see A. Giuliano, *Arco di Constantino* (Milan, 1955), pls. 44, 45. The closest
comparanda for the coins in July are three sixth-century consular diptychs; see Volbach,
Elfenbeinarbeiten, nos. 16, 24, 32. Do these sixth-century diptych representations preserve
accurately the distribution of certain kinds of contorniates and medallions at the consular
games, or is the addition of a groove a distinctive late-antique way of depicting coins? This
second possibility makes the identification with the contorniates only hypothetical for now.
For *liberalitas*, see R. Brilliant, *Gesture and Rank in Roman Art*, Memoirs of the Connecticut
Academy of Arts and Sciences, no. 14 (New Haven, Conn., 1963), pp. 170–173.

his disposal to benefit his clients and friends. The more magnificent the display, the greater the patron's power. Such munificence was accepted practice, from the time of the republic down through the Ostrogothic period. The coins, then, would represent the generosity of the praetor, traditionally a Roman senator, toward his clients, the citizens of Rome, at the *ludi Apollinares,* the premier occasion for ostentatious senatorial display in the fourth century.

According to A. Alföldi, the bronze pseudomedallion contorniates begin to appear in 356, just two or so years after the creation of the Calendar.[197] This timing may be merely coincidental, but perhaps not. Perhaps the designer of the Calendar was inspired by the same aristocratic and festival associations that produced the contorniates. In any event, the coins depicted in the illustration of July should be read as an allusion to aristocratic *liberalitas* at the all-important *ludi Apollinares.*

September

665.17–18
Tempora maturis September vincta racemis
    velate; ⟨e⟩ numero nosceris ipse tuo.

September, although you veil your head, covered with ripe grape clusters, you are recognized from your place [in the order of months].[198]

395.33–36
Turgentes acinos varias et praesecat uvas
    September, sub quo mitia poma iacent,
captivam filo gaudens religasse lacertam,
    quae suspensa manu mobile ludit opus.[199]

September cuts off the swelling berries and the variegated grapes, under whom [i.e., under whose feet] lie soft fruit. He [September] rejoices at having tied up the lizard, held captive on a string, the lizard which, suspended from his hand, plays a fast-moving game.

September survives in R., V., and B. (Figs. 20, 40, 48). September in R. (Fig. 20) is depicted as a male figure wearing only a light cloth. In his

197. Alföldi 1943, pp. 14–15, dates the contorniates from 356–359, in connection with the prefectureship of Orfitus, 353–355 or 357–359. For further discussion, see Chapter 5. It is noteworthy that certain contorniates represent Apollo; e.g., Alföldi 1976, no. 219, Fig. 88.7. Were these struck for the *ludi Apollinares?*

198. *Numerus* in line 18 probably refers to the order of the months. In my translation I follow Riese's reading of line 17 as a concessive.

199. Line 33: *turgentes* Riese: *surgentes* mss. Line 36: *opus* Riese: *onus* Housman.

right hand is a lizard on a string, which he holds over a jar that is sunk into the ground; in his left hand he holds, over another jar sunk into the ground, a basket from which protrude five skewers (?) bearing rectangular objects. In the background to the man's right is depicted a cluster of grapes; to his left is a basket of what appear to be figs.[200] Voss. (Fig. 53) verifies that the central image is a single male who holds in his left hand a basket with skewers, but here the lizard becomes a sack (?) filled with fruit or herbs.[201]

The grape cluster, the figs, the jars to receive the new fall wine—these illustrate the fall grape harvest. Although the male figure with the lizard on a string is also interpreted as symbolizing the harvest,[202] the precise significance of this image is disputed: it may portray the use of a magic charm to scare off enemies of the grape,[203] some medicinal or magical practice that required the lizard to be dropped into a receptacle and then removed,[204] or the capture and destruction of the lizard, a creature that was believed to damage the grape harvest.[205] In any case, the association of a man holding a lizard on a string with the grape harvest led ultimately to the inclusion of this motif (without any particular seasonal allusion) in Bacchic imagery, where it has been interpreted as representing evil defeated by Dionysus.[206]

---

200. Akerström-Hougen 1974, p. 132, suggests that these "figs" were small wine bottles.

201. As is its custom, Voss. omits the secondary attributes of the grape cluster and basket with figs(?). The significance of the alteration of the lizard is discussed in Appendix 1.

202. Stern 1953, pp. 263–266. The *Menologia Rustica* note September as the month to pitch the jars for the new wine, as does the calendar from S. Maria Maggiore; see Degrassi 1963, pp. 284–298; and Magi 1972, pp. 1ff.

203. See Pliny *N. H.* 29.12.72–73; Stern 1953, pp. 263ff. Stern 1981, p. 460, n. 115, cites two North African mosaics that depict a crown of millet stalks as comparanda for the basket with skewers, and he argues that the crown and basket, like the lizard, had an apotropaic function. See also L. Foucher, *Inventaire des mosaïques de Tunisie* (Sousse, Tunisia, 1960), nos. 57095, 57097. Stern 1981, p. 460, n. 115, notes that the basket with skewers held fruit, as is indicated by the designer of V.

204. Pliny *N. H.* 30.17.52; see 29.12.76 for the positive benefits of eating a ground-up lizard. More medical texts are cited in Stern 1953, p. 265, n. 4; and Hanfmann, *The Season Sarcophagus* 2:184.

205. Pliny *N. H.* 29.23.74 records the belief that if salamanders crawl into a fruit tree, they infect all the fruit with venom.

206. For this interpretation, see Stern 1953, pp. 263–266. A. Merlin and L. Poinssot, "Deux mosaïques de Tunisie à sujets prophylactiques," *Monument et mémoires Piot*, vol. 34 (1934), pp. 162–176; and K. Dunbabin, *The Mosaics of Roman North Africa* (Oxford, 1978), pp. 184–185, similarly interpret the mid-fourth-century mosaic from the Maison de Bacchus at El-Djem, Tunisia (Fig. 87). In this mosaic, Bacchus is depicted holding a lizard on a

The Dionysian and grape harvest associations of the lizard-on-a-string motif may explain the use of this image to illustrate autumn—with the addition of wine jars—on fourth-century seasonal and funerary sarcophagi.[207] Regardless of the motif's exact meaning, moreover—whether apotropaic, magical, or medicinal—the previous association of the lizard on a string with Dionysus and with the autumn grape harvest makes it appropriate iconography for September, when, as the Calendar records, on the fifth the *Vindemial* festival was celebrated in Rome.[208]

The contemporary popularity of *Vindemial* festivals is well attested, although the date of their celebration varied according to local custom and climate.[209] The festivities were "Dionysian" and perhaps required a visit to the countryside; at one such revelry, noble Romans were invited to drink and sit on baskets (*corbes*), with drinking and lewd joking following.[210] The popularity of these festivals insured their continuance even at the end of the fourth century, after the Christian emperors had outlawed the celebration of pagan holidays.[211]

The autumnal *Vindemial* festivals were devoted to Liber, the Roman Dionysus.[212] Since the lizard-on-a-string motif appears in Dionysian contexts, it still might convey this Dionysus/Liber meaning in the Calendar, representing the joyful celebration of the successful grape harvest in September and the triumph of Dionysus over the forces that threaten the harvest. The lizard is a potent symbol of that struggle: although the lizard

---

string—but not over any jars—as he dominates the fighting wild beasts around him. Dunbabin suggests that the Dionysian association for this motif led to its depiction with other members of the Dionysian entourage, as on a mosaic of the vintaging Erotes from Dugga in which one of the Erotes holds a gecko on a string.

207. See autumn on the sarcophagus of Junius Bassus, in Stern 1953, pl. 49.4; on the Sarcophagus of the Seasons (Fig. 86); and on the lost Carthage mosaic (App. 2, no. 17; Fig. 88).

208. Cf. September in the Acton mosaic (App. 2, no. 14; Fig. 100). The Calendar records *Mammes Vindemia* on 5 September. The precise meaning of *Mammes* is unknown. Mommsen reads the two words separately, which V. supports by inserting a large space between the two words. Degrassi 1963, p. 508, plausibly suggests that *Mammes* had a topographical reference.

209. The *Menologia Rustica* record vindemial festivals on 15 October, as does the *Feriale Capuanum* (A.D. 387); see Degrassi 1963, pp. 281–293.

210. See, for example, the *H.A. Elag.* 11.2. The emperor and his entourage may have left the capital for the celebration.

211. *C.Th.* 2.8.19 (A.D. 389).

212. For the autumn vindemial festivals as being sacred to Liber in the Roman calendar, see Degrassi 1963, pp. 508, 521–522. For Liber in the fourth century, see esp. J. Collins-Clinton, *A Late Antique Shrine of Liber Pater at Cosa* (Leiden, 1977) (= *EPRO* 77).

can be an evil creature, if his power is tamed it can be used for the good, as for magical and medicinal purposes.[213] This victory of Dionysus/Liber over evil was celebrated in September in Rome.

March

665.5–6
Condita Mavortis magno sub nomine Roma
  non habet *errorem*; Romulus auctor erit.

Rome, which was founded under the great name of Mars,
  makes no mistake; Romulus will be the author.[214]

395.9–12
Cinctum pelle lupae promptum est cognoscere mensem.
  Mars olli nomen, Mars dedit exuvias.
Tempus ver⟨num⟩ hedus petulans et garrula hirundo
  Indicat et sinus lactis et herba virens.[215]

It is easy to recognize this month, girded in the skin of a wolf. Mars gave his name to it, and his spoils. The impudent goat and the chattering swallow indicate the spring season, as does the milk pail and green grass.

March (Figs. 18, 33, 46) survives in R., V., and B., as well as in the miniatures in Voss. (Fig. 53). In R., the best copy, March is illustrated as a young male shepherd with shaggy hair, dressed in the skin of a cloven-footed animal; his left arm is around the neck of a goat that is raised on its hind legs, partly turned away from the shepherd. Pictured above the goat and to the shepherd's right in R. and B. are three baskets (for cheese?) and a large bird with outspread wings. The shepherd points to a smaller bird, which is placed in a framed rectangle (a window or a cage?). At the feet of the shepherd are depicted a pail, grass, and flowers. Voss. confirms the shepherd motif for March, but here, instead of pointing to a bird, the figure stretches his right arm out to grasp a long, thin object, identified as a lance or staff. Even the goat may have been depicted in Voss., but if so it is no longer visible.[216]

213. A.D. Nock, "The Lizard in Magic and Religion," in *Essays on Religion and the Ancient World*, ed. Z. Stewart, vol. 1 (Cambridge, 1972), pp. 271–276; reprint of "Magical Texts from a Bilingual Papyrus in the British Museum," *Proceedings of the British Academy* 17 (1931): 235–287.
214. Housman, "Disticha de Mensibus," p. 131, would interpret line 6 as "Romulus will be the author of this doctrine." But *auctor* is probably a pun, referring also to Romulus as "author" or founder of the city.
215. Line 11: *tempus ver⟨num⟩* Scaliger: *primum ver* Baehrens: *tempus ver* mss.
216. Stern 1953, p. 29, saw the depiction of the goat in Voss. as well. The substitution of a lance, an attribute associated with March as warrior, may be due to an error of the

March has been interpreted in two contradictory ways: as a purely seasonal illustration of the coming of spring[217] or as a reference to the cult and festivals of Mars through a depiction of the shepherd Romulus or Faustulus.[218] The iconography, festival context, Roman provenance, and traditional associations of Mars with this month argue strongly for the latter interpretation, with Romulus, son of Mars and the Vestal Virgin Rhea Sylvia, here representing the cult of Mars, whose festivals are noted in the Calendar on 1, 9, 19, and 23 March.[219]

In canonical Roman legend, Romulus was celebrated as the first king of Rome, albeit a king of shepherds.[220] Depictions of him as a shepherd—as in the Calendar for March—appear in Roman art and literature from the time of the early republic. Romulus is described as a young, idealized shepherd (*pulcher*) in Ennius's *Annales* and is represented on republican coinage as a shepherd with shaggy hair, dressed in a wolf- or lionskin.[221] The image of Romulus as a shepherd survives into the imperial period.[222] Perhaps the best-known Roman representation of Romulus and Remus as shepherds is that on the Temple of Quirinus in Rome; the fragments of a Flavian monument, identified as representing

---

copyist or to a conflation of sources. For a second type of illustration of March as warrior, see the fifth-century Argos mosaic (App. 2, no. 28; Fig. 90). It is also possible that the Voss. miniaturist utilized another model for this illustration; Stern 1953, p. 29, argues, not convincingly, that the copyist was inspired by the tetrastichs.

217. Stern 1953, pp. 239–245; Stern 1981, pp. 457–458, n. 108, cites as support C. Nordström, "Some Iconographical Problems in the Argos Mosaics," *Cahiers archéologiques* 25–26 (1976–1977): 73–80.

218. Akerström-Hougen 1974, pp. 77ff.

219. The *N(atalis) Martis* on 1 March; *Arma, ancilia movent(ur)* on 9 March; the *Mamuralia* on 14 March; the *Quinquatria*, originally to Mars but popularly associated with Minerva, on 19 March; and the *Tubilustrium* on 23 March (now associated also with the cult of the Magna Mater). See Degrassi 1963, pp. 420ff.

220. See, among others, Livy 1.3–16; Plutarch *Life of Romulus*; the fourth-century *Chronicle of the City of Rome*, section XVI of the Codex-Calendar of 354, discussed in Chapter 2. Varro, in *De re rustica*, asked: "Romanorum vero populum a pastoribus esse ortum, quis non dicit?"

221. Ennius *Ann.* 1.80–85, ed. Vahlen, frag. 80 (1928; repr. Amsterdam, 1967). For Romulus *pulcher*, see A. Alföldi, *Der Vater des Vaterlandes in Römischen Denken* (Darmstadt, 1971), pp. 14–27; reprint of "Die Geburt der kaiserlichen Bildsymbolik," *Mus. Helv.* 8 (1951): 190–215. For Romulus's depiction as a shepherd on coinage of the republic, a type identified by Alföldi as being close to the illustration of March in the Calendar of 354, see Alföldi, *Der Vater*, pp. 15–17, including n. 9, and pls. 1 and 2; for Romulus in a lion skin, see pls. 3.2–5.

222. *Encyclopedia dell'arte antica classica e orientale* (1965 ed.), s.v. "Romuleo," for representations of Romulus as a shepherd, noting especially that in the Columbarium on the Esquiline Hill (1st cent. A.D.). See Alföldi, *Der Vater*, pl. 3.1, for a silver vase with Romulus as shepherd (imperial period).

this temple frieze, show Romulus as a shepherd in a short tunic, holding a cornucopia.[223] This traditional iconography for Romulus and the significance of the Roman foundation myth continued, for both writers and artists, into the fourth century.[224] A shepherd hut, believed to be that of Romulus, was even maintained on the Palatine Hill in Rome.[225]

The depiction of the shepherd Romulus with a goat and dressed in the skin of a cloven-hoofed animal represents the special association of this animal with Romulus and with the cult of Mars in Roman myth and ritual.[226] Romulus was associated with the *Lupercalia*, celebrated in February with the sacrifice of a goat that, some scholars say, supplied the skins worn by the Luperci.[227] Moreover, Romulus's apotheosis occurred in Rome in the area of the Campus Martius known as the "Goat's Marsh."[228] A goat was also, in certain contexts, an appropriate sacrifice to Mars.[229]

The bird depicted in March to the right of Romulus has been identified as a *picus*, or woodpecker, the bird sacred to Mars. The *picus* played

223. P. Hartwig, "Ein römisches Monument der Kaiserzeit mit einer Darstellung des Tempels des Quirinus," *MDAIR* 19 (1904): 28, 19ff., pl. IV; P. Hommel, *Studien zu den römischen Figurengiebeln der Kaiserzeit* (Bonn, 1954), dates the monument to the Flavian period and proposes the identifications noted in the text. Romulus with *cornucopia* may allude to *divus pater Quirinus*.

224. Only the inscription survives (*CIL* 6.33856) from a statuary group of Mars, Romulus, and Remus, which Maxentius is said to have erected in the Roman Forum on the anniversary of the foundation of Rome. Presumably these images followed traditional iconography. See E. Talamo, "Raffigurazioni numismatiche. Il tempio di Romolo a Foro romano," *Quaderni dell'Istituto di Storia dell'Architettura* 26 (1980): 23–34; and *BC* 27 (1899): pp. 213–214. See also Alföldi 1976, no. 55, p. 198, pl. 112.9, for Mars and Rhea Sylvia; new no. 92 (= old no. 85), p. 202, pl. 12.1, *lupa* with twins; Ausonius *Eclog.* 10.5, ed. Prete. For the contemporary importance of the myth, see discussion below and Chapter 4.

225. So it appears in the fourth-century Regionary Catalogue of Rome, the *Notitia* (section XIV of the Codex-Calendar). See Chapter 2; also Platner-Ashby, *Topo. Dict.*, pp. 101–102.

226. See, for example, the obverse of a republican coin dedicated to one of Rome's early kings, Numa Pompilius, by L. Pomponius Molo, on which is depicted a goat being led to sacrificial slaughter; on the reverse is the shepherd Romulus, identified by inscription in Alföldi, *Der Vater*, p. 15, pl. 1, fig. 4. I. S. Ryberg, *Rites of the State Religion in Roman Art*, *MAAR* 22 (1955), p. 37, n. 77, fig. 19c, pl. IX, identifies the coin with a sacrifice to Apollo, but without any justification.

227. Degrassi 1963, pp. 409–411; Festus *Epit.* pp. 75ff. ed. Lindsay (Leipzig 1913).

228. Platner-Ashby, *Topo. Dict.* s.v. "Caprae palus"; Livy 1.16.1; Plutarch *Life of Romulus* 27; Ovid *Fasti* 2.491, Zon. 7.4, Flor. 1.1.16. This version of Romulus's death appears in the *Chronicle of the City of Rome*, section XVI in the Codex-Calendar. See Chapter 2, note 83.

229. Apuleius *Met.* 7.11, records the pseudomilitary group of bandits sacrificing a goat to Mars. Cf. the goat depicted on a Roman altar to Mars and Venus, in Ryberg, *Rites of the State Religion*, p. 22, n. 18, fig. 14, plate VI. For goats on the gems, see note 232 below. For Mars, see Wissowa 1912, p. 144.

a significant role in the foundation myth of Rome as well, for it fed the twins Romulus and Remus after they were abandoned by the she-wolf.[230] The *picus* in March may also bespeak the augural powers attributed to Romulus and Mars.[231] The most striking visual parallels for March in the Calendar appear on certain gems, which depict a shepherd pointing to a bird on a column, at the foot of which is a bound goat, identified as a sacrificial offering;[232] other gems vary this iconography by replacing the goat with a sacrificial altar. These gems have been identified with an oracle of Mars at Tiora, and the goat as a sacrifice to that deity.[233]

The remaining attributes—the pail and grass—illustrate Romulus within an appropriate pastoral and seasonal setting. March, the beginning of the spring season, was placed under the special tutelage of Mars allegedly because of the god's agricultural associations; only after Mars acquired a military aspect was this tutelage explained by pointing to March as initiating the military season.[234] As the beginning of both spring and the military season, March became the first month of the new year in the pre-Julian calendar.[235]

The New Year associations with March were popularly recalled in connection with the *Natalis Martis*, recorded in the Calendar on 1 March. At Rome, this festival included hanging laurel wreaths on the Regia, feasting, and holding ceremonies and such martial activities as a mock battle to honor Mars in the Campus Martius—practices that continued into the eighth century.[236] The traditional New Year association of 1 March with Mars was widely known in the fourth and fifth centuries, as

230. Roscher, *Lex.*, s.v. "Picus."

231. The augural powers of Romulus explain his seeing the twelve vultures, the sign that he would be the founder of Rome. See Alföldi, *Der Vater*, p. 19, pl. 2, fig. 1–8, for republican coins with depictions of the augural staff of Romulus; cf. Ennius *Ann.* 1.80, ed. Vahlen.

232. A. Furtwänger, *Die antiken Gemmen*, vol. 2 (Berlin, 1900), pp. 119ff. and pl. 24.10; cf. pls. 24.11, 24.12 for variations.

233. Dionysius of Halicarnassus *Ant. Rom.* 1.14–15, ed. C. Jacoby, vol. 1 (Stuttgart, 1967).

234. Mars originally had an agricultural role in Roman religion; see, for example, G. Dumézil, *Archaic Roman Religion*, rev. ed., vol. 1 (Chicago, 1970), pp. 213–345.

235. Ovid devotes to Mars the entire third book of the *Fasti* and discusses March (3.97–98) as the original beginning of the New Year; see Degrassi 1963, pp. 417ff.

236. Degrassi 1963, pp. 417–418; Atto of Vercelli *Sermo* 3, *PL* 134, col. 836: "similiter [to 1 January] etiam Kalendis Martiis huius modi homines moltis solent debacchare praestigiis." Rites included renewing the sacred fire of Vesta on this day and hanging fresh laurel wreaths on the doors of the Regia, Curia, and the houses of the Flamens, as described by Macrobius *Sat.* 1.12.6, Solin. 1.35; Ovid *Fasti* 3.135. Ceremonies and mock battles in honor of Mars were also described; see *Anth. Lat.* 117.5, 847a.5–6; *AP* 9.383.7; Lydus *De Mens.* 4.42.

Macrobius, Ausonius, and the *Anthologia Latina* attest.[237] Fourth-century astrologers began their calculations from 1 March, and Christians sporadically tried to revive this New Year.[238] Because the New Year association with 1 March was so well known, the Panegyrist of A.D. 297 plays on this New Year theme in his panegyric to Constantius Chlorus, delivered on that date.[239] Finally, the New Year associations of 1 March, together with the martial and traditional Roman ones, led the fourth-century emperors to adopt this date for the designation of their caesars.[240]

The importance of Mars and of Romulus as *patres patriae* explains the political play given these figures in the fourth century. The usurper Maxentius even named his son Romulus and commemorated his dynastic hopes by erecting monuments and striking coins in the legendary king's honor.[241] With Romulus's premature death and Maxentius's fall, the Panegyrist of A.D. 313 thanked the Tiber for the fall of this "false Romulus" and the arrival of the "true Romulus," Constantine.[242] Indeed, these dynastic associations led Themistius, the spokesman for the Senate of Constantinople, to salute Constantius in A.D. 357 as a greater founder (ἀρχηγέτης) than Romulus.[243]

The fourth-century emphasis on Mars and Romulus as founders of Rome reinforced the traditional and popular New Year celebration of the cult of Mars, noted in the Calendar on 1 March. The illustration for this

237. Ausonius *Eclog.* 9.3, 10.5–6, ed. Prete; *Anth. Lat.* 394.3, 665.5–6, according to Courtney 1988; Solin. 1.35; Macrobius *Sat.* 1.12.5.

238. On ancient astrologers, see Nigidius Figulus, in Servius *Ad Georg.* 1.43; and see Stern 1953, pp. 230ff., for Christian attempts to substitute 1 March for 1 January.

239. *Pan. Lat.* 4(8).3, ed. Galletier: "O Kalendae Martiae, sicuti olim annorum volventium, ita nunc aeternorum auspices imperatorum."

240. Stern 1953, pp. 77–78.

241. Maxentius's devotion to Mars is recorded in *CIL* 6.33856; and see note 224 above. See also J. Gagé, "Le *Templum Urbis* et les origines de l'idée de *Renovatio*," in *Mélanges à F. Cumont*, vol. 1 (Brussels, 1936), pp. 151–187 (= *Annuaire de l'Institute de Philologie et d'Histoire Orientales de l'Université de Bruxelles*, vol. 4); J. Doignon "Le titre de *nobilissimus puer* porté par Gratien et la mystique littéraire des origines de Rome à l'avènement des Valentiniens," *Mélanges à A. Piganiol*, ed. R. Chevallier (Paris, 1966), pp. 1693–1709. For the circus of Maxentius and the temple of Romulus, see G. Pisani Sartorio and R. Calza, *La villa di Massenzio sulla Via Appia* (Rome, 1976); F. Coarelli, *Dintorni di Roma* (Rome, 1976), pp. 36–37.

242. *Pan. Lat.* 9(12).18, ed. Galletier.

243. Themistius *Orat.* 3.43c (A.D. 357), ed. W. Dindorf (Hildesheim, 1962), p. 52. For the fourth-century revitalization of Romulus with Neoplatonic associations, see Julian *Orat.* 4.154c, ed. Wright; and C. Lacombrade, "L'empereur Julien et la tradition Romane," *Pallas* 9 (1960): 155–164; and idem, "Notes sur *Les Césars* de l'empereur Julien," *Pallas* 11 (1962): 59–60. For Gratian's revitalization of this myth, see J. Doignon, "Le titre de *nobilissimus puer*"; and its reuse by Theodosius, P. Bruggisser, *Romulus Servianus. La légende de Romulus dans les "Commentaires" à Virgile de Servius* (Bonn, 1987) (= *Antiquitas*, 1st ser., vol. 36).

month—of the shepherd Romulus, son of Mars and founder of Rome—
is thus especially appropriate to the cult as it was celebrated in Rome
and, consequently, to the Calendar. Yet the appeal of the Roman foundation myth and of the festivities in that city contrast markedly with the
way the cult of Mars was honored in the Greek East, for there it was the
martial aspects of the god that were commemorated on 1 March[244]—as
the illustration of March as a warrior in several Eastern cycles (see Fig.
90) reflects.[245] Thus, the diverging iconography for March—the warrior
in the Greek East versus the shepherd in the Latin West—highlights
quite different beliefs and practices across the empire.

DIACHRONIC AND LOCAL ICONOGRAPHIC VARIATION IN THE ILLUSTRATIONS OF THE MONTHS

The illustrations of the months in the Calendar of 354 result from a
complex interweaving of themes. Each month is inspired by the accompanying Calendar text and depicts a season, a holiday, a popular belief,
or some combination of these. Since the text is the product of fourth-
century Rome, the illustrations reflect that world as well—as other
fourth-century archaeological and literary remains amply corroborated.

The contemporary inspiration for the Calendar of 354 becomes clear
when we compare it with extant cycles from the Latin West.[246] Comparison with second- and third-century calendars, for example, reveals
that the iconography for religious festivals in the Calendar often varied
according to local practice, even though the festival represented was the
same. The (November) depiction of the popular cult of Isis in three early
cycles differs in detail from that in the Calendar of 354 (Fig. 22), an illustration that coincides precisely with fourth-century practice.[247] Similarly, the popular festival of the *Saturnalia*, the inspiration for the
Calendar's December image (Fig. 23), is depicted by iconography quite

244. For example, the *Feriale Duranum* notes the sacrifice of a bull to Mars Pater Victor
on this day, commemorating Mars in his martial role; see Degrassi 1963, p. 417, with
bibliography.

245. Akerström-Hougen 1974, pp. 76–80, first suggested this interpretation.

246. For a list of these mosaics, see Appendix 2, nos. 1–26.

247. The three early cycles are those from Trier, Germany (App. 2, no. 3; Fig. 95);
Hellín, Spain (App. 2, no. 4; Fig. 106); and El-Djem, Tunisia (App. 2, no. 9; Fig. 69). In
five other extant monuments—at S. Maria Maggiore; mosaics from Thina, Sousse (North
Africa), and St.-Romain-en-Gaul; and the Reims relief (App. 2, nos. 5, 6, 10, 11, 13)—
November is represented by seasonal activities.

unlike that found in any earlier cycle.[248] Such variation reflects both changes in ritual over time and the essentially local nature of pagan practice.

Not only can the iconography for a pagan festival vary over time and space, but the subject matter itself can change too. As one festival becomes more popular or meaningful, its imagery may replace that of another celebration, now grown less important or even obsolete. For example, two mosaic cycles from the second or third century[249] illustrate the month of May with Mercury, whose festival is noted on 15 May in Roman calendars. The Calendar of 354 (Figs. 35, 53), however, replaces Mercury with an image inspired by the popular Rose Festival, recorded in the Calendar on 23 May. The economic importance of this particular harvest to the fourth-century aristocracy probably contributed to this substitution. And the continuing popularity of this celebration explains why later cycles of the months pictorialize May with Rose Festival imagery,[250] with iconographic variations in late-fourth- and early-fifth-century cycles attributed largely to differing local practices.

Two other months in the Calendar of 354 depict local Roman festivals with revised iconography appropriate to the Calendar's provenance. The illustration for April, newly identified as representing the festival of the Magna Mater, celebrated in Rome from 4 to 10 April, replaces the Venus imagery found in earlier second- and third-century mosaic cycles, as do other cycles from the late fourth century.[251] In these later cycles, moreover, the iconography varies according to local practice. A mosaic from Carthage, for instance, depicts a priestess of Dea Syria-Atargatis for April, probably because in North African practice this goddess was included in the cult of the Magna Mater. The second month reflecting local Roman practice is July, which refers to the summer heat but also to the *ludi Apollinares,* the popular aristocratic games celebrated at Rome in July. This iconography replaces Neptune, who is depicted in an earlier cycle;[252] even the depiction of summer heat differs from earlier cycles

248. Cf. the El-Djem Mosaic (App. 2, no. 9; Fig. 70).

249. See the mosaics of Hellín (App. 2, no. 4; Fig. 103) and El-Djem (App. 2, no. 9; Fig. 63).

250. See the fourth-century mosaic of May now in Rome (App. 2, no. 19; Fig. 36) and the Dominus Julius mosaic from Carthage (App. 2, no. 21; Fig. 83).

251. See the second–third-century mosaics from Hellín (App. 2, no. 4; Fig. 102) and El-Djem (App. 2, no. 9; Fig. 62). For the fourth century, see the mosaics from Ostia (App. 2, no. 15; Fig. 76) and Carthage (App. 2, no. 16; Fig. 74).

252. See the Trier mosaic (App. 2, no. 3; Fig. 97), which alludes to Neptune, whose festival falls on 23 July.

and contemporary fourth-century illustrations, which use the eating of fruit or the gathering of straw as motifs for this month.[253] July in the Calendar of 354, then, reflects its Roman provenance in its seasonal iconography as well as in its festival imagery.

Two other months in the Calendar of 354, January and March, indicate the vitality of paganism in the Latin West, and their iconography can similarly be explained by reference to local cult practices and beliefs. This becomes especially apparent after comparison with these same months in cycles from the Greek East. A synthesis of imagery from the cult of the Lares (a consul burning incense, for example) and the *ludi Compitales* depicts the January New Year festivities in Western calendar cycles.[254] In cycles from the Greek East, however, the New Year festivities are symbolized by a consul throwing down the *mappa* to start the circus games. Such iconography, showing the magistrate performing the secular duties at the New Year, was more appealing in the Greek East, where the *ludi Compitales* and cult of the Lares had no strong tradition and where Christianity was more deeply entrenched. A similar differentiation characterizes March, which is frequently represented by a warrior in Eastern cycles but by a shepherd in Western ones. This divergence may be attributed to Roman pagan traditions that associated March with Romulus and Mars as founders of Rome. In the fourth-century West, and especially in Rome, these associations were still significant; in the East, however, the military associations carried far more weight.

Contemporary practice is to be seen in the Calendar's seasonal imagery as well. So, for example, August and October incorporate motifs that appear first on monuments, dating from 330–360, from the Latin West. Moreover, October depicts hunting, and September, grape festivals, because these are activities appropriate to the climate and the season.[255]

Comparable cycles of the months verify the fourth-century date for the Calendar iconography and indicate how motifs for the months traveled across the empire and in different media. Even though comparison with later cycles reveals a certain amount of shared iconography, there is no need to look for an archetypal source for these images, whether in

253. The El-Djem Mosaic (App. 2, no. 9; Fig. 65) depicts July with a seasonal reference to a man carrying a bundle of sticks on his back; for fruit eating, see note 190 above.

254. See January as a New Year's celebration in the mosaic from El-Djem (App. 2, no. 9; Fig. 59).

255. The Bacchus and Vindemial festivals are the subject of October in the mosaic from Trier (App. 2, no. 3; Fig. 94). Vindemial festivals can fall any time within a two-month period, from mid August to mid October; see *C.Th.* 2.8.19 (A.D. 389).

the Calendar of 354 or elsewhere.[256] The continued use of various motifs does, however, indicate their enduring vitality, albeit reinterpreted within a local context to fit contemporary and regional rites and beliefs. Such local variations are especially noticeable with regard to pagan festivals.

A striking aspect of the Calendar of 354 is the illustrator's tendency to assemble numerous motifs on the page. October (Figs. 21, 41, 50) and March (Figs. 18, 35, 46), for example, represent the fullest range of graphic themes for these two months as compared to other cycles, both earlier and later, and November is unparalleled in the fullness of its iconography of Isis worship. This same tendency may also explain the mixing of religious, popular, and seasonal themes in one image—as in July with its amalgam of pagan religious imagery (*ludi Apollinares*), popular motifs (the sacks and containers, for instance), and summer imagery (the plant). Even the distichs alongside each month's illustration may have been inspired by this same encyclopedic bent, for the verses illustrate the month in yet another way.

The accumulation and scattering of motifs in the field behind the central figure may stem from the "Asaroton" tradition, which can be traced, via the mosaics of S. Costanza in Rome, to Hellenistic times.[257] Yet this tendency to depict as many secondary attributes and motifs as possible, which I call encyclopedic, is noticeably heightened in the Calendar as compared with other extant cycles. Although this encyclopedic tendency has ancient roots, it blossomed in fourth-century literary, artistic, and scholarly circles. Moreover, this trend was continued with a passion by late-antique writers such as Macrobius, Martianus Capella, and Nonius Marcellus—for the essentially scholarly concern of the encyclopedist, so prominent a figure in late antiquity, was based in and supported by an educational system that saw much merit in compiling lists from many sources.[258] In a fundamental way, then, this encyclopedic tendency is the organizing impulse—its raison d'être, as it were—behind the Codex-Calendar as a whole.

---

256. Stern 1981, pp. 455ff., groups these cycles under the heading "Le Calendrier de 354 et ses dérivés."

257. M. Henig, "Late Antique Book Illustration and the Gallic Prefecture," in *Aspects of the De Rebus Bellicis*, British Archaeological Reports International Series, no. 63 (Oxford, 1979), pp. 17–18.

258. See W. H. Stahl, *Roman Science: Origins, Development, and Influence to the Later Middle Ages* (Madison, Wis., 1962); L. G. Whitbread, *Fulgentius*, pp. 21–22; M. Schanz and C. Hosius, *Geschichte der römischen Literatur*, vol. 8 (Munich, 1914), pt. 4.1, s.v. "Nonius Marcellus," pp. 142–148; and Nonius Marcellus *De compendiosa doctrina*, ed. W. M. Lindsay (Oxford, 1901). For the popularity of compendia in the educational system, see H. I. Marrou, *A History of Education in Antiquity*, trans. G. Lamb (1956; repr. Madison, Wis., 1982), pp. 242ff.

The encyclopedic tendencies observed here help to elucidate the fullness and complexity of this Calendar cycle in contrast to other comparable pictorial cycles, mainly in mosaic form and dating from the late fourth and early fifth centuries.[259] These later cycles, it should be emphasized, reproduce neither the full range of iconographic detail nor the subject matter of the Calendar of 354. Yet even if the elaborately illustrated Calendar was unusual in the abundance of its imagery, it nevertheless reflects the contemporary world for which it was created. While the codex as a medium was at the height of its development, the art of illustration in codices appears to have been a somewhat more recent innovation, providing a new area for artistic development.[260] This fact suggests one explanation for the more elaborate and complex imagery of the Calendar relative to other cycles, a level of treatment befitting a special, deluxe codex. The encyclopedic tendencies and literary associations of this cycle, too, give further insight into this complexity.

The illustrations of the months indicate the Calendar's mid-fourth-century provenance in one other way. Although paganism is presented as the dominant religion in both illustrations and text, we can nevertheless see in them the beginnings of a movement to accommodate the rise of Christianity. Earlier calendar cycles depicted four months—August, June, October, and September—with deities or religious festivals;[261] the substition of seasonal imagery for these months in the Calendar of 354 reflects contemporary trends in pictorial and textual cycles and points the way to the secular cycles of later centuries.[262] This secular influence is also evident in the omission of sacrificial depictions and the substitution of less offensive scenes of incense burning, not only in the Calendar but perhaps in other fourth-century art as well. Thus, through artistic accommodation, the first hints of the rise of Christianity in mid-fourth-century Rome appear.

By understanding the illustrations of the months in the Calendar of 354 within their own unique context, we may use these images to provide reliable evidence (in conjunction with other archaeological, literary, and epigraphic sources) for late Roman cultic practices and festivals. Interpretation of the text of the Calendar will elucidate that reality more fully.

---

259. See Appendix 2; and Stern 1981, pp. 462–469.

260. C. H. Roberts and T. C. Skeat, *The Birth of the Codex* (Oxford, 1983), pp. 70ff.

261. October is represented by Mars in the Hellín Mosaic (App. 2, no. 4; Fig. 105) and by Bacchus in the Trier Mosaic (App. 2, no. 3; Fig. 94); August by the *Natalis Dianae* in the Hellín (Fig. 104) and El-Djem (App. 2, no. 9; Fig. 68) mosaics; June by Juno and September by Vulcan in the Trier Mosaic (Figs. 96 and 93).

262. Stern 1981, pp. 470ff.

· IV ·

THE TEXT OF THE
CALENDAR OF 354

He [the Emperor Constantius II] stripped nothing from the privileges of the Vestal Virgins, he filled the priesthoods with men of noble rank, he did not refuse expenditure for the ceremonies of Rome. Through all the streets of the Eternal City he passed, preceded by a joyful senate, and viewed, with no anger on his face, the holy shrines; he read the names of the gods inscribed on the pediments; he inquired about the origins of the temples, expressed admiration for their founders and preserved these as part of the empire, even though he followed a different religion himself.[1]

The visit of the Emperor Constantius II to Rome in A.D. 357 was a momentous occasion. Symmachus, in his famous *Third Relatio* of 384 (quoted above), described the city and its pagan religion, which so impressed this Christian emperor that he willingly gave his support to the pagan cult, its rituals, and its priesthoods. Whatever moved Symmachus to describe the visit in such glowing terms, his account is corroborated by a large body of contemporary evidence that highlights the vitality of late Roman paganism. But what was the nature and appeal of that paganism? What did Constantius II see that so awed him during his visit to the city? If we look at the text of the Calendar of 354 (e.g., Figs. 24–

---

1. "Nihil ille decerpsit sacrarum virginum privilegiis, replevit nobilibus sacerdotia, Romanis caerimoniis non negavit inpensas, et per omnes vias aeternae urbis laetum secutus senatum vidit placido ore delubra, legit inscripta fastigiis deum nomina, percontatus templorum origines est, miratus est conditores, cumque alias religiones ipse sequeretur, has servavit imperio"; Symmachus *Rel.* 3.7, in O. Seeck, ed., *Symmachus. Opera, MGH Auctores Antiquissimi* (Berlin, 1883); all citations are from this edition. Trans. B. Croke and J. Harries, eds., *Religious Conflict in Fourth-Century Rome: A Documentary Study* (Sydney, 1982), p. 80.

26)—the round of pagan holidays, imperial anniversaries, and astrological events—we can gain a clearer vision of the religion that this Christian emperor found so moving.

The Calendar text includes the holidays and festivals that were officially recognized and celebrated every year at state expense—that is, the most important public celebrations in Rome. From this text, then, we can infer which were the most important cults in the city. Afterward I will discuss specific holidays, festivals, and cults within their contemporary religious, social, and historical context.

In this chapter, my goal is to arrive at not only a more accurate but also a more synthetic understanding of the nature and appeal of the paganism recorded by the Calendar. I will therefore conclude by analyzing the salient aspects of late Roman paganism, as revealed in Roman calendars from the first four centuries of the imperial period. A comparison of calendars will show how the traditionalism and apparent conservatism of the paganism recorded therein effectively obscure the religion's flexibility and vitality. Yet the very ability of late Roman paganism to add new cults, rites, and meanings while remaining evidently unchanged—call it tradition and originality, continuity and change, conservatism and flexibility—goes far in explaining the longevity of the religion.[2] Of even greater import, in my view, are the ties that paganism enjoyed with the most important groups and institutions in Rome: the emperor and the imperial bureaucracy, as well as the senatorial aristocracy, so closely aligned to the urban and state government. These ties are reflected in the text of holidays in the Calendar.

Because my aim is to read the Calendar within its context, I have tried to restrict discussion of contemporary evidence to that from Rome for the period beginning with Aurelian and ending in the last quarter of the fourth century. Nevertheless, the limitations in the extant evidence have at times forced me to to expand my chronological and geographical boundaries. Further, while I will supply here corroborative testimony for the celebrations noted in the Calendar text, the legal status of paganism and subsidiary historical documentation will be addressed at greater length in Chapter 5.[3]

---

2. See, for one, J. H. W. G. Liebeschuetz, *Continuity and Change in Roman Religion* (Oxford, 1979).

3. Suffice it here to note that the evidence is convincing that the text of the Calendar of 354 reflects contemporary cult practice and the civic round of holidays still celebrated in the mid-fourth-century city. The predominance and particulars of imperial cult in the text of the Calendar reinforce this conclusion.

FESTIVALS, HOLIDAYS, AND CULTS
IN THE CALENDAR OF 354: AN OVERVIEW

An official Roman calendar recorded the public holidays (*feriae publicae*) recognized by the Roman state. Thus, the Calendar of 354 included all fixed annual, state-supported public celebrations (*feriae stativae*). In addition to these holidays, some were celebrated annually but without fixed dates (*feriae conceptivae*), as Easter is today, and others were proclaimed for special reasons (*feriae imperativae*)—to commemorate a triumph or a ritual act of purification (*lustratio*), for example. Yet these last two types, as well as festivals held only irregularly (i.e., not annually), were not included in official Roman calendars, and they do not appear in the Calendar of 354.

The Latin terms for holidays—*feriae, dies festi,* or *dies feriati*—include the basic notion not only of honoring the gods but also of abstaining from work.[4] As legally defined, Roman holidays required that certain rites be performed and the law courts be officially closed[5] (a definition that remained intact in the fourth century).[6] Because the activities associated with a Roman holiday were for the benefit of the people, whether as a whole or some subgroup, they were funded by the state.[7] And while the priests (*sacerdotes publici* or *pontifices*) were charged with carrying out prescribed rites to fulfill the human part of the bargain,[8] there was no obligation for the public at large to perform any specific acts of worship.[9]

Most often, cultic rites included a sacrifice, usually performed in front of the temple of the divinity by the priests of the cult. A banquet

---

4. Cicero *De Leg.* 2.19, 29, 55; Cato *De Agr.* 138, 140; Servius Auctus, *Ad Georg.* 1.270; Macrobius *Sat.* 1.16.10, 11, 24, 25, 28.

5. Macrobius *Sat.* 1.16.2; Cicero *De Leg.* 2.19, 29; on *feriae,* see Latte 1960, pp. 198–199; Michels 1967, pp. 69–73, esp. p. 69, n. 29; Dar.-Sagl., s.v. "Feriae"; A.D. Nock, "The Roman Army and the Roman Religious Year," *HTR* 188 (1952); reprinted in *Essays on Religion and the Ancient World,* 2 vols. (Oxford, 1972).

6. *C.Th.* 2.8.19 (A.D. 389) restates the fact that legal actions were not allowed on *feriae* and stipulates a new group of *feriae* requiring the cessation of legal action. Cf. *Just. Dig.* 2.12.2, .6, .9. Of course, this 389 law had no impact on the giving of *ludi,* which were not legislated against until 392; *C.Th.* 2.8.20.

7. Festus 284L: "Publica sacra, quae publico sumptu pro populo fiunt"; cf. Macrobius *Sat.* 1.16.4–8; Festus 282L.

8. Nock, "Roman Army," pp. 188ff.

9. This is the view of the majority of historians of Roman religion, including R. M. Ogilvie, *The Romans and Their Gods in the Age of Augustus* (London, 1969); Wissowa 1912; and Nock, "Roman Army." However, M. P. Nilsson, "Pagan Divine Service in Late Antiquity," *HTR* 38 (1945): 63–70, argues from the change in Greek cult that daily divine service was of widespread import in late antiquity.

frequently followed,[10] as in the event of a *natalis*, an anniversary celebration, such as that on the birthday of an emperor or on the dedication of a temple.[11] In the case of a *natalis*, the banquet and games were optional; only a public sacrifice performed by priests was mandatory. The dedication of a new temple often coincided with the public holiday to honor the god in question, but not necessarily: in the Calendar of 354, the indication *natalis* can refer to both or either event.[12]

The public games, or *ludi*, were not strictly speaking holidays, or *feriae*. Hence, law courts were not always closed for them, nor was there an official day of rest. Still, the games were celebrated as festivals (*dies festi*), were funded by public monies, and were administered by state magistrates on behalf of the people. And, because they were public celebrations, the games were recorded in official Roman calendars. The public nature of *ludi* derives from their origin and development in the republic, where they are generally believed to have begun as votive offerings by victorious generals to honor Jupiter Optimus Maximus. During the early republican period a series of games was instituted to bolster the confidence of the people and to win divine favor. Public games were also held to celebrate military victories and the individuals responsible for the successes.

Festivals and Holidays in the Calendar of 354

The text of the Calendar of 354 informs us of the most important holidays and festivals in the fourth-century city. Two consistent indicators of importance can be identified: the length of the celebration and the kind—namely, *ludi scaenici*, theatrical games or spectacles (hereafter referred to as *ludi*); *ludi circenses*, circus races (hereafter referred to as *circenses*); or *munera*, gladiatorial combats. Those festivals that were celebrated with *ludi* and *circenses* are shown in Tables 1, 2, and 5. In a separate grouping are holidays commemorated with rites or celebrations but not with *ludi* or *circenses*. This second category is divided chronologically

10. For banquets, see Macrobius *Sat.* 1.16.3; K. Latte 1960, pp. 198ff., 275ff., 298–299; Liebeschuetz, *Continuity and Change*, pp. 80ff.; Wissowa 1912, pp. 419ff.

11. See Wissowa 1912, pp. 474ff. For a dedication by the emperor, see, for example, Dio Cass. 54.26; for a dedication to the emperor on the occasion of a *natalis*, see, for example, *ILS* 154.10; for a temple dedication, see, for example, *CIL* 12.3058.

12. See Wissowa 1912, p. 474, on the dedication day of an *aedes sacra*. In the Calendar of 354, however, *natalis* does not mean "dedication day"; rather, it is a generic term for any sort of anniversary or celebration. For example, *Natalis chartis* on 25 January indicates the celebration of the day the papyrus shipment arrived in Rome; see Degrassi 1963, p. 402. See n. 22 below.

according to those festivals attested in calendars from the times of Augustus into the mid first century A.D. (Table 3) and those that apparently entered the Roman calendar at a later date (Table 4).[13] By this first step of analysis we may determine the city's most important holidays and festivals, for those celebrated by *circenses* correspond to the most influential cults, followed by those with *ludi* and finally those with merely cultic ritual.[14]

In the Calendar, 177 holiday or festival days are devoted to *ludi* and *circenses*, including 10 days of gladiatorial shows. The sheer number is at first glance astonishing. Yet it would be wrong to think that all Rome came to a standstill for 177 days of the year. Participation in these events was, after all, limited; like the saints' days of the Roman Catholic church in modern Italy, the festivals and holidays in the Calendar of 354 did not require universal observance. Rites had to be performed in conjunction with the games by priests or magistrates or both, but attendance at any particular set of games was limited to those who could and would attend. Moreover, an observer did not have to stay all day. Nor did the law courts close for all 177 days; *ludi* required no such observance. Nevertheless, the number of *ludi* and *circenses* in the Calendar does indicate the contemporary popularity of these celebrations, and the appeal of many a Roman festival results in good measure from the games attached to it.

By far the greatest single recipient of festivals and holidays celebrated with *ludi* and *circenses* was the emperor and his family (hereafter referred to as the imperial cult). Thus, if we exclude the ten days of gladiatorial games, the imperial cult accounts for an impressive ninety-eight days of games and circuses.

The remaining sixty-nine days are devoted primarily to festivals and holidays in honor of the pagan gods of the Greco-Roman pantheon. Thirty-seven of these days are taken up by the six great public games, which had also been celebrated in the republican period (Table 1). Of these, the most important were the *ludi Romani* and *ludi Plebeii*, in honor of Jupiter Optimus Maximus; a banquet in his honor, a traditional component of the *ludi Plebeii*, is also noted on 13 November.[15] The remaining games in commemoration of pagan deities are the *ludi Megalesiaci* for the

---

13. Since there is only one fragmentary calendar from S. Maria Maggiore in Rome that dates after the mid-first-century calendars and before the Calendar of 354, it is often difficult to determine when a festival entered the Roman calendar. See Chapter 1, note 14.

14. Mommsen, *CIL* 1893, p. 300. This distinction was already true in the third century; see Fink, Hoey, and Snyder 1940, p. 127.

15. Degrassi 1963, p. 530.

TABLE 1: PUBLIC *LUDI* RECORDED IN CALENDARS OF THE MID FIRST CENTURY A.D. AND THEIR APPEARANCE IN THE CALENDAR OF 354[a]

Ludi Name	1st-Century Calendars	Calendar of 354	354 Holiday Replacing First-Century *Ludi*	Change[b]
Romani	5–19 Sept.	12–15 Sept.	9/5 Mammes vindemia 9/9 N. Aureliani 9/11 N. Asclepi 9/18 N. Traiani; Ludi Triumphales 9/19 N. Pii Antonini	red. to 4
Plebeii	4–17 Nov.	12–17 Nov.	11/8 N. Nervae et Constantii 11/9 Ludi votivi	red. to 5
Apollinares	6–13 July	5–13 July		incr. to 9
Cerialici	12–19 April	12–19 April[c]		s. = 8
Megalesiaci	4–10 April	4–10 April		s. = 7
Florales	28 April–3 May	30 April–3 May[d]	4/28–29 *no notation*	red. to 4
Victoriae Sullanae	26 Oct.–1 Nov.	omitted	10/28 Isia. Evictio tyranni 10/29 Adventus Divi. Isia 10/30 Ludi votivi. Isia 10/31 Ludi. Isia 11/1 Ex se nato. Isia	omitted
Victoriae Caesaris	July 20–30	omitted	7/20 Ludi Francici 7/21 Adventus Divi 7/22 Ludi (votivi) 7/23 (Ludi) Neptunalici 7/25 N. Divi Constantini 7/26 Ludi votivi 7/27 Vict(orias) Sarmaticas 7/30 Vict(orias) Marcomannas	omitted

[a] In this table I include the evidence of the *Menologia Rustica* and the *Ferialia* dated to the Julio-Claudian period (nos. 44–45 and 47–48 in Degrassi 1963) as well as the mid-first-century calendars (nos. 2–41 in ibid.). For further discussion, see Scullard 1981; Degrassi 1963, pp. 372ff.; and Chapter 1 above.

[b] All figures in this column refer to the number of days noted in the Calendar of 354: red. = number of days *ludi* were reduced to; incr. = number of days *ludi* were increased to; s. = same number of days in first-century calendars and the Calendar of 354.

[c] The characteristic -*ici* ending appears in the fourth-century Calendar, as opposed to the -*alia* in the first-century calendars. So the *ludi Cerialici* = *Cerialia*, the *Megalesiaci* = *Megalesia*, etc. This does not signify a change in festival. See also Stern 1953, pp. 96–98.

[d] According to Degrassi 1963, pp. 449–451.

January

3	Ludi Compitales.[b] Votorum nuncupatio
4	Ludi Compitales
5	Ludi Compitales
7	Iano Patri. Circenses
13	Iovi Statori. Circenses

February

1	N(atalis) Herculis. Circenses
11	Ludi Genialici
12	Ludi Genialici

March

1	N(atalis) Martis. Circenses
13	Iovi Cultori. Circenses
17	Ludi Liberalici. Circenses

April

3	N(atalis) d(ei) Quirini. Circenses
8	N(atalis) Castor(is) et Pollu(ci)s. Circenses
21	N(atalis) urbis. Circenses

May

12	[Ludi Martialici. Circenses][a]
29	Ludi Fabarici
30	Ludi Fabarici
31	Ludi Fabarici

June

1	Ludi Fabarici
4	Ludi in Minicia

July

23	(Ludi) Neptunalici

August

4	Vict(oria) Senati. Circenses
5	N(atalis) Salutis. Circenses
23	(Ludi) Vulcanalici. Circenses
28	[N(atalis)] Solis et Lunae.[c] Circenses

[a] The majority of extant calendars date no later than the mid first century A.D.; see Chapter 1 above and Degrassi 1963, pp. 375–376. Hence, the festivals with *ludi* in this table were mostly added to the Roman calendar after that time. In this table are also included those festivals noted in mid-first-Century calendars without *ludi*, such as the *ludi Liberalici*, which earlier appeared as the *Liberalia*. The only exception is the *ludi Martialici*, recorded as *ludi* only in the *Fasti Maffeiani* (A.D. 4–14); see Degrassi 1963, pp. 456–457. I have included these *ludi* in Table 2 with brackets, since they are neither an ancient republican holiday (noted in Table 1) nor part of the imperial cult (noted in Table 5); the origin and annual celebration of these games are open to question.

[b] The *ludi Compitales* were celebrated as *feriae conceptivae* in the late republic and early empire, though they were not officially recorded by the Calendars of this period. See note 18 below.

[c]N(atalis) fell out or should be supplied. For further discussion, see Degrassi 1963, p. 503.

TABLE 2   (*CONTINUED*)

	September
29	Ludi Fatales
30	Ludi Fatales
	October
19	Ludi Solis
20	Ludi Solis
21	Ludi Solis
22	Ludi Solis
	November
1	Ex se nato. Circenses; Isia[d]
	December
2	Initium muneris[e]
4	Munus arca
5	Munus arca
6	Munus arca
8	Munus kandida
19	Munus arca
20	Munus kandida
21	Munus arca
23	Munus arca
24	Munus consummat(ur)
25	Natalis Invicti. Circenses

[d] I have included the *Ex se nato* and *Isia* here. Although the *Ex se nato* is probably the equivalent of the *Heuresis* noted in the *Menologia Rustica* on 15 November, neither it nor the *Isia* nor the accompanying *circenses* were recorded there.

[e] The gladiatorial combats, 2–24 December intermittently, are recorded here but are not included in the calculations of the "holidays and festivals" discussed in Chapter 4 because they were the privilege of the emperor. Only the two days of *Munus kandida* (8 and 20 December) were the responsibility of the quaestors.

Magna Mater, the *ludi Cerialici* for Ceres, the *ludi Florales* for Flora, and the *ludi Apollinares* for Apollo.[16]

Thirty-one of the remaining thirty-two Calendar days celebrated with public *ludi* and *circenses* (Table 2) were added after the mid first century A.D.;[17] yet these, too, are reserved primarily for the gods and

16. These are the *ludi* names as they appear in the Calendar of 354. Spelling changes do not indicate a change in festival. See Table 1, note c, above. The remaining *ludi* in Table 1 were instituted for the victories of Sulla and of Caesar.

17. This dating is based on the fact that none of the extant first-century calendars or their notes date after the reign of Claudius (A.D. 41–54); see Chapter 1, note 14. Neither the *ludi Iovi Liberatori*, commemorating what were considered imperial victories, nor the *ludi Palatini* or *Augustales*, established in the Julio-Claudian period and also associated with imperial cult, are included in Table 2. Only the *ludi Martialici*, celebrated with games according to their sole notation in the *Fasti Maffeiani* (A.D. 4–14), were included in brackets here; see Table 2 note a.

January

11	Dies Carmentariorum = Carmentalia
15	Carmentalia

February

13	Virgo Vesta(lis) parentat = Parentalia
15	Lupercalia
17	Quirinalia
21	Feralia
22	Caristia = Cara Cognatio
23	Terminalia
24	Regifugium

March

5	Isidis navigium
14	Mamuralia = Sacrum Mamurio[b]
19	Quinquatria
23	Tubilustrium
27	Lavatio

April

25	Serapia = Sarapia

May

June

9	Vestalia
11	Matralia
15	Vesta cluditur = Q.St.D.F (Quando stercum delatum fas)
18	Annae sacrum = Annae Perennae (15 March)
24	Fortis Fortunae. Solstitium

July

August

13	Natalis Dianes = Feriae Diana[e]

September

October

November

13	Iovis epulum = Iovi epulum

December

11	Septimontia = Septimontium[c]
17	Saturnalia

---

[a] If a festival or ceremony noted in mid-first-century calendars is identified with a fourth-century one, both names are given. The first one is that found in the text of the Calendar of 354; the name after the equal sign is that found generally in the earlier calendars and in Degrassi 1963, pp. 364ff.

[b]*Sacrum Mamurio* is noted in the *ferialia*.

[c]*Septimontium* is recorded in the *Fasti Guiddizzolenses*.

TABLE 4: FESTIVALS AND CEREMONIES WITHOUT *LUDI*
OR *CIRCENSES* ADDED TO ROMAN CALENDARS AFTER
THE MID FIRST CENTURY A.D. AND RECORDED
IN THE CALENDAR OF 354.

	January
[25	N(atalis) chartis][a]
	February
	March
7	Iunonalia
9	Arma, ancilia movent(ur)
15	Canna intrat
20	Pelusia
21	N(atalis) Minerves
*22	Arbor intrat*[b]
*24	Sanguem*
25	Hilaria
26	Requetio
28	Initium Caiani
	April
1	Veneralia
	May
15	N(atalis) Mercuri
[18	N(atalis) annonis]
19	Zenziarius
23	Macellus rosa(m) sumat
29	Honor et Virtus. Zinza
	June
6	Colossus coronatur
7	Vesta aperit(ur)
13	N(atalis) Musarum
	July
	August
12	Lychnapsia
17	Tiberinalia
	September
5	Mammes vindemia
11	N(atalis) Asclepi
	October
15	Equus ad Nixas fit
28	Isia
29	Isia
30	Isia
31	Isia
	November
2	Ter novena
3	Hilaria
24	Bruma
	December

[a] The holidays noted in brackets may also be considered under the rubric of the imperial cult in the fourth century. See discussion below.

[b] The holidays noted with asterisks are attributed to the Emperor Claudian (Table 6) and are noted here because they do not appear in extant Roman calendars of the early first century.

goddesses of the Greco-Roman pantheon. Moreover, eight of these holidays (taking up some twelve days) were celebrated in the first century A.D., and seven of these eight (taking up some nine days) were recorded in first-century Roman calendars[18]—but all eight were without *ludi* or *circenses*.

The addition of *ludi* and *circenses* to eight holidays from the early empire indicates not only the fourth-century passion for this sort of celebration but also the contemporary significance of these festivals and cults. The eight holidays are[19]

ludi Compitales	3–5 January (honoring the Lares Compitales and the *genius Augusti*)
Natalis Martis	1 March (honoring Mars)
ludi Liberalici	17 March (honoring Liber)
ludi in Minicia	4 June (honoring Hercules at the temple to Hercules Custos in the Porticus Minucia)[20]
ludi Neptunalici	23 July (honoring Neptune)
ludi Vulcanalici	23 August (honoring Vulcan)[21]
Natalis Salutis	5 August (honoring *Salus Publica*)
Ex se nato. Isia	1 November (honoring Osiris and Isis; identified with the first-century A.D. *Heuresis*)

Most often, *ludi* and *circenses* were added to these early imperial festivals as part of a celebration, or *natalis*,[22] commemorating the dedication of a temple in Rome.

Indeed, the same rationale holds for the remaining twenty-two days in this category (holidays celebrated with *ludi* and *circenses* added to the

18. The *ludi Compitales* were *feriae conceptivae* in the republic and early empire and so were not recorded in Julio-Claudian calendars; they were celebrated in the first century A.D. without *ludi* and *circenses*. See Scullard 1981, p. 59.

19. The following festivals and holidays are listed as recorded in the Calendar of 354; the names of the deities honored are not included in the Calendar but are added for clarification where known.

20. Scullard, 1981, p. 146.

21. Although disputed, there is no evidence for *ludi* associated with this festival to Vulcan in the Julio-Claudian period; see Degrassi 1963, pp. 500–501. The *ludi Vulcanalici* are the fourth-century name for the *Volcanalia*.

22. A *natalis* indicates a general celebration or commemoration in the Calendar of 354. It can indicate the commemoration of a dedication of a temple, as does the *Natalis urbis*, identified with the temple of Venus and Rome; Degrassi 1963, pp. 443ff. It can also refer simply to any sort of commemorative celebration, as the *Natalis Divi Constantinii*. Confusion about this term has led certain scholars to identify incorrectly all *natales* with temple dedications, as, for example, Wissowa 1912, p. 367, n. 4, who identifies the dedication of the temple of Sol with the *Natalis Invicti* on 25 December, though without any evidence from the sources; see Salzman 1981, pp. 223ff.

Roman calendar after the mid first century).[23] In this group, temple *natales* are commemorated for the following deities:

Hercules	1 February
Jove (Jupiter) Cultor	13 March
Quirinus	3 April
Castor and Pollux	8 April
Urbs Roma Aeterna	21 April[24]
Sol and Luna	28 August
Sol Invictus	25 December

These cults ranked among the most popular in the fourth century, for all these *natales*, with the exception of that for Sol Invictus, were celebrated with twenty-four races in the circus; Sol Invictus, being even more important, received thirty races.

In addition to the *natales* associated with particular temples, the following festivals with *ludi* or *circenses* were added to the Roman calendar after the mid first century A.D.:

ludi Solis	19–22 October (honoring Sol)
Iano Patri	7 January (honoring Janus Pater)
Iovi Statori	13 January (honoring Jupiter Stator)
ludi Fatales	29–30 September (honoring the Fates?)
ludi Genialici	11–12 February
ludi Fabarici	29 May–1 June (honoring Dea Carna?)

The inclusion of *ludi* and *circenses* in the Calendar to honor the first three deities is readily understood, for these popular cults are well attested. The last three, however, are surprising, because these festivals cannot even be tied securely to any deity.

As for the festivals and holidays that were not celebrated by *ludi* and *circenses* (Tables 3 and 4), clearly the Greco-Roman pantheon dominates. These celebrations go back to the archaic Roman religious year; indeed, the very antiquity of these *feriae* made their significance obscure even to writers of the early empire, and by the fourth century A.D some had changed so much as to be incorporated into the cults of other deities. For example, the old rites of Sol in the Circus Maximus and of the *Armilustrium* played a role in Aurelian's new cult of Sol Invictus. In other cases, the traditional rites (or rites thought to be traditional) continued

23. Thirty-one days minus nine days for the seven holidays of the Julio-Claudian period makes twenty-two days. I omitted the *ludi Compitales* from this calculation.

24. The *Natalis urbis*, held on the same date as the ancient *Parilia*, honored the new deity Roma Aeterna; see pp. 155–156 and 177.

to be practiced as they always had been, but their meaning had changed. Sometimes enough evidence exists to disclose how the holiday had come to be interpreted—for example, in the case of the *Lupercalia*.[25] Unfortunately, this is not always true. The *Feriae Mamurio*, for instance, are described as a popular New Year festival, but neither its connection with the cult of Mamurius (an archaic doublet for Mars) nor the cult of Mamurius itself is attested in the fourth century.[26]

The festivals in this last group are often the most difficult to interpret in a fourth-century context. Perhaps some of these archaic celebrations had become so loosely connected with their gods that they assumed the status of, in Wissowa's terms, *sacra popularia*, "soon to be celebrated with all the festivities of the carnival."[27] But others, such as the *Saturnalia* and the *Lupercalia*, were among the most popular and long-lived festivals of the Roman calendar year. Their association with a deity may well have been vital. I therefore cannot accept the view, advanced by Wissowa and others, that many of the archaic festivals in this last group were different in religious emphasis from the other *feriae*—that one sacrificed to Saturn, for example, merely because he was the god with whom the *Saturnalia* was traditionally connected but that his cult was no longer vital. This formulation is anachronistic. As long as the rituals of the cult of Saturn continued to be practiced, they would be valid and, at least for some pagans, have real religious meaning.[28] I emphasize this point because there is a tendency to dismiss popular festivals as nonreligious if they do not conform to modern ideas of solemnity. Yet we cannot assume that the festivals in this group about which we lack information were devoid of cultic ritual in the mid fourth century.

Included in this group of archaic festivals and holidays[29] is a celebration to honor Fors Fortuna on 24 June; the *Matralia* to Mater Matuta on 11 June; the *Tiberinalia* to Tibur on 17 August; the *Saturnalia* to Saturnus on 17 December; the *Quirinalia* to Quirinus/Romulus on 17 February; the *Terminalia* to Terminus on 23 February; the *Mamuralia* (= *Sacrum Ma-*

---

25. See my discussion in Chapter 6.

26. For Mamurius, see Degrassi 1963, pp. 422–423, and the discussion of the illustration of March, Chapter 3.

27. See Wissowa 1912, p. 399, n. 4, re *Saturnalia*; and Fink, Hoey, and Snyder 1940, pp. 170–172, for further discussion and bibliography. Even among the most archaic and arcane festivals, it is not possible to affirm that festival ceremonies or rites were modified by Christianity; see Stern 1953, pp. 105–107.

28. The author of the *Carmen contra Paganos* is characterized as a "cultor Saturni," line 69; cf. Macrobius *Sat.* 1.7.18–37. This is the view taken also by Stern 1953, pp. 105ff.

29. The names in parentheses are those recorded in earlier calendars or the *Menologia Rustica*. The names given are otherwise those found in the Calendar of 354. See Degrassi 1963 for discussion of individual days.

murio) to Mamurius on 14 March; the *Carmentalia* to Carmenta on 11 and 15 January; the *Tubilustrium* on 23 March (although this day was traditionally in honor of Mars, in the fourth century it was associated with Attis and Cybele); and the *Lupercalia* on 15 February, to a deity of uncertain identity. Three holidays—the *Virgo Vestalis Parentat* (= *Parentalia*) on 13 February, the *Feralia* on 21 February, and the *Cara Cognatio* (= *Caristia*) on 22 February—are associated with the worship of the Manes, the ancestral spirits of the dead; and the 13 February notation included a Vestal Virgin in the rites for that day. In addition to these early Roman cults, this group of festivals includes days, noted in calendars from the first century A.D., to honor gods of the Greek pantheon, including Mercury, Diana, and Aesculapius.

Four holidays recorded in the rustic calendars—the *Isidis navigium* in March, the *Sacrum [Isidi] Phariae* and the *Sarapia* in April, and the *Heuresis* in November—can be correlated to three holidays in the Calendar of 354: the *Isidis navigium* on 5 March, the *Serapia* on 25 April, and the *Ex se nato. Isia* on 1 November, referring respectively to the Egyptian cults of Isis, Serapis, and Osiris. The growth of these cults in the first three centuries of the empire is reflected in the calendars and helps to explain the illustration for November (Fig. 22) in the Calendar of 354.

This last group of holidays (celebrated without *ludi* or *circenses*) includes celebrations that do not honor any particular deity. Several commemorate historic or mythic events associated with the beginnings of Rome and its institutions; so, for example, the *Regifugium* on 24 February celebrates the expulsion of the Etruscan king Tarquinius Superbus. Others are seasonal festivals that owe their inclusion to a growth of interest in astrology and astronomy or an association with certain civic institutions. Many seasonal celebrations occur for the first time only in calendars from the second half of the first century A.D. For example, the Rose Festival (*Macellus rosa[m] sumat*), 23 May in the Calendar of 354, popularly commemorated the rose harvest; its earliest recorded appearance is in the *Feriale Duranum,* where it was celebrated as a military lustration of arms.[30] The *Bruma,* on 24 November, and the *Vindemial* festival, on 5 September, also appear as seasonal celebrations.[31] Still other commemorations appear for the first time in the Calendar because of their importance to the civic life of Rome, as, for example, the *Natalis chartis* (25 January) and *Natalis annonis* (18 May), celebrations of the arrival of papyrus and grain shipments in the city. In my view, though, these festi-

30. For details, see discussion of the illustration of May, Chapter 3.
31. See Degrassi 1963, pp. 508, 532.

vals gain a place in the Calendar because they are tied to the imperial cult as well. Two new festivals are still of unknown intent: the *Zenziarius* and the *Zinza,* on 19 and 29 May, respectively.

In sum, the *feriae* without *ludi* and *circenses* in the Calendar of 354 represent a somewhat different range of cults from those commemorated with such activities. The festivals of Attis, Isis, and Serapis are predominant, especially among those added after the mid first century (see Table 4); but the high percentage of Roman festivals from the republican period, together with the prominence of the cults of Vesta and the Manes in this last grouping, indicates the conservative nature of the Roman calendar.

The Cults in the Calendar of 354

> convenit inter publicos sacerdotes, ut in custodiam civium publico obsequio traderemus curam deorum. benignitas enim superioris, nisi cultu teneatur, amittitur.[32]

> It has been agreed among the public priests, that we should commit the care of the gods to the guardianship of the citizens as a public trust. For the benevolence of the gods, unless it is maintained by ritual, will be lost.

The results of our inquiry thus far have led to the following groupings of cults based on the kind and frequency of celebration associated with them, and thus on popularity.

Group 1. The Imperial Cult
Group 2. Cults celebrated with *ludi* and *circenses*
  A. Cults with *ludi* and *circenses* on more than one day:
    Mars
    Sol Invictus
    Hercules
    Quirinus/Romulus
    Ceres
    Flora
    Apollo
    Jupiter
    Magna Mater
  B. Cults with *ludi* and *circenses* on one day only:
    Salus
    Osiris

32. Symmachus *Ep.* 1.46.2 (ca. A.D. 381).

Castor and Pollux
Janus Pater
Liber
Vulcan
Roma Aeterna
Neptune
Group 3. Cults not celebrated with *ludi* or *circenses*
  A. Cults recorded with celebrations on more than one day:[33]
    Isis (including Serapis, Osiris, and Hippocrates)
    Attis
    Vesta
    Minerva
    Manes
    Carmenta
  B. Cults recorded with celebrations on one day only:
    Tibur
    Juno
    Diana
    Aesculapius
    Venus
    Fors Fortuna
    Mercury
    Mater Matuta
    (Mamurius ?)
    Honor and Virtus

I will not analyze all the cults listed here in detail; rather, I will focus on those festivals whose connection with a particular deity is attested by both contemporary evidence and the Calendar of 354.

GROUP 1. THE IMPERIAL CULT

The festivals and ceremonies associated with the emperor and his family are the most frequent and most important of all those noted in the Calendar of 354, with ninety-eight days of *ludi* and *circenses* in honor of the imperial cult recorded throughout the year (see Table 5).[34] Of

33. Cults celebrated with *ludi* or *circenses* that have already been mentioned are not repeated here. These are the cults of Mars, Quirinus, Jupiter, and Sol.

34. This figure assumes that the *Equit(um) Ro(manorum) probatio*, 15 July, and the *Evictio tyranni*, 28 October, included *ludi*. For imperial cult in general, see P. Herz, "Kaiserfeste der Prinzipatszeit," *ANRW* II 16.2 (Berlin, 1978), pp. 1135–1200; and idem, "Bibliographie

these, the majority, some sixty-nine days, are devoted to the House of Constantine; the remaining twenty-nine days commemorate earlier emperors or historical events associated with them. In its tendency to focus on the living emperor and the reigning dynasty, the Calendar of 354 echoes trends in earlier paganism and calendars.[35]

Imperial festivals entered the Roman calendar in the early years of the empire, gradually replacing the days devoted to other gods and goddesses. The predominance of the imperial cult, however, is clear as well in an extant third-century calendar list of the military garrison at Dura-Europos, the *Feriale Duranum*, in which twenty-seven of forty-one entries relate to the imperial cult.[36] Although the *Feriale* reflects the needs of a military detachment at Dura-Europos, where the primacy of the imperial cult would be expected, it may also reflect general tendencies in calendars of the third century.[37] Unlike the *Feriale Duranum*, however, where imperial predominance was marked only by a larger proportion of entries, the Calendar of 354 includes various distinctive patterns for festivals in honor of the reigning dynasty. Such celebrations are distinguished from the festivals of the pagan gods or of earlier emperors not only in terms of frequency but also by the nature and length of the festivities.

The Roman imperial cult involved two traditional aspects that essentially explain the festivals in the fourth-century Calendar—namely, the worship of the living ruler, including his identification with the divine, however formulated; and the apotheosis of the dead emperor. Articulation of the relationship of the emperor to the divine changed according to political and geographical context. Under Augustus, for

---

zum römischen Kaiserkult (1955–1975)," ibid., pp. 833–910; D. Fishwick, "The development of Provincial Ruler Worship in the Western Roman Empire," ibid., pp. 1201–1253; and *The Imperial Cult in the Latin West: Studies in the Ruler Cult of the Western Provinces of the Roman Empire, EPRO,* no. 108 (Leiden, 1987), vol. 1.1.

35. The victory celebrations of a particular dynasty seem rarely to have survived the dynasty that instituted them, as indicated by the *Feriale Duranum* and the Calendar of 354. See Fink, Hoey, and Snyder 1940; Nock, "Roman Army," pp. 186–252; Stern 1953, p. 70; and Fishwick, "Provincial Ruler Worship," pp. 1201–1253.

36. See Nock, "Roman Army," p. 778; Fink, Hoey, and Snyder 1940, pp. 173ff. Also of value are the reviews of the *Feriale Duranum* by S. Weinstock, *JRS* 32 (1942): 127ff.; A. A. Boyce, *CP* 38 (1943): 64ff.; L. R. Taylor, *AJA* 46 (1942): 310ff. The final report on the *Feriale* is R. Cavenaile, ed., *Corpus Papyrorum Latinarum,* vol. 4 (Wiesbaden, 1958), no. 324, "Papyrus Doura 2: Feriale Duranum," pp. 412–416. Cf. Herz, "Kaiserfeste," pp. 1135–2000.

37. J. Heigeland, "Roman Army Religion," *ANRW* II 16.2, pp. 1470–1505; and E. Birley, "The Religion of the Roman Army: 1895–1977", ibid., pp. 1506–1541.

Festival Occasion	Natalis	Victory[a]	Other[b]
January			
17–19, 21, 22		[L. Palatini][c]	
20	N. Gordiani. C.		
24	N. D(ivi) Hadriani. C.		
26–30		[L. Adiabenis victis.]	
31		Adiabenis victis. C.[d]	
February			
4–8		L. Gottici.	
9		Gottici. C.	
25			Lorio. C.
27	N. D(ivi) Constantini. C.		
28	Ludi votivi		
March			
31	N. Constanti(n)i. C.[e]		
April			
1	Ludi [votivi][f]		
11	N. Divi Severi. C.		
26	N. M. Antonini. C.		
May			
4–8		L. Maximati.	
9		Maximati. C.	
10	N. Claudi. C.[g]		
13–16		L. Persici.	
17		Persici. C.	

[a] A victory is any victory associated with the imperial cult. Each festival associated with the ruling dynasty was followed by a day of *ludi votivi*, which is recorded in the same column. L. = *ludi* or games; C. = *circenses* or circus races; N = *natales* or the celebration of birth or elevation to caesar.

[b] "Other" includes a variety of occasions that in the fourth century fell under the rubric of the imperial cult.

[c] I have attributed this holiday to the imperial cult in the fourth century because this celebration is tied to the death of Augustus, whose significance for all subsequent dynasties is unique. The *Natalis chartis* (25 January) and *Natalis annonis* (18 May) may also be part of the imperial cult, but since there is less evidence for these dates, I have recorded them in Table 4.

[d] These victory *ludi* were omitted from the Calendar, probably owing to a scribal error; see Stern 1953, pp. 83ff.; and Degrassi 1963, p. 375.

[e] This is the *natalis* of Constantius Chlorus (293–306); the notation Constantini is a scribal error.

[f] The term *votivi* was omitted, probably owing to scribal error. See note 57 below.

[g] This is the *natalis* of Claudius Gothicus (268–270).

TABLE 5   (*CONTINUED*)

	Natalis	Victory[a]	Other[b]
June			
July			
3			Fugato Licinio. C.
15			Equit(um) Ro(manorum) prob(atio)[h]
15–17, 20		L. Francici.	
18			Adventus D(ivi). C.
19			Ludi votivi
20		Francici. C.	
21			Advent(us) Divi. C.
22			Ludi [votivi][e]
25	N. D(ivi) Constantini. C.		
26	Ludi votivi		
27		Vict(orias) Sarmaticas. C.	
30		Vict(orias) Marcomannas. C.	
August			
1	N. D(ivi) Pertinacis. C.		
7	N. Constantii. C.		
8	Ludi votivi		
19	N. Probi. C.		
September			
9	N. Aureliani. C.		
18	N. Traiani.	[L.] Triumphales. C. [i]	
19	N. Pii Antonini. C.		
20–22		L. Triumphales.	
23	N. Divi Augusti. C.		

[h] Although this ceremony is attributed to Augustus, it does not appear in the calendars of the mid first century. Its appearance here is probably the result of newly reinstated festivals associated with the imperial cult in 305; see Stern 1953, pp. 362ff.; and my discussion below.

[i] Forty-eight circus races are recorded on this date. There is good reason for this exceptionally large number of games; this is the *Natalis Traiani* and the beginning of the *ludi Triumphales*, which commemorated Constantine's victory over Licinius in 324, according to Stern 1953, p. 82. Degrassi 1963, pp. 510–511, would also associate this day with the preceding *ludi Romani*, on 12–15 September in the Calendar.

TABLE 5 (*CONTINUED*)

	Natalis	Victory[a]	Other[b]
September			
27			Profectio Divi. C.
28			[Ludi votivi][j]
October			
1	N. Alexandri. C.		
5–9		L. Alamannici.	
10		Alamannici. C.	
12			Augustales. C.
13–17		[L. Iovi Liberatori.]	
18		[Iovi Liberatori. C.][k]	
28			Evictio tyranni
29			Advent(us) Divi. C.
30			Ludi votivi
31			Ludi [votivi][l]
November			
8	N. Nervae et Constantii C.		
9	Ludi votivi		
17	N. Vespasiani. C.		
25–30		L. Sarmatici	
December			
1		L. Sarmatici. C.	
12–14		L. Lancionici.	
15	N. Divi Veri. C.		
16–17		L. [Lancionici]	
18		Lancionici. C.	
30	N. Divi Titi. C.		

[j] The notation *ludi votivi* was omitted from the manuscripts of the Calendar, probably owing to scribal error. See note 57 below.

[k] A victory celebration ascribed to a pre-Constantinian dynasty by Degrassi 1963, p. 520.

[l] The Calendar notes "Ludi. Isia" on 31 October. The *ludi* should refer to the preceding festivals, the *Advent(us)Divi* and *Evictio tyranni*, which would have necessitated two days of *ludi votivi*. Thus, the *ludi* on 31 October should not be associated with the *Isia*, as Degrassi 1963, p. 376, would read them, reversing the order of the words in the text. The *Heuresis*, the joyful discovery of Osiris, is not recorded until 1 November, as the *Ex se nato*, in the Calendar of 354. Until that day there was a period of mourning, during which *ludi* would not have been appropriate.

example, the imperial cult, as officially defined for citizens in Rome, combined the cult of the *divi* with that of the genius of the reigning emperor; in the Greek East, however, Augustus was worshiped in his own right, following the precedent of the Hellenistic ruler cults. Later emperors adapted the imperial cult to their times and needs. Septimius Severus, for one, justified his new dynasty by proclaiming his role as emperor as that of a deified oriental savior who, with his house, would bring about a new golden age.[38]

Constantius II followed imperial precedent when he shaped the imperial cult according to his views and the needs of his time. We see his personal handiwork in the imperial festivals, as they appear in the Calendar of 354, for the essential framework of the imperial cult was constructed by means of the festival:

> It was at festivals and in their ritual that the vague and elusive ideas concerning the emperor, the "collective representations" were focussed in action and made powerful. As Geertz puts it, "For it is in ritual . . . in some sort of ceremonial form . . . that the moods and motivations which sacred symbols induce in men and the general conceptions of the order of existence which they formulate for men meet and reinforce one another." Here the conceptual systems of temple, image and sacrifice had their living embodiment.[39]

The imperial festival was not just a passing ceremony; in the fourth century it generally lasted several days. Public ceremonial was at its core, including processions, *ludi* and *circenses*, vows, and, until Constantine, sacrifices. Often a *supplicatio* was ordered, with prayers required of the entire city. The ability to involve the whole community in its celebration was what made the imperial cult so vital in the life of the empire; for, like ancient religion in general, the cult drew its strength from the fact that it was primarily public: "It was in the public arena that cities decided to establish [imperial] cults and that individuals manifested their civic virtues by serving as priests. The city also expected participation in festivals by its members and made prescriptions for their attendance."[40] The strictures concerning attendance and the legal status of imperial cult festivals as official public holidays on which court action was prohibited continued throughout the fourth century; even after Gratian withdrew

38. Fishwick, "Provincial Ruler Worship," pp. 1243ff.; S. R. F. Price, *Rituals and Power: The Roman Imperial Cult in Asia Minor* (Cambridge, 1984), pp. 56–57.

39. Price, *Rituals and Power*, p. 102.

40. Ibid., pp. 120–121.

state subsidies for the pagan cults and his successors outlawed their festivals and holidays, the official status and celebration of certain of the imperial cult festivals remained intact.[41]

Imperial cult occurred at three levels: provincial, municipal, and private. Under Constantius II, civic properties and revenues were taken over by the state. As a consequence, the state shouldered many burdens formerly met by the city; it therefore appears likely that the imperial cult festivals at Rome were subsidized from the imperial treasury. And although chariot racing in the fourth century was a public duty required of private persons, it was so expensive that at times emperors had to lend a hand.[42] For the wealthy, then, the imperial cult still provided room for private initiative and civic munificence. Thus, while the Calendar of 354 may be said to reflect most directly the municipal level of imperial cult and the initiative of private individuals, the very fact that this was Rome required that the emperor intervene to support the cult.

The imperial festivals noted in the Calendar of 354, which outline a regular cycle of celebration, can be divided according to the occasion commemorated.

Victory *Ludi* and *Circenses*

Nine imperial military victories, taking up some fifty days, are recorded in the Calendar of 354; all but one can be securely identified with the Constantinian dynasty.[43] Moreover, these victories are elaborately celebrated, with five days of *ludi* preceding one day of *circenses* in which twenty-four races are noted (see Table 5). This pattern characterizes the *ludi Gottici, Alamannici, Maximati, Lancionici,* and *Adiabenis victis.* Three other victory festivals fit this general pattern as well, although the *ludi Francici* and *Triumphales* last longer because of interruptions by other imperial festivals, while the *ludi Persici* include only four days of *ludi* and one of *circenses.*[44] Only the *ludi Sarmatici* extend for an unprecedented

41. *C.Th.* 2.8 passim and 2.8.19, A.D. 389 in particular. See also Chapter 6.

42. Libanius *Ep.* 381 (A.D. 358), ed. Foerster (Leipzig, 1903–1913); J. H. W. G. Liebeschuetz, *Antioch: City and Imperial Administration in the Later Roman Empire* (Oxford, 1972), pp. 141ff.; A. Cameron, *Circus Factions: Blues and Greens at Rome and Byzantium* (Oxford, 1976), pp. 217ff.

43. The *ludi Francici* may be identified as a victory either of Maximian or of Constantine or Constantius II; see Degrassi 1963, p. 483.

44. The *ludi Triumphales* began with one day of circus games, marked by an unusually large number of races, forty-eight, on 18 September. This number and pattern may be the result of the combination of celebrations on this one day. In addition to this victory cele-

seven days; the precise reason for this unusual length is not known, but a very important celebration seems indicated: I would say, the joint victory of Constantine and Constantius II in A.D. 334 over the Sarmatians.[45]

In Roman calendars in general, victory celebrations rarely survive the dynasty that instituted them;[46] accordingly, the Calendar of 354 includes only two celebrations that refer to victories of dynasties prior to the house of Constantine: the *Victorias Sarmaticas* and the *Victorias Marcomannas*, celebrated with twenty-four circus races on 27 and 30 July, respectively. Both follow a pattern quite different from that outlined above, being referred to in the Calendar by archaic formulas and involving only one day of games.

By not commemorating earlier dynasties and by extending the festivities centering on the reigning dynasty, the imperial cult in the fourth-century calendar focused on the living emperor and his family, as it had in the third century as well. Thus, of the eight victory celebrations securely identified with the house of Constantine, three attach to Constantius II, namely, the *ludi Adiabenis victis, Persici,* and *Sarmatici.*[47] A large number of victory *ludi* are recorded for Constantius's father, Constantine, who is tied to the *ludi Alamannici, Triumphales, Gottici, Maximati,* and *Lancionici,* and, I suggest, to the joint victory of the *Sarmatici.*[48] This last group of *ludi* serves a double purpose: not only is Constantine honored, but Constantius's *pietas* toward his father and claim to the throne are also emphasized through celebration of these paternal victories.

The importance of imperial victory in the fourth century, and in the political ideology of Constantius II in particular, will reappear in our discussion of the *adventus* ceremony.[49] We can note here that, according to the text of the Calendar of 354, it is a dominant element in Constantius's articulation of the imperial cult. This emphasis is understandable, given the significance of victory for an emperor who was involved in

---

bration is noted the *Natalis Traiani,* and the *ludi Romani*—recorded in first-century calendars for 4–19 September and for 12–15 September in the Calendar of 354; both may have contributed to the importance of the day as well, as Degrassi 1963, pp. 510–511, suggests.

45. The lengthy celebration of these games is an argument in support of J. Arce's interpretation in "The Inscription of Troesmis (*ILS* 724) and the First Victories of Constantius II as Caesar," *ZPE* 48 (1982): 245–249. Controversy over this inscription has continued: see T. D. Barnes, "Two Victory Titles of Constantius," *ZPE* 52 (1983): 229–235; and J. Arce, "Constantius II Sarmaticus and Persicus: A Reply," *ZPE* 57 (1984): 225–229.

46. See note 35 above.

47. For these *ludi,* see Degrassi 1963, pp. 404, 457, and 532; and note 43 above.

48. See identifications in Degrassi 1963, pp. 406, 454, 510–511, 517, and 537. Only the *ludi Francici* are disputed; see note 43 above.

49. See pp. 144–146.

almost constant warfare, both on the borders of the empire and deep inside.

Ludi ob Natales Imperatorum

The *natalis,* or celebration of the emperor's birthday, was commemorated by circus games even during Augustus's reign and continued to be observed over the course of the empire. The *Feriale Duranum* followed other Roman calendars in including the *natales* both of certain *divae,* or deified empresses, and of the *divi,* the deified emperors;[50] these *divae,* however, are absent from the Calendar of 354, as are some of the *divi.*[51] The dubious character of Caracalla and Commodus may explain the omission of their *natales.* The absence of the *natalis* of the nonconsecrated Germanicus, too, is explicable, though that of Claudius is not. The Calendar does include eighteen *natales divorum imperatorum,* which coincide with the listing of the *Natales Caesarum* in section III of the Codex-Calendar.[52]

Ludi ob Natales Imperii

The celebration of the emperor's accession to the throne was traditionally commemorated with *ludi,* and on this day vows (*vota*) for the future were taken. The *Feriale Duranum* records these *ludi* not only for the accession of the living emperor, but also for some five deceased emperors;[53] in the Calendar of 354, in contrast, *ludi* for the *natales imperii* are recorded only for the ruling emperor and his father, Constantine. Moreover, *ludi* in the Calendar commemorate the date of these rulers' accession not to the position of augustus, but to that of caesar. The designation of such an event as a *natalis* occurs for the first time in the fourth-century Calendar. Some have attributed this change to reforms carried out under the tetrarchy and established by Diocletian sometime after

50. Fink, Hoey, and Snyder 1940, pp. 185ff. The anniversaries of the *divae* were included in the public calendars, although, as the Calendar indicates, they were omitted sooner than those for the corresponding *divi*; see Wissowa 1912, pp. 344–345.

51. The fifth-century calendar of Polemius Silvius includes the *natalis* of a Faustina, wife of some Antonine, according to Degrassi 1963, pp. 374–375. The only other indication of the fourth-century importance of this *diva* is a contorniate with the legend "Diva Faustina Aug."; the reverses include representations of Nero, Apollonius of Tyana, and Faustina Iunior. See Alföldi 1976, no. 239.

52. See Chapter 2.

53. Fink, Hoey, and Snyder 1940, pp. 181ff.

54. Stern 1953, pp. 74ff., and Degrassi 1963, p. 375.

293.[54] Although emphasis on the position of caesar is a posttetrarchic development, commemoration of a ruler's accession to caesar is noted as cause for celebration already in the *Feriale Duranum*—in which regard the *Feriale* no doubt follows contemporary trends in both imperial cult and public calendars.[55] Thus, Diocletian's emphasis on this position builds on tendencies already present in third-century imperial cult.

In selecting *natales*, the imperial cult under Constantius focused on the living emperor and his deified father. In the Calendar of 354, then, two *natales* are recorded for Constantine: 27 February, commemorating his birthday; and 25 July, commemorating his elevation to caesar. Similarly, we find two *natales* for Constantius, referring to parallel events: on 7 August and 8 November.

Ludi Votivi

In the Calendar of 354, the anniversaries of members of the reigning dynasty are regularly recorded with a second day of votive games, or *ludi votivi*—a temporal extension that distinguishes the *natales* of the ruling emperor and his family from those of earlier *divi*. No evidence tells us whether this practice goes back to the third century or further.[56]

Nine anniversaries associated with the house of Constantine are recorded with a subsequent day of *ludi votivi*.[57] Five commemorate the birth or accession of a caesar: the four *natales imperii* noted above, plus the *natalis* of the birthday of Constantius's grandfather, Constantius Chlorus, on 31 March. The *adventus*, or arrival, ceremony appears prominent in this regard, for it too received an extra day of *ludi votivi*; it is recorded on three dates in the Calendar of 354: on 21 July, commemorating Constantine's entry into Rome; on 18 July, celebrating the decennial (315) and vicennial (326) of his rule; and on 29 October, celebrating his victory over Maxentius (312). His ceremonial departure, *Profectio Divi*, in 315 is recorded on 27 September.[58]

55. Fink, Hoey, and Snyder 1940, p. 180, col. 2.16. For honors to the caesars at Lugdunum, see Fishwick, "Provincial Ruler Worship," pp. 1246–1249, who suggests that such honors were dropped after this period but acknowledges that no evidence exists to support this view.

56. Degrassi 1963, pp. 374ff.; Stern 1953, pp. 73ff.

57. Six of these explicitly record *ludi votivi* on the day following the celebration. For 21 July (*Adventus Divi C.*) and 31 March (*Natalis Constantii [Chlori]*), only the word *ludi* appears on the following day, but the adjective *votivi* should be added for 22 July and 1 April because it was probably omitted due to scribal error. The notation *ludi votivi* after 27 September (*Profectio Divi*) is probably also a scribal error; see Stern 1953, pp. 71–74; and Degrassi 1963, pp. 487, 434, and 515.

58. See Degrassi 1963, p. 514; and note 57 above.

Two additional notations refer to anniversaries of Constantine but lack the distinguishing *ludi votivi*: *Evictio Tyranni* on 28 October, referring to the defeat and departure of Maxentius from Rome; and *Fugato Licinio* on 3 July, commemorating Constantine's defeat of Licinius in 324. Since neither of these is technically a victory, because not involving a foreign enemy, the omission of *ludi votivi* is explicable; nonetheless, these notations in the Calendar highlight its Roman provenance.

Imperial Anniversaries Established by Earlier Emperors

As noted, the victory celebrations of earlier dynasties were not generally retained in Roman calendars. A few exceptions do exist, however. The *Lorio*, a holiday established by Hadrian to commemorate the adoption of Antoninus Pius as caesar, is recorded on 25 February. Its appearance may derive from the contemporary importance of the role of caesar, as the Codex-Calendar documents.[59] The *ludi Augustales*, established by Augustus, also survived but were reduced to a single day, 12 October. The retention of this festival is attributable to the unique significance of Augustus for all subsequent imperial dynasties. The Augustan role may also explain the survival of the *ludi Palatini*, noted on 17–19, 21–22 January, which are thought to have been established after the death of Augustus.[60] The *ludi Iovi Liberatori*, recorded on 13–18 October, probably represent a victory celebration of some earlier dynasty.[61] The *Equitum Romanorum probatio*, on 15 July, is a traditional parade of knights, which, although revived under Augustus, did not appear in first-century calendars. Its celebration in the fourth century can be best explained by its inclusion in the imperial cult.[62]

The Imperial Cult in the Fourth Century

The imperial cult, focusing as it did on the ruling emperor and his family, was constantly being revised and reinvented—as the corrections in the Calendar to eliminate all memory of the sons of Constantine except

59. See the *Natales Caesarum* discussion in Chapter 2; and Stern 1953, pp. 87ff.; and Degrassi 1963, p. 416.

60. Degrassi 1963, pp. 400–401.

61. Ibid., p. 520.

62. Stern 1953, pp. 362–363, analyzes the dates for Constantine's entries into Rome and demonstrates the error of Mommsen's view that this festival was the occasion for the ceremony mentioned in Zosimus *Hist. Nova* 2.29.5 as a *pátrios heorté*, an ancestral or traditional ceremony. The association with the emperor rather than the army is suggested by the Augustan reforms. See Scullard 1981, pp. 164–165.

for the sole victorious survivor, Constantius II, demonstrate. Therefore, one would expect the imperial festivals and cult in the Calendar of 354 to reflect especially the views of Constantius II. And since Constantius II largely followed the policy of his father as regards imperial cult, the Calendar also reflects Constantine's views.

The famous reply of Constantine to the town of Hispellum, in Umbria (*CIL* 11.5265), succinctly sketches his official policy. The rescript records the establishment of a new provincial imperial cult center with a temple of the Second Flavian (i.e., Constantinian) house. A *flamen* (priest) and games were established, but the dedication explicitly stipulated that *superstitio* be absent from this cult. While the precise meaning of this word in this context is open to interpretation,[63] Constantine's continued support for imperial cult, along with its *ludi* and *circenses*, is indisputable. His coins, too, continue to show his support for the cult by carrying the legend *Genio Augusti*.[64] At the same time, however, Constantine did attempt to prohibit those aspects offensive to Christians—which meant, first and foremost, the performance of public sacrifice.[65]

Constantius pursued this same policy, continuing imperial support for aspects of the imperial cult redefined in an increasingly secular and civic way while attempting to remove its pagan religious backbone. The distinction was at times a fine one. For example, Constantius allowed the *consecratio* of his father—and his own as well. The continuation of this pagan rite, which traditionally indicated the elevation of the emperor to the status of a god in some pagan Olympus, was clearly problematic in a Christian context.[66] The Christian Eusebius, for one, redefined this ceremony to include Constantine's ascent to a Christian heaven, using language that comes close to implying cult.[67] Yet one thing was definite: pagan sacrifice was not allowed as part of the *consecratio*. This restriction and subsequent attempts at redefinition allowed Constantius and certain Christians to view the *consecratio* ceremony, and imperial cult in general, more as a secular than a religious honor.[68] This shift was due in part to Constantius's beliefs and in part to pressure from Christian leaders who,

63. For discussion and bibliography, see M. Salzman, "*Superstitio* and the Persecution of Pagans in the *Codex Theodosianus*," *Vigiliae Christianae* 41 (1987): 172–188.

64. *RIC* 7, pp.637; 643, nos. 1.1, 1.2; 698.

65. See Chapter 5.

66. L. Cerfaux and J. Tondriau, *Un concurrent du christianisme: Le culte des souverains dans la civilisation gréco-romaine*, Bibliothèque de théologie, 3d ser., vol. 5 (Tournai, 1957), p. 379.

67. See Eusebius *Vita Constantini* 1.9, 4.40; and discussion by S. MacCormack, *Art and Ceremony in Late Antiquity* (Berkeley and Los Angeles, 1981), pp. 117–121.

68. Price, *Rituals and Power*, pp. 125–126.

after Constantine, assumed an increasingly hostile stance vis-à-vis the imperial cult.

The imperial cult flourished in the fourth century, as evidenced by the reformed cult of the Second Flavians in Rome, North Africa, and throughout the provinces.[69] At Rome, the head priest, or *pontifex Flavialis*, served the Temple of the Flavian Gens (*Templum gentis Flaviae*);[70] in Africa, Christians are recorded as holding the office of the *Flamen Perpetuus* of the imperial cult into the late fourth century;[71] and in early-fifth-century Novempopulania, Gaul, an imperial priest, who was also a Christian, demonstrated traditional civic beneficence by giving a *venatio* in the public theater.[72] The position of civil priest continued until the end of the fourth century; a law of 386 only bans the office of *"chief* civil priest" for Christians, and inadvertently attests the vitality of the imperial cult:

> In obtaining the office of chief civil priest [*archierosyna*], that person shall be considered preferable who has performed the most services for his municipality, and who has not, however, withdrawn from the cult of the temples by his observance of Christianity. Indeed it is unseemly, and further, that We may speak more truly, it is illicit, for the temples and the customary rites of the temples to belong to the care of those persons whose conscience is imbued with the true doctrine of divine religion, and who ought properly to flee such compulsory public service, even if they were not prohibited by law from performing it.[73]

Constantius continued the provincial assemblies as well, even though their principal role was the celebration of games at a temple dedicated to Rome and the emperor. Delegates to the provincial assembly were called *sacerdotes provinciae*. Both these offices and the assemblies, needless to say, had inherently pagan associations.[74]

69. Cerfaux and Tondriau, *Concurrent du christianisme*, pp. 379ff.

70. *CIL* 6.1690, 6.1691; E. Kornemann, "Zur Geschichte der antiken Herrscherkulte," *Klio* 1 (1901): 51–146; *RE*, suppl. 4, s.v. "Kaiserkult," col. 852.

71. *CIL* 8.450, 8.10516. See too Aurelius Victor *Caesars* 40.28; and in *Dictionnaire d'archéologie chrétienne*, vol. 5 (Paris, 1923), s.v. "*Flamines* Chrétiens," pp. 1643ff.

72. Diehl, *ILCV*, no. 391, dates this inscription to the fifth century on the basis of its lettering; E. Le Blant, *Inscriptions chrétiennes de la Gaulle antérieures au VIII siècle* (Paris, 1956–1965), 1:xcv and no. 595A dates it to the reign of Honorius (393–423).

73. *C.Th.* 12.1.112 (A.D. 386), Valentinian and Valens, Augg. to Florentius; translation by C. Pharr, *The Theodosian Code and Novels and the Sirmondian Constitutions* (Princeton, 1952).

74. *C.Th.* 12.1.46 (A.D. 358). See A. H. M. Jones, *The Roman Economy: Studies in Ancient Economic and Administrative History*, ed. P. A. Brunt (Oxford, 1974), p. 33; J. A. O. Larson, "The Position of Provincial Assemblies in the Government and Society of the Late Roman Empire," *CP* 29 (1934): 209–224. Constantius's issuance of mandates directly to municipal *curiae* may represent an attempt to bypass the provincial assemblies, but his motivation appears to be a desire for more direct control over the cities.

In sum, the imperial cult in the West—its festivals, rites, and institutions—was continued by Christian rulers until the end of the fourth century. The Christian emperors, however, and Constantius especially, altered their formulation of how the emperor related to divinity. Constantius followed the policy established by Constantine, who had in turn followed that set by Diocletian—for it was in conjunction with Diocletian's reorganization of government that the imperial cult was promulgated as a "sacred" monarchy. Constantius fostered the view (found since Diocletian, if not earlier in the third century) that it was not so much that the emperor himself was divine as that he was under divine protection and a channel through which divine favor could be secured for the state.[75] (Indeed, even in the early empire the emperor was at times viewed as "chosen by the gods.")[76] Constantius followed Diocletian too in attempting to enhance the emperor's position by removing him from the human sphere and imposing formal court ceremonial and insignia. At the same time, he centered the cult on specific moments in his or his father's rule by celebrating not only their imperial victories but also the *adventus* and *profectio* of Constantine—occasions on which he could both demonstrate his relationship to the divine Constantine and reestablish ties between himself and his subjects.[77]

These general lines of the development of imperial cult can be seen in the Calendar of 354. The number of festivals that celebrate moments in the life of the ruling emperor or his father—*adventus, profectio, natales*—reflect the attempt to focus on the living emperor as a conduit to higher divinities. Under Constantius, however, these ceremonies took on a very particular interpretation, especially if they took place in Rome. And Rome, after all, was where this Calendar came from.

In discussing Ammianus's well-known account of the visit to Rome by Constantius in A.D. 357, an *adventus* that assumes almost mythic dimensions, S. MacCormack summarizes well those aspects of Constantius's imperial cult that appear in the Calendar:

> What becomes clear from Ammianus' account is that [ceremonial] arrival [*adventus*], when it took place in Rome, the "mother city of trophies" of Themistius, had the special significance of expressing imperial victory.

75. See W. Seston, "Jovius et Herculius ou l'*épiphanie* des tétrarques," *Historia* 1 (1950): 257–266; W. Seston, *Dioclétien et la tétrarchie* (Paris, 1946), pp. 193ff., on Diocletian's divine status; and significant criticism by N. Baynes, *JRS* 38 (1948): 109–113, and 25 (1935): 84. This is a very abbreviated discussion of a complex topic. I indicate here only the outlines of Diocletian's policy relevant to discussion of Constantius's approach.

76. J. R. Fears, *Princeps a Diis Electus,* Papers and Monographs of the American Academy in Rome, no. 26 (Rome, 1977); MacCormack, *Art and Ceremony,* p. 106 and n. 66.

77. MacCormack, *Art and Ceremony,* pp. 106ff.

The fourth century was the time when, on the coinage, imperial titles such as UBIQUE VICTOR had become frequent. They expressed on a general level what *adventus* in Rome expressed on a particular level: the universal victoriousness of the emperor, a theoretical quality upon which concrete historical victories were based; not, as formerly, the other way round. Victory . . . was an innate imperial quality. . . . Under Constantius . . . *adventus*, especially in Rome, became the vehicle for expressing within the walls of the city imperial victory, both universal and particular.[78]

Ammianus explicitly denied that the 357 *adventus* could be viewed as a triumph, since Constantius had merely won a civil war.[79] Themistius, in contrast, openly played on the idea of this defeat of the Alamanni and Magnentius and Decentius when, for example, he envisioned himself offering a wreath of victory to Constantius.[80] Ammianus's denial is rhetorical, not historical; the occasion, the coinage, and the Calendar—in which imperial victories and *adventus* into Rome are so frequently recorded—indicate that victory was indeed intended to be viewed as an inherent imperial quality.[81]

Moreover, as the Calendar shows, Constantius's emphasis on the *adventus* ceremony was exceptional. Although inclusion of the *adventus* and *profectio* of the ruling emperor was apparently normal calendrical practice, the recording of such ceremonies for past emperors is not otherwise attested.[82] Thus, the notation of Constantine's *adventus* and *profectio* suggests a special emphasis on imperial victory, viewed as an inherent imperial quality, as well as on the *pietas* of a son. In addition, this ceremony was congenial to Constantius's Christianity: since it focused on the actions of the living emperor, it avoided aspects of imperial cult that would be more problematic for Christians.

Perhaps the most obvious indication of the ongoing reformulation of imperial cult to meet the current emperor's needs is the omission from the Calendar of offending members of the Constantinian house. The flexibility of imperial cult helps to explain its survival in new political

78. Ibid., pp. 41–42.
79. See my discussion of Ammianus's account in Chapter 5.
80. Themistius *Or.* 3.41A, 40A–C, 41C–D, 42B, ed. Dindorf (Leipzig, 1832). Cf. J. Straub, *Vom Herrscherideal in der Spätantike* (Stuttgart, 1939; repr. Darmstadt, 1964), pp. 175–204.
81. Victoria and the legend "VICTORIAE DD AUGGQ NN" appear on the coinage of Constantius (*RIC* 8, pp. 34–35), and from Rome (pp. 243ff.). It is noteworthy how frequent are dedications to Constantius as "Victor ac triumfator", as, for example, *ILS* 730–732. See also J. R. Fears, "The Theology of Victory at Rome: Approaches and Problems," *ANRW* II 17.2 (Berlin, 1981), pp. 736–826.
82. S. Eitrem and L. Amundsen, *Papyri Osloenses* 3.1, no. 77 (Oslo, 1936), pp. 45–55.

and religious circumstances; so too a ceremony like *adventus*, which provided a "vocabulary for the encounter of different types of persons, and for their convergence into one group," was of obvious value, for it provided a critical means of cementing social relations within the city and between ruler and ruled.[83] These positive social and communal benefits should not downplay the powerful personal religious significance that imperial cult retained in the fourth century; the imperial cult was omnipresent, not only at public festivals and in imperial temples, but also in civic centers and individuals' homes. The emperor's aid was invoked at private ceremonies, as, for example, prior to marriage, and in moments of extreme crisis.[84] Imperial cult "was not simply a game to be played in public. . . . Private imperial images were not out of keeping with the [private] significance of the imperial cult."[85]

It is the importance of the imperial cult that explains its dominant presence in the Calendar of 354.[86] But imperial cult was so significant because it received the attention and funding of the emperor. Imperial favor also emerges as a key factor in explaining the popularity and importance of the next group of festivals and cults, those celebrated by *ludi* and *circenses*.

GROUP 2. FESTIVALS AND CULTS CELEBRATED WITH *LUDI* AND *CIRCENSES*: THE MOST IMPORTANT CULTS

The number and frequency of *ludi* and *circenses* are extremely reliable indicators of the importance of festivals and holidays recorded in the Calendar; hence, we can easily deduce which cults were most important in the fourth century. In the first rank, in descending order, are Jupiter, Sol, Mars, Hercules, and Salus, all recipients of imperial support or attention in the period after Aurelian. Imperial support was demonstrated

83. MacCormack, *Art and Ceremony*, pp. 42–43.
84. See Price, *Rituals and Power*, pp. 117–120, for evidence.
85. Ibid., p. 120. Contra is the view of Fishwick, "Provincial Ruler Worship," pp. 1202–1253.
86. On imperial cult in the fourth century, see M. De Dominicis, "Un intervento legislativo di Costantino in materia religiosa (Nota à *CIL* XI.5265)," *Revue internationale des droits de l'antiquité* 10 (1963): 199–211; T. Pekáry, "Der römische Bilderstreit," *Frühmittelalterliche Studien* 3 (1969): 13–26; and, in general, P. Batiffol and L. Bréhier, *Les survivances du culte impérial romain* (Paris, 1920); Cerfaux and Tondriau, *Concurrent du christianisme*, pp. 408ff.; F. Taeger, *Charisma. Studien zur Geschichte des antiken Herrscherkultes* (Stuttgart, 1957–1960), 2:678ff.

in the building of temples or altars and the financing of commemorations of their dedications; in the choice of iconography and legends for imperial coins and medallions; in the establishment of certain priesthoods; and, finally, in the inclusion of holidays in the official Roman calendar.

To achieve the status of a public holiday or festival, a celebration required public monies. In the late empire, such disbursements required the approval of the emperor or his administrator;[87] this meant, in effect, that only those cults with imperial sanction could be publicly celebrated and so appear in the official calendar.

Imperial control over the calendar took many forms. The emperor's approval was necessary for a new cult to be incorporated into the calendar, although technically the Senate and the people had to acquiesce in its adoption as well.[88] The scheduling of festivals for both new and old cults, moreover, required governmental affirmation; in the 160s, for example, the proconsul at Ephesus responded to a community request and, following the precedent of earlier proconsuls, issued an edict indicating which days were to be festival days.[89] Occasionally we hear of emperors restricting the numbers of holidays; Constantine, for instance, forbade the institution of new festivals by judges.[90]

Imperial control over the pagan cults attested in the Calendar is noticeable as well in the appointment of priests—those people responsible for the performance of appropriate ritual acts in conjunction with the public holidays and festivals—and in the administration of the priestly colleges, which in 354 included the pontifices, augurs, the men designated *sacris faciundis*, and the *epulones*.[91] These positions, in the fourth century held generally by Roman aristocrats, were considered a public honor and a duty.[92] Three other bodies, practically speaking, were included in the pontifical college as well: the Vestal Virgins; the *flamines*, or priests of certain named gods; and the *Rex Sacrorum*. Although inscriptional evidence attests to the survival of the Vestal Virgins and the *flamines* of certain cults (notably the imperial cult and the cult of Sol) into

87. Symmachus *Rels.* 6, 8, 9 esp.; *CJ* 3.12.3.

88. Wissowa 1912, p. 406.

89. *SIG*, no. 867; *AE* (1933), no. 123.

90. *CJ* 3.12.3 (A.D. 323) appears in part motivated by a desire to restrain the powers of the judges.

91. The pontifices and augurs traditionally were of more distinguished status; the other members inside each college were of equal rank.

92. The position of a priest of a pagan public cult or of the imperial cult is viewed positively by contemporary writers, e.g. Firmicus Maternus *Mathesis* 4.21.5; cf. Artemidoros Ὀνειροκριτικά 2.30, ed. R. Pack (Leipzig, 1963). The last attested augur at Rome appears in A.D. 390 (*CIL* 6.503 = *ILS* 4151).

the fourth century, the *Rex Sacrorum* and the *flamines* of lesser deities are not attested after the second century.[93] At the head of the colleges of priests was the emperor, who, although a Christian, held the position and title of *pontifex maximus* into the fourth century, until the reign of Gratian. Even in the appointment of priests, imperial control was exercised; so, for example, in the 170s the priest of Hercules Augustus in Apulum, Dacia, was installed by the governor, and other priests in Smyrna by the emperor and the Roman Senate.[94] When the Emperor Julian set out to reform paganism, he did so in part by attempting to alter the requirements and attitudes of the priests.[95]

In Rome in 354, state funding was necessary for the upkeep of temples, the purchase of ceremonial garlands, incense, and sacrificial animals, and general cult and ceremonial expenses.[96] Not until 382 was there a significant interruption in state funding.[97] Public monies were also required for *ludi* and *circenses*, although in some cases the magistrates in charge of the specific set of games would have to contribute as well. Thus, the six public games of the early empire (Table 1), which were among the most popular festivals in Group 2, were considered great national holidays and were held at state expense, while in the fourth century the magistrates—the consul and urban prefects—also contributed significant funding for the games to Ceres and Apollo. In all cases, though, the celebration of the cult, including the games to honor Jupiter, the Magna Mater, and Flora, as well as Ceres and Apollo, required imperial monies, and that meant imperial approval, whether implicit or explicit.[98]

Because the Roman government intervened in the financing and organization of holiday and festival celebrations in ways both small and large, imperial approval (albeit indirect) is implied by the presence of a cult in the public civic calendar of Rome. I would therefore argue that

93. The *Rex Sacrorum* is attested under Trajan (*CIL* 14.3604 = *ILS* 1043); for further discussion, see Ogilvie, *The Romans and Their Gods*, pp. 108ff.; Wissowa 1912, pp. 23, 103, 504ff. The three major *flamines* were devoted to Jupiter, Mars, and Quirinus; the twelve minor *flamines* are not well attested. There were also *flamines* for the imperial cult and for Sol (e.g., *CIL* 11.5265). If the *Rex Sacrorum* and these minor *flamines* continued into the fourth century, they left no trace.

94. *CIL* 3.7751; *IGR* 4.1431.

95. Julian *Ep.* 22, ed. W. C. Wright (London and Cambridge, 1913–1923). See A. Wardman, "Pagan Priesthoods in the Later Roman Empire," in *Pagan Gods and Shrines in the Roman Empire*, ed. M. Henig and A. King, Oxford University Commission for Archaeology, Monograph no. 8 (Oxford, 1986), pp. 257–262.

96. Wissowa 1912, pp. 406ff.

97. See Chapter 6.

98. Any discussion of the fourth-century popularity of the cult of Magna Mater and to some extent that of Ceres should, however, take into account the private rites of initiation associated with these cults. See pp. 164–169, 176ff.

imperial support or preference was the critical factor in promoting either acceptance of a new cult, such as that of Sol Invictus, or continuation of a traditional one, such as that of Jupiter. Imperial patronage was all the more effective if it was sustained over time by several rulers.

Jupiter, Hercules, Mars, Sol

The support of the tetrarchic rulers for Jupiter, Hercules, Mars, and Sol is well documented. Diocletian and Maximian, by adopting the titles Jovius and Herculius, found a way of intimately relating their imperial office to these national deities.[99] Both deities appear on the coinage of these emperors, as does Mars, a favorite of the army who was also particularly favored by Maxentius and Constantine.[100] Constantius Chlorus, who had been "carried to the councils of the gods" in the chariot of Sol, was devoted especially to Sol Invictus.[101]

Constantine inherited both this devotion to Sol (through his father, Constantius Chlorus) and the association with Hercules (through his father-in-law, Maximian). "It was during the rule of Constantine (306–337) that the cult of Deus Sol Invictus reached extraordinary heights, so that his reign was even spoken of as Sun emperorship."[102] Constantine struck coins with representations of Sol Invictus until 323, and with Mars Conservator and Mars Propugnator until 316;[103] in his early years, he struck coins to Jupiter Conservator Augustorum as well.[104] In my opinion, the impact of this recent imperial attention helps to explain the prominence of these four cults in the Calendar of 354.

The development of the cult of Sol Invictus is perhaps the most in-

99. Seston, "Jovius et Herculius"; and idem, *Dioclétien*, pp. 193ff.

100. For Mars on the coinage of Diocletian, see *RIC* 5.2, p. 245, nos. 249–250; p. 222, no. 2; p. 231, nos. 113–114; for Maximian, see *RIC* 6, p. 130, nos. 93, 96, 100; p. 170, nos. 59, 60, 62–63. Maxentius honored Hercules, Jupiter, and especially Mars, as *RIC* 6, pp. 345, 347, 379, 423, and *CIL* 6.33856 indicate. Portrait bust types of Mars appear for Constantius and Galerius, as observed in *RIC* 6, p. 144. For Constantine's coins to Mars, see *RIC* 7, p. 48, n. 2, and nos. 6–11, 25–26, from the mint of Rome (to A.D. 314); London: nos. 4, 24–25; Lyons: nos. 10–14; Trier: nos. 49–55, 177–183, 108–118 (to A.D. 316); Arles: nos. 23–29, 47: Ticinum: nos. 5, 6, 11–13, 18, 19.

101. *Pan. Lat.* 6(7).3 (A.D. 307), ed. E. Galletier (Paris, 1949–1955): "illius ad deorum concilia translati"; and *Pan. Lat.* 6(7).14; 7(6).8. Cf. MacCormack 1981, p. 109.

102. G. Halsberghe, *The Cult of Sol Invictus, EPRO*, no. 23 (Leiden, 1972), p. 167.

103. Ibid., p. 167. For Mars on coins, see note 100 above. Constantine's devotion to Sol Invictus is well attested; see *RIC* 6, pp. 111ff., for Rome; and *RIC* 7, pp. 392–393, nos. 368–377, and pp. 751–752, for types. According to P. Bruun (*RIC* 7, p. 48), Sol Invictus disappears only in A.D. 318–319.

104. *RIC* 6, Rome, p. 385, no. 282, dated A.D. 312–313; Aquileia, p. 309; Thessalonica, pp. 516–519, nos. 44c, 45, 47B, 52B.

teresting of this group, for it alone is new (i.e., post Julio-Claudian) to the Roman calendar. Four festivals or celebrations are recorded to honor Sol in the Calendar of 354. On 19–22 October the *ludi Solis* are noted, culminating with thirty-six circus races on the final day. These games are understood as one component of the religious reforms of Emperor Aurelian, instituted in 274 to unite Roman pagan cults under the banner of Deus Sol Invictus.[105] Aurelian had coins struck proclaiming Sol "Dominus Imperii Romani," the official deity of the Roman Empire. He also founded a new temple in Rome, whose *natalis* has been associated with the Calendar notation *Natalis Invicti* on 25 December. Although this dedication is uncertain, the unusually large number of circus races on this day indicates the importance of the holiday;[106] wrongly supposed to have been the winter solstice, the *Natalis Invicti* has been seen as having its Christian counterpart in the celebration of the birth of Christ.[107]

Aurelian's creation and dating of the *ludi Solis* represent the continuity of Roman festival traditions through incorporation into a new cult. The *ludi Solis* were held on the same day as the ancient festival of the *Armilustrium*, a traditional lustration of arms (*ambitus lustri*) by the *Salii*, the priests of Mars. The *ambitus lustri* was often confused by Romans with the *pompa* (ceremonial procession) in the Circus Maximus, associated with the old Roman Sol;[108] by placing his festival on this date, then, Aurelian linked the new Deus Sol Invictus with not only the priestly *Salii* but also the old Roman Sol of the Circus Maximus.

Another holiday, too, the *[Natalis] Solis et Lunae,* celebrated on 28 August with circus races, may owe its popularity at least in part to Aurelian's attempts to associate the new Deus Sol Invictus with the traditions of the old Roman Sol, whose temple in the Circus Maximus this festival is assumed to commemorate.[109] Tertullian attests that the Cir-

---

105. Halsberghe, *Cult of Sol Invictus,* p. 144; L. Homo, *Essai sur le règne de l'empereur Aurelien* (Paris, 1904), pp. 122–124, 186.

106. Wissowa 1912, p. 367, suggested that the *Natalis Invicti* be associated with the dedication of the temple of Sol Invictus established by Aurelian. In the Calendar of 354, however, the term *natalis,* while it may indicate a temple dedication, has a less specific meaning; see notes 12 and 22 above. Hence, Wissowa's identification is not convincing.

107. Halsberghe, *Cult of Sol Invictus,* pp. 122–126, 186ff.

108. Q. Schofield, "Sol in the Circus Maximus," *Latomus* 102 (1969): 640–650, observes: "Far from indicating a change of thought on the part of the Romans, we believe this later festival (*ludi Solis*) shows how immediately the *Armilustrium* and the *Salii* were connected with Sun-worship" (p. 644). Concerning the confusion between the *pompa* and *ambitus lustri,* see J. W. Crous, "Florentiner Waffenpfeiler und *Armilustrium,*" *MDAIR* 48 (1933): 1–119; Varro *De Ling. Lat.* 5.153; *TLL,* s.v. "Pompa," "Ambitus."

109. Tacitus *Ann.* 15.74: " . . . Soli, cui est vetus aedes apud Circum." Scullard 1981, p. 182.

cus Maximus was dedicated primarily to the old Roman Sol; and in the fourth-century Catalogue of the Region of Rome (section XIV of the Codex-Calendar) the deity's temple is noted in the middle part of the Circus Maximus.[110] The commemoration with circus races, however, appears only in the fourth-century Calendar, where the holiday's popularity derives, in my view, to some extent from Aurelian's successful religious program, which built on earlier Roman traditions of Sol in the Circus Maximus. These associations also fed the popular theology revolving around the Circus and the seasons that arose in the late empire.

One final notation in the Calendar of 354 refers to ceremonies held in honor of Sol: *Colossus coronatur*, on 6 June. This commemoration can be identified with the colossal statue of Nero that Vespasian had dedicated to Sol at the opening of the Colosseum.[111] It therefore seems likely that the ceremonial crowning of this statue in the fourth century was associated with Sol, and perhaps with the imperial cult as well, since the ties between these two cults were quite strong, especially in the early years of the century.[112]

The Calendar reinforces other evidence for the enduring vitality of the cult of Sol. The college of his priests, *pontifices Dei Solis*, continued to enroll the most important Roman aristocrats into the last quarter of the century.[113] The author of the *Expositio Totius Mundi et Gentium*, dated to 350, says of the Romans: "And indeed they honor the gods, especially Jupiter and Sol."[114] The cult of Sol had so many devotees that Augustine considered it necessary to preach against them.[115]

Although much of the popularity of Sol can be attributed directly to imperial support, some of the cult's appeal derives also from its ability

110. Tertullian *De Spect.* 8.1ff. For the Catalogue of the Regions of Rome, see Valentini and Zucchetti I, 1940, pp. 132, 178. This location assumes that the fragment of the Praeneste calendar belongs here, as was argued by Wissowa 1912, p. 316, n. 3; and Degrassi 1963, p. 503. (Contra was the view of Latte 1960, p. 232, n. 4.) The temple may also be associated with the Severan attentions to the moon; see R. E. A. Palmer, "Severan Ruler-Cult and the Moon in the City of Rome," *ANRW* II 16.2, pp. 1085–1120.

111. Some scholars have identified this statue with the *signum dei* dedicated by the Senate to Constantine in A.D. 313; *Pan. Lat.* 9(12).25, ed. Galletier. So, for example, Halsberghe, *Cult of Sol Invictus*, p. 167, n. 3; and Cerfaux and Tondriau, *Concurrent du christianisme*, p. 379, n. 4, observe that Constantine, following Aurelian's precedent, was seen as "un double du Soleil." The statue described by the Panegyricist of 313, however, has no particular solar attributes; it is more likely a statue of Victory given its *scutum* and *corona*.

112. Halsberghe, *Cult of Sol Invictus*, p. 167.

113. Cf. *CIL* 6.1778 (A.D. 387); Wissowa 1912, p. 367.

114. *Expositio Totius Mundi et Gentium*, in Valentini and Zucchetti I, 1940, p. 265: "Colunt autem et deos ex parte Iovem et Solem."

115. Augustine *Sermo de Vetere Testamento* 12 (*CCL* 41, 1961); *Enarratio in Psalmum* 25, esp. chap. 2 (*CCL* 38–40, 1956).

to incorporate other deities into its generalized system. So it seemed to the Emperor Julian.[116] Macrobius's statement of this syncretism in the *Saturnalia,* while late and somewhat hyperbolic, is indicative of the beliefs of the age. Praetextatus states: "Certainly, it is not empty superstition but divine reason that makes them [the poets] relate almost all the gods—at any rate the celestial gods—to the sun."[117] This view coincides with Praetextatus's known affiliations: inscriptions attest that he was a devotee of Sol Invictus and of numerous other pagan cults. His willingness to embrace so many of the pagan deities makes him the appropriate person to have repaired, in 367, the *Porticus Deorum Consentium* in the Forum, the *porticus* that housed the twelve gods of the Roman pantheon.[118]

Through its syncretism, the cult of Sol demonstrates one of the great strengths of late Roman paganism. Yet not all cults were absorbed into that of Sol; many were merely associated with it, thereby receiving certain positive benefits.[119] In the West, Sol had always been linked with Apollo, whose cult—celebrated at the *ludi Apollinares*—is in my view the subject of the July illustration in the Calendar (Fig. 38). Indeed, around this time, in 356–359, the urban prefect, Memmius Vitrasius Orfitus, dedicated a temple to Sanctus Apollo in Rome.[120]

The association of Sol with Jupiter Optimus Maximus and with Sarapis is attested in Rome at the end of the third century by a marble altar dedicated by the Roman aristocrat Scipio Orfitus.[121] This connection is not surprising; all three divinities had received imperial support in the late third and early fourth centuries. Medallions of Maximinus and Constantine exist, for example, that depict the emperor on one side and Sol holding a Sarapis head on the other.[122] Both cults, moreover, appear in the list of festivals in the Calendar of 354 (see Tables 2 and 3).

116. Julian *Or.* 4, ed. Wright.

117. Macrobius *Sat.* 1.17.2: "Quod omnes paene deos, dumtaxat qui sub caelo sunt, ad solem (poetae) referunt, non vana superstitio sed ratio divina commendat"; trans. P. V. Davies (New York, 1969).

118. See *CIL* 6.102 = *ILS* 4003 for the *porticus;* see also *CIL* 6.1778, 1779 = *ILS* 1259.

119. Julian's unsuccessful attempt to associate the Greek Helios-Mithras with Sol is not directly relevant to our discussion, since it occurs after the Calendar of 354.

120. *CIL* 6.1.45 = *ILS* 3222.

121. *CIL* 6.402 = *SIRIS* 394. The iconography of this altar fits well with the imperial associations of Sarapis, discussed below. The altar apparently reused a triumphal scene, and the main figure, in a general's cuirass, enters Rome in triumph on the back of a bull. This is appropriate iconography for the cult of Jupiter Dolichenius as well. See W. Helbig, *Führer durch die öffentlichen Sammlungen klassischer Altertümer in Rom,* vol. 2, pt. 4 (Tübingen, 1966), pp. 226–228, no. 1421.

122. Cohen, *Méd.* 7 for Constantinian medallions, p. 288, no. 507; for those of Maximinus see p. 158, nos. 157–158, 160–161.

I have discussed the cult of Sol at some length because its success elucidates the appeal and importance of cults listed in Group 2 (i.e., cults celebrated with *ludi* and *circenses*). Consistent imperial favor, especially during the period after Aurelian, was the single most salient factor in explaining the popularity of a cult or festival in Group 2. An additional element was the cult's ability to incorporate or be associated with other popular gods and cults.

Salus, Quirinus/Romulus, Roma Aeterna, Castor and Pollux

The factors of imperial support and association with a popular cult are relevant in explaining the appeal of several other cults in Group 2. A good example is provided by the cult of Salus (*Salus publica populi Romani*), one of the most prominent abstract virtues of cult life during the imperial period. In its original sense, *salus* meant safety and welfare, both private and public. It is the public form of *Salus publica populi Romani* that was deemed essential for the well-being of the state; consequently, the cult received considerable imperial support. *Salus publica populi Romani* was celebrated by the dedication of a temple to Salus, presumed to have been on the Quirinal Hill in Rome.[123] The dedication date of this temple has been associated with the *natalis* of *Salus publica*, recorded on 5 August in the Calendar of 354.[124] While the twenty-four circus races held on that day attest to the festival's contemporary popularity, even in the third-century *Feriale Duranum* its importance for the state was indicated, for then both circus races and an official sacrifice were required.[125] The festival also attracted imperial attention, as seen in the legends "Salus Rei Publicae" and "Salus et Spes Rei Publicae" on coins and medallions of both Constantine and Magnentius.[126]

The fourth-century cult of Salus was strengthened by its association with imperial cult. In the early republican period, Salus was linked with divine salvation and with the charismatic leader who brought about such

123. J. R. Fears, "The Cult of Virtues and Roman Imperial Ideology," *ANRW* II 17.2, pp. 827–948; Scullard 1981, pp. 170ff.

124. Degrassi 1963, pp. 492–493.

125. Ibid., p. 492; Fink, Hoey, and Snyder 1940, pp. 150–151, records: "o[b circenses Sa]lutares Salut[i b(ovem)] f(eminam)."

126. See *RIC* 7, p. 283, and *RIC* 7, Rome, p. 331, no. 298, for a bronze medallion under Constantine dated A.D. 328, with legend "Salus Rei Publicae"; and *RIC* 7, Rome, p. 328, no. 280, for a bronze medallion with the legend "Salus et Spes Rei Publicae." See too *RIC* 7, Lyons, p. 137, no. 235, for a bronze folles with Fausta depicted on the reverse. Magnentian examples include *RIC* 8, p. 136; p. 163, nos. 318–319, from Trier; and *RIC* 7, p. 328.

salvation.[127] Under the empire, Salus came to be associated with the imperial cult as *Salus Augustorum*, as inscriptions and dedications attest.[128] Tetrarchic coins used this legend to proclaim the stability of the regime, as did the coins of Licinius, Constantine, Decentius, and Magnentius.[129] Although Constantius preferred "Spes Rei Publicae" to "Salus," late-fourth-century emperors favored "Salus": the legend "Salus Rei Publicae" appears on the coins of Valentinian II, Theodosius, Arcadius, and Eugenius, where it was often also joined with the Christian *chi-rho* symbol.[130] The easy assimilation of this imperial virtue by Christians, indeed, contributed to its continued support; thus the *Feriale* from Capua, dated to 387, includes the *circenses Salutares* as one of the seven festivals still authorized by the Christian emperor.[131] Pagans, however, could still view Salus as the recipient of cult.

The fourth-century popularity of Quirinus/Romulus also reflects the importance of imperial support and attention. Quirinus/Romulus was often joined with Mars and Jupiter, the official protectors of the state, and had been identified with the emperor as well.[132] Building on these associations, Maxentius, for example, identified his new dynasty with Mars and Quirinus/Romulus and proclaimed that he was founding a "new Rome."[133] Maxentius's association of the cult of Quirinus/Romulus with that of Roma Aeterna, too, had precedents going back to the early empire.[134] Maxentius realized these ties in many ways: most graphic is a dedication to Mars Invictus Pater and to the founders of his eternal city ("aeternae urbis suae conditoribus") on the *Natalis Urbis*, 21 April.[135]

Maxentius's ideology did not prevent his defeat, but neither did his defeat put an end to this nexus of associations. Imperial attention to the cult of Quirinus/Romulus, especially in association with Roma Aeterna, continued into the fourth century. For example, medallions of *Urbs Roma*, beginning in 330 and continuing until the end of the century, depict the

127. See Fears, "Cult of Virtues," pp. 860ff.

128. Ibid., pp. 860ff.; *AE* (1962), no. 232.

129. *RIC* 6, pp. 144–145, for tetrarchic coins from Trier; *RIC* 6, p. 411, from Carthage for Constantine and Licinius; *RIC* 8, pp. 172, 576, for Decentius and Magnentius.

130. *RIC* 9, Rome, pp. 133–134, no. 64; the legend is joined with the *chi-rho* symbol on coins from Constantinople, nos. 48, 49, 72; and from Nicomedia, no. 28.

131. Degrassi 1963, pp. 282–283.

132. Scullard 1981, pp. 78–79; D. Porte, "Romulus-Quirinus, prince et dieu, dieu des princes. Etude sur le personnage de Quirinus et sur son évolution, des origines à Auguste," *ANRW* II 17.1 (Berlin, 1981), pp. 300–342.

133. See also my discussion of the illustration of March, Chapter 3.

134. Fink, Hoey, and Snyder 1940, pp. 102–126.

135. *CIL* 6.33856 = *ILS* 8935.

founding of Rome with the wolf suckling Romulus and Remus.[136] The addition of twenty-four circus races to the notation *Natalis dei Quirini* on 3 April suggests the contemporary importance of this day; and if the festival is also associated with the dedication of a temple in Rome, this event occurred after the middle of the first century A.D., since no such dedication appears in calendars from the first half of the century (see Table 2).

The appeal of Quirinus/Romulus was due in part to his association with Roma Aeterna, a goddess whose own popularity was facilitated by her ties to the emperor and imperial cult in the Western empire.[137] Although Roma was still accorded cult honors from pagans, she was also conceived as one of the electors to empire; it is in this guise that she appears, for example, in the Panegyric of A.D. 307, delivered at the festival in her honor, the *Natalis Urbis*.[138] This popular celebration, noted on 21 April with twenty-four circus races, is identified with the dedication of Hadrian's temple of Venus and Rome and with the establishment of the cult of Roma Aeterna, the version worshiped in the city.[139] Her cult was served by a priesthood, the *duodecemviri urbis Romae*, who are attested into the fourth century.[140] Although Christians rejected the *goddess* Roma Aeterna, the idea of the eternity of the city and the emperor was acceptable to all.[141] Hence, Roma Aeterna, like the imperial cult in general, served as a bridge between pagans and Christians. The Christian emperors Valentinian, Theodosius, and Arcadius showed their support by allowing the continued celebration of the *natales* of Roma and Constantinopolis even after the suppression of other pagan public festivals in 389.[142] The *Natalis Urbis* continued to be celebrated with games as late as 444.

The fourth-century emergence of Roma Aeterna as a preeminent

136. *RIC* 8, p. 236, n. 7; p. 282, nos. 336–337, from A.D. 337; medallions of Constantius II, pp. 287–288, nos. 390–391, 402–403 (dated A.D. 340–347); and on contorniates, Alföldi 1976, no. 92.

137. S. MacCormack, "Roma, Constantinopolis, the Emperor, and His Genius," *CQ* 25 (1975): 131–150.

138. C. Koch, "Roma Aeterna," in *Religio. Studien zu Kult und Glauben der Römer*, Erlanger Beiträge zur Sprach- und Kunstwissenschaft 7 (Nüremberg, 1960), pp. 142–175.

139. R. Mellor, "The Goddess Roma," *ANRW* II 17.2, pp. 950–1030; and Athenaeus *Deip.* 8.361E–F.

140. *CIL* 6.500 = *ILS* 4148 (A.D. 377); *CIL* 6.1700 = *ILS* 1249. Perhaps the *sacerdotes sacrae urbis* are also to be identified with the cult of Roma as well as of Vesta; see *CIL* 6.2136, 2137, 250.

141. Prosper *Epitoma Chronicon*, in *MGH, Auctores Antiquissimi* 9.1 (Berlin, 1892), pp. 343–499; F. Paschoud, *Roma Aeterna. Etude sur le patriotisme romain dans l'Occident latin à l'époque des grandes invasions*, Bibliotheca Helvetica Romana, no. 7 (Rome, 1967).

142. *C.Th.* 2.8.19.

deity owes much to imperial support and to the gradual dropping of other deities from imperial favor. Yet certain other deities or abstract concepts associated with Roma probably also benefited from imperial patronage—which may explain their presence in the Calendar. Abundance (*Abundantia*), so important in imperial ideology, is represented on various coin types with the legends "Annona Aug." and "Abundantia Aug."[143] *Annona Augusti* was even the recipient of dedications, both public—at Rome—and private.[144] It thus seems likely that the festival noted in the Calendar as the *Natalis annonis* was also associated with the worship of this virtue, which was seen as an imperial attribute and was the recipient of imperial favor.[145]

A combination of factors may explain the addition, after the mid first century, of a commemoration to Castor and Pollux, celebrated with circus races on 8 April.[146] Castor and Pollux are also depicted on the fourth-century contorniates.[147] This cult, associated with Rome's earliest foundations, has traditional and historical associations of great venerability; its contemporary appeal may also be attributed to its ancient association with the horse races, so popular in the late empire. The continued celebration of this cult would be further explained if it attracted imperial favor; I have found no specific evidence for such attention, however.

To sum up, sustained imperial support in the period after Aurelian emerges as the single most important factor in the great popularity of Group 2 cults, which included those of Mars, Hercules, Jupiter, and Sol Invictus. Even some of the more obscure Roman festivals and cults may be traced to imperial patronage in this period. For example, the dedication to Tiberinus by Diocletian and Maximianus probably accounts for a renewed interest in that cult, whose festival, appearing for the first time on 17 August in the fourth-century Calendar, was known as the *Tiberinalia*.[148] Imperial favor also helps to explain the popularity of the

143. *RIC* 5.1, pp. 132, 145, 180, 213, 230, for "Annona Aug." or "Augg."; *RIC* 5.2, p. 236, on coins of Diocletian from Rome. Similar ideology lies behind Constantinian coins from the Trier mint with the legend "Ubertas Augg."; *RIC* 7, p. 193, nos. 335–336.

144. *CIL* 6.22; *AE* (1925), no. 74; Fears, "Cult of Virtues," pp. 936ff.

145. Degrassi 1963, pp. 459–460, notes that no known temple dedication occurred on this day; cf. the fourth-century contorniates with "Annon-a-Augusta-Ceres" in Alföldi 1976, nos. 113–115. Similarly, the *Natalis chartis* is probably tied to imperial cult.

146. Perhaps it was in conjunction with this temple that in 359 the urban prefect Tertullus made the customary sacrifice to Castor at Ostia as Amm. Mar. 19.10.4 indicates.

147. Alföldi 1976, no. 45; and with Helena, no. 56.

148. *CIL* 6.773. I agree with Degrassi 1963, pp. 496–497, that Tiberinus and the *Tiberinalia* should not be equated with Portunus and the *Portunalia* recorded in the first-century calendars on this date, 17 August. See also note 186 below. For an opposing view, see Stern 1953, p. 96.

cults celebrated by *ludi* and *circenses* that were added to the Roman calendar after the mid first century A.D. (see Table 2). Significantly, other new cults that lacked sustained imperial support, even though they were popular and attested in private inscriptions, were not incorporated into the public calendar (e.g., those of Sabazius, Belenus, and Mithras).[149]

GROUP 3. FESTIVALS AND CULTS NOT CELEBRATED WITH *LUDI* AND *CIRCENSES*: OLD AND NEW CULTS

Of the festivals and cults commemorated without *ludi* and *circenses* (Group 3), approximately half date from the first half of the first century (Table 3), while the remainder were added after the middle of that century (Table 4). The appearance of many ancient festivals and cults of the Greco-Roman pantheon in Group 3 should not obscure the significance of imperial favor for this category as well: even though no *ludi* or *circenses* were involved in these celebrations, they still received public funding in 354. This meant that, at the very least, they had implicit state—or rather, imperial—approval, if not active support. Within this group, however, those cults that were preeminent did receive active imperial patronage in the years after Aurelian.

Ancient Festivals and Cults

A second factor in the popularity of the ancient festivals and cults, in addition to imperial support, is the conservative nature of the Roman calendar. The calendar embodies a veneration of tradition. Part of that respect for precedent focuses on Rome's early cults and rituals, as well as on its history and myth.

The Cult of Vesta. The cult of Vesta dominates the ancient cults in Group 3 (see Table 3), with four days given over to its celebrations and rituals in the fourth-century Calendar. More remarkable still, all four calendar notices indicate festivals or cult activities recorded in the calendars of the mid first century A.D., and two of those refer back to the early republican

---

149. Belenus, the protector of Aquileia, Italy, introduced to the Romans in the third century, was the recipient of rites by Diocletian; see *CIL* 5.732 = *ILS* 625; Wissowa 1912, p. 297. Sabazius was worshiped in Rome and Italy toward the middle of the third century; see *CIL* 6.31164 (A.D. 241); and Wissowa 1912, p. 376. Mithras (as opposed to Sol Invictus) was not officially embraced, except perhaps later under Julian; see Halsberghe, *Cult of Sol Invictus*, pp. 165–166, 117–121; and M. Simon, "Mithra et les empereurs," in *Mysteria Mithrae*, ed. U. Bianchi, *EPRO*, no. 80 (Leiden, 1979), pp. 411–425.

calendar.[150] This conservatism surely underscores the vitality of traditional public Roman paganism.

Vesta had always been viewed as essential for maintaining the very existence of the state, and her cult was of critical importance in insuring the *Salus publica* and the *Aeternitas imperii*. So, in the mid fourth century, the writer of the *Expositio Totius Mundi* notes: "There are, moreover, at Rome seven virgins, both noble and of the most distinguished class [i.e., the *clarissimate*]; these perform the sacred rites of the gods on behalf of the well-being of the state according to the custom of the ancients, and they are called the Virgins of Vesta."[151] Later in the century, this view is rearticulated by Symmachus in his *Third Relatio*, addressed to the emperor: "Their virginity has been dedicated to the public good [*Salus*]"; he continues: "What is the use of their dedicating a chaste body to the public good and supporting the everlasting empire with divine aid . . . ?"[152] The importance of the cult of Vesta for the well-being of the state explains its high status in Roman society and lies behind Symmachus's call for proper punishment of a Vestal Virgin whom a court had found guilty of adultery: "And therefore you will deem it worthy, once you consider the benefit to the state and the [nature of the] laws, that this evil deed, which until today throughout all the centuries has been most severely avenged, be suitably punished."[153]

Until the actions of Gratian in A.D. 382, the cult of Vesta had received imperial support and public monies: as Symmachus states in his *Third Relatio*, Constantius stripped nothing from the privileges of the Vestal Virgins.[154] Vesta's fourth-century status owed much to the cult's revival by several emperors in the preceding century. A long series of dedica-

---

150. The festival of the *Vestalia* on 9 June and the notation *Vesta cluditur* on 15 June = Q. ST. D. F., or *Quando stercum delatum fas,* were noted in republican calendars; see Degrassi 1963, pp. 467–471.

151. *Expositio Totius Mundi*, in Valentini and Zucchetti I, 1940, p. 264: "Sunt autem in Roma et virgines septem ingenuae et clarissimae, quae sacra deorum pro salute civitatis secundum antiquorum morem perficiunt, et vocantur virgines Vestae."

152. Symmachus *Rel.* 3.11, 3.14: "Saluti publicae dicata virginitas. . . . Quid iuvat saluti publicae castum corpus dicare et imperii aeternitatem caelestibus fulcire praesidiis?" For further bibliography on this *Relatio* and the controversy that provoked it, see Chapter 6, note 3. For the virgins of Vesta, see M. Beard, "The Sexual Status of Vestal Virgins," *JRS* 70 (1980): 26ff.; A.D. Nock, "A diis electa," *HTR* 23 (1930): 251–274. On Vesta as the most important religious symbol of Rome's eternity, see Mellor, "The Goddess Roma," p. 1020.

153. Symmachus *Ep.* 9.147: "Et ideo dignaberis, reipublicae utilitatem legesque considerans facinus cunctis usque ad hunc diem saeculi severissime vindicatum conpetenter ulcisci." We do not know if the traditional punishment—entombing the Vestal Virgin alive—was actually carried out in the fourth century.

154. Symmachus *Rel.* 3.7. The argument that Symmachus was essentially interested in the restoration of lands and subsidies to priests and the Vestal Virgins and that the

tions in the Atrium of Vesta in Rome, for example, dating mostly from 200–300, praises the services of several *Virgines Vestales Maximae* both to the state and to private individuals.[155] Apparently, the cult of Vesta in the Forum had regained its former importance by the second or third century, while that of Vesta on the Palatine (founded by Augustus and for the first two centuries the dominant cult) had become simply the household cult of the imperial family.[156] Given the importance of imperial support for paganism in general, it is not surprising that this shift has been traced to an emperor, Trajan, whose coins contain the legend "Vesta p[opuli] R[omani]. Quiritum."[157]

It therefore stands to reason that a public festival of the cult of Vesta should be recorded in the third-century military *Feriale Duranum*: after all, the army, like Vesta, was responsible for the survival of the state. For the 9 June *Vestalia*, the *Feriale* records a *supplicatio*, although the records of the *Fratres Arvales* indicate a blood sacrifice on this day. And indeed, the public cult act—be it a *supplicatio* or a sacrifice—in conjunction with the *Vestalia* is one of the oldest of Roman rites, noted in the earliest calendars of the republic.[158] These rites continued to be performed well into the fourth century—as the Calendar attests for 9 June.

The *Vestalia* and the cult of Vesta had a popular private side as well as an official public one. The *Vestalia* as the festival of millers and bakers is how this holiday is most prominently presented in the literary tradition; also well documented is the private household cult of Vesta, which was the responsibility of the women in the family.[159] The combination of public cult act and private devotion appears on two days in the Calendar of 354. The notation *Vesta aperit[ur]* on 7 June, although attested for the first time in a Roman calendar in the fourth century, indicates an ancient rite: on this day the inner sanctum of the Temple of Vesta was

---

concern of the pagan aristocracy lay in the erosion of the basis of their wealth is not convincing. For a forceful modern exposition of this erroneous view, see F. Paschoud, "Réflexions sur l'idéal religieux de Symmaque," *Historia* 14 (1965): 215–235, reiterated in his *Roma Aeterna*. For the compelling counterargument, see N. Baynes, "Review," *JRS* 36 (1946): 177ff.

155. Nock, "A diis electa"; list on pp. 270–274.

156. Fink, Hoey, and Snyder 1940, pp. 138ff. The disappearance of Vesta from the coin types of the third-century emperors does not, according to Nock, "A diis electa," pp. 251–174, indicate the diminution of her cult.

157. Fink, Hoey, and Snyder 1940, p. 139.

158. Degrassi 1963, pp. 467–468; and see note 156 above on the cult act.

159. See Roscher, *Lex.*, s.v. "Vesta," cols. 256–257, for the popular side of this cult; cols. 244–247 for its private side. See too Degrassi 1963, pp. 467ff.

opened, but only for women.[160] Thus commenced a period of activity, including the *Vestalia*, that ended on 15 June. On this final day the Calendar records *Vesta cluditur*, which corresponds to the ritual noted in first-century calendars as *Q.ST.D.F.*, or *Quando stercum delatum fas*,[161] when the Temple of Vesta was ritually cleansed, "the dirt swept away," and the temple closed. Once the impurities were thrown into the Tiber, the activity centered on the cult was over and the Vestal Virgins could return to their normal routine.

The final notation for Vesta, on 13 February—*Virgo Vestalis parentat*—is especially interesting, for it allows us to see another side of the cult's public activities. This is the first indication in a Roman calendar of the participation of the Vestal Virgins in the rites associated with the Manes, the ancestral spirits of the dead.[162] In his *Contra Symmachum*, Prudentius describes their role as follows: "And below the ground in presence of ghosts [the Vestals] cut the throats of cattle over the flames in propitiatory sacrifice, and mutter indistinct prayers"[163]—a passage that has been understood to describe the descent into an underground sanctuary (*subter humum*) and the performance of a bloody sacrifice of purification, as is appropriate for chthonic deities.[164]

The fourth-century *Virgo Vestalis parentat*, the equivalent of the first-century *Parentalia*, was the first of a series of days devoted to the worship of the Manes. During this period, groups of mourners would visit the tombs of dead relatives and perform *sacra privata*; it concluded with either the public festival of the *Feralia* on 21 February or the *Caristia* on 22 February, noted in the Calendar of 354 as the *Cara Cognatio*. The importance of the Manes and of private ancestral worship continued well past the fourth century. A church canon of 567 from Tours, for instance, reports attempts to put an end to such worship.[165] And the family feast and offering to the Lares on 22 February was probably transformed into the

160. Scullard 1981, pp. 148–150.

161. Noted in *Fasti Venusini* and *Fasti Tusculani*; see Degrassi 1963, p. 471.

162. The *Fasti Farnesiani* records only that the *Parentatio* begins on this day. The *Menologium Rusticum Colotianum* and *Fasti Vallenses* note only a *Parentalia* in the month of February. For further discussion, see Scullard 1981, pp. 74ff.

163. Prudentius *Contra Symm.* 2, vv. 1106–1107ff.: "Et quia subter humum lustrales testibus umbris / in flammam iugulant pecudes et murmura miscent?" trans. H. J. Thomson, vol. 2 (Cambridge, 1949–1953).

164. Stern 1953, p. 105; Macrobius's reference to this month, *Sat.* 1.13.3, remarks only the lustration to the Manes. The *Parentalia* is the title of Book 3 of the *Opuscula Magni Ausonii*, ed. S. Prete (Leipzig, 1978).

165. Council of Tours, Canon 23 (22), ed. C. de Clecq, *CCL* 148A (Turnholt, 1963); Polemius Silvius's fifth-century entry states, "Parentatio tumulorum [incipit] quo die Roma liberata est de obsidione Gallorum"; Degrassi 1963, pp. 408–409.

Christian festival of St. Peter's Chair, which continued the ancient rites with a Christian framework.[166]

The association of the Vestal Virgins with the Manes and with their popular private rites indicates the sort of flexibility that gave vitality to a traditional public cult. In the case of Vesta, the cult's role in maintaining state security was significant in encouraging imperial support as well. This particular sort of public/private conjunction may be seen also in other cults.

The Capitoline Triad: Jupiter, Juno, Minerva. One would expect an emphasis on the cults of the Capitoline Triad in a calendar from Rome. We have already remarked on the importance of Jupiter in our discussion of Group 2 cults, for his cult was the recipient of numerous games and circuses. In addition, Jupiter was commemorated at the *Iovis epulum* on 13 November, a ritual banquet held at the time of the *ludi Plebeii*.[167] The inclusion for the first time of a festival to Juno, the *Iunonalia* on 7 March, in this fourth-century Calendar may be due to a strictly local emphasis on this cult and the Capitoline Triad;[168] yet while this holiday may have been associated with a particular site in Rome, no temple is attested.[169]

The cult of Minerva overshadows that of Juno in the Calendar, for in addition to her official significance as part of the Capitoline Triad, she had considerable popular appeal as well. Her cult was considered traditional by the fourth century, with the festival of the *Quinquatria* (the fourth-century name for the first-century *Quinquatrus*) popularly celebrated in her honor on 19 March (see Table 3). Although this festival originally lasted for five days and honored Mars, as the *Fasti Vaticani* state, by the first century B.C., if not sooner, it had come to be associated with Minerva too, as indicated in the *Fasti Antiates Maiores*.[170] A second festival in honor of Minerva, the *Natalis Minerves* (Table 4), is noted in the Calendar of 354 on 21 March, perhaps commemorating the dedication of a temple to Minerva in Rome; but if so, the identification of this temple—whether with the Aventine, Esquiline, or Caelian temple of the goddess—is uncertain.[171] Whatever the *natalis* connotes, this second fes-

---

166. See Scullard 1981, pp. 76ff; and Chapter 2 above.

167. Degrassi 1963, p. 530.

168. The only other attestation for this holiday is a poem entitled *De Iunonalibus*, attributed to Claudian; see *Carm. Min.*, ed. J. B. Hall (Leipzig 1985), app. 8, p. 421.

169. Degrassi 1963, p. 421

170. Minerva was worshiped with and eventually replaced Mars at the *Quinquatria*; the notation *Minervae* appears in the *Fasti Antiates Maiores* and the *Fasti Farnesini*; it is listed as *Feriae Marti* in the *Fasti Vaticani*. See Degrassi 1963, pp. 426–428; and Scullard 1981, pp. 92ff., for the growth of a mythology connecting the two deities.

171. Degrassi 1963, pp. 426ff., assumes an error and would place the festival to Mi-

tival to Minerva may have been so placed because of chronological associations with the *Quinquatria,* celebrated just two days before. Indeed, the popular aspects of the *Quinquatria* largely overshadow its cultic associations in our literary sources; there is no evidence to suggest, however, that in the eyes of fourth-century pagans the festival was not still tied to the cult of Minerva.[172]

The dual role of Minerva was commemorated at the *Quinquatria.* In her peaceful aspect, she was worshiped by artisans as the patroness of craftsmanship. But she also had a martial side, which explains her inclusion in the Capitoline Triad, as well as the legend "Minerva Victrix" on coins of the Severan period.[173] It was certainly Minerva, Giver of Victory, whom the military detachment in receipt of the *Feriale Duranum* honored.[174] The martial aspect of the goddess explains her association with the emperor, too, attested for example by the legend on the coins of Aurelian, "Miner[vae] Aug[usti]," and of Postumus, "Miner[vae] Fautr[ici]," Minerva the protectress.[175] Under the tetrarchy, Minerva appears as a protector and companion (*comes*) of the emperor, in which role she came to be associated with Hercules, but in a subordinate position.[176] Although Minerva is not depicted on fourth-century imperial coinage, she is represented in martial attire and accompanying Hercules on contorniates from that era.[177]

The conjunction of Minerva with Hercules calls up another popular aspect of the goddess, for Minerva was equated with the Greek goddess Athena, who "invoked the capacity of mind, the function of the intellect under the control of reason. As patroness of Athens and Athenian philosophy, Athena stimulated the intellectual strength of Hercules."[178]

---

nerva on the nineteenth instead of the twenty-first. There is no reason to do this. A *Natalis Minerves* may be associated with the *Quinquatria,* which in the early imperial period lasted five days. The Greek spelling, *Minerves,* is that in the Codex-Calendar of 354.

172. Wissowa 1912, pp. 100ff., 207; p. 212, n. 11, argues that the *Quinquatria,* like the *Neptunalia* and the *Saturnalia,* was only a popular diversion without ties to its cult. But this is an argument *ex silentio*—and silence does not allow one to draw such a conclusion. The cult rites probably continued. On this point I agree with Stern 1953, p. 105.

173. *RIC* 4.1, p. 381; *RIC* 4.2, p. 97, no. 322.

174. Fink, Hoey, and Snyder 1940, pp. 98–99.

175. For coinage of Aurelian, see *RIC* 5.1, p. 302, no. 334, from Cyzicus. For Postumus, see *RIC* 5.2, p. 354, no. 210, and, with the legend "Miner[vae] Fautr[ici]," p. 339, no. 29; p. 343, no. 74; p. 350, no. 150; p. 354, no. 210—all from Lyons.

176. MacCormack, *Art and Ceremony,* pp. 173ff., discusses the late-third-century Igel Monument, which, although a private work, imitates imperial apotheosis imagery.

177. Alföldi 1976, nos. 40, 41.

178. *Age of Spirituality: Late Antique and Early Christian Art, 3rd–7th Century* (Catalogue

Thus is demonstrated the role of Minerva/Athena in contemporary Neo-platonic thought.[179] This side of the goddess also helps to explain the popularity of the *Quinquatria* among school pupils—as Symmachus suggests when he refers to the festival as "pueriles feriae"—a children's holiday.[180] The popular, school connections of this festival may also explain its appearance in the fifth-century calendar of Polemius Silvius.[181] Moreover, the Greek spelling of the goddess's name at another festival noted in the Calendar—*Natalis Minerves*—and the frequent reference to her in literature of the late empire as the "Tritonian maiden" suggest an appeal that owed something to Hellenic associations.[182]

Festivals and Cults Important in Early Roman History or Myth. There are several other festivals and cults whose continued celebration in the fourth century can be largely attributed to their association with the early history or myths of the city. We have already remarked on the cult of Quirinus/Romulus, honored at the *Natalis d[ei] Quirini*, on 3 April, and the *Quirinalia*, recorded on 17 February in calendars of the republic. The fifth-century chronographer Polemius Silvius glosses the significance of the latter date as follows: "The *Quirinalia* [commemorated] the day on which the fiction was invented that Romulus disappeared, though [in reality] he was killed by his own people; he was called Quirinus after the Sabine term for a spear, *curis*."[183] The historical associations of this date with Quirinus/Romulus are emphasized, and his divinity is treated rather cynically—indicating one way in which a particular cult festival was viewed by Christians in the fifth century. Quirinus/Romulus, as we have seen in relation to the illustration of March, was an important fourth-century figure, especially in Rome.

The commemoration of moments in Rome's historical or mythical

---

of the Exhibition, Metropolitan Museum of Art), ed. K. Weitzmann (New York and Princeton, N.J., 1979), chap. 2: R. Brilliant, "Mythology: The Classical World," pp. 126–132; see p. 114, no. 118, for Athena and Hercules depicted together.

179. Macrobius *Sat.* 1.17.70, 3.4.8.

180. Symmachus *Ep.* 5.85.

181. Degrassi 1963, pp. 426–428.

182. There is a reference to a consultation of Tritonia in the *Carmen contra Paganos, Anth. Lat.*, vol. 1, pt. 4, pp. 20–25, l. 90 : "What responses could the Tritonian maiden give?" For Minerva as Tritonia, see, for example, Claudian *De consulatu Stilichonis* 3.169. Minerva's association with Hercules, the god of oracular responses, might have contributed to this late development. Minerva is popularly represented on late Roman works of art, such as the Corbridge Lanx, illustrated in *Age of Spirituality*, ed. Weitzmann, pp. 132–133, no. 110; and a gold bracelet of early-fifth-century Rome, p. 308, no. 282.

183. "Quirinalia quo die Romulus, occisus a suis, Qui[rinus] ab hasta, quae a Sabinis curis vocatu[r], non apparuisse confictus est"; text from Degrassi 1963, p. 411.

past appears as the overriding factor in explaining the survival of several festivals whose cultic reality is not otherwise securely attested. So, for example, the two festivals to Carmenta, the *dies Carmentariorum* on 11 January and the *Carmentalia* on 15 January, are identified with the mother of Evander, a figure from early Roman history.[184] The *Regifugium* on 24 February also fits into this category, for it commemorates the expulsion of the Etruscan king Tarquinius Superbus, which event marked the beginning of the Roman Republic.[185]

New Festivals and Cults

Study of the most prominent festivals and cults not celebrated by *ludi* and *circenses* that were added to the public calendar after the mid first century A.D. (see Table 4) reveals just how important imperial favor was in the period after Aurelian. If a new cult appeared in Rome, it might attract imperial sanction and then be included in the calendar. For example, the cult of Tiberinus Pater, in whose honor a public festival appears for the first time in the Calendar of 354, had only recently received an imperial dedication.[186]

The new festivals cluster around two cults: that of Attis (worshiped with the Magna Mater) and that of Isis (including her consorts, Sarapis and Osiris, and her child, Harpocrates). The popularity of these new cults and the nature of their festivals point up some of the dominant trends in late Roman public paganism, in particular, certain soteriological aspects of fourth-century mystery cults, an area that we will discuss when we examine the appeal of these cults more closely. One further indication of these two cults' popularity is that they provided the inspiration for the illustrations of April and November in the Calendar. Yet even for these cults, imperial favor was a key factor in their inclusion in the public calendar.

The Festivals and Cult of Attis. Although archaeological evidence exists for the worship of Attis in the first century B.C. in Rome at the Palatine

184. Ibid., pp. 394ff.

185. Ibid., pp. 415ff.

186. *CIL* 6.773 = *ILS* 626, dedicated by Diocletian and Maximian. As observed earlier (note 148 above), the *Tiberinalia* on 17 August should not be equated with the *Portunalia*. The evidence from Varro is important; see *De Ling. Lat.* 5.7.29–30, ed. G. Goetz and F. Schoell (Leipzig, 1910). Section 5.71 indicates that Tiberinus is named after the river Tiber; and 6.19–20 indicates that the *Portunalia* was named after Portunus, whose temple was in "portu Tiberino" and for whom the temple and festival were established. Cf. Ennius *Ann.* 54, ed. Vahlen (Leipzig 1928; repr. Amsterdam, 1967); Servius *Ad. Aen.* 8.31. See J. Le Gall, *Recherches sur le culte du Tibre* (Paris, 1953).

TABLE 6:   INCORPORATION OF CULT FESTIVALS
OF ATTIS AND THE MAGNA MATER INTO THE
ROMAN CALENDAR

	Claudius	Antoninus Pius	Antoninus Pius or Later
15 March		Canna intrat	
22 March	Arbor intrat		
24 March	Sanguem		
25 March			Hilaria
26 March			Requetio
27 March	Lavatio		
28 March			Initium Caiani [= Gaiani]

temple of the Magna Mater, it was not until Emperor Claudius (A.D. 41–54) that public holidays in honor of Attis were distinguished in the Roman calendar from the games honoring the Magna Mater.[187] Imperial attention to the cult of Attis, the young male consort of the Magna Mater, continued under Antoninus Pius (138–161), and new festivals were added at that time or soon thereafter. (Table 6 gives one possible reconstruction of the gradual incorporation of these festivals into the Roman calendar.)[188]

These festivals repeat annually the mythical death and rebirth of Attis in the early spring, the time of vegetative regeneration. Attis's fate demonstrated his triumph over death and the renewal of life in a happier mode of existence—at least, that is essentially the explanation of the fourth-century astrologer turned Christian Firmicus Maternus. While his euhemeristic interpretation does not coincide in every respect with the sources, the mythic outline that he presents is fairly consistent with them. The Magna Mater, the Roman name for the Anatolian goddess Cybele, loves a young man who rejects her. The goddess takes her revenge and drives Attis mad. In his rage, he commits self-castration and

187. P. Pensabene, "Nuove acquisizioni nella zona sud-occidentale del Palatino," *Quaderni del centro di studio per l'archeologia etrusco-italica* 5, Archeologia Laziale 4 (Rome, 1981), pp. 101–118. For the most recent report, see P. Pensabene, "Sesta e settima campagna di scavo nell'area sud-ovest del Palatino," *Quaderni del centro di studio per l'archeologia etrusco-italica* 8, (Rome, 1984), pp. 149–158.

188. This reconstruction is by D. Fishwick, "The *Cannophori* and the March Festival of Magna Mater," *TAPA* 97 (1966): 193–202; D. Fishwick, "*Hastiferi*," *JRS* 57 (1967): 142–160. I have altered the identification of the *Initium Gaiani*. See note 194 below and further discussion by M. J. Vermaseren, *Cybele and Attis: The Myth and the Cult* (London, 1977), pp. 113ff.

dies. He is buried, but so that he may comfort the Magna Mater, he comes back to life. (In some accounts, the goddess herself, mourning his loss, revives Attis.) Firmicus Maternus's explanation of the myth makes clear the symbolic identification of Attis with the grain that is sown (*mors*) every year and then comes back to life (*vita*) in the spring.[189] In the fourth century, and especially after Julian, this myth was a favorite subject for Neoplatonic interpretation: the death and rebirth of Attis were identified as the ascension of the soul to its place of origin or the return of sunlight.[190]

The details of the rites that reenacted this myth convey both the soteriological aspects and the appeal of the public celebration of the cult of Attis in fourth-century Rome; they therefore warrant a close examination.[191] The cycle of holidays began on 15 March with the festival *Canna intrat*, a solemn procession of "reed bearers" into the city. This day commemorated the first days of Attis's life, when he was abandoned in the reeds on the bank of the River Gallus and then miraculously saved, either (depending on the version of the myth one follows) by shepherds or by the Magna Mater. A week later, at the time of the spring equinox on 22 March, was the entry of the pine tree, *Arbor intrat*; this evergreen, next to which Attis is often depicted and a symbol of eternal life, is worshiped and mourned as a symbol of the god himself.

Then, on 23 March at the *Tubilustrium*, the tree, decked with purple ribbons and an effigy of Attis, was laid to rest—as the god Attis—in the temple of the Magna Mater (perhaps that on the Palatine Hill in Rome) and his death was mourned with loud cries and lamentations. In the calendars of the mid first century, this holiday connoted the day on which the *Salii*, the priests of Mars, performed with their shields and cleansed their trumpets in a ritual lustration prior to the military campaigning season. In the fourth century, however, and probably earlier, these priests flourished their trumpets and marched around the temple of Magna Mater, martially beating their shields—like the *Corybantes* represented on the Tholus of the Magna Mater on the Sacra Via in Rome.[192] The assimilation of the *Salii* of Mars and the *Corybantes* of Attis was easy:

189. Firmicus Maternus *De Err. Prof. Rel.* 3.2
190. Julian *Or.* 5.8.168c–D, 169c–D, ed. Wright; Sallustius *De diis et mundo* 4.10, ed. A.D. Nock (Cambridge, 1926); Macrobius *Sat.* 1.21.10.
191. For further discussion, see Degrassi 1963, pp. 429–431.
192. Julian *Or.* 5.168c–D, 169D, ed. Wright; Martial *Ep.* 1.70.9–10 indicates that the *Corybantes* were linked with the cult of the Magna Mater in Rome: "Flecte vias hac qua madidi sunt tecta Lyaei / Et Cybeles picto stat Corybante tholus." See further L. Musso, *Manifattura suntuaria e committenza pagana nella Roma del IV secolo. Indagine sulla lanx di Parabiago*, Studi e materiali del Museo della Civiltà Romana, no. 10 (Rome, 1983), pp. 24ff.

the *Corybantes* were often represented with Rhea, who since time immemorial was identified with the Magna Mater.[193] Thus the rites of the
Roman god of war were integrated into the spring festivals of Attis.

The mourning became more violent on the following day, 24 March,
Sanguem, when the devotees flagellated themselves until they bled,
sprinkling the altars and effigy with their blood. This was also the day
when certain devotees of the goddess, carried away by their emotion,
would perform self-castration. During the "sacred night" of the twenty-
fourth, Attis was ritually laid to rest in his grave and the new *galli* were
inducted into the priesthood (presumably symbolizing the god's rebirth);
at dawn, then, a day of rejoicing—*Hilaria*—could begin. A day of rest,
Requetio, was observed on the twenty-sixth, followed the next day by a
ritual procession and bathing of the statue of the goddess, the *Lavatio.*
This act commemorated as well her historic entry into Rome, as goddess
of victory in the Hannibalic war. The notation *Initium Caiani* (or *Gaiani*),
on 28 March, may indicate a period of initiations into the cult of the
Magna Mater and Attis at the Gaianum, near the Phrygianum, the cult's
Vatican sanctuary.[194]

The public celebrations of the cult of Attis and the Magna Mater in
March indicate a belief in the resurrection of the god and associate his
return with that of springtime vegetation. The return of Attis evidences
his own salvation; it also conveyed the promise of a good harvest to his
followers or, more metaphorically, the promise of a happier life with the
arrival of spring. So Attis and Cybele were worshiped as saviors, that is,
as deities who could assure their followers a favorable future life in this
world. Dedications to *Mater deum salutaris*[195] must be understood as conveying this soteriological hope.

The question then arises, did this mean people thought that such a
blessing as Attis's own triumph over death and return in a happier new
life was possible for themselves as well? The most solemn private rites
of the cult of Attis and the Magna Mater, the *taurobolium* (ritual cleansing

193. Vermaseren, *Cybele and Attis,* p. 49. Inscriptions from fourth-century Rome indicate the ritual linking in dual dedications to Rhea and the Magna Mater: *CIL* 6.509,
6.30780, 6.30966.

194. In contrast to Vermaseren, *Cybele and Attis,* pp. 45ff., 124, *Initium Caiani* (or
Gaiani) should refer to activities in the Gaianum, the field of Gaius in the area of the Vatican,
and not to the Phrygianum, the Vatican sanctuary of the cult. See G. Lugli, "Il Vaticano
nell'età classica," in *Vaticano,* ed. G. Fallani and M. Escobar (Florence, 1946), pp. 1ff.; F.
Coarelli, *Guida archeologica di Roma* (Rome, 1974), p. 319.

195. F. di Capua, "Un epigrafe stabiese e il culto della 'Deum Mater' presso le sorgenti
di acque minerali," *Rendiconti dell'Accademia di Archeologia, Lettere, e Belle Arti di Napoli* 21
(1941): 75–83; G. Sfameni Gasparro, *'Soterioligici e aspetti mistici nel culto di Cibele e Atti'*
(Palermo, 1979).

in the blood of a bull) and, for the less wealthy, the *criobolium* (ritual cleansing in the blood of a ram), have been interpreted as conveying this message. Originally, the *taurobolium* was undertaken for public vows and as part of the imperial cult; only in the fourth century did it take on a private meaning, promising the dedicant long life (i.e. salvation) in a state of ritual purity. This is the meaning attached to a series of altars found near the Vatican sanctuary of the cult in Rome, dating from 295 to 376.[196] But these altars indicate a purification rite intended for a limited period of time, which is why the *taurobolium* was generally repeated after a period of ten or twenty years.

One altar from the Vatican sanctuary, however, bears a *taurobolium* inscription indicating that an initiate has been "renatus in aeternum"; these words have been interpreted as promising the initiate eternal rebirth.[197] Sextilius Agesilaus Aedesius, a devotee of several cults and head priest in the cult of Mithras, dedicated this altar in 376, some twenty years after the Calendar was compiled. The inscription suggests the incorporation into cultic belief of the idea of salvation for eternity, an idea found both in other mysteries and in Christianity. Indeed, it seems quite likely that the cult of Attis was developing along these lines: the similarities between the mythic rebirth and the rites to Attis on the one hand and the springtime festival and resurrection of Christ on the other strongly suggest the interaction of these two religions in the Greco-Roman world. The only other indication that the cult of Attis may have been developing a promise of salvation for eternity is the late witness of Damascius, who noted a link between the *Hilaria* and liberation from Hades.[198] Until better evidence comes to light, however, it remains doubtful that in 354 the public or private rites of Attis can be read as leading to eternal salvation. Salvation and purification understood as limited to this world, though, cannot be disputed; these constituted the overwhelming soteriological promise of this cult.

The *Initium Caiani*, noted in the Calendar on 28 March, may refer to

196. There is a twenty-eight-year interval within which no *taurobolia* are attested at the Vatican sanctuary. This gap has been explained as the result of the cult's interruption at this site due to the work on St. Peter's. See M. Guarducci, *Cristo e S. Pietro in un documento preconstantino della necropoli Vaticane* (Rome, 1953), pp. 66ff.; M. Guarducci, "L'interruzione dei culti nel *Phrygianum* durante il IV secolo d. Cr.," in *La soteriologia dei culti orientali nel'Impero Romano*, ed. U. Bianchi and M. J. Vermaseren, *EPRO*, no. 92 (Leiden, 1982), pp. 109–122; J. M. C. Toynbee and J. B. Perkins, *The Shrine of St. Peter and the Vatican Excavations* (New York, 1957).

197. The evolution of this rite has been documented by R. Duthoy, *The Taurobolium: Its Evolution and Terminology* (Leiden, 1969). The inscription is *CIL* 6.510 = *ILS* 4152.

198. Damascius *Vita Isidori excerpta a Photio Bibl. (Cod. 242)*, ed. R. Henry (Paris, 1971), p. 131.

a period after the public celebrations to Attis when private *taurobolia* were performed. Graillot, for one, detected this tendency:[199] of thirty-two dated *taurobolia* and *criobolia* known to him, twelve were dated 7 April and 5 May—after the public holidays of the cult. At Rome, out of the twenty-three *taurobolium* altars recorded by Duthoy, two are dated 5 April, during the games to the Magna Mater; three are dated at the time of the games to Ceres, whose cult was closely associated with the Magna Mater; and two fall in the period 12 March–14 April.[200] The chronological separation of the public and private rites to Attis correlates to the topography of the cult in Rome: the private rites of initiation were presumably held either at the Phrygianum, the Vatican sanctuary of the goddess and Attis, or, when access to the Phrygianum was disrupted owing to the construction of St. Peter's, at the nearby Gaianum (which explains the *Initium Caiani* notation in the Calendar of 354), whereas the public games and rites in honor of Attis were held at the temple of the Magna Mater on the Palatine Hill.

The appeal of the cult of the Magna Mater and Attis in the fourth-century city lies in its joining of the traditional cult of the Magna Mater, celebrated publicly with games since the Second Punic War, to the powerful soteriological message of Attis, whose private rites offered the hope of renewed life in a purified state, at least in this world. This merging of private and public elements appears as well on the late-third-century *taurobolium* altars dedicated by the Roman aristocrat Scipio Orfitus—private commemorations that suggest a very intentional harking back to the traditions of his alleged ancestor, P. Cornelius Nasica, who first brought the goddess to Rome in the third century B.C.[201] By melding public and private, the festivals of Attis and the Magna Mater established this cult, especially among the aristocracy, as one of the most vital cults in the fourth-century city.[202]

The Festivals and Cult of Isis. The cult of Isis and her consorts, Sarapis and Osiris, emerges as the second most popular new cult in the Calendar (see Table 4). Like that of the Magna Mater and Attis, it succeeded in joining a public cult, long favored by emperors, to private rites of initiation that offered salvation.

The first notices of the public festivals of Isis and her consorts occur

199. H. Graillot, *Le culte de Cybèle. Mère des dieux à Rome et dans l'Empire Romain* (Paris, 1912), p. 168.

200. Duthoy, *The Taurobolium*, nos. 1–34. Vermaseren, *Cybele and Attis*, p. 105, sees no pattern.

201. *CIL* 6.505 = 6.30781; *CIL* 6.506 = 6.30782.

202. *Carmen contra Paganos, Anth. Lat.* 1.1, pp. 20–25, ll. 106–107, cites the aristocrats especially in connection with this cult, which continues a more ancient connection; see Cicero *Har. Resp.* 12.24; Valerius Maximus 2.4.3; Aulus Gellius *Noctes Atticae* 2.24.2, 18.2.11.

TABLE 7:   FESTIVALS OF THE CULTS OF ISIS,
SARAPIS, AND OSIRIS AS THEY WERE ADDED TO THE
ROMAN CALENDAR

Menologia Rustica[a]	*Hermeneumata*[b]	Calendar of 354	Misc. Attestations[c]
March Isidis navigium[d]		5 Isidis navigium 20 Pelusia	Pelusia[e]
April Sacrum Phariae item Sarapia[f]	25 Serapia	25 Serapia	
August		12 Lychnapsia	
October	28 Isia	28 Isia	28 Castu Isidis[g]
	29 Isia	29 Isia	
	30 Isia	30 Isia	
	31 Isia	31 Isia	
November Heuresis[h]	1 Isia	1 Ex se nato. Isia	
	2 Isia	2 Ter novena	
	3 Isia	3 Hilaria	

[a] The *Menologia Rustica* refer to two rural calendars dated to A.D. 19–65: the *Menologium Rusticum Colotianum* and *Vallense*; see Degrassi 1963, pp. 284–291.

[b] *Hermeneumata*, or lists of holidays, which I would associate with the schools, can be dated to the second or third century.

[c] A variety of sources, including literary and calendrical texts, attest these names.

[d] Celebrated before the *Sacrum Mamurio*, that is, before 14 March; it probably fell on 5 March, as in the Calendar of 354.

[e] Attested by the *H. A. Marc. Ant.* 23.8.

[f] Celebrated after *Oves lustrantur*, which can be identified with the *Parilia*, of 21 April; it may have fallen on 25 April, as in the Calendar of 354.

[g] Noted in the calendar from S. Maria Maggiore in Rome, which should be dated to 176–224/275; see Salzman 1981.

[h] Celebrated after *Iovis epulum*, that is, after 13 November; although it probably fell on 15 November in the *Menologia Rustica*, the *Heuresis* is equated with the *Ex se nato* in the Calendar of 354.

in the *Menologia Rustica*, rural calendars from Italy that have been dated to the reign of either Gaius (36–39) or Claudius (41–54) because of these emperors' efforts in support of this cult.[203] Thus, although the cult of Sarapis and Isis originated in Egypt and entered the Roman world in the Hellenistic period, its official incorporation into the Roman calendar of

203. Degrassi 1963, pp. 526–527, sees these festivals as entering the Roman calendar sometime between A.D. 19 and 65 because Tiberius restricted this cult (Tacitus *Ann.* 2.85)

holidays did not occur until the Julio-Claudian period, 19–65 at the earliest.

Imperial favor fell especially on Sarapis. This city god of Alexandria—the Egyptian king, as well as husband and brother of Isis—was worshiped with Sol/Helios, Jupiter/Zeus, and Neptune as a deity who could endow the emperor with success and victory.[204] The ready assimilation of Sarapis into imperial ideology is underscored by the epithets that accrue to him—Dominus, Magnus, Invictus[205]—and may indeed be a factor in explaining why the *sacrum* to Sarapis, noted in the *Menologia Rustica* in April, survives as the festival *Serapia*, recorded on 25 April in the Calendar of 354.

The incorporation of Osiris, also an Egyptian king, and husband and brother of Isis, into Roman belief occurred along very different lines. The mythic contours of the god's life emphasize his consistent funerary character and the soteriology of his cult. Aided by his wife, Osiris taught the benefits of culture to man. His brother, Seth, however, fired by envy, put Osiris in a coffin and had it carried off to Syria. Isis wandered the world, finally finding Osiris and bringing him back to life. But Seth stole Osiris again. This time, Osiris was completely dismembered. Isis found all parts except for his genitalia and, once more, brought him back to life.

This myth is reenacted in the festivals of the cult, noted in the Calendar of 354 in late October and early November. The public and private rites recreate Isis's loss, her mourning, and her joyful discovery of Osiris on his return to life. In Egypt, Osiris's disappearance was associated with the recession of the Nile, and his rebirth with the rising water that brought the return of vegetation.[206] In the Roman Empire, liturgical practice focused on the god's presence in the water, the sacred substance.[207]

---

and Lucan (dead by 65) attests in the *Pharsalia* 8.831ff. to its acceptance in Rome. See M. Malaise, *Les conditions de pénétration et de diffusion des cultes égyptiens en Italie*, EPRO, no. 22 (Leiden, 1972), pp. 221–244, who sees these festivals as due to the imperial support of Gaius or Claudius. No evidence secures the dating of these festivals, nor does the *Menologia Rustica*. But the known policies of the emperor Gaius did favor this cult, as his rebuilding of the Iseum Campense, for one, demonstrates. See E. Köberlein, *Caligula und die ägyptischen Kulte* (Meisenheim/Glan, 1962). It seems probable that Gaius was responsible for their appearance in the public calendar. At the very least, the festivals and the *Menologia Rustica* are Julio-Claudian.

204. J. Gwyn Griffiths, *The Isis Book (Metamorphoses XI)*, EPRO, no. 39 (Leiden, 1975), p. 44, n. 4.

205. Malaise, *Conditions de pénétration*, pp. 194, 357.

206. Ibid., pp. 221–244.

207. Ibid., pp. 352ff. Cf. the Osiris-Canopus vases on the columns of the Iseum in

Literary accounts describe some of the rites associated with the Isis festivals of 28 October–3 November. The author of the fourth-century *Carmen contra Paganos*, Prudentius, and Plutarch describe a "mourning" atmosphere and the grieving of Isis, whose joy abounds at the return of Osiris.[208] This tone coincides with the notation in the Calendar from S. Maria Maggiore in Rome of a one-day festival, the *Castu Isidis*, a day of abstention and loss on 28 October.[209] The Calendar of 354 notes the *Isia* on 28–31 October. The joyful return to life of Osiris has been identified with the notation *Ex se nato*—literally meaning "Osiris has been born from himself"—recorded in the Calendar on 1 November and celebrated with twenty-four circus races. This celebration, the culmination of the Isis-Osiris cycle, is identified with the *Heuresis* ("a finding out") in the *Menologia Rustica*.[210] On 2 November, the Calendar indicates a joyful choral singing of twenty-seven men, called the *Ter novena*; on 3 November, the notation *Hilaria* indicates the joy at Osiris's return to life.

Isis appears in these October–November festivals as the sister and wife of Osiris, a mother goddess and the Egyptian equivalent of Demeter insofar as she, too, is the recipient of mysteries: secret initiations, the prohibition against divulging ceremonies, and the claim to rebirth are all associated with her cult.[211] Yet here again, the nature of salvation (or rebirth) is open to question: does it apply only to this world, or did it involve a hope for a happier life in the hereafter? In her famous revelation to Lucius, Isis speaks in the language of Greek myth, promising him that

---

the Campus Martius; and R. Wild, *Water in the Cultic Worship of Isis and Sarapis*, EPRO, no. 87 (Leiden, 1981).

208. *Carmen contra Paganos, Anth. Lat.* 1.1, pp. 20–25, ll. 95–102; Prudentius *Contra Symm.* 1.629ff. Plutarch *De Iside et Osiride* 39 describes this festival fully but ascribes only four days to these activities, while the Calendar gives it five days. This discrepancy may be due to the fact that Plutarch, although writing in the first century A.D., is representing myth and cult from the third and second centuries B.C. Nonetheless, much of his description fits with the myth and cult known from the Roman calendar and from later Roman sources.

209. Magi 1972, p. 25, also notes that no indication is given on the next line for a festival.

210. I follow Degrassi 1963, pp. 527–531, for the identification of these festivals. In the *Menologia Rustica*, the *Heuresis* occurs in November, probably on the fifteenth of the month and certainly after the *Iovis epulum* on 13 November. The change in date and nomenclature must reflect changes in cult over time. Cf. Malaise, *Conditions de pénétration,* pp. 217ff.

211. Apuleius *Met.* 11.21. Apuleius twice uses the term *renatus* in Book 11, chaps. 16 and 21. According to Griffiths, *Isis Book*, pp. 51ff., the term has both physical and spiritual reference: "It denotes an end and a new beginning, and the concern with a spiritual sense is borne out by the emphasis on death in the First Initiation."

he will find her ruling in the underworld while he inhabits the Elysian fields. This passage, in keeping with the suggestion of comfort after death that is connected with worship of Osiris, emphasizes peace for the deceased.[212] Indeed, a small number of Greek inscriptions from Rome invite Osiris to give refreshing water and urge the deceased to take courage[213]—not as a promise of rebirth or resurrection, but as a wish for solace in death.[214] The soteriological aspect of Osiris worship appears, but, compared with the Christian doctrine of resurrection, it is of limited intent.

The *Isidis navigium*, noted in the Calendar of 354 on 5 March, also appears in the *Menologia Rustica*. This holiday honors Isis Pelagia, Isis as a goddess of the sea, as well as of grain and fertility. These aspects of Isis are neatly combined in a hymn attributed to the poet Claudian, ''De Isidis Navigio'':

> Isis, abundant with the new fruit which you have now deemed it worthy to [make] appear, you who do not seek help for [bringing forth] the gifts of Ceres. (For you are our goddess, nor does the god himself—the one accustomed to remaining silent and who carries your sails—deny you; for Zephyrus and winged Mercury favor you): May you not flee from our region![215]

In the fourth century, this festival maintained the Alexandrian associations of Isis and Sarapis as the protectors of navigation—ritually symbolized by the ceremonial launching of a ship. Yet they were also considered the special protectors of the emperor,[216] and their dual role

---

212. Apuleius *Met.* 11.6.5; cf. W. Burkert, *Ancient Mystery Cults* (Cambridge, Mass., 1987), pp. 26–27.

213. Malaise, *Conditions de pénétration*, pp. 206–207; *IG* 14.1782 = *SIRIS* 461; *IG* 14.1488 = *SIRIS* 459; *CIL* 6.20616 = *IG* 14.1705 = *ILS* 8171 = *SIRIS* 460; *BC* 61 (1933): 211 = *SIRIS* 462. Further discussion by M. Malaise, *Inventaire préliminaire des documents égyptiens découverts en Italie*, EPRO, no. 21 (Leiden, 1972).

214. See R. MacMullen, *Paganism in the Roman Empire* (New Haven, Conn., 1981), pp. 54–56; Burkert, *Ancient Mystery Cults*, pp. 17–18 and passim.

215. Claudian *Carm. vel spuriorum vel suspectorum app.* 11, ed. Hall (Leipzig 1985), ''De Isidis navigio'':

> Isi, o fruge nova quae nunc dignata videri
> plena nec ad Cereris munera poscis opem
> (nam tu nostra dea es nec te deus ipse tacendi
> abnegat expertus, quis tua vela ferat;
> namque tibi Zephyrus favet ac Cyllenius ales):
> ne nostra referas de regione pedem!

216. See A. Alföldi, *A Festival of Isis in Rome under the Christian Emperors of the Fourth Century* (Budapest, 1937), pp. 59ff.; and Degrassi 1963, pp. 419–420.

appears in the ceremonies performed on this day: after the launching of the ship, the chief priest would say a prayer for the Roman emperor, the Senate, the knights, and the people at large.[217]

The association of Isiac and imperial cult is attested by coins, beginning with Commodus, that depict Isis Pelagia and Sarapis. Diocletian revived the imperial associations with the cult by striking coins that bear on the obverse the bust of the emperor and on the reverse the words *VOTA PUBLICA* (the imperial vows taken on 3 January), accompanied by Isiac imagery—most commonly, the ship of Isis (*Isidis navigium*). These coins were struck in an unbroken series until the reign of Gratian, in A.D. 378–379, when portraits of Sarapis and Isis replaced the image of the Christian emperor, although the reverses remained the same. Even this late series, however, invokes Isis and Sarapis as guarantors of the "Safety of Augustus" (*Salus Augusti*). The numismatic evidence for the continuing connection between the Isiac cult and the emperor[218] receives further support from archaeology: the Temple of Isis at the Port of Ostia was restored under imperial orders around 376, with funding approved by the Emperors Gratian, Valens, and Valentinian.[219]

Two other festivals associated with the cult of Isis are actually recorded for the first time in a Roman calendar in the Calendar of 354. The *Pelusia*, on 20 March, entered the Roman calendar sometime after the mid first century (since no earlier calendar notes it) but prior to the reign of Marcus Aurelius.[220] This festival, as explained by John Lydus, owes its name to the "mud" from which a god rises; the god announces the fertility of the Nile, which puts an end to drought and hunger. The *Pelusia* most likely commemorates the birth of Harpocrates, the child of Isis, who is depicted holding a cornucopia and emerging from the mud.[221]

217. Apuleius *Met.* 11.5–17.

218. Alföldi, *A Festival of Isis*, pp. 17ff., argued that these later coins were part of the pagan reaction after A.D. 379. This view of a pagan reaction is questionable; see Chapter 6 below. Alföldi modified his view that the rites of the *navigium Isidis* were imitated in detail on 3 January, in connection with the *Vota publica*, and not on 5 March (where the Calendar of 354 records it) and also acknowledged the importance of Sarapis in this festival in "Die alexandrinischen Götter und die *Vota publica* am Jahresbeginn," *JAC* 8–9 (1965–1966): 53–87.

219. *SIRIS* 562 = *AE* (1961), no. 152: "Ddd. nnn. Valens, Gratianus et Valentinianus Augusti / aedem ac porticus deae Isidis restitui praeceperunt / curante Sempronio Fausto v(iro) c(larissimo) praefecto annonae."

220. The *H.A. Marc. Aur.* 23.8 records it under this emperor. Unless this is an anachronism, the festival should be considered as having a *terminus ante quem* of the rule of Marcus Aurelius.

221. Lydus *De mens.* 4.57; P. Courcelle, "Sur un passage énigmatique des *Confessions* de Saint Augustin (VIII.2.3): Harpocrate et Anubis," *REL* 29 (1951): 306. The alternative identification of Harpocrates as the god of Pelusia would not easily explain the presence

The *Lychnapsia*, the last Isiac festival noted in the Calendar, was celebrated on 12 August. Assumed to be Egyptian in origin, it is associated with lamps and their role in the Egyptian cult. This date sanctified the birth of the goddess.[222]

The growing emphasis on Isis as the recipient of mysteries or in conjunction with the imperial cult may explain the omission of one Isiac festival from the Calendar. In April, the *Menologia Rustica* recorded a *sacrum* to *(Isis) Pharia*, a festival in honor of Isis as goddess of the Pharos harbor[223]—an aspect of Isis that was evidently no longer relevant in the Rome of 354.

By the fourth century, the cult of Isis, like that of the Magna Mater and Attis, was considered traditionally Roman. Both cults had been admitted among the *sacra Romana* by the Senate according to regular procedure, sometime in the mid first century as the *Menologia Rustica* attest.[224] The festivals increased in frequency as their cults spread. The *Isia* was expanded and the date of the *Heuresis* changed at some point between A.D. 20 and 175–225, as the notation *Castu Isidis* on 28 October in the calendar from S. Maria Maggiore indicates.[225] The *Pelusia* was presumably added by the time of Marcus Aurelius. And by the reign of Caracalla the cult of Sarapis was no longer considered foreign, since that emperor built his temple to Sarapis on the Quirinal, not outside the *pomerium*.[226]

At each step in the growth of the festivals of Isis, Osiris, and Sarapis, imperial patronage was a key factor in the cult's appeal and public acceptance. In addition, its private rites of initiation and its soteriological message made the cult a favorite of fourth-century aristocrats; inscriptions attest to the prominence of this class in dedications to Isis and her consorts and in its priesthood.[227] For these reasons, Isiac iconography

---

of this festival in a Roman calendar; for this, see C. Bonner, "*Harpokrates* (Zeus Kaisios) of Pelusium," *Hesperia* 15 (1946): 51–59.

222. M. Salem, "The '*Lychnapsia* Philocaliana' and the Birthday of Isis," *JRS* 27 (1937): 165–167. The *Fasti Amiternini* (A.D. 20) notes a festival to Hercules Invictus on this day, giving a *terminus ante quem* for the *Lychnapsia*. See Degrassi 1963, pp. 493–494.

223. Degrassi 1963, p. 288, *Menologium Rusticum Colotianum*; p. 292, *Menologium Rusticum Vallense*.

224. Wissowa 1912, pp. 45, 406.

225. When exactly this occurred is not known. It must have been before the calendar from S. Maria Maggiore (A.D. 175–225) but after A.D. 20, since calendars from that time record the *ludi Victoriae Sullae* for 26 October to 1 November; see Degrassi 1963, pp. 526–527; and Table 7 below, note h.

226. Wissowa 1912, p. 355.

227. Alföldi, *A Festival of Isis*, pp. 59ff. and passim. At the turn of the third century,

provided especially suitable subject matter for the illustration of November (Fig. 22) in the Calendar of 354.

CONTINUITY AND CHANGE: CALENDARS AND CULTS IN THE LATE EMPIRE— THE APPEAL OF A ROMAN HOLIDAY

A comparison of our fourth-century Roman Calendar with those of the mid first century A.D. reveals the dominant characteristics of late Roman paganism.[228] The conservatism of public paganism is a salient feature of the Calendar of 354. All six of the great public games of the Roman Republic were still celebrated in the fourth-century city (Table 1). Moreover, out of a total fifty-four days of public holidays and festivals recorded without *ludi* or *circenses* in the Calendar of 354 (Tables 3 and 4), fully twenty-four—or almost half—had been celebrated since the mid first century. And the equivalent of seven holidays (some nine days) noted in first-century calendars without *ludi* were now celebrated with *ludi* (Table 2).[229] In all, some thirty-seven of eighty-six days of holidays in honor of the pagan deities recorded in the Calendar of 354 (excluding the public games) had been celebrated in the first century—a conservative trend indeed.[230]

The conservatism of the Calendar reflects the essence of Roman paganism, a religion predicated on a sense of being in harmony with the past of one's family, group, and wider community:

---

the aristocrat L. Cornelius Scipio Orfitus dedicated an altar to I(ovi) O(ptimo) M(aximo) Soli Sarapidi (*CIL* 6.402 = *SIRIS* no. 394) in Rome along with altars to honor the Magna Mater and Attis (see notes 121 and 201 above). For the inscriptions, see *CIL* 6.1780 = *ILS* 1260; *CIL* 6.846 = *ILS* 4413; *CIL* 6.512 = *ILS* 4154; *CIL* 6.504 = *ILS* 4153. Others are listed in *SIRIS*. For further discussion, see Malaise, *Conditions de pénétration*, pp. 217ff.; R. Merkelbach, *Isisfeste in griechisch-römischer Zeit: Daten und Riten* (Meisenheim/Glan, 1963).

228. The small number of extant calendars restricts our knowledge of the chronological growth of the Roman calendar (see Chapter 1). The reader may recall that the majority of extant Roman calendars date from the Julio-Claudian period; only the calendar of S. Maria Maggiore, which I have dated to 175–225, postdates these. Extant *ferialia* help to fill in the gaps in our information. That from Dura-Europos is especially helpful in this regard, since it is dated to 225–227.

229. This figure omits the *ludi Compitales*, since these were *feriae conceptivae* in the early empire. See the list on p. 126.

230. The figure thirty-seven includes the twenty-four days without *ludi* and *circenses*, the nine days with *ludi* and *circenses*, the three days of the *ludi Compitales*, and the one of the *ludi Martialici*. The public games (Table 1) are omitted from this total.

> These are the religious institutions handed down to them by their ancestors, which they persist in maintaining and defending with the greatest obstinacy. Nor do they consider what character they are; but they feel assured of their excellence and truth on this account, because the ancients have handed them down; and so great is the authority of antiquity that it is said to be a crime to inquire into it.[231]

Conservatism reinforced the appeal of the traditional in religion and in society. Even the format and appearance of the Calendar text evidences these traits, for it transfers from wall calendars to a codex the traditions of the Roman calendar.

The traditionalism of the Roman calendar militated against overt change. While change did occur, it tended to do so with the proviso, observable in calendars, that the innovation appear rather as a continuation. Indeed, a great strength of the pagan religious system was its ability to absorb new cults and ideas by appearing to follow established custom.[232] So, for example, the name and date for the festival of the *Tubilustrium* remain the same in calendars three hundred years apart. Yet in the Roman calendars of the mid first century, the *Tubilustrium* was a holiday to commemorate Mars; in the mid fourth century, it was a holiday when the *Salii*, the priests of Mars, danced and shook their spears in honor of Attis and the Magna Mater. The name, date, and some functionaries remained the same, but the deity and meaning of the holiday had changed.

This incorporation of new rites and deities under the rubric of old festivals was an important means of validating new cults. So, for example, Hadrian chose to celebrate the dedication of the new temple and cult of Roma Aeterna on 21 April, the date both of an ancient agricultural festival, the *Parilia*, to honor the obscure deity Pales and, by popular association, of the anniversary of Rome's foundation. Thus Hadrian was able to link his new cult of Roma Aeterna with the ancient festival commemorating Rome's birthday.[233]

Such flexible conservatism contributed to the predominance of the traditional Greco-Roman gods in the Calendar. Yet at the same time, many of these familiar deities had acquired new rites and meanings. This kind of accretion—as opposed to syncretism—constitutes another im-

---

231. Lactantius *Inst.* 2.6.7: "Hae sunt religiones quas sibi a maioribus suis traditas pertinacissime tueri ac defenderi perseverant, nec considerant quales sint, sed ex hoc veras ac probatas esse confidunt quod eas veteres tradiderunt, tantaque est auctoritas vetustatis ut inquirere in eam scelus esse ducatur."

232. Liebeschuetz, *Continuity and Change*, pp. 1ff.

233. Scullard 1981, pp. 103–105; Mellor, "The Goddess Roma," pp. 1016ff.

portant aspect of the mid-fourth-century Calendar, one that is apparent as well in the encyclopedic tendencies in the illustrations.

Changes in the Roman Calendar

Continuities like these make change difficult to assess. But comparison of the Calendar of 354 with earlier calendars does highlight some major developments. Perhaps the most striking change is a significant increase in the number of days devoted to holidays and festivals, an increase that bespeaks the widespread support throughout Roman society for these celebrations. At Rome under Augustus, approximately 77 days a year were devoted to public games, and 45 to public holidays.[234] Indeed, by the time of Domitian, some eighty years later, the number of public games and festivals to honor the emperor as well as the pagan gods had so swollen the Roman civic calendar that a senatorial commission was established to rid the Calendar of undesirable festivals.[235] Despite individual emperors' efforts, however, the number of holidays continued to increase. Marcus Aurelius, in the late second century, attempted to reform the calendar by setting aside 230 days for carrying out business and lawsuits and 135 days for festivals and games[236] His reform did not last; in 322–323, Constantine found it necessary to forbid the institution of new festivals by judges (*iudices*).[237] This law appears well advised: in 354 in Rome, 177 days were devoted to festivals and holidays celebrated with *ludi* and *circenses* (including the 10 days of gladiatorial games), plus 54 days for festivals or holidays without.

Not only were more days devoted to public festivities in the fourth-century Calendar, but the kind of celebration had also changed, with many more days given over to *ludi* and *circenses*: 177, versus 77 under Augustus. Even some seven traditional festivals (totaling 9 days) noted without *ludi* and *circenses* in first-century calendars were now commem-

234. E. De Ruggiero, *Dizionario epigraphico di antichità romane*, vol. 4, fasc. 63–66 (Rome, 1975–1977), s.v. "Ludi." Degrassi 1963, p. 373, discusses the changing number of public holidays celebrated under Augustus and in the imperial period.

235. Tacitus *Hist.* 4.40.

236. Imperial opposition to the growing number of festivals and holidays recorded in calendars resulted in imperial reforms by Claudius, Dio Cassius 60.17.1; by Nerva, Dio Cassius 68.2.3; by Domitian, see note 235 above; and by Aurelian *H.A. Marc. Aur.* 10.10.

237. *CJ* 3.12.3. The law is directed against *iudices*; in the late empire, *iudices* included all imperial officials or functionaries who were charged with the right to adjudicate affairs inside and outside the courts; see A. Berger, *Encyclopedic Dictionary of Roman Law, Transactions of the American Philosophical Society*, n. s., vol. 43, pt. 2 (Philadelphia, 1953). Cf. *C.Th.* 1.16.9 on restrictions placed on *iudices* seeking popularity by attending games.

orated with games. Such activities were by far the most popular means of celebration in the fourth-century city.

The Central Role of the Emperor

The key development evidenced by Roman calendars over the first four centuries of the empire involved the increasing centrality of imperial prerogative. Among the cults commemorated by public games in the Calendar of 354, that of the emperor and his family dominated the year. The numbers tell part of the story: ninety-eight days were reserved for anniversaries and ceremonies of the imperial house that included *ludi* and *circenses* (excluding the ten days of gladiatorial games). In contrast, sixty-nine days were reserved for *ludi* and *circenses* to honor the pagan gods.

The predominance of the imperial cult was attested as well by the number of gladiatorial combats, the most expensive and most moving of festival rites. Eight of the ten fixed days for gladiatorial combat in December were devoted to the imperial cult. The imperial treasury financed these games, and the priests of the imperial cult were in charge of their celebration. Although the holding of gladiatorial games had been the emperor's prerogative in the early empire, the tendency to focus all honors on the emperor and his family reached its logical culmination in the fourth century with the setting aside of specific dates in the Calendar solely for this purpose. Another aspect of this change is seen in the fact that, in the late empire, magistrates performed their inaugural sacrifices not to the traditional gods but to the emperor or empress.[238]

The importance of the emperor and imperial cult in late Roman public paganism, however, is even greater than the numbers suggest. Although the six great public games of the republic were still celebrated in the fourth century, the total number of days devoted to them decreased: from fifty-nine days in the first century to thirty-seven days in the fourth (Table 1). Moreover, this decrease can be explained by the temporal and financial encroachments on the Roman year by the imperial cult.

Again, in looking at holidays and festivals to honor the pagan deities or mythical and historical events (69 days with *ludi* and *circenses* plus 54 days without, for a total of 123), numbers can mislead. At first sight it would appear that the gods were holding their own against the imperial cult. Yet on closer examination it becomes clear that the most important

238. See, for example, J. H. Oliver, "Julia Domna as Athena Polias," *HSCP*, supp. 1 (1940): 528–529, ll. 15–18.

festivals and cults (i.e., the ones with the greatest number of *ludi* and *circenses*) are those that had received imperial support, especially in the period after Aurelian.

The impact of imperial preference or affiliation was especially critical when it came to incorporating new festivals and cults into the Roman calendar (Tables 2 and 4). The number of cults new to the fourth-century Calendar as compared to first-century one are relatively few. Only three appear with any frequency: Sol Invictus, Isis (with her associated consorts, Sarapis and Osiris), and Attis, the young consort of the Magna Mater. Each of these cults had received imperial support for some time. In marked contrast, other new cults that gained only sporadic imperial support do not appear in the Calendar. For example, the cult of Dea Caelestis, favored by Septimius Severus, received a temple in Rome, and her image appeared on imperial coins under his reign; yet her cult was not integrated into the Calendar, even though it is popularly attested in Rome into the fourth century.[239] Similarly, although Vortumnus's statue in Rome was restored by Diocletian and Maximian and this deity received imperial attention, his cult finds no place in the Calendar.[240]

The importance of sustained imperial support for the integration of new cults into the public calendar can be explained, in part, in institutional terms: to become a public cult required state monies, which, in the empire, generally required the approval of the emperor. Of course, technically the Senate had to approve a new cult as well, and the people had to acquiesce in its adoption.[241] Nonetheless, it is indicative that only those new cults with imperial support were recorded in the official Calendar.

Imperial affiliation was important for the "older" cults (i.e., those also found in first-century calendars) as well (Tables 1 and 3). Significantly, the deities honored most often and with the greatest expense were also those supported by emperors within the seventy-five-year period after Aurelian. The impact of the attempted "pagan revival" initiated by the rulers of the tetrarchy is apparent in the popularity of the cults of Mars, Hercules, and Jupiter. Even some of the more obscure festivals and cults may be traced to this period: the dedication to Tiberinus by Diocletian and Maximian, for instance, may account for renewed

239. Wissowa 1912, p. 374, n. 6. *CIL* 6.77–80, 6.545, 6.2242, indicates a shrine in the city in A.D. 259. Worship of Dea Caelestis continued into the fourth century, according to Firmicus Maternus *De Err. Prof. Rel.* 4; cf. Wissowa 1912, pp. 374ff.

240. *CIL* 6.804 = *ILS* 3588; cf. *CIL* 6.803. Games to Vortumnus are identified in the inscription from Hispellum, Etruria, from the time of Constantine, *CIL* 11.5265.

241. Wissowa 1912, p. 406.

interest in that cult, whose festival appears, for the first time in a Roman calendar in the Calendar of 354, under the name of *Tiberinalia*.[242]

Given the institutionalized importance of the emperor in determining the allocation of resources and attention, it is not surprising that the most expensive and frequent celebrations were those devoted to the imperial cult. They were funded largely from the imperial fisc, though often with the willing participation of wealthy individuals. And, as noted above, eight of the ten days reserved for gladiatorial games—the most expensive of the celebrations—in the fourth-century Calendar were financed by the imperial treasury and held in honor of imperial cult.

The political, social, and religious appeal of the imperial cult and its holidays explains why the Christian emperors of the fourth century, including the pious Constantius, willingly maintained them. Nevertheless, Constantius, like his predecessors, altered imperial cult to reflect his views. In the Calendar, I noted a narrowing of focus onto the ruling emperor and his dynasty, with particular emphasis on Constantius and his father, Constantine. This may explain the omission of celebrations in honor of the *divae*; yet the absence of such festivities is also consistent with Constantius's general policies toward paganism and his attempt to redefine the rites of imperial cult as secular honors while outlawing aspects especially offensive to Christians.[243] In this way, Constantius tried to use imperial cult as a bridge between pagans and Christians; after all, both groups could participate in festivals to honor the emperor.

The Increased Role of *Ludi* and *Circenses*

The increased role of *ludi* and *circenses* in the Calendar is evident. Some have argued that this change is due to the political interests of the emperor. There is some truth in this: the great public games did allow the emperor direct contact with the populace at large. Even Maxentius, short-lived emperor that he was, built a hippodrome at Rome out of a desire to display his power.[244] But the appeal of the *ludi* and *circenses* was more than merely political.[245] These games were the single most important occasions for uniting the community, either in honor of the gods or, increasingly in the late empire, in honor of the emperor. Their

242. See note 148 above.
243. For Constantius's actions against sacrifice, see Chapter 5.
244. See Cameron, *Circus Factions*, p. 182.
245. Viewing the games as merely political is most common. See, for example, J. P. V. Balsdon, *Life and Leisure in Ancient Rome* (London, 1969), pp. 244ff.; A. Wardman, *Religion and Statecraft Among the Romans* (Baltimore, 1982), pp. 27ff.; Fink, Hoey, and Snyder 1940, pp. 167–173ff.; De Ruggiero, *Dizionario epigraphico*, vol. 4, fasc. 63–66, s.v. "*Ludi*."

function, then, was as much social and civic as it was political and religious.

The following paragraph highlights the social significance of the public games, be they to honor the gods or the emperor:

> Within the games, [which were] a significant part of the cult, typically administered by an imperial high priest, competition was obviously fundamental. These competitive values were also a crucial part of the value system of the elite who organized the games. To be an imperial priest was a mark of distinction, as was true of priesthoods in general. . . . This world of competition and display . . . is summed up in the term *philotimia,* "love of honor."[246]

In the fourth century, the games offered an arena for the display of civic prominence: competition within the elite was matched by that between the circus factions. Although the competition was real enough, it also held symbolic connotations, cosmic meanings derived from the associations of the circus with Sol and the planets—astrology being, as the Codex-Calendar has shown, a contemporary passion.

It would be anachronistic to view these moments of contact at games and festivals as mere political rallies or social events, devoid of religious significance. Despite Constantius's attempts to reshape imperial cult, the games and circuses held in conjunction with the festivals of imperial cult and certainly of the pagan gods were considered *inter res divinas.*[247] As such, of course, they were opposed by Christian leaders. Yet aside from their appeal on religious and traditional grounds, the public games offered satisfaction on more personal terms: in short, they were exciting. Few modern readers find it difficult to understand, for example, why Alypius, Augustine's earnest Christian companion, was seduced by the games.[248]

Contemporary Popular Trends in the Calendar of 354: Soteriological Intent, the Army, Astrology, and Rome

Although imperial support was the single most important factor influencing a pagan cult's popularity, in the case of the three major cults new to the fourth-century Calendar certain other contemporary devel-

---

246. Price, *Rituals and Power,* pp. 122ff.

247. Augustine *De Civ. Dei* 4.26: "Ludi scaenici . . . inter res divinas a doctissimis conscribuntur." See further W. Weismann, *Kirche und Schauspiele. Die Schauspiele im Urteil der lateinischen Kirchenväter unter besonderer Berücksichtigung von Augustin* (Würzburg, 1972), pp. 243ff.; and O. Pasquato, *Gli spettacoli in Giovanni Crisostomo. Paganesimo e cristianesimo ad Antiochia e Constantinopoli nel IV Secolo,* Orientalia Christiana Analecta, vol. 201 (Rome, 1976).

248. Augustine *Conf.* 6.8.

opments played a noteworthy role as well. Soteriological intent, for a start, had a major impact on the growth of the cults of Attis and Isis. In the fourth century, their public celebrations were reinforced by—and they in turn reinforced—popular private rites.[249] Small wonder, then, that these cults soon became the most popular of the Roman year, inspiring the illustrations of April and November in the Calendar.

Another significant new trend evident in the calendar of the fourth century as compared to that of the first is the fixing of dates for ceremonies and holidays that had earlier been movable festivals. These include ten days for gladiatorial combat, as well as the festivals and ceremonies of the *Vindemiae*, noted on 5 September; the *ludi Compitales*, on 3–5 January; *Vesta aperitur*, on 7 June; and *Arma, ancilia moventur*, on 9 March. This development coincides with increased governmental centralization and control over all aspects of life under the *dominate*; in this sense, to be sure, the Calendar reflects the state it served.

Increasing state militarization owing to the crises of the third century, too, has left its mark on the Calendar. Hence, the cults and festivals attached to Mars, Quirinus/Romulus, and Jupiter, as well as to Minerva and Vesta (important in military contexts), are noted more frequently in the fourth-century Calendar than in first-century ones. The association of the emperor with the imperial virtue of victory is but one more aspect of this trend.

Among the festivals new to the fourth-century Calendar, one notes the tendency to record and at times celebrate seasonal and astrological events. The *Bruma*, on 24 November, and the Rose Festival (*Macellus Rosa[m] sumat*), on 23 May, for example, were publicly celebrated, whereas the summer solstice (*Solstitium*), on 24 June, and the astrological location of the sun in the sky were merely noted. Seasonal changes, tied to agricultural cycles, of course informed the very earliest layer of paganism and the first Roman calendars; but this emphasis on astrology ties in with other sections of the Codex-Calendar, which evidence a widespread contemporary interest in such information. Moreover, the ascription of religious meaning to astrological events coincides with recent discussions of other pagan cults worshiped in the empire. The popular cult of Mithras, for instance, may be explained to some extent in terms of astrology.[250]

---

249. It may be difficult to assess the private cult's impact on the popularity of the public cult and its celebration; it is impossible to say to what degree the participant distinguished between the private rites of initiation into the cult of Attis and the public games in honor of the Magna Mater. For further discussion, see J. Matthews, "Symmachus and the Oriental Cults," *JRS* 63 (1973): 175–195.

250. Roger Beck, "Mithraism Since Franz Cumont," *ANRW* II 17.4 (Berlin, 1984), pp. 2002–2015; and David Ulansey, *The Origins of the Mithraic Mysteries: Cosmology and Salvation in the Ancient World* (Oxford, 1989).

Attention to Rome and the cult of Roma Aeterna emerges as a significant change in the fourth-century Calendar.[251] Not only is the *Natalis urbis,* the anniversary of the city's foundation, recorded and commemorated with twenty-four circus races on 21 April, but several other notations point to events in honor of Roma Aeterna as well: the *Natalis annonis,* the celebration of the arrival of grain at Rome; the *Natalis chartis,* the celebration of the arrival of papyrus; and the *Septimontia,* the holiday in honor of the seven hills of Rome.[252] The number of *natales* of temple dedications and the prominence of deities associated with early Rome—Quirinus/Romulus, Castor and Pollux, and Vesta—also suggests the popular appeal of Roma Aeterna. The importance of Roma in symbolic religious ideology was seen as well in the stress laid on the *adventus* and *profectio* ceremonies by the imperial cult, for these ceremonies took on a different meaning when they were performed in Rome.[253] Although the association of Roma with imperial cult was centuries old,[254] the increased emphasis on the emperor and his family in the fourth century probably contributed to this goddess's new prominence. Moreover, Roma was particularly suited to the times: even if Christian emperors and their subjects were not able to accept Roma Aeterna as a divinity, they could accept the civic and patriotic ideology that accompanied her cult. Thus, Roma, like the imperial cult, assumed a role as mediator between pagans and Christians—as her illustration in the Codex-Calendar of 354 (Fig. 2), given to a Christian aristocrat, shows so well.

The focus on Rome and the commemorations of its history and civic institutions contributed to the great number of temple anniversaries that appear for the first time in the fourth-century Calendar (Tables 2 and 4). The exact location in the city of many of these temples, ones dedicated sometime between the mid first century and 354, is not known, nor is the date or identity of the donor. Nonetheless, the continued commemoration in the fourth century of earlier ceremonies focusing on Rome is itself indicative of the popular veneration of the city.

The Senatorial Aristocracy and Roman Religious Life

The celebration of the dedication day of a cultic temple is perhaps the second most prominent occasion for a festival in the Calendar (Tables

251. For the development of the cult of Roma Aeterna in the Latin West, see F. Paschoud, *Roma Aeterna,* Bibliotheca Helvetica Romana, no. 7 (Rome, 1967).

252. For the *Septimonia,* see P. Harmon, "The Public Festivals of Rome," *ANRW* II 16.2, pp. 1440–1468.

253. In addition, certain cults had to perform their ritual at Rome for it to be effective; see Wissowa 1912, pp. 474ff.

254. Mellor, "The Goddess Roma," pp. 952–1030.

2, 3, and 4). The importance of such an anniversary for commemorating the gods highlights the key role of the senatorial aristocracy in the religious life of Rome.

The building or dedication of a new temple to the gods was a religious act;[255] the commemoration of an *aedes sacra* by a *natalis* included a *sacrificium publicum,* whose offering (which was not part of the public rites) was under the care of a few priests or a society specifically charged with this task.[256] According to the Calendar of 354, the *natalis* of a temple in Rome was most popularly commemorated by means of *ludi* and *circenses*; this appealed not merely to the populace at large, but especially to the rich and powerful, for it offered them an opportunity to demonstrate their *philotimia*—civic munificence—within an appropriate social and ceremonial setting. In the fourth-century city, these men were the senatorial aristocracy.

After the reforms in government administration carried out by Constantine, the Roman senatorial aristocracy played a greater role in city administration and state government than it had in the third century. The resurgence of this class is indicated, for example, in the laws of Constantius that attempted to restore the Senate to its preeminent position of respect and honor.[257] There is also perhaps some evidence for the revived status of this body in the notation, recorded for the first time in the Calendar of 354, of the *Vict[oria] Senati* on 4 August, commemorated by twenty-four races in the circus—a celebration that is not connected with any known victory.[258] (Perhaps this notation can be

255. In the republic, the *votum* and dedication of a new temple could be undertaken without the approval of the Senate, although traditionally approval was given. In the imperial period, the approval of the emperor and probably the Senate were required. See Wissowa 1912, pp. 474ff.

256. Wissowa 1912, p. 474; cf. *Fasti Vallenses* on 5 August: "Saluti in colle Quirinale sacrificium publicum." The precinct then remained under a special statute, *lex*, and the *natalis* was celebrated annually. Instructive is the statute of the Collegium Cultorum Dianae et Antinoi at Lanuvium, *CIL* 14.2112, col. ii.11ff. = *ILS* 7212; and at Rome that of the Collegium of Aesculapius and Hygiae, *CIL* 6.10234, ll. 11ff. = *ILS* 7213.

257. *C.Th.* 6.4.8, 9, 10, and 6.4 passim indicates that Constantius allowed only *clarissimi* (members of the hereditary senatorial class) to become senators and that he removed decurions from the Senate. *Zon.* 13.22c, in *PG*, col. 1142, indicates that Constantius required literacy and rhetorical skill of all senators. For the reforms of Constantine and their impact on the senatorial class, see A. Chastagnol, "La carrière sénatoriale du bas-empire (depuis Dioclètien)," *Titulus* 4 (1982): 174ff.; and A. Chastagnol, "L'évolution de l'ordre sénatorial aux III et IV siècles," *Revue Historique* 496 (1970): 305ff. For Constantius's government, see C. Vogler, *Constance II et l'administration impériale* (Strasbourg, 1979).

258. Degrassi 1963, pp. 491–492; *senati* is the spelling in the manuscripts. It may be an archaic genitive: see Lewis and Short, *Lat. Dict.,* s.v. "Senatus." For Constantine's vicennial (A.D. 326), the multiple with the reverse legend "Senatus" was struck at Rome. See *RIC* 7, p. 282 and p. 326, no. 272, for a gold medallion from Rome; p. 490 and p. 517, no. 146, for one from Thessalonica; and p. 593 and p. 616, no. 102, for one from Nicomedia.

associated with the famous altar and statue of Victory in the Roman Senate house?)

The urban senatorial aristocracy was prominent in the building, maintenance, dedication, and celebration of *natales* of temples. It was this aristocracy, too, that traditionally held the most prestigious pagan priesthoods and magistracies. The responsibility for financing and organizing the public games was, under Constantius II (as always), largely that of the magistrates; quaestors, praetors, and suffect consuls, as well as consuls, occupied primarily ceremonial offices divorced from their former political duties. In Rome, their major obligation upon entering office was the giving of games. Certain of these games were held in conjunction with traditional Roman holidays. So, for example, the urban prefect arranged the games to Apollo in July; the candidates for the quaestorship were responsible for the gladiatorial games held on two days in December, traditionally associated with the *Saturnalia*;[259] the suffect consul, whose duties are otherwise unknown, had certain formal obligations at the *Natalis urbis* on 21 April; and the consul was responsible for games on 3 January, the *ludi Compitales* and *Votorum nuncupatio*, on 7 January games to Janus Pater, on 13 January to Jove Stator, and on 19 April to Ceres.[260]

The magistrate faced with arranging a set of games could receive some financial help from the public treasury (*aerarium Saturni*). Actors for the *ludi scaenici* seem to have been paid straightforwardly from public funds.[261] For only modestly well off senators, however, the games, a virtual tax on their wealth, were a burden—even though attempts were made to aid them and to limit the amount that they could spend on the games. In the second century, for example, Antoninus Pius gave the impoverished Gavius Clarus a large sum from his private exchequer to help him with his games.[262] Julian donated to Antioch three hundred lots of land tax free to assist councillors faced with the prospect of paying for chariot races.[263] There is even some evidence to suggest that in the

259. Eight days of gladiatorial combat in December were paid for with monies from the imperial treasury (*arca fisci*); the remaining two were paid for largely by the magistrate. This distinction was marked in the names of the spectacles: *candida* or *arca*, unsubsidized or subsidized.

260. See *C.Th.* 6.4, on the games required of praetors and quaestors; Symmachus *Ep.* 6.40 and discussion by Seeck, p. clxvi; J. Matthews, *Western Aristocracies and Imperial Court A.D. 364–426* (Oxford, 1975), p. 14, n. 1; Degrassi 1963, on the consular role for the days cited; Balsdon, *Life and Leisure*, pp. 262–263.

261. J. H. W. G. Liebeschuetz, *Antioch: City and Imperial Administration in the Late Roman Empire* (Oxford, 1972), p. 146; John Chrysostom *Hom. 12 ad Cor. I, PG* 61.103.

262. Fronto *Ep. ad L. Ver.* 2.7.5–6, ed. Naber (Leipzig, 1867) = 2:154, ed. C. R. Haines (London, 1957).

263. Julian *Misopogon.* 370D–371A, ed. Wright.

fourth century the poorer senators had to give only one set of games, their quaestorian games;[264] yet this could still be a burden, and some senators tried to avoid it. As a result, Constantine was forced to reestablish the penalty for quaestors, praetors, and consuls who failed to appear for their games, and in 354 Constantius ordered the praetorian prefect of Rome to round up all senators who were due to give games and compel them to return to the capital,[265] demanding as well that all *clarissimi* be prepared to finance games and civic services if nominated to the Senate.[266]

If a magistrate was to give truly spectacular games, however, he had to dig into his own pocket. For the wealthy Roman aristocrat with a bent for largesse, the giving of games was a welcome opportunity to make his mark on the city. And the elite, by and large, continued to support this arrangement, with enthusiasm that mounted in proportion to their wealth. As A. H. M. Jones remarks: "At Rome, members of great families, who had a tradition of munificence and ample fortunes to indulge their tastes, sometimes squandered fabulous sums on them. Symmachus is said to have spent 2000 lb. of gold on his son's praetorian games, and Petronius Maximus, one of the richest men in the empire, double that sum on his own."[267] Some aristocrats were no doubt inspired to give games beyond their means, for the competitive quality, as Ambrose remarks, was indeed still vital: "It is prodigality to exhaust one's own fortune for the sake of popularity, which is what those men do who destroy their patrimony by giving circus races or even theatrical performances or gladiatorial contests or even wild beast hunts, so that they may surpass the festal celebrations of their predecessors."[268]

Although Ambrose may be accused of rhetorical exaggeration, the civic and communal aspects of Roman games and festivals that inspired such competition among the elite were very much alive in the fourth century. No wonder that contemporary Christian polemicists attacked

264. Seeck believed, on the basis of Symm. *Rel.* 8, and especially *Or.* 8, that the poorest senators at Rome might be let off with one set of games, the quaestorian, which were the least expensive: "Nam certe potuerat convenientem censibus suis, ut nunc facimus, petere quaesturam, sed inopiae suae conscia hoc quoque ut gravissimum timuit, quo minus nihil est" (*Or.* 8.2). At Constantinople, only praetorian games were required by Constantius: *C.Th.* 6.4.5 (A.D. 340).

265. *C.Th.* 6.4.4 (A.D. 354), 6.4.7 (354), 6.4.18 (365), reiterates a law of Constantine no longer extant.

266. *C.Th.* 6.4.7; see too 6.4.1.

267. A. H. M. Jones, *The Later Roman Empire,* A.D. 284–602 (Oxford, 1964), pp. 537–538; *Olymp. frag.* 44, in *FHG* 4.

268. Ambrose *De Off.* 2.109, *PL* 16, pp. 23–184: "Quod faciant qui ludis circensibus vel etiam theatribus et muneribus gladiatoribus vel etiam venationibus patrimonium dilapident suum, ut vincant superiorum celebritates."

the ties between the urban aristocracy in their civic role and paganism: "Tell me, what benefit to the City was your prefect, when, a plunderer in ceremonial attire, he had reached the throne of Jupiter. . . . How, I ask you, did your [pagan] priest help the city?"[269]

However great was the role of the aristocracy in celebrating the *natales* of temples and pagan public cult festivals in general, the role of the emperor was still greater. Not only did the temples of the gods fall under state jurisdiction, and hence under the legal control of the emperor, but the emperor was still the *pontifex maximus* of all the pagan cults as well. Thus, any temple *natalis* recorded in the Calendar would, by definition, involve the implicit approval and explicit support of the state, and hence of the emperor—even if he did not take part in the celebration directly.

Discussion of the nature and appeal of late Roman holidays and cults has allowed us to delimit the two dominant groups with which Roman paganism was intimately linked in the fourth century capital. First was the senatorial aristocracy of Rome. In 354, these men were enjoying a renewed sense of importance in the state. Moreover, since the emperor was very seldom in Rome, their role in the celebration of public festivals and games was greater than ever before.

This class, however, was overshadowed in the Calendar by the second group: the emperor and his family. The critical role of imperial favor was indicated not only by the frequent celebrations recorded in the Calendar in honor of the imperial cult but also, and more surprisingly, by the number and nature of the pagan cults and festivals listed. Indeed, imperial preference, especially in the years after Aurelian, was decidedly the key factor in determining which of the pagan cults would survive both in public celebration and, consequently, in the Calendar.

CHRISTIAN EMPERORS AND PAGAN PRACTICES

The close ties between late Roman public paganism and the emperor that can be traced in the Calendar are at first surprising, for the emperors involved—beginning with Constantine—were all Christian. Moreover, Christianity, by the mid fourth century a major institution in Rome, had made its mark on the Codex, even if Christian festivals were not yet of sufficient public import to be included in a civic calendar for A.D. 354.

If my analysis is correct, the significance of imperial approval and of

269. *Carmen contra Paganos* 29–30, trans. B. Croke and J. Harries, *Religious Conflict*, p. 80.

the emperor's role in effecting the public celebration of pagan cults is far greater than previously thought. Hence, the decision of a sequence of fourth-century emperors to support Christianity emerges as a major institutional explanation for the ultimate decline of paganism and the rise of the new religion of imperial preference, Christianity. Indeed, this may be the critical reason for the Christianization of the Western Roman Empire as a whole.

Yet in the mid fourth century, the ties between public cult, the senatorial aristocracy, and the emperor were still strong. When confronted with the new cult of imperial choice and the growth of a new and powerful institution in Rome—Christianity—how would the Roman senatorial aristocracy react? Given the ties that bound them, it would be surprising to find pagan aristocrats in 350s Rome involved in an overt political movement against the religion of the emperor. But certain scholars have made precisely this argument. Did this happen in Rome? To answer this question, we must broaden our view and discuss the world that produced and used the Calendar of 354.

· PART III ·

THE WORLD: ROMAN SOCIETY AND RELIGION AND THE CODEX-CALENDAR OF 354

· V ·

CONSUETUDINIS AMOR: ROME IN THE MID FOURTH CENTURY

Consuetudinis amor magnus est . . .

The love of custom is a powerful thing . . . [1]

usque ad illam aetatem venerator idolorum, sacrorumque sacrilego-
rum particeps, quibus tunc tota fere Romana nobilitas inflata, spirabat
prodigia iam et omnigenum deum monstra et Anubem latrato-
rem . . . et a se victis iam Roma supplicabat.

He [Victorinus] had always been a worshipper of idols and had taken
part in the sacrilegious rites which were then in vogue amongst most
of the nobility of Rome. Rome, in fact, had become the suppliant of
the gods whom she had once defeated, for her leaders now talked
only of "prodigies, monstrous deities of every sort, and Anubis who
barked like a dog."[2]

CONFLICT OR ACCOMMODATION: TWO THEORETICAL MODELS

The Codex-Calendar of 354 with its yearly round of pagan holidays
and illustrations was produced in Rome for a Christian aristocrat living
under the reign of Constantius II. The content and the circumstances of
production of this codex reflect its contemporary world. That world—

---

1. Symmachus *Rel.* 3.4, ed. O. Seeck, in *MGH, Auctores Antiquissimi* 6.1 (Berlin, 1883);
translation by author.
2. Augustine *Conf.* 8.2.3, trans. R. S. Pine-Coffin (Middlesex, Eng., 1961; repr. 1981).

mid-fourth-century Rome—has been interpreted according to two very different theoretical models.

The first model focuses on the points of conflict, especially political conflict, between pagans and Christians. Like two modern superpowers, these two groups are seen as locked in a struggle to the death in a city polarized along religious lines. In drawing this conflictual model, scholars have been much influenced by the writings of A. Alföldi. In his fundamental study of the contorniates—those bronze pseudomonetary medallions with pagan iconography that appeared ca. A.D. 356–358 and continued to be issued through the fourth century—Alföldi in 1943 argued for interpreting the contorniates as pieces of pagan propaganda produced by the Roman aristocracy against Christianity. Thus, these medallions marked the beginning of the pagan reaction that would lead to the so-called pagan revival of Symmachus and his circle in the 380s and the uprising of Eugenius.[3]

Alföldi's views rang especially true for the generation of scholars who had lived through World War II. F. Poulsen, for one, compared the pagan contorniates, "hated and persecuted by the government," with the liberal propaganda and illegal writings of the war, which he thought had been "called to life by the unbearable strain on thought and the expression of opinions."[4] Many scholars accepted Alföldi's thesis, in both general and specific terms.[5] Although some disagreed with him regarding the particular use of the contorniates, Alföldi's vision of the period (which was based on a wide survey of evidence, including the numismatic) as one of overt political conflict has remained influential.[6]

3. The *locus classicus* for interpretation of 350s Rome as a city polarized by conflict was advanced in detail by A. Alföldi, as indicated by the title *Die Kontorniaten: Ein verkanntes Propagandamittel der stadtrömischen heidnischen Aristokratie in ihrem Kampfe gegen das christliche Kaisertum* (Budapest, 1943). The revised catalogue was reprinted by A. Alföldi and E. Alföldi, *Die Kontorniat-Medaillons*, vol. 1 (Berlin, 1976). Unfortunately, A. Alföldi died before publishing his more recent interpretation of the contorniates. Alföldi continued to expound his conflictual view of the fourth century; see, for example, *A Conflict of Ideas in the Late Roman Empire: The Clash Between the Senate and Valentinian I* (Oxford, 1952) and *The Conversion of Constantine and Pagan Rome* (Oxford, 1948; repr. 1969). For the alleged pagan revival in the 380s, see Chapter 6.

4. F. Poulsen, *Glimpses of Roman Culture*, trans. J. Dahlmann Hansen (Leiden, 1950), p. 276.

5. A. Piganiol, *L'empire chrétien*, 2d ed. (Paris, 1972); F. Paschoud, *Roma Aeterna. Etudes sur le patriotisme romain dans l'Occident latin à l'époque des grandes invasions*, Bibliotheca Helvetica Romana, no. 7 (Rome 1967), p. 94; B. Kötting, *Christentum und heidnische Opposition in Rom am Ende des 4. Jahrhunderts*, Schriften der Gesellschaft zur Förderung der westfälischen Wilhelms-Universität zu Münster, no. 46 (Münster, 1961); H. Bloch, "The Pagan Revival in the West at the End of the Fourth Century," in *The Conflict Between Paganism and Christianity in the Fourth Century*, ed. A. Momigliano (Oxford, 1963), pp. 193–218; K. S. Painter, *The Mildenhall Treasure* (London, 1977), p. 94.

6. For scholars who were critical of Alföldi's interpretation of the contorniates, see

Recently, a group of "revisionist scholars" has sketched the outlines of an alternative model for interpreting the period in Rome under Constantius II, one that highlights the processes of accommodation and assimilation in the capital. In his thoughtful criticism of Alföldi's publication on the contorniates, S. Mazzarino observes: "La Roma tardo-imperiale, e in molti casi Roma in genere, è la città del compromesso paganeggiante e dell'umana tradizionale tolleranza."[7] While Mazzarino does not analyze the historical evidence in full, his approach has been pursued by other "revisionist" scholars. They argue that Rome is best described as an ambience of compromise and that this period was critical for facilitating the gradual assimilation of pagan culture into a Christian framework.[8] Assimilation necessarily altered the very form and content of the new religion, creating, for the first time in the fourth-century city, a respectable, aristocratic Christianity.

The outlines of this alternative model can only be traced in the individual studies of scholars that reinterpret the bits and pieces of the evidence. To my knowledge, no one work has yet attempted systemati-

---

notes 81–85 below. Alföldi's work has greatly influenced interpretation of this period by other scholars, some of whom are named in note 5 above. Others are recorded in A. Cameron's essay "The 'Pagan Reaction' 1943–1983," which will appear in vol. 2 of *Die Kontorniat-Medaillons*, ed. E. Alföldi (forthcoming). The bibliography on the conflict between paganism and Christianity in the fourth century is vast; relevant specific works are cited in the notes below. Scholars who viewed this period as one of pagan-Christian conflict and pagan revival include Geffcken, 1978; Piganiol, *L'empire chrétien*; H. Lietzmann, *From Constantine to Julian*, vol. 3 of *A History of the Early Church*, trans. B. L. Woolf (London, 1950); Bloch, "The Pagan Revival"; and J. Wytzes, *Der letzte Kampf des Heidentums in Rom*, *EPRO*, no. 56 (Leiden, 1977).

7. S. Mazzarino, "La propaganda senatoriale nel tardo impero," *Doxa* 4 (1951): 142. In his article, Mazzarino remarked the commemoration of Christ's birthday on 25 December instead of 6 January as a compromise with the traditional pagan festival of Sol by the Christian church; this was the only evidence he adduced for the period before the death of Constantius II (pp. 142–143).

8. See, for example, the still-fundamental study by P. Brown, "Aspects of the Christianization of the Roman Aristocracy," *JRS* 51 (1961): 1–11. A general introduction to this period that reflects this "new" view is D. Bowder, *The Age of Constantine and Julian* (London, 1978). Noteworthy prosopographical works that exemplify the reinterpretation of this period include D. Novak, "Anicianae domus culmen, nobilitatis culmen," *Klio* 62, no. 2 (1980): 473–493; D. Novak, "Constantine and the Senate: An Early Phase of the Christianization of the Roman Aristocracy," *Ancient Society* 10 (1979): 271–310; R. von Haehling, *Die Religionszugehörigkeit der hohen Amtsträger des Römischen Reiches seit Constantins. Alleinherrschaft bis zum Ende der Theodosianischen Dynastie (324–450 n. Chr.)*, Antiquitas, 3d ser., vol. 23 (Bonn, 1978); R. MacMullen, *Paganism in the Roman Empire*, (New Haven, Conn., 1981); A. Wardman, *Religion and Statecraft Among the Romans* (Baltimore, 1982), pp. 135–174; and R. Wilken, *John Chrysostom and the Jews* (Berkeley and Los Angeles, 1983). An excellent collection of documents and bibliography can be found in B. Croke and J. Harries, *Religious Conflict in Fourth-Century Rome: A Documentary Study* (Sydney, 1982).

cally to refute the conflictual model of Rome under Constantius II advanced by Alföldi.

The aim of this chapter, then, is to demonstrate the veracity of the second model of interpretation. First, I shall examine the evidence provided by the Codex-Calendar itself and the circumstances of its production; then I shall question the principal proofs and the other contemporary evidence from Rome in the 350s that were used to buttress Alföldi's conflictual model. My analysis will show that Rome under Constantius II was a place where pagans and Christians had reached a modus vivendi by means of accommodation. By 354, the assimilation of pagan aristocratic traditions into a Christian framework was well under way in Rome—a reality that is amply reflected in the pages of the Codex-Calendar.

THE CODEX-CALENDAR OF 354:
THE CONTENTS AND CONTEXT AS EMBLEMATIC
OF ROMAN SOCIETY

The Codex-Calendar evidences the close interconnections among the three dominant institutions in the city of Rome: the Roman aristocracy, grounded in traditional paganism; the emperor with his bureaucracy and imperial cult; and the Christian church at Rome. As we have seen, the Codex presents these three institutions in a similar light, indicating the shared concerns and values of the people in positions of authority in each area. In Rome, these people were drawn predominantly from the senatorial aristocracy or had close ties to it. In my view, it was this shared aristocratic culture that cut across religious differences and supported a climate of accommodation and assimilation in the Rome of Constantius II. Analysis of the contents and the circumstances of production—involving creator, donor, and recipient—of the Codex-Calendar of 354 further reinforces this estimation.

The Contents of the Codex-Calendar:
Evidence for Accommodation and Assimilation

The text and illustrations of the Calendar attest to the ongoing importance of paganism for both the imperial government and the Roman senatorial aristocracy; the support of these two institutions helps to elucidate the vitality of paganism in the urban life of mid-fourth-century

Rome. To reiterate, the senatorial aristocracy under Constantius II enjoyed considerable economic and political strength; as holders of high civic offices, this aristocracy—especially after the divisive civil wars under Magnentius and the restoration of peace—was in a position not only to prevent the enforcement of laws unfavorable to paganism but also to protect their own pagan traditions.

In addition to aristocratic attention, imperial backing for the public state cults recorded by the Calendar contributed greatly to the endurance of late Roman paganism. Pagan festivals and holidays, games and circuses, were funded by imperial monies and celebrated with imperial approval. As I have argued, imperial support in the years after Aurelian was critical for determining the most popular pagan holidays in the mid fourth century. Moreover, the imperial cult remained a vibrant aspect of the annual calendar of events, favored by emperor and aristocracy alike. Its celebration thus offered pagans and Christians numerous occasions to share easily the pleasures of games and circuses and a common cultural heritage.

Certain pagan festivals were especially important in this respect. Holidays commemorating abstract civic ideals, such as the celebrations in honor of Roma Aeterna, or those tied to great moments in Roman history, such as the *Regifugium,* which commemorated the expulsion of the Etruscan kings and the beginning of the Roman Republic, were thus important as both state occasions and pagan festivals. Pride in Roman aristocratic traditions, in short, could be shared by all inhabitants of Rome, regardless of religious affiliation.

Although the Calendar indicates the vitality of the pagan and imperial round of holidays in 350s Rome, it also evidences the beginnings of Christian and pagan accommodation to the changing times. The emphasis on festivals in which both pagans and Christians could participate, especially those of the imperial cult and those commemorating civic and historical events, suggests just such a process. And the illustrations of the months, although focusing on contemporary pagan festivals, include no scenes of animal sacrifice, the rite most objectionable to Christians; only January (Fig. 30) involves any image of sacrifice, but here it is the relatively inoffensive rite of incense burning within an official context. Moreover, fewer representations of pagan festivals are included in the Calendar of 354 than in its counterparts from the third century, while the number of seasonal illustrations appears to have grown proportionally.

The inclusion of a veritable calendar of Christian holidays within the Codex, the lists of the Depositions of Bishops and Martyrs (sections XI and XII), also underscores the accommodative nature of the Codex-Calendar. With this second calendar, the man for whom the Codex was prepared could participate in a traditional Roman secular timeframe and hence world view, as well as in Christian ones. Presuming that the recipient of this work was typical of other Roman aristocrats, moreover, these lists of Christian observances also highlight the importance of this religion and its institutions in the city. Nevertheless, the Christian calendar is still, in 354, separate from the civic calendar of Rome; its holidays are not yet integrated into the life of the city, even if they are to be noted and tolerated.

The other Christian lists added to the pagan, imperial, and aristocratic sections of the Codex-Calendar further reinforce the idea of accommodation, as well as indicate the growth of Christianity. Two separate but equal chronographic and historical systems, one Christian, one traditionally Roman and pagan, are both parts of a shared aristocratic culture that cuts across religious differences.

The Codex-Calendar of 354 reveals more than mere accommodation, however: it attests as well to the assimilation of aristocratic, traditionally pagan culture into a Christian framework and, simultaneously, of Christianity into aristocratic, traditionally pagan Roman society. The new religion was indeed being changed by its contact with Roman aristocratic values. Indeed, one of the earliest, securely dated examples of this two-way process of assimilation lies in this very Codex—in its style, format, and content, for instance, conceived to appeal to a classically educated, aristocratic Roman who was also a Christian, and in its attempt to present Christianity on a par with paganism. Thus are explained the ornate and classicizing tendencies observed in the representations of the months, in the representations of civic subjects such as city goddesses, and in the representations of the consuls (which derive from imperial secular sources). Similarly decorative and appealing are the Christian monogram and dedicatory vows designed by Filocalus to convey the wish that the recipient should "flourish in God."

Perhaps most interesting is the attempt to portray Christian institutions as commensurate with traditional Roman pagan and secular ones. The addition of Christian information to the consular annals suggests such an attitude, as does the unbroken list of bishops of Rome going back to St. Peter and the apostles, which seems to indicate a Christian past as venerable as the Roman one recorded by the lists of consuls and emperors. On the other side of the coin, the pagan festivals and traditional Roman calendar were clearly thought to be as important to this Christian aristocrat as the Christian holidays and information. Certainly this was a man who not only could tolerate religious differences but also could participate in two worlds, one pagan aristocratic, the other Christian.

The Context of the Codex-Calendar: Who Was Valentinus?

Surely Valentinus was a Christian. A codex-calendar specifically designed to include sections of an emphatically Christian character—the Easter Cycle, the Depositions of Bishops and Martyrs, the List of Bishops of Rome, and the *World Chronicle*—would only have been of interest to a Christian reader, as would the inclusion of four Christian holidays within the list of Consuls. The dedicatory inscription on the book's title page—"Floreas in Deo"—reinforces this identification, for the addition of *in Deo* to the nonspecific wish *Floreas* is a formula peculiar to Christianity.[9] The use of Christian symbols and monograms on inscriptions, unless by order of the emperor, is further evidence for Christianity.[10] Although the specific phrase "Floreas in Deo" is unique, it is similar to the admonition "Vivas" or "Vivatis in Deo" inscribed on certain fragments of gold glass, where expressing an intimate wish for well-being within a familial context.[11] The formula here noted, then, conveys a familiar note and implies that the donor was of equal social status; it also supports Valentinus's Christianity.

The information provided by the ornate, personalized dedication of this deluxe Codex-Calendar indicates that its recipient belonged, most likely, to the aristocracy at Rome. This was, it seems, a man of wealth and rank, an impression borne out by his patronage of the artist Filocalus, who was known to have been patronized by a pope and perhaps by the Christian aristocrat Melania the Elder as well. As we read past

9. Stern 1953, pp. 113–115.

10. Von Haehling, *Religionszugehörigkeit*, pp. 19–49. This conclusion is noted with approval by J. R. Martindale in his review of von Haehling's book, *JRS* 69 (1979): 194–196. In contrast, Cameron, "The 'Pagan Reaction,' " pp. 143–144, argues that Christian dedications could be used to address a pagan member in a mixed marriage. The evidence, however, is problematic; and in any case, here the sole addressee is Valentinus.

11. F. Cabrol and H. Leclercq, *DACL*, s.v. "Fonds d'or," nos. 450, 451, 482; C. Morey, *Catalogo del Museo Sacro della Bibliotheca Apostolica Vaticana* 4, (Vatican City, 1936), nos. 42, 447. Interestingly, many of the inscriptions on the fragments of gold glass have been derived from the Christian wedding service; see *Age of Spirituality: Late Antique and Early Christian Art, 3rd–7th Century* (Catalogue of the Exhibition, Metropolitan Museum of Art), ed. K. Weitzmann (New York and Princeton, N.J., 1979), no. 261. J. Weitzmann-Fiedler notes that the inscription on a gold glass reads "Vivatis in Deo," a formula used since Clement of Alexandria in the Christian wedding ceremony.

the title page, the high status of Valentinus is reinforced: the illustrations of Rome, Constantinople, Trier, and Alexandria, followed by the imperial dedication "Salvis Augustis Felix Valentinus," a list of the *Natales Caesarum* (at the top of which is an imperial nimbed portrait), and the portraits of the two consuls that close the illustrated portion of the Codex, are all visual symbols of social preeminence in fourth-century Rome. Comparable objects, such as ivory consular diptychs, illustrated with official and semiofficial portraits and distributed as a means of indicating the status not only of the donor but also of the recipient have long been known. A study by R. Grigg of the portrait-bearing codicils in the illustrations of the *Notitia Dignitatum* has convincingly demonstrated the function of imperial portraits to specify the recipient's rank: "The presence of the portrait, in fact, may have been partly a means of distinguishing the codicil-diptych of the *illustres* from that of the consuls. Moreover, even among the *illustres,* a higher or lower status is expressed by the use of two different patterns of gold trim."[12] Although the Codex-Calendar is not an official, appointive document, as those illustrated in the contemporary *Notitia Dignitatum* were, the inclusion of imperial portraits may make a similar statement about the status of the recipient—and of the donor. The recipient's status is further elucidated by the fact that the designs for sections I–VII derive from precisely such official and semiofficial documents as the appointive *codicilli.*

As a visual symbol of status, then, the Codex-Calendar strongly suggests that Valentinus was an aristocrat. This personalized edition, with depictions of the months that allude to the visual and literary traditions of the Roman calendar, is illustrated in a manner consistent with his social standing and implies that he is a man of learning and of culture. The unillustrated lists of consuls and urban prefects and the *Chronicle of Rome* carry a similar message. The combination of education and good breeding was a most important mark of status in late Roman aristocratic society. This is what Paulinus of Nola means when he refers to "honos, litterae, domus"—office, letters, and family—as the "tokens of prestige in the world," or what Jerome has in mind when he talks of the "man who is noble, eloquent, and wealthy."[13] Funeral elogia consistently record the learning of the deceased to denote social status.[14] And since

12. R. Grigg, "Portrait-bearing Codicils in the Illustrations of the *Notitia Dignitatum?*" *JRS* 69 (1979): 107–124.

13. Paulinus of Nola *Carm.* 24, vv. 481ff.; Jerome *Ep.* 66.6. For further discussion see R. A. Kaster, *Guardians of Language: The Grammarian and Society in Late Antiquity* (Berkeley and Los Angeles, 1988), pp. 26ff.

14. See, for example, Petronius Probus's epitaph, which refers to him as "Nobilitatis culmen / litterarum et eloquentiae lumen"; *CIL* 6.1751 = *ILS* 1265.

Valentinus was probably a Christian, it is understandable that he would have—or seek to appear to have—an appreciation not only of Roman history and culture but also of Christian history and culture.

The question then arises, which known "Valentinus" might have received the Codex-Calendar? Peiresc proposed identifying our Valentinus with a certain Valentinus cited in the List of Bishops (section XIII) as having received a basilica.[15] Peiresc's identification, however, confuses this Valentinus with the saint Valentinus, martyred in the period of Emperor Claudius.[16]

Of the eleven Valentini recorded in the *Prosopography of the Later Roman Empire,* five have dates that fit ours. Mommsen identified the Calendar recipient with the Valentinus who held the offices of *primicerius protectorum* or *tribunus* in 359 and of *dux* in Illyricum sometime thereafter (*PLRE* 1:935, no. 3). Yet Mommsen then goes on to state, incorrectly, that this *dux* could be identified with a certain Valentinianus found on a consular list in Picenum.[17] Hence, Mommsen's identification can be discarded, since this *dux,* a military man, was not of the aristocracy (*vir clarissimus*), nor can he be located in Rome. For similar reasons of status and geography, another Valentinus (*PLRE* 1:935, no. 5) can be removed from consideration.

Two know Valentini remain who fit comfortably within the outlines suggested by the Calendar: M. Aurelius Valerius Valentinus (*PLRE* 1:936, no. 12), consular of Numidia in 330; and Avianius Valentinus (*PLRE* 1:936, no. 7), consular of Campania under Valentinian I from 364 to 375. Both these men apparently belonged to the same family, that of the aristocratic Symmachi: M. Aurelius Valerius Valentinus was uncle of the famous orator Symmachus (*PLRE* 1:865, no. 4), and Avianius Valentinus has been identified as this same Symmachus's brother because of his unusual cognomen, Avianius, which repeats that of Symmachus's father (*PLRE* 1:863, no. 3; see also *PLRE* 1:1146, stemma 27). Moreover, the orator Symmachus also had a nephew called Valentinus (*PLRE* 2:1139, no. 2), probably named after the same Avianius Valentinus, Symmachus's brother. The name Valentinus, then, lived on within the aristocratic Symmachus family through the fifth century; and since these three are about the only aristocratic Valentini we find in the fourth century,[18]

15. "Basilicam in via Flaminia mil. II quae appellatur Valentini"; text in Mommsen, *MGH* 1892, p. 76. This basilica, according to Valentini-Zucchetti II, 1942, p. 73, was erected by Pope Julius I.

16. Stern 1953, p. 46, n. 1.

17. Mommsen, *MGH* 1892, p. 13

18. The only other aristocratic Valentinus is that listed in *PLRE* 1:936, no. 11, but he is a generation before the Calendar's recipient. This man's name is badly damaged in the

one of them was most likely the recipient of the Codex-Calendar. Perhaps the most plausible identification, based on chronology and geography, is Symmachus's brother, Avianius Valentinus. But unfortunately, little is know about this man other than that he held the prestigious consular post in Campania from 364 to 375 and that he died before 380.[19]

The implications of this suggested identification of Valentinus as a member of the Symmachus family are many. For one thing, it would indicate that at least one male member of this very important Roman aristocratic family became a Christian much earlier than is otherwise known, since the first attested Christian Symmachus is Aurelius Anicius Symmachus, urban prefect in 419–420. The Christianity of a Symmachus family member, too, would provide a striking example of the tolerance and degree of personal religious choice found in Rome in the 350s— elements traditional in Roman aristocratic society and perhaps expressive of the climate of accommodation in the Rome of Constantius II. These tendencies also highlight the complexity of social relations among the city's aristocracy.

What Do We Know About the Creator and Donor of the Codex?

The identities of the creator and donor of the Codex-Calendar of 354 underscore the view of Rome advanced above. The person who penned this Codex was the famous calligrapher Furius Dionysius Filocalus[20]— the same man who carved the epigrams composed by Pope Damasus (366–384) for the renovated tombs of Christian martyrs and aristocrats at Rome. Damasus has been described as the first "social pope"; his cultivation and learning made him a favorite of the aristocracy and

---

one surviving inscription concerning him, which notes that he was consular of Campania A.D. 324–337. Identified as (IU?)NIUS VALENTINUS, this Valentinus may also have been linked to the Symmachus family.

19. The post of consular of Campania was highly prestigious, according to G. Clemente, "Le carriere dei governatori della diocesi italiciana dal III al V secolo," *Latomus* 28 (1969): 632ff. My proposed identification for Valentinus was suggested but not demonstrated by M. T. W. Arnheim, *The Senatorial Aristocracy in the Late Roman Empire* (Oxford, 1972), p. 81, n. 14.

20. Filocalus was omitted from *PLRE* 1 but noted by T. D. Barnes, "More Missing Names (A.D. 260–395)," *Phoenix* 27 (1973): 148, who (in my view) erroneously identified Filocalus with the grammarian of the same name. See also Ferrua 1939, pp. 35–42; and Ferrua 1942, pp. 21–35. Filocalus was most likely a nickname awarded in virtue of his skill. See A. Cameron, "Polyonomy in the Late Roman Aristocracy: The Case of Petronius Probus," *JRS* 75 (1985): 176, for Musonianus and Tullianus.

earned him, according to a contemporary Christian document, the dubious distinction of being an "ear scratcher" (*auriscalpius*) of Roman matrons.[21] Under his tutelage, Christianity became increasingly fashionable among Roman aristocrats.[22] How appropriate, then, that Filocalus—himself probably a Christian[23]—presented Christianity for both Damasus and Valentinus in ways appealing to a cultivated eye.

These may not be the only Christians of social prominence for whom Filocalus labored. A late Latin poem describing baths (*Anth. Lat.* 120, ed. Riese) cites a certain Melania and Filocalus in an acrostich and telestich. Based on dating and prosopography, the most likely identification of these two names is Melania the Elder, the aristocratic Christian famous for her generosity and asceticism, and the calligrapher Filocalus[24]—providing one more instance of Filocalus's role within Christian elite circles at a date roughly contemporary with the Codex-Calendar. The dating of this poem is uncertain, but since Melania was born ca. 340 and probably had the poem inscribed in baths built prior to her departure for the Holy Land (ca. 372), the late 350s or 360s are a reasonable estimation.[25] Given the vitality of paganism within the Roman upper class in the middle decades of the century, Filocalus's patronage by Christian aristocrats is striking.

This raises the interesting question of who the donor of the Calendar was. The donor's name is not included on the title page, an unusual omission as compared with the consular diptychs. Three possible explanations can be advanced here: (1) the name was inserted in the original manuscript, either on the title page or on a separate page or cover, but has been lost owing to the vagaries of transmission; (2) the Codex-Calendar had no donor but was commissioned at Valentinus's request for his personal use; or (3) the dedication by Filocalus to Valentinus may be analogous to the inclusion of *titulavit* on sepulchral elogia (e.g., *ILS* 3703), meaning, in fact, that Filocalus himself was the donor. What evidence exists favors the second or third possibility: Filocalus was involved in the

21. See A. Cameron, "The Date and the Owners of the Esquiline Treasure," *AJA* 89 (1985): 136; the Christian document, *Collectio Avellana*, ed. O. Guenther, *CSEL* 35.1 (Vienna, 1895), 1:4.

22. R. A. Markus, *Christianity in the Roman World* (London, 1974), pp. 151–156, for an interesting discussion of Damasus's role.

23. See note 26 below for inscriptions attesting Filocalus as *cultor* and *amator* of Pope Damasus; these inscriptions indicate Filocalus's Christianity as observed by Ferrua 1942, pp. 124–134; and Ferrua 1939, pp. 35ff.

24. A. Cameron, "Filocalus and Melania," *CP* (forthcoming).

25. The chronology for Melania the Elder is indeed problematic. The dates cited here are from Cameron, "Filocalus and Melania," and *PLRE* 1:592–593. See N. Moine, "Melaniana," *Recherches augustiniennes* 15 (1980): 3–79.

leading Christian aristocratic circles at the time the Codex-Calendar was created, and he copied the poems of Damasus on stone and probably inscribed (and perhaps composed) a poem for the baths of a Melania.

Yet Filocalus was no ordinary professional calligrapher. In the epitaph for the martyr Eusebius composed by Damasus, Filocalus inscribes his name and states that he is "an admirer and personal friend" (*cultor* and *amator*) of the pope. No mere workman could have claimed such intimacy.[26] When that inscription was damaged, its replacement panel recopied the names of Damasus and the martyr along with Filocalus's personal words.[27] In the *Latin Anthology* poem cited above, Filocalus appears on personal terms with a Melania—probably the Christian aristocrat Melania the Elder.[28]

Like the inscriptions in stone, the dedication of the Codex-Calendar proclaims Filocalus's role with a formula that indicates his familiarity with Valentinus. Visually, his name is joined with that of Valentinus on the page. No other late-antique codex includes the name of the calligrapher here.[29] Thus, the Codex reinforces the view that Filocalus was a man of "respectable, if not aristocratic origins who simply spent his time doing what he did so well. Others of his class wrote letters and poems; Filocalus copied their work whether on vellum or stone."[30] Since neither his social status nor his religion stands in the way, either Filocalus himself was the donor or else he was approached by Valentinus to create or copy the Codex-Calendar, in part or in whole. Even in the latter event, Filocalus may well have been the creator;[31] however, it is possible that some unknown third party compiled the texts, which Valentinus then asked Filocalus to copy.

To conclude, the Codex-Calendar of 354, assuming that it and the circumstances of its production are emblematic of the situation in Rome under Constantius II, reveals a world in which the peaceful coexistence of the city's two powerful religious groups has been achieved. In this atmosphere of tolerance, fundamental changes in thought and religion

26. Ferrua 1942, pp. 129–134, no. 18, emphasizes the friendship implied by the terms *cultor* and *amatur*. Filocalus proclaims his name in two other fragmentary epitaphs, published in Ferrua 1942 as nos. 27 and 18.2.

27. Ferrua 1942, pp. 129–134, no. 18, dates the recopying to the sixth century.

28. Cameron, "Filocalus and Melania."

29. At least, no surviving codices or later copies dating from the fourth–fifth centuries include the calligrapher's name; nor is this the practice for early medieval manuscripts.

30. Cameron, "Filocalus and Melania," also observes that other amateur calligraphers of aristocratic status in this age earned renown in similar fashion. For example, the fame of Theodosius II's calligraphy spread far and wide.

31. The term *titulavit* in section I of the Codex-Calendar also implied that Filocalus was the creator of the Codex-Calendar; see Chapter 2.

were taking hold, and in such a way as to preserve rather than destroy pagan aristocratic culture. This world fits comfortably within the second model of interpretation discussed above, with its emphasis on accommodation and assimilation. While arguments for the conflictual model may appear strong at first, close examination shows that the evidence from Rome buttressing this view neither supports a pagan-Christian conflict nor indicates a pagan political reaction or revival in Rome under Constantius II.

THE EVIDENCE FOR PAGAN-CHRISTIAN CONFLICT

The Laws Against Paganism

The interdiction of pagan sacrifice, as it is documented by the Theodosian Code for the years 341–357, is considered the focal point of the Christian attack on paganism. Analysis of legislation against pagan sacrifice, its enforcement, and the pagan reaction to it typically provides the yardstick for measuring the pagan-Christian conflict in Rome. These laws are seen as having had an "inflammatory effect on Christians,"[32] "led to the destruction of many temples,"[33] and revealed "the strength of the pagan party in Rome."[34] As I will show, however, this legislation did not directly affect the pagan senatorial aristocracy and Rome; it therefore did not give rise to a uniform pagan political reaction in the middle of the century, nor does it indicate conflict between pagans and Christians.

The first extant code outlawing pagan sacrifice, dated A.D. 341, reads: "Superstition [*superstitio*] shall cease; the madness of sacrifices shall be abolished. For if any man in violation of the law of the sainted Emperor, Our father, and in violation of this command of Our Clemency, should dare to perform sacrifices, he shall suffer the infliction of a suitable punishment and the effect of an immediate sentence."[35] This code has been much debated, in terms of both its content and its intent. Argument

32. Geffcken 1978, p. 121.
33. D. Bowder, *Age of Constantine*, p. 81.
34. A. Alföldi, *A Festival of Isis in Rome under the Christian Emperors of the Fourth Century* (Budapest, 1937), p. 31.
35. C.Th. 16.10.2: "IMP. CONSTANTIUS A. AD MADALIANUM AGENTEM VICEM P(RAEFECTORUM) P(RAETORIO). Cesset superstitio, sacrificiorum aboleatur insania. Nam quicumque contra legem divi principis parentis nostri et hanc nostrae mansuetudinis iussionem ausus fuerit sacrificia celebrare, conpetens in eum vindicta et praesens sententia exeratur. ACC(EPTA) MARCELLINO ET PROBINO CONS"; trans. C. Pharr, *The Theodosian Code and Novels and the Sirmondian Constitutions* (Princeton, N.J., 1952).

centers on what was meant by the term *superstitio* and, consequently, what precisely was being prohibited.

In one piece of Constantine's earlier extant legislation, a code prohibiting private consultation of *haruspices* and *sacerdotes*, *superstitio* referred to the art of divination.[36] This usage harkens back to earlier legal usage, which sought to prohibit *superstitio* when associated with illicit divination and magical practices.[37] A second Constantinian code uses *superstitio* in a Christian sense: Christians are not to be forced to participate in lustral sacrifices, also termed rites of an "alien superstition."[38]

These earliest instances of the use of the word *superstitio* in the Theodosian Code reveal the two meanings that coexisted in legislative language of this period, implying at once divination and magic and paganism.[39] Sympathetic pagan administrators, then, may quite well have interpreted the 341 code, like the extant codes of Constantine, as directed primarily at divination and magical sacrifice. For pagans, the "insanity of sacrifices" would be a restatement and clarification of *superstitio*, defined by its context to refer to the "insanity of sacrifices" associated with divination and magic. But Christian administrators in predominantly Christian areas could easily have read *superstitio* as applying to paganism in general and therefore to all pagan sacrifice.[40]

Hence the critical importance of knowing who would interpret and enforce the code.[41] This code, issued in 341 when Constantius controlled the Eastern empire and Constans the Western, was directed to Madali-

36. *C.Th.* 9.16.1 (A.D. 319/320).

37. Cf. *C. Gr. in Mos. et. Rom. Legum Collat.* 15.3.1, a law of A.D. 297 under Diocletian and Maximian against the Manichees as a *superstitio*; the rescript of Marcus Aurelius, *Dig.* 49.19.30; and Ulpian's remarks, *Dig.* 28.7.8.

38. *C.Th.* 16.2.5 (A.D. 323). This connection between *superstitio* and sacrifice is remarked in the *Scholia Vaticana*: "Sed hoc inrisive dicit, ut tempta conducta publica secundum ritum pristinum sacrificare"; and *C.Th.* 16.10.1. (A.D. 320/321) outlaws "sacrificis domesticis" because, according to Pharr, *The Theodosian Code*, p. 472, n. 4, they were "secret and antisocial; they might be used against the Emperor."

39. M. R. Salzman, "*Superstitio* in the *Codex Theodosianus* and the Persecution of Pagans," *Vigiliae Christianae* 41 (1987): 172–188.

40. It is interesting that this 341 law corroborates Eusebius's statement, *Vita Constantini* 2.45, that Constantine legislated against pagan sacrifice by those above the rank of provincial governor. Since Eusebius does not quote this law verbatim, it is tempting to posit that it repeats the language of Constantine's law, including the term *superstitio*, which is found often in Constantinian documents.

41. Cf. the legislation requiring magistrates to enforce laws under penalty of death, such as *C.Th.* 16.10.4. The degree to which individual magistrates could influence the enforcement of legislation is indicated by an anecdote about Praetextatus, who, as proconsul of Greece in A.D. 364, intervened to persuade the emperor to allow nocturnal cult practices; attested by Zosimus *Hist. Nova* 4.3.2–3.

anus, vicar of Italy and Africa; thus, Constans was responsible for its promulgation, despite the two imperial names in the manuscript heading.[42] These facts indicate that the code was not intended for Rome, since legislation so intended was directed to the urban prefect or praetorian prefect of the city. In this city, with its predominantly pagan aristocracy, enforcement of such a law would seem unlikely.

A code of 342, directed to the prefect of Rome, appears to specify the nature of certain sanctions imposed for the first time on the pagans in Rome while simultaneously protecting the pagan temples outside the city walls:

> Although all superstitions must be completely eradicated, nevertheless, it is Our will that the buildings of the temples situated outside the walls shall remain untouched and uninjured. For since certain plays or spectacles of the circus or contests derive their origin from some of these temples, such structures shall not be torn down, since from them is provided the regular performance of long established amusements for the Roman people.[43]

The destruction and despoliation of temples and monuments for religious reasons or for profit was a fourth-century phenomenon of increasing frequency; we encounter it elsewhere in the Theodosian Code in legislation protecting tombs—both pagan and Christian—lying outside the city walls.[44] This law may reflect an effort to curb religious zealots, or possibly zealous robbers—we cannot know which.

In any case, the language of the 342 code is decidedly ambiguous. Pagans charged with enforcing the code—including Catullinus, the urban prefect—could, with good conscience, choose to read *superstitio* in

42. *C.Th.* 16.10.2; text cited above. Every imperial pronouncement included both Augusti in the heading, even if only one emperor issued it. One can tell who was responsible for the issuance of a law and the area of the empire actually affected by it from the recipient. Madalianus's (*PLRE* 1:530) religious beliefs are not known, but he was a careerist who was indebted to the house of Constantine for his advancement.

43. *C.Th.* 16.10.3: "AD CATULLINUM P(RAEFECTUM) U(RBI). Quamquam omnis superstitio penitus eruenda sit, tamen volumus, ut aedes templorum, quae extra muros sunt positae, intactae incorruptaeque consistant. Nam cum ex nonnullis vel ludorum vel circensium vel agonum origo fuerit exorta, non convenit ea convelli, ex quibus populo Romano praebeatur priscarum sollemnitas voluptatum. DAT. KAL. NOV. CONSTANTIO IIII ET CONSTANTE III AA. CONS"; trans. Pharr, *The Theodosian Code*; directed by Constans and Constantius Augusti to Catullinus, prefect of the city. For Catullinus, see *PLRE* 1:187–188.

44. *C.Th.* 9.17.1 (A.D. 340), 9.17.2 (A.D. 349), 9.17.3 (A.D. 356), 9.17.4 (A.D. 356), 9.17.5–7 (A.D. 363, 381, 386). Certainly, tomb robbing and despoliation of temples for personal gain and benefit was an age-old Roman problem.

the older meaning of the term, namely, divination.[45] Moreover, this code is impressive for what it accepts in pagan culture as well as for what it attempts to outlaw. The temples were to be reserved for those very games, circuses, and festivals that constituted the traditional pagan religious celebrations. It is worth noting, too, how apt the term *superstitio* was for the mid fourth century, since the coexisting definitions certainly facilitated accommodation to the laws.[46]

After the defeat of Magnentius in 353, Constantius at first continued earlier policy, rescinding only Magnentius's edict permitting nocturnal sacrifice.[47] After 356, however, his policy toward paganism became more forceful. A code (*C.Th.* 16.10.6), securely dated to 356, prohibits sacrifice and the veneration of pagan images under pain of death; another code (*C.Th.* 16.10.4), dated to 356–361, is the harshest of all, for it not only prohibits sacrifice under pain of death but also closes the temples.[48] Codes of 357 and 358 (*C.Th.* 9.16.4–6) prohibit divination, astrology, and magic; they also reveal how—conceptually—Constantius's attack on pagan sacrifice, divination, and magic was in essence an attack on *superstitio*.[49]

If the laws against sacrifice—here understood to include all pagan sacrifice—and the closing of the temples had actually been enforced in Rome with capital punishment, then this legislation would indeed have been cause for alarm. Yet examination of these codes reveals that only the prohibition of nocturnal sacrifice (*C.Th.* 16.10.6–9) was directed to the prefect of Rome; all other injunctions were directed to vicars or praetorian prefects of Italy and Africa and, therefore, were not intended for enforcement in Rome. In fact, it is not until 391 (*C.Th.* 16.10.10) that sacrifice was prohibited in Rome proper.[50]

Independent literary and archaeological evidence attests to the policy of tolerance for paganism at Rome. As Libanius, in *Oratio* 30, dated 386, notes: "They [the officials] have not yet dared rob Rome of its sac-

---

45. *Superstitio* was applied in the Code to magic and astrology and divination; see *C.Th.* 9.16.1; and Salzman, "*Superstitio.*"

46. For further discussion, see Salzman, "*Superstitio.*"

47. *C.Th.* 16.10.5.

48. *C.Th.* 16.10.4 is addressed to Taurus, praetorian prefect of Italy and Africa from 356–361, but is incorrectly dated in the manuscripts to a consulship of Constantius II and Constans in 346. The most likely solution is that "Constans" is a mistake for Julian, in which case the law was actually issued in the consulship of Constantius and Julian in 356, that is, during Taurus's prefecture. This sort of error is frequent in the Code.

49. See *C.Th.* 9.16.4–6 for laws of A.D. 357–359.

50. *C.Th* 16.10.5 (AD. 353) was directed to Cerealis, prefect of Rome; *PLRE* 1:197. Legislation dated 391, *C.Th.* 16.10.10. was directed to Albinus, prefect of Rome.

rifices" (*Or.* 30.33–34). Libanius's statement, admittedly rhetorical, is supported by the testimony of Symmachus, who similarly remarked that Constantius did not disrupt pagan cult practices.[51] And Ammianus Marcellinus records a sacrifice to the Dioscuri by the urban prefect Tertullus at Ostia in 360 or 361, without any suggestion that the act was illegal.[52]

The evidence indicates that Constantius's antipagan codes were not enforced at Rome and that pagan reaction to such legislation has been greatly exaggerated, both in modern scholarship and in ancient rhetoric.[53] Julian's claims of "unheard-of calamities" (*Or.* 7.228B) and Libanius's descriptions of persecution (*Or.* 7.10, 18.23, 30.34–38, 17.7) under these codes are countered by Christian writers who claim absolute victory.[54] Both sides are suspect.

The Uprising Against Constans and the Usurpation of Magnentius

The uprising against Constans in 349–350 and the usurpation of Magnentius in 350–353 provide the second set of evidence for the conflict between pagans and Christians.[55] Yet again, on close examination neither action supports this interpretation.

The revolt against Constans was not mounted because of his religious policies. His prohibitions against pagan sacrifice (noted above) stopped after 342, and they were never intended for Rome; his orthodox Christianity did not prevent him from appointing numerous pagan aristocrats to office,[56] nor do his antipagan policies seem to have aroused particular pagan hostility.[57] Rather, the uprising was the result largely of army dissatisfaction with the emperor's conduct of military and economic affairs, including his contempt for his generals, his meanness,

51. Symmachus *Rel.* 3.7; text cited above, p. 116. See too *Rel.* 7 and 15.
52. Ammianus Marcellinus 19.10.1–4.
53. Modern scholars who claim the destruction of pagan buildings as a result of these laws include Bowder, *Age of Constantine*, p. 81; and Piganiol, *L'empire chrétien*, pp. 107–108.
54. Christian claims that paganism was destroyed are belied by the small number of actual shrines noted. Eusebius, for example, cites only four shrines (*Vita Constantini* 3.53–58); Socrates *H. E.* 1.18 cites the same shrines.
55. See, for example, Geffcken 1978, p. 122; Piganiol, *L'empire chrétien*, pp. 95, 109–110; Alföldi, *A Festival of Isis*, pp. 31–34, 50ff.; E. Kornemann, *Römische Geschichte*, 5th ed., vol. 2 (Stuttgart, 1965), p. 399; Chastagnol 1960, p. 424.
56. Von Haehling, *Religionszugehörigkeit*, pp. 524–527.
57. In *RIC* 8, p. 9, Kent notes the complete loss of support for Constans in the civilian population as well as in the military in explaining the revolt.

and perhaps his devaluation of coinage.[58] Even the senatorial aristocrats who at first supported Constans turned against him for similar reasons; ancient authors cite in particular his economic policies, his preferential treatment of barbarians, and his moral vices.[59] Hostility toward Constans led the praetorians to turn for leadership to Marcellinus, a treasury prefect, and to Magnentius, then in command of two important legions.[60] Magnentius's usurpation drew support primarily from the army and his fellow Gauls,[61] which in turn enabled him eventually to win recognition in Italy, Gaul, Britain, Spain, and Africa.[62]

Magnentius did not succeed in using religious differences to fuel his uprising against Constantius II (350–353). Indeed, His religious policies are accurately described as opportunistic, for he favored pagans and Christians alternately in order to attract members of both sects to his cause.[63] To please Roman traditionalists, for instance, he supported pagan cult and permitted nocturnal sacrifice, which Constantius II had outlawed.[64] At the same time, however, he struck coins with the Christian symbols *Alpha* and *Omega*. Whether this latter act was an attempt to win the support of orthodox Christians in Gaul against the Arian Constantius[65] or a demonstration of his own religious beliefs is disputed,

58. Aurelius Victor *Caes.* 41.23.

59. Zosimus *Hist. Nova* 2.42; Aurelius Vict. *Caes.* 41.23–24; Eutropius 10.5–6; Libanius *Or.* 14.10, ed. R. Foerster (Leipzig, 1909–1927); Zonaras 13.5–6, in *PL*, cols. 1119, 1864; Piganiol, *L'empire chrétien*, p. 94. In *RIC* 8, p. 9, Kent adds Constans's novel administrative practice of appointing an easterner to the joint post of prefect of Rome and praetorian prefect of Italy and Africa rather than giving the prefecture of Rome to a Western aristocrat, as previously was the custom. For his morality, see *C.Th.* 9.7.3, legislating against homosexual marriage.

60. Zosimus *Hist. Nova* 2.42; Magnentius, in *PLRE* 1:532; Marcellinus, in *PLRE* 1:546, no. 8.

61. J. Bidez, "Amiens, ville natale de l'empereur Magnence," *REA* 27 (1925): 312–318. At the battle of Mursa, Magnentius's men demonstrated their support by fighting on with outstanding devotion against great odds. See Zosimus *Hist. Nova* 2.51–53; P. Bastien, *Le monnoyage de Magnence, 350–353*, 2d ed. (Wetteren, Belg. 1983), pp. 1–25.

62. His position was shaken in Italy by the uprising of Flavius Popilius Nepotianus, who held Rome 3–30 June A.D. 350 before falling to Magnentius's army. Nepotianus's brief rule was marked by the execution of many prominent senators and supporters of Magnentius. This man, a nephew of Constantine's, was apparently taking the city for Constantius II and based his revolt not on religious but on dynastic claims. See Aurelius Victor *Caes.* 42.6–7; Eutropius 10.6; and Zosimus *Hist. Nova* 2.43.3. Nepotianus's motivations are discussed by R. T. Ridley, *Zosimus: New History* (Sydney, 1982), p. 164, n. 113.

63. *RIC* 8, p. 11, gives Kent's view of Magnentius's opportunism. The religious policies of this man are particularly difficult to trace, because of the bias of the sources against the loser in a divisive civil war.

64. *C.Th.* 16.10.5.

65. The times made for strange alliances; Magnentius is said to have secretly intrigued with the Christian orthodox Athanasius of Alexandria and with Paul of Constantinople to win their support against the Arian Constantius. See Athanasius *Apol. ad Const.* 8.9.

but in any event, these coins add little to the notion that Magnentius's revolt was fueled by pagan-Christian conflict.[66]

Support for Magnentius among the Roman senatorial aristocracy was never very strong: only a minority followed the usurper, but it was a minority composed of both pagans and Christians.[67] Some pagan senators went over to his camp, namely Fabius Titianus, Valerius Aradius Proculus, Clodius Celsinus Adelphius, and Aurelius Celsinus, all of whom became prefects of Rome under his rule. These men, though, were probably discontented because they had not held positions under Constantius.[68] Christian senators, too, rallied to Magnentius's cause, including the Anicii.

Moreover, his opportunistic religious policies aside, Magnentius lost the allegiance of many senatorial supporters because of his political and economic policies; taxation of the wealthy, the use of denunciations by slaves against their masters, and death sentences for senators quickly alienated the aristocracy.[69] Many senators, pagan and Christian alike, fled from Magnentius and Rome to Constantius in Pannonia, perhaps as early as July 350. Later, in the autumn of 351, they fled the city en masse, persuaded by Magnentius's defeat at Mursa and Constantius's promised amnesty.[70] In the end, Rome, though still predominantly a pagan city, turned against Magnentius and hailed the Christian Constantius as its liberator.[71]

Magnentius seems to have tried to exploit religious differences to his

66. See Bastien, *Le monnoyage de Magnence*, p. 8, for the first view; and J. Ziegler, *Zur religiösen Haltung der Gegenkaiser im 4. Jahrhundert*, Frankfurter althistorische Studien, no. 4 (Kallmünz, 1970), pp. 53–61, 71ff., for the second view. Magnentius's own religious affiliations have been much disputed. Some scholars claim that he was a pagan, others that he was a Christian and orthodox. Ziegler, pp. 64–65, gives the positions of modern scholars on this question; at p. 68 he states his belief that Magnentius was a Christian who was compelled to seek support from pagans.

67. Chastagnol 1960, p. 420, notes that the number of Magnentian supporters must have been small because three of the five urban prefects under Magnentius held this position for the second time, a rare phenomenon in the fourth century and probably the result of a small pool of qualified aristocrats.

68. Chastagnol 1960, pp. 420ff., raised this as a plausible motivation for these men; cf. *CIL* 6.1166. Although Clodius converted to Christianity, he was probably a pagan in 351; see p. 229 and note 165 below.

69. Socrates *H.E.* 2.32; Sozomen *H.E.* 2.13; Themistius *Or.* 3.43A, ed. W. Dindorf (Leipzig, 1928); Julian *Or.* 1.38c–D, ed. W. C. Wright (Cambridge, Mass., 1913–1923); Eutropius 10.6.

70. Bastien, *Le monnoyage de Magnence,* pp. 18–20; Julian *Or.* 1.38c, 2.97B–c, ed. Wright, indicates that the flight was prior to Mursa.

71. Zosimus *Hist. Nova* 2.53.2 claims that Magnentius did not take refuge in Italy after Mursa because he knew Rome was for Constantius; cf. Socrates *H.E.* 2.32.

advantage, but with little success.[72] Evidence that such a conflict may have played a role in the uprising is in fact scanty, and nothing exists to suggest a pagan political party reacting to the usurper's overtures. Although Christian sources would depict Magnentius as a pagan tyrant defeated by the good, pious Constantius, the evidence from Rome does not show that he had won the support of many pagans. Other considerations were of greater import for winning aristocratic support in this conflict.[73]

The Urban Prefect Orfitus and the Contorniates

Among the pagan aristocrats welcoming Constantius to Rome was Memmius Vitrasius Orfitus, a trusted and loyal supporter who had served the emperor well at the imperial court.[74] Constantius appointed Orfitus to two 2½-year terms as urban prefect, an unprecedented action.[75] Orfitus's promotion and his deeds in office, together with Constantius's subsequent treatment of the pagan senatorial aristocracy, have been alleged to indicate a specifically pagan political reaction, spearheaded by Orfitus.[76] Yet this interpretation likewise is unsupportable.

Immediately after the civil war, according to Ammianus Marcellinus's history, Constantius treated the senatorial supporters of Magnentius with cruel vindictiveness, despite his proclaimed policy of amnesty. This policy, however, was directed against all of Magnentius's supporters, regardless of religion,[77] since the emperor's primary concern was to protect his position against usurpers.

72. His attempts were aimed as much at alienating orthodox Christians from Arians as at alienating pagans from Christians.

73. Even the pagans Julian and Zosimus have little good to say of this man; see Julian *Caesares* 316A, ed. Wright; Zosimus *Hist. Nova* 2.54.

74. Orfitus, *PLRE* 1:651–653, no. 3.

75. Chastagnol 1960, p. 423, explains this unprecedented action as a compromise because the emperor's chosen candidate for urban prefect in 355, the Christian Anatolius, had refused. There may be some truth in this, but the retention of Orfitus for so long and the turning to him a second time remain unprecedented actions and indicative of the trust Constantius placed in Orfitus.

76. See Piganiol, *L'empire chrétien*, pp. 109ff.; Alföldi 1943, pp. 50ff.; Chastagnol 1960, p. 424, sees 357 as the turning point for the pagan revival at Rome.

77. Ammianus Marcellinus 14.5.1 cites only one victim of Constantius, a certain Gerontius, a man of unknown religious persuasion. There is no evidence of Constantius waging a vendetta against pagan senators at Rome or elsewhere (an action that might have politicized them) later in the decade. The trials of 359, instigated by Constantius and recorded by Ammianus Marcellinus (19.12.1–16), were held in Egypt and so fall outside our

Similarly, Orfitus's appointment as urban prefect for 353–355 and 356–359 was owed primarily to his loyalty to the emperor.[78] Yet this same man is credited with spearheading the pagan political reaction in Rome and identified as the official responsible for the sudden appearance in the city on 1 January 356, 357, or 358 of those mysterious novelties, the contorniates. In Alföldi's view, the contorniates, lacking official mint marks but utilizing dies found for earlier medallions and coins, must have been made surreptitiously in the *officinae* of the government's mint at Rome.[79] Their iconography—representations of pagan gods, myths, literati, emperors, and circus games—were, Alföldi claims, part of a systematic body of political propaganda aimed by the Roman aristocracy at the ever-darkening cloud of Christianity. These aristocrats passed the message on to the populace, then, in the guise of New Year's gifts at the games on 3 January, much as imperial Roman medallions would have been given to convey imperial propaganda during New Year festivities.[80]

Alföldi's interpretation of the contorniates has been very influential, though levels of acceptance of his theory vary markedly. For instance, Toynbee, one scholar who expressed reservations, wondered "whether so elaborate a system was necessary or practical"; she suggested instead that the contorniates were merely mementos distributed on the occasion of the games.[81] In his review of the 1976 edition of Alföldi's *Die Kontorniat-Medallions*, Metcalf reiterated Toynbee's question, stating that the anti-Christian elements and the connection with the New Year's games—the last being at least "well-documented for medallions—remain to be demonstrated for the contorniates".[82] Mazzarino made the astute ob-

---

range. However, the men who were tried and condemned were brought up on charges of high treason (*laesae maiestatis*) for consulting diviners or for plotting against the emperor for their own self-advancement. Ammianus names only three men so charged (19.12.9–19.13); not one belongs to the Roman senatorial aristocracy, though one man, Phillipus, appears to be an aristocrat. While Ammianus says that many more men were charged and condemned, he includes no names. I follow R. C. Blockley, *Ammianus Marcellinus: A Study of His Historiography and Political Thought* (Brussels, 1975), pp. 119–120 and apps. B and C, and find no basis for arguments about the specifics of these trials. But see R. Von Haehling, "Ammianus Marcellinus und der Prozess von Sythopolis," *JAC* 21 (1978): 74–101.

78. Orfitus's loyalty is emphasized by A. Cameron, "The 'Pagan Reaction.' "

79. Alföldi 1943; as an alternative, J. M. C. Toynbee suggested in *Roman Medallions* (1944, repr. New York, 1986), p. 243, n. 27, that they were made in workshops owned or controlled by noble families.

80. Alföldi 1943, pp. 1–25; Alföldi, *A Festival of Isis*, p. 39, n. 59, and p. 253.

81. J. M. C. Toynbee, review of Alföldi 1943, *JRS* 35 (1945): 115–121.

82. W. Metcalf, review of Alföldi 1976, *AJA* 81 (1977): 406–407.

servation that, regardless of their "pagan" meaning, the contorniates continued to be struck with pagan iconography until the time of Anthemius in the 470s; according to Mazzarino, the contorniates may in fact have been entrance tickets to the games, distributed from the office of the urban prefect.[83] Cameron, too, has argued that Orfitus was a most unlikely person to initiate any political action that might offend his Christian patron, Constantius.[84]

Other scholars see the contorniates as evidence for a pagan revival and of a rapprochement between the emperor and the pagan Senate. This view implies, of course, that the period in fact was one of pagan-Christian conflict. Chastagnol, for one, has called the contorniates souvenirs of the Roman past, orchestrated by Orfitus with the approval of the emperor and distributed at the time of Constantius's visit to Rome.[85] But Alföldi's analysis, together with his model of pagan-Christian conflict (carried out on both a political and religious level), has set the framework for discussion. Nonetheless, there are many conjectural elements about the meaning and function of the contorniates in his analysis.

Indeed, study of the Calendar of 354 has led me to question Alföldi's interpretation of the contorniates. I would suggest that the contorniates—like the Calendar itself—fit comfortably within the framework of late Roman aristocratic patronage, fulfilling a traditional function at Roman games and festivals. Antique sources record the distribution of nonmonetary gifts at festivals and games continuing into the fourth century.[86] Such gift giving—on the part of the emperor, the president of the festival, or the city itself—was a traditional means of advertising. In the East, cities, prompted by a "mixture of sins, pride and avarice," issued small bronze coins depicting their most characteristic religious beliefs.[87] In Rome it was the aristocracy who, with the emperor out of town most of the time, took over as givers of games and circuses. Thus, one

---

83. Mazzarino, "La propaganda senatoriale"; and S. Mazzarino, *Enciclopedia dell'arte antica, classica e orientale* (Rome, 1959), s.v. "Contorniati," 11:784–791.

84. See A. Cameron, "The Pagan Reaction."

85. See Chastagnol 1960, p. 425. Similarly, A. Piganiol, in his review of Alföldi 1943, *Journal des savants* (1945): 19–28, connected the contorniates with the 357 visit of Constantius II to Rome.

86. Usually the gifts of the emperor were noted. These included birds, pets, silk vestments, ivory tablets, food, paintings, slaves, and animals. Cf. Suetonius *Domitian* 4; *Nero* 11; Seneca *Ep.* 74–78; *H. A. Elag.* 22. But others who were not emperors were also known to have distributed gifts of coins and other objects; *C.Th.* 15.9.1 (A.D. 381) restricts the giving of gold coins and ivory tablets to consuls and emperors. See Alföldi 1943, pp. 57ff., for a fuller discussion.

87. Quote from R. MacMullen, *Paganism in the Roman Empire*, p. 25; he cites examples on page 153, n. 32, such as *Sylloge numis. Graec. von Aulock, Nachträge* 4 (1968), no. 8348.

would expect to find the impetus for such gift giving precisely in this group, the recipients being the aristocrats' clients, the citizens of Rome.

The pagan iconography on the contorniates suggested long ago an intimate connection with the traditional Roman games,[88] as this cursory listing of obverse types shows:

1. Alexander the Great with his mother, Olympias
2. Deified emperors and empresses
3. Ruling emperors
4. Circus games (e.g., charioteers, dancers, musicians, masks, musical instruments, athletes)
5. Sacral types
6. Portraits of Roman literati

The reverses include the same categories, with the addition of one type with captive barbarians.[89] Obverse types 2–6 refer either to the games themselves, with their literary and theatrical performances, or to the imperial anniversaries and religious festivals that were the occasions for said games. Many of the contorniates depicting famous mythical scenes from Roman history may in fact represent reenactments of those scenes in the Roman circus or theater; one image found on Constantius II's medallions, showing the rape of the Sabine women taking place before three obelisks, probably depicts such a performance in the Circus Maximus.[90] Even the Alexander and Olympias contorniate type is appropriate to the games, for these medallions augured good luck to the competitors.[91]

The contorniates mirror the very same amalgam of concerns—astrological, imperial, and pagan religious—as the Calendar of 354, and both were occasioned by the traditional Roman games and festivals. The variety of iconography on the contorniates, alluding to several pagan deities and festivals, would seem to suggest that the medallions were distributed at more than one festival, perhaps at the discretion of the games' donor.[92] In any case, given the scanty New Year associations of the legend and iconography on the contorniates, the New Year's hypothesis should probably be discarded.[93]

---

88. So Toynbee observed in the 1945 *JRS* review of *Die Kontorniaten*.

89. Mazzarino, *Enciclopedia* pp. 784–791.

90. *RIC* 8, p.246.

91. Toynbee, review of Alföldi 1943, p. 120.

92. The range of deities includes Roman gods associated with traditional festivals such as Mars, but also Apollo, Isis, Cybele and Attis, Minerva, and Hercules; see Alföldi 1976, passim.

93. V. M. Brabic, "Contorniates and Public Festivals in the 4th and 5th Century," *TE*

While pagan iconography—gods, myths, writers, and *divi*—is depicted on the contorniates, this is in itself no reason to argue, as Alföldi did, that the medallions conveyed a strident and exclusively religious message; such imagery is entirely consonant with the contorniates' association with the traditional games and festivals of Rome. Pagan iconography, moreover, is often found even on Christian objects from this period—for example, the representation of Venus on the casket of the Christian bride Projecta, or the Bacchic imagery in the mosaics at S. Constanza in Rome and on the sarcophagus of Iunius Bassus.[94] A lovely fresco of Diana decorated a Christian baptismal font in the Hypogaeum on the Via Livenza in Rome in this period.[95] Even the Calendar of 354, though commissioned for a Christian and designed by a Christian artist, includes illustrations of pagan festivals.

It would be anachronistic to suppose that the Christian emperor opposed the traditional Roman games. On the contrary, Constantius, a devout Christian, issued a law requiring senators to return to Rome so that they might devote their customary attention to the compulsory public services enjoined upon them, that is, to "produce the promised shows."[96] His circus medallions also point to his desire to continue the traditional games.[97] After a divisive civil war, Constantius's policy indicates a return to life as usual—and life in Rome usually included *ludi* and *circenses*.

The appearance of the contorniates in the middle decades of the fourth century can be connected with the enduring Roman aristocratic traditions of *largitio* at the games. Alföldi's work supports this interpretation, for he convincingly demonstrated, through analysis of die links and legends, that several pagan scenes depicted on the contorniates were inspired by those on the imperial medallions distributed by the emperor

12 (1971): 10–15, observes the association of the contorniates with several different festivals and suggests that they were gifts as were given at the *Saturnalia*.

94. K. Shelton, *The Esquiline Treasure* (London, 1981), would redate the Proiecta of the Proiecta casket to the 350s. The argument for the conventional dating in the 380s is convincingly made by A. Cameron, "The Esquiline Treasure," pp. 135–145; Shelton's rejoinder is "The Esquiline Treasure: The Nature of the Evidence," *AJA* 89 (1985): 147–155. The mosaics from S. Constanza and the sarcophagus of Iunius Bassus are securely dated to the 350s and Rome.

95. L. Usai, "L'ipogeo di Via Livenza," *Dialoghi di archeologia* 6 (1972): 363–412.

96. *C.Th.* 6.4.7.

97. Most interesting is the Constantius II medallion depicting the rape of the Sabine women, which may be a representation of an actual theatrical scene in the Circus Maximus; see *RIC* 8, p. 246.

to commemorate the New Year or his own vows.[98] A great output of large bronze imperial medallions marked Constantius II's reign, but that was "the swansong of this particular genre,"[99] for in his later years these bronze medallions came to an abrupt end.[100] Almost simultaneously, the contorniates began. Perhaps with the imperial bronze medallions no longer in circulation, some Roman aristocrats saw an opportunity to enhance their position and social prestige by striking a new form of the small bronze commemorative medallions, the contorniates. Indeed, given similar iconography on both imperial medallions and the contorniates, their function may have been similar as well: to symbolize the generosity of their donor, whether emperor or senator.[101]

Because the donor was not the emperor, or even a member of the emperor's court, the contorniates were made of bronze and not more valuable metals, as befitted the lower status not only of the donor but also of the recipients.[102] Small medallions enabled the donor to avoid being in competition with the emperor, but they could nevertheless serve as gifts—*sportulae*—precisely because of their association with imperial patronage. Nor should inferior artistic quality discount this theory; although mass produced, the contorniates of the early period—and especially the Alexander and Olympias type—were well crafted and worth keeping.[103]

If the contorniates were distributed at Rome as gifts during the *ludi*, as I suggest, it is difficult to imagine the urban prefect disapproving; it

98. Alföldi 1943, pp. 37ff., 57ff., remarks the *Sabinae* type. Toynbee, review of Alföldi 1943, p. 116, observes that "the likeness of certain Pius Caracalla portraits to the portrait of Priscus Attalus on the latter's silver medallions is very striking." Toynbee then argues contra Alföldi that the contorniate with "SABINAE" in the exergue was copied—as was the medallion of Constantius II—from the original large bronze medallion of Faustina I. Toynbee may be right about the source of the iconography, but the association with the imperial medallions posited by Alföldi remains feasible. In *RIC* 8, pp. 246, Kent sees this die ("SABINAE") as an important link to the contorniates.

99. *RIC* 8, p. 246.

100. Ibid., pp. 246–247; Toynbee, *Roman Medallions*, p. 21.

101. C. Clay, "Roman Imperial Medallions," in *Actes du 8e Congrès international de numismatique* (New York–Washington, 1973; Paris, 1976), pp. 253–264, made this same association.

102. See the strict regulations according to rank concerning the giving of gifts (*sportulae*) in *C.Th.* 15.9.1 (A.D. 384); and cf. 15.9.9 (A.D. 384), restricting coins distributed by others than the emperor to silver.

103. The earliest emission, A.D. 356–395, includes scenes of the rites of Bacchus and images of Minerva, Hercules, the Magna Mater, and Attis. The last two cults' iconography appears on high-quality aristocratic pieces of art. See further Piganiol, review of Alföldi 1943, p. 23. The division into three periods was stated originally by Alföldi 1943 and then worked out in greater detail by C. Clay in Alföldi 1976.

is more difficult to interpret the contorniates as exclusively or primarily political propaganda aimed at Christians. As gifts at the games, the contorniates would fit within the framework of traditional patronage; moreover, they would be the natural successors of the now defunct bronze imperial medallions. Indeed, as Clay points out, the contorniates increased in size over the course of the fourth century, another indication that they essentially replaced the imperial medallions.[104] Finally, the use in the first grouping of contorniates of dies found on official imperial medallions, as well as the appearance of consuls and contemporary emperors on later issues, suggests that they were produced in the official mint.

If the contorniates began in 356–358, as Alföldi and others have argued on numismatic grounds, they might well have coincided with Constantius II's visit to Rome.[105] And in fact, their appearance and iconography do appear specifically intended to advertise Rome and to commemorate the occasion of the emperor's visit. But any association with pagan-Christian conflict or pagan propaganda seems highly unlikely.

Constantius II's Visit to Rome, 28 April to 29 May 357

The visit of Constantius II to Rome in 357 has been interpreted by some as connoting a reconciliation between the pagan senatorial aristocracy and the Christian emperor, and the beginning of "a new attitude toward paganism" on the part of the "bigoted" emperor.[106] The visit also,

104. C. Clay made this observation to me in a conversation in Vienna in the fall of 1984.

105. The evidence for their initial dating was the active role of Orfitus as urban prefect in 353–356 and 357–359, as Alföldi 1943, pp. 55ff., argues. Alföldi also utilizes two numismatic pieces of evidence that point to the period 355–361: (1) A contorniate die cutter experimented with a design on the blank back of a small coin proof on which the emperor was shown spearing a barbarian; the legend read "FEL TEMP REPARATIO." This piece with the mint mark "RM" appears only after 357; *RIC* 8, p. 278. Toynbee, review of Alföldi 1943, p. 116, however, argues that this "proof" could have found its way into the contorniate maker's hands at a later time. (2) The "SABINAE" medallions of Constantius II, which are similar iconographically to the contorniates, begin in 354–361; *RIC* 8, p. 297. Again, however, Toynbee (p. 116) argues that since both the contorniate and the medallion may derive from an earlier medallion of Faustina I, these iconographic associations do not secure the beginning date of the contorniates.

106. Constantius is described as bigoted by Alföldi, *A Festival of Isis*, p. 33; Bowder, *Age of Constantine*, p. 81, in more contemporary psychological terms, ascribes a "new attitude" to Constantius. Other scholars who argue for reconciliation include Geffcken 1978, pp. 90ff.; Piganiol, *L'empire chrétien*, p. 109; J. Ceska, "En marge de la visite de Constance à Rome en 357," *Sborník Prací Filosofické fakulty Brnenské Univ.*, ser. E10, 14 (1965): 111; H. Lietzmann, *From Constantine to Julian*, p. 137.

these scholars maintain, sparked a pagan revival in 350s Rome, which in turn fueled pagan reactions in the 380s.[107] Analysis of the events does not, however, support this view. Constantius's visit and subsequent actions reveal an emperor eager to play the appropriate role, but they do not indicate any change in policy. Implicit support for Roman traditions —as distinct from Roman paganism—had always been part of his program.

Discussion of Constantius's visit has focused on the primary source for these events, the *History* of Ammianus Marcellinus, written under Theodosius the Great. Yet the evidence Ammianus provides for either a reconciliation or a pagan revival is slender indeed. Moreover, his account of the visit is clearly colored to suit his own rhetorical and contemporary purposes.

In describing Constantius's visit and the effect that Rome had on the emperor, Ammianus concentrates more on appropriate imperial comportment than on historical accuracy. According to Ammianus, Constantius's visit was motivated by a curiosity to see Rome and a desire to celebrate a triumph against the proper ceremonial background. In the view of Ammianus, however, he did not deserve such recognition, because the defeat of Magnentius was nothing but a civil war victory and otherwise Constantius had performed no feats of military import.[108] Other sources disagree with Ammianus and credit Constantius with triumphs, not only over Magnentius but also over the Alamanni.[109] Ammianus, then, presents his own view of the "true dignity of a Roman emperor through a criticism of the false conception of Constantius."[110]

107. See, for example, Chastagnol 1960, p. 424; Mazzarino, "Propaganda senatoriale," pp. 121ff.

108. Ammianus Marcellinus 16.10.1–2: "Constantius quasi cluso Iani templo stratisque hostibus cunctis, Romam visere gestiebat, post Magnenti exitium absque nomine ex sanguine Romano triumphaturus. Nec enim gentem ullam bella cientem per se superavit, aut victam fortitudine suorum comperit ducum, vel addidit quaedam imperio aut usquam in necessitatibus summis primus vel inter primos est visus, sed ut pompam nimis extentam, rigentiaque auro vexilla, et pulchritudinem stipatorum ostenderet agenti tranquillius populo, haec vel simile quicquam videre nec speranti umquam nec optanti."

109. J. Straub, *Vom Herrscherideal in der Spätantike* (1939; repr. Stuttgart, 1964), pp. 177–178. The inscription on the obelisk (*CIL* 6.1163 = *ILS* 736) commemorating triumphs is identified with the defeat of the Alamanni (perhaps already celebrated in 355) and of Magnentius. Others speak of this visit as a triumph: see especially Themistius *Or.* 3.42B–c, ed. W. Dindorf (Leipzig, 1828). This oration was certainly delivered in Rome: *RE*, s.v. "Themistius," col. 1658; Straub, *Vom Herrscherideal*, pp. 175ff.; and Sozomen *H. E.* 4.11.

110. N. Baynes, in his review of J. Vogt and E. Kornemann, *Römische Geshichte*, in *JRS* 25 (1935): 87, makes this point as he criticizes the view that this passage (Amm. Marc. 16.10.1–17) was based on two sources and was not the result of Ammianus's rhetoric, a theory advanced, for example, by R. Laqueur, "Das Kaisertum und die Gesellschaft des

While Ammianus praises Constantius for fulfilling the traditional duties of a Roman emperor as regard the pagan cults, these activities do not, he says, indicate a reconciliation or a reversal of earlier legislation against pagan sacrifice. Thus Ammianus notes with approval the emperor's maintenance of state subsidies for cults and temples. As *pontifex maximus,* too, Constantius filled the pagan priesthoods.[111] He gave games as befitted his position, conducted himself appropriately by accepting the crowd's heckling and by allowing the contests to be terminated by chance.[112] Constantius also expressed proper admiration for Rome's pagan monuments, just as earlier emperors had done; even his father, Constantine, had included pagan statuary in his new Christian capital, Constantinople.[113]

Constantius's gift of an obelisk to Rome is noted positively as well, for this donation, in which he was urged not only to emulate Augustus but also to complete a project begun by Constantine,[114] accords with the established pattern of emperor as patron. The inscription on the obelisk—stating that although Constantine had originally wanted to place the obelisk in his new capital, Constantius desired that it be given to Rome instead[115]—differs from the explanation given in Ammianus's account, however. If Ammianus is correct, Constantius was merely reminded by his advisers of unfinished business and so deserves less credit than the actual obelisk inscription gives him.[116] Yet if in fact Constantine had intended the obelisk as a gift to commemorate his vicennalia, cele-

---

Reiches," excursus no. 4 in *Probleme der Spätantike,* ed. R. Laqueur, H. Koch, and W. Weber (Stuttgart, 1930), pp. 33–36.

111. Symmachus *Rel.* 3.7; text cited above, p. 116. *CIL* 3.3705 = *ILS* 732 (A.D. 354), a milestone, calls Constantius II Pontifex Maximus.

112. Ammianus Marcellinus 16.10.14. The contrast between the emperor's formal entry (16.10.9) and the relaxed performance of his duties while in Rome fits within the conventions of an *adventus* ceremony; and Ammianus Marcellinus represents his entrance as this sort of ceremony. See S. MacCormack, *Art and Ceremony in Late Antiquity* (Berkeley and Los Angeles, 1981), pp. 106ff.

113. G. Dagron, *Naissance d'une capitale: Constantinople et ses institutions de 330 à 451* (Paris, 1974), pp. 37–47, 92–102. Cf. Eusebius *Vita Constantini* 3.54.

114. Ammianus Marcellinus 16.10.17, 17.4.12–14.

115. "Patris opus munusqu[e suum] tibi, Roma, dicavit / Augustus [toto Constan]tius orbe recepto . . . / Hoc decus ornatum genitor cognominis urbis / esse volens, caesa Thebis de rupe revellit." The last line indicates that Constantine, wishing this ornament to adorn the city that bears his name, cut and tore it from the Theban rock; *CIL* 6.1163 = *ILS* 736. The inscription is now lost but was carefully copied at the end of the sixteenth century.

116. G. Fowden, "Nicagoras of Athens and the Lateran Obelisk," *JHS* 107 (1987): 51–57.

brated in Rome in 326, what better precedent for Constantius than finally to erect the obelisk for what amounted to *his* vicennalia, also celebrated in Rome but some thirty years later.[117] Thus, the actual obelisk inscription probably does reflect the truth, insofar as Constantius likely donated the obelisk on his own initiative.[118] Moreover, since all obelisks were associated with the cult of Sol/Apollo-Helios, the favored cult of the Constantinian family, this gift underscored Constantius's dynastic claims. In short, the donation of an obelisk to Rome conveyed numerous messages intended to advertise Constantius's dynastic associations, imperial benefactions, and military triumphs. But whatever else it was, it was not an act of reconciliation to win over Rome, nor was Rome uniquely honored by this gift—another obelisk, after all, had been intended by Constantius for Constantinople.[119]

Although the emperor may well have been pleased to reach a working relationship with the pagan senatorial aristocracy before leaving Rome for his Eastern campaigns, Ammianus's account gives no evidence of an overt attempt at reconciliation with a politicized pagan party.[120] On the contrary, certain of Constantius's actions (not noted by Ammianus) argue explicitly against such an interpretation. During his visit, for instance, the emperor removed the altar of Victory from the Roman Senate,[121] and he may have suspended the custom of sacrificing prior to the Senate's opening sessions.[122] Constantius probably also refused to sacrifice to Jupiter on the Capitol Hill, following his father's exam-

117. R. Klein, "Der Rombesuch des Kaisers Konstantius II im Jahre 357," *Athenaeum* 57 (1979): 99–103.

118. The text of the inscription supports this view by emphasizing the difficulty of this task and the military triumphs of Constantius. See Fowden, "Nicagoras of Athens," for discussion.

119. *ILS* 736 merely mentions Rome in ll. 1–4, but ll. 7–24 convey the idea of honoring Rome; Julian *Ep.* 59.443B, ed. J. Bidez, *L'Empereur Julien, Oeuvres complètes* (Paris, 1932), notes the obelisk intended for Constantinople.

120. It is unnecessary and in any case there is no room to analyze here the entire account in Ammianus Marcellinus. The interested reader is directed to Straub, *Vom Herrscherideal*, pp. 175–204.

121. Symmachus *Rel.* 3.4–3.6; and Ambrose *Ep.* 17–18, ed. R. Klein, *Der Streit um den Victoriaaltar* (Darmstadt, 1972). For Ammianus's omission, see R. O. Edbrooke, Jr., "The Visit of Constantius II to Rome," *AJP* 97 (1976): 58. F. Paschoud, "Réflexions sur l'idéal religieux de Symmaque," *Historia* 14 (1965): 219, holds that since this act did not affect the economic power of the aristocracy, it was not noted by contemporaries. This argument is not convincing; see the effective refutation by J. Matthews, *Western Aristocracies and Imperial Court* A.D. 364–425 (Oxford, 1975), pp. 208–209. The altar was returned to the Senate house, perhaps during the reign of Julian; see G. Lo Menzo Rapisarda, "La personalità di Ambrogio nelle Epistole XVII e XVIII," *Orpheus* 20 (1973): 130–132.

122. Ambrose *Ep.* 18.32.

ple.[123] These actions, of course, were consistent with legislation outlawing pagan sacrifice.

Constantius's concern for ecclesiastical politics in Rome was probably greater than his desire for a rapprochement with the pagan senatorial aristocracy.[124] Pope Liberius's support of Athanasius and claim to independence had led Constantius to remove Liberius from his see in 355.[125] Both the church historian Theodoret and the pagan historian Ammianus Marcellinus report that the emperor was actively trying to effect a reconciliation with this influential bishop.[126] In the midst of preparing for his triumphal entry, then, Constantius called the exiled Liberius to him; and when in Rome, he restored the bishop to his see by popular petition. Nevertheless, he refused to remove Liberius's successor, Felix, from office, and so the controversy continued,[127] the unfeasibility of this "solution" being met by the heckling of the crowds in the hippodrome. Only when Felix left Rome was peace restored.[128]

Analysis of the aftermath of Constantius's visit to Rome does not support theories of a reconciliation either. Prior to his departure for the East, Constantius took certain precautions to insure loyalty. He minimized the powers of the urban prefect—at that time the pagan Orfitus—taking away the right of hearing appeals for most of Italy, Sicily, and Sardinia and reserving it (with the exception of Latium, Tuscia, Umbria, and Valeria) for the praetorian prefect of Italy.[129] (By contrast, in a law of 361 he granted the right of hearing appeals for the nine provinces near Constantinople to the urban prefect of that city, the same privilege he had removed from the urban prefect of Rome.)[130] Moreover, Constantius decided that the provinces of Achaea, Macedonia, and Illyricum should thenceforth send their senators to Constantinople and not Rome—perhaps another attempt to undermine the influence of Rome and its aris-

123. See J. Straub, "Konstantins Verzicht auf den Gang zum Kapitol," *Historia* 4 (1955): 297–313.

124. See M. Meslin, *Les Ariens d'Occident, 335–430*, Patristica Sorbonensia, no. 8 (Paris, 1967), pp. 29–44.

125. Ammianus Marcellinus 15.7.6–10, 21.16.18. Politics then, as now, made for flexible alliances; if the Christian historian Theodoret (*H.E.* 2.13) is correct, Liberius was accused at his trial of opposing the emperor to win favor with the Roman Senate. Theodoret's veracity, however, has been called into question. For further discussion, see Pietri 1976, pp. 238–268. It is plausible that Liberius did view the pagan senatorial aristocrats, with their tradition of political independence, as allies in withstanding imperial pressure.

126. Theodoret *H.E.* 2.13–14; Ammianus Marcellinus 15.7.10.

127. Socrates *H.E.* 4.12.

128. Theodoret *H.E.* 1.17.

129. *C.Th.* 11.30.27 (A.D. 357).

130. *C.Th.* 1.6.1 (A.D. 361).

tocracy. Indeed, the favoring of Constantinople at the expense of Rome became somewhat more common in general after this time.[131]

No revival of pagan aristocratic fortunes seems to have occurred following Constantius's 357 visit to Rome; both before and after, appointments to office in the West were almost evenly divided between pagans and Christians.[132] He consistently placed officials according to the needs of the areas to be governed, with predominantly pagan areas generally receiving pagan officials, and likewise for the Christian areas. In the West, paganism was the norm until Gratian.[133]

Constantius's appointments to the urban prefecture in Rome were consistent with his general policy of equilibrium: he alternated pagan and Christian.[134] Although this practice probably did not please pagan traditionalists, it conforms to what we know about the growth of Christianity in Rome and may reflect the mixed religion of the population at large.[135] It also undoubtedly facilitated the ambience of toleration in the mid-fourth-century city.

OTHER EVIDENCE FOR ACCOMMODATION AND ASSIMILATION

The relationship between religion and politics in Roman society in the 350s is too fluid to make religion the key to interpretation of this period. Inhabitants of Rome would likely have found our modern categorization of iconography, politics, and legislation from the reign of Constantius into simply pagan or Christian slots of little relevance. Even within a profoundly serious context—the burial of the dead—these categories are not necessarily meaningful, as the interment of pagans and

131. See *C.Th.* 6.4.11 for senators sent to Constantinople instead of Rome; discussed by Piganiol, *L'empire chrétien*, p. 117. Laws favored Constantinople. For example, Constantius raised the chief official of Constantinople from the rank of proconsul to prefect in 357; see Chastagnol 1960, p. 38. Constantius aided the office holders in the new center of government; see *C.Th.* 1.6.1, 1.28.1, 6.4.12–13, 7.8.1, 11.1.7, 11.15.1. See, too, Edbrooke, "The Visit of Constantius," pp. 55ff.

132. Edbrooke, "The Visit of Constantius," pp. 40–61; although von Haehling, *Religionszugehörigkeit*, pp. 527–536, did note some favoring of Arians in Constantius's appointments, the overall pattern did not reflect a pro-Christian bias.

133. Von Haehling, *Religionszugehörigkeit*, pp. 569–575.

134. Chastagnol 1960, p. 426.

135. Chastagnol (ibid.) viewed these appointments as an insult to pagans, as well as an indication of the growth of Christianity. This position is unduly polemical; Christians were appointed to the urban prefecture by Constantine, and Constantius's attempt at equilibrium may as easily be viewed positively as intended to satisfy the needs of two large populations in the city.

Christians side by side in the Via Latina catacomb, where pagan mytho-logical scenes are juxtaposed to biblical ones, suggests.[136] Rather, evi-dence from mid-fourth-century Rome reflects a much wider range of attitudes, values, and affiliations than a simple model of religious conflict suggests.

Pagan aristocratic response to the new religion in Rome under Con-stantius II was not monolithic, of course: some pagans probably stood in steadfast opposition to this new system of belief. Others, though, assimilated themselves to Christian culture through conversion. Valen-tinus, the recipient of the Calendar, may have been one such recent con-vert, from one of the most notable pagan aristocratic families in Rome. In the 350s we can begin to see a movement toward Christianity by other aristocratic males, including Iunius Bassus signo Theotecnicus (*PLRE*, 1:155), Gaius Marius Victorinus (*PLRE* 1:964), and, albeit a few years earlier (343–346), Iulius Firmicus Maternus Iunior (*PLRE*, 1:567–568)[137]—to name but a few of the most prominent converts.

Gaius Marius Victorinus is perhaps the best-known convert of the 350s. This noted rhetor of Rome, honored by a statue in the Forum of Trajan for his eloquence, had before his conversion been a forceful de-fender of the pagan gods.[138] But according to Augustine, Victorinus's reading of the Holy Scriptures gradually led to his conversion—even though, Augustine says, Victorinus was afraid to manifest his new faith in public lest he offend his proud pagan friends at Rome.[139] We cannot know whether this concern was Victorinus's or was attributed to him by Augustine to highlight the dramatic conversion of this famed rhetor. In any event, Victorinus's public proclamation of his faith in 355–357[140] must have made a strong impression on many pagans, and especially on his numerous students, as did his subsequent writings on Christian Neoplatonism.

Whatever his fears of reprisal, Victorinus's conversion was tolerated,

---

136. See W. Tronzo, *The Via Latina Catacomb: Imitation and Discontinuity in Fourth Cen-tury Roman Painting,* Monographs on the Fine Arts, no. 38 (University Park, Penn., 1986); A. Ferrua, *Le pitture della Nuova Catacomba di Via Latina,* Monumenti di antichità cristiana, 2d ser., vol. 8 (Rome, 1960).

137. Other famous rhetors such as Hecebolius and Prohaeresius, Julian's teachers, converted in the 350s as well; see Eunapius *Vitae Sophist.* 485–93, ed. J. F. Boissonade (Paris, 1849).

138. Augustine *Conf.* 8.2 describes Victorinus as defending paganism with an "ore terricrepo." For discussion of this term and Victorinus's conversion, see P. Hadot, *Marius Victorinus: Recherches sur sa vie et ses oeuvres* (Paris, 1971), pp. 28–32, 52ff.

139. Augustine *Conf.* 8.2.

140. I follow Hadot, *Marius Victorinus,* pp. 28–33, for the date of Victorinus's conver-sion. Victorinus was called *vir clarissimus* in the manuscripts.

and Augustine does not indicate that he suffered in any way from the reaction of his pagan friends. Victorinus maintained his position as rhetor of Rome throughout the 350s, stepping down only in 362, when Julian proscribed Christian rhetors.[141] Thus, although some pagans may indeed have been offended by Victorinus's new faith, their religious concerns did not alter the rhetor's public position. Again we see the influence of aristocratic accommodation on public affairs at Rome.

The vast majority of pagans no doubt took this middle road of accommodation. Pagan tolerance for new cults was traditional, especially if the cult had imperial support. The willingness of pagan aristocrats to live side by side with their Christian neighbors was certainly eased by the fact that both groups, at least in 350s Rome, shared the same aristocratic values and life-style. At least this is what the Codex-Calendar of 354 suggests.

Even within the most intimate relationships—in marriage and the family—the norm, especially among aristocrats, appears to have been toleration of religious differences. In mixed marriages, husband and wife apparently retained their own religions. This accommodation is especially understandable for elite circles, where marriage was not about personal fulfillment or a way of life: huge estates and inheritances were at issue. Moreover, from a pagan point of view, religion was, after all, a personal choice. Even Christians demonstrated a noticeable change in attitude toward mixed marriages, which, Augustine claims, were no longer avoided as sinful.[142] Although the Christian partner may have tried to influence his or her spouse, toleration was recommended.

Many mixed marriages are attested in the fourth century. The Christian poetess Proba was married to the prominent pagan Clodius Celsinus Adelphius.[143] The aristocratic Christian Adelfia may have been the wife of the pagan Lucius Aradius Valerius Proculus, consular in Sicily ca. 330 and praised by Symmachus for his devotion to religion.[144] The Christian bride Proiecta of the Esquiline casket may also have married a pagan.[145] Perhaps the most striking example of familial accommodation to religious

141. Augustine *Conf.* 8.5.

142. Augustine *De Fide et Operibus* 19, 35, in *CSEL* 41, ed. J. Zycha (Vienna, 1900), p. 80.

143. See note 165 below.

144. Adelfia, *CIL* 10.7123, from Syracuse, Sicily; Proculus, *PLRE* 1:747–748, no. 11; praised by Symmachus in *Ep.*12.4.

145. Proiecta's mixed marriage was proposed by E. Weigand, "Ein bisher verkanntes Diptychon Symmachorum," *JDAI* 52 (1937): 128–129. See too the remarks of Cameron, "The Esquiline Treasure," pp. 142–145, about the religion of Proiecta's husband; Cameron, however, would date Proiecta to the 380s, not the 350s.

differences is from the Ceionii Rufii. In the middle of the century, a pagan couple in this family had four sons. Two sons, Ceionius Rufius Albinus and Publilius Caeionius Caecina Albinus, remained pagan although married to Christian women, and the daughters of both grew up devout Christians.[146]

Pagan-Christian accommodation is also suggested by mid-fourth-century Roman artifacts with markedly pagan iconography. No scenes of animal sacrifice, for example, are depicted on the contorniates,[147] in the pagan scenes from the Via Latina catacombs, in the *opus sectile* work from the house of Iunius Bassus, or on objects from the Esquiline Treasure.[148] The Calendar of 354, unlike earlier calendars, depicts only scenes of incense burning.[149] In fourth-century mosaic cycles of the months, too, the less offensive rite of libation was substituted for animal sacrifice (see Appendix 2). Scenes of sacrificial incense burning (thurification) are found on contorniates and other Roman mosaics as well.[150]

That such accommodation in terms of pagan ritual did occur is attested later; animal sacrifice was banned once again by the emperor Theodosius, although pagan rituals—including thurification—continued. Libanius describes one such celebration: "Summoned on the usual day, they [the pagans] dutifully honoured it [the feast day] and the shrine in a way that involved no risk."[151] He notes that the people "were in the habit of drinking together amid the scent of every kind of incense," arguing further that the emperor, by banning the performance of one specific action—animal sacrifice—automatically permitted everything else.[152] In other words, as long as the pagans complied with that law, the less controversial ritual practices could continue, among which thuri-

146. A. Chastagnol, "Le sénateur Volusien et la conversion d'une famille de l'aristo-cratie romaine au Bas-Empire," *REA* 58 (1956): 241–253, remains an excellent analysis of this family.

147. Accommodation may also account for the omission from the contorniates of scenes of the gladiatorial games, which had been outlawed by Constantine; *C.Th.* 15.12.1 (A.D. 325).

148. Shelton, *The Esquiline Treasure*, pp. 1ff. This dating for the Treasure follows that suggested by Shelton.

149. By contrast, the late-second–early-third-century calendar from St.-Romain-en-Gaul and the third-century one from S. Maria Maggiore do depict scenes of animal sacrifice in illustrating pagan festivals in November and January. See Chapter 3 and Appendix 2.

150. The lack of scenes of animal sacrifice on artifacts from Rome in the period under Constantius may be purely accidental, given the fragmentary nature of the remains. But it may be significant; as a reflection of changing tastes or as a reflection of real religious practice, this lack suggests the accommodation of Roman pagans to legislation during this time.

151. Libanius *Or.* 30.19, trans. A. F. Norman (Cambridge, Mass., 1977).

152. Ibid., 30.18.

fication was perhaps the most appealing for its ease and economy.[153] This speech by Libanius indicated that symbolic substitution could and did satisfy traditional Roman religious scruples, as is attested elsewhere in Roman literature: Plutarch, for example, records that during the siege of Cyzicus, when the inhabitants could not sacrifice their customary black cow to Persephone, they sacrificed instead an image made of wool; and Servius, discussing the substitution of victims made of wax and bread for the animals themselves, notes that "in sacrifices those things which could not be presented were simulated and they were treated as if they were the real things."[154] Indeed, incense burning became so identified with paganism in the fourth century that Prudentius defines pagan idolaters as "the incense-bearing crowd" (*turifera grex*), and St. Cyprian applies the term "incense offerer" (*turificatus*) to a Christian who recanted.[155]

Active adaptation to the "Christian times" under Constantius was not, however, the universal rule. Many Roman pagans merely continued their traditional cult practices without perceiving their activities as controversial. Temples were still dedicated, sacrifices still performed, and religious festivals and games still celebrated.[156]

The extent and vitality of the paganism practiced in this period in Rome has only recently been appreciated.[157] Indeed, some scholars have read the continuity of paganism after the antipagan laws of Constantius as bespeaking, if not a pagan political reaction, then a pagan religious revival, which in Rome was lent added weight by Constantius's visit in 357. In my opinion this view, too, is misleading, for it suggests a uniform

153. In 386, animal sacrifice continued for *vota publica* if performed away from the site of an altar, without burnt offerings, and without the accompanying ceremony; it continued to be legally allowed for this purpose until 399. See *C.Th.* 16.10.17 (A.D. 399); and Libanius *Or.* 30.17.

154. Servius *Ad Aen.* 2.116: "In sacris . . . quae exhiberi non poterant simulabantur, et erant pro veris"; see too Plutarch *Lucullus* 10.1. For further discussion of the frequency of animal substitution, see G. Capdeville, "Substitution des victimes dans les sacrifices d'animaux à Rome," *MEFR* 83 (1971): 283–323.

155. The derogatory nature of these remarks by Christians indicates the degree to which this practice was identified with paganism; cf. Prudentius *Apoth.* 292; and St. Cyprian *Ep.* 55.2. G. J. Laing, *Survivals of Roman Religion* (New York, 1931), pp. 210ff., suggests that the identification of incense with paganism prohibited its use by Christians until the end of the fourth century.

156. For temple dedications, see *CIL* 6.45: temple of Apollo dedicated by Orfitus, A.D. 356–359 (or after). For sacrifices, see Ammianus Marcellinus 19.10.4, for Tertullus's sacrifice to Castor and Pollux at Ostia; for a *taurobolium* dedication of A.D. 350, see *CCCA* 3.1, no. 227 = *CIL* 6.498 (though this occurred during the reign of Magnentius).

157. See, for example, MacMullen, *Paganism in the Roman Empire*; Wardman, *Religion and Statecraft*, pp. 135–168; Wilken, *John Chrysostom*, pp. 1–34; and Liebeschuetz, *Antioch and Continuity and Change*.

restoration of non-Christian practices owing to either a deliberate revitalization or a spontaneous resurgence of pagan beliefs and practices. The evidence for the 350s, however, indicates no such thing. Comparison with the pagan revival under the Emperor Julian (361–363) will be instructive here.

To turn people back to the old religion, Julian restored the temples, encouraged and performed sacrifices, and tried to reform such pagan institutions as the priesthood.[158] He then launched an aggressive ideological campaign, writing speeches and encouraging notable pagan literati and philosophers like the Neoplatonist Sallustius and the rhetoricians Libanius and Priscus to publicize their religious views. The extent of the pagan resurgence inspired by Julian is debatable, but its intent is unmistakable.

The indicators of Julian's attempted pagan revival are absent from 350s Rome. No spontaneous or deliberate widespread revival of religious practices occurred; while pagan sacrifices were still performed and temples dedicated, their numbers are not great.[159] Nor did any one individual promulgate a particular set of beliefs, as Julian did for Sol; many pagan cults coexisted in the city.[160] Since paganism survived in Rome largely unaffected by the antipagan laws, no religious issue arose to unite pagan aristocrats, and no one leader stepped forth, as did Julian, to champion the cause. Certainly Orfitus was no such intellectual or religious figure.[161]

The literature and art from this period do not suggest a pagan revival either. Pagans and Christians alike read classical literature in the 350s, as before, as part of their education. And as before, writers continued

---

158. See Wardman, *Religion and Statecraft*, pp. 157ff., for further discussion.

159. The inscriptional evidence adduced for the pagan revival in the 350s is slim indeed. (1) Mithraic dedications and establishment of a temple in the area of S. Sylvestro in Rome, 357–362; *CIL* 6.749–754. Although this Mithraic sanctuary is newly established, it is not clear why it represents a revival and not the survival of worship of Mithras. Cf. the worship at the Mithras shrine at S. Prisca in Rome, *CIMRM*, nos. 476, 500, beginning in the second century and continuing to the end of the fourth. *CIMRM*, no. 388 (Rome), in the house of the Nummi Albini, attests this family, one of whom, Nummius Albinus, was consul in 345. (2) *Taurobolia* altars to the Magna Mater and Attis from the Phrygianum recommence in great number in 370; *CCCA* 3.1. The Phrygianum inscriptions begin somewhat later than our discussion, but one inscription exists dating from 350; *CIL* 6.498. (3) Orfitus dedicated a temple to Apollo in 357–359 or later; *CIL* 6.45.

160. See the array of deities honored by Orfitus. *PLRE* 1:651–653 records his priesthoods: Pontifex Deae Vestae, Quindecimvir S. F., Pontifex dei Solis, and (from Symmachus *Ep.* 1.1.3) "Attica . . . palla tegit socerum . . . praefuit iste sacris." Cf. the assortment of holidays in the Calendar, discussed in Chapter 4.

161. Cameron, "The 'Pagan Reaction,' " highlights Orfitus's lack of intellectual or religious fervor; see too Ammianus Marcellinus 14.6.1.

to produce works according to classical canons.[162] Some of these writers were Christian. In fact, it is in this period that pagan classical literature begins to be assimilated into a Christian framework. Perhaps the most striking example of this phenomenon is the poetry of Faltonia Betitia Proba. Proba Christianized the classical epic with her *Cento Vergilianus de laudibus Christi*, on the creation of the world and the life of Jesus Christ, constructed entirely using lines from Virgil. In the proem to this work, she proclaims that she writes so "that Virgil put to verse Christ's sacred duties."[163] In this, the first Christian *cento*, or patchwork poem, we have, Aeneas is a prototype for Christ. Proba may well have written her epic to familiarize Christian children with biblical stories; nonetheless, she desired children to learn these stories via the language of the greatest of all Latin pagan poets.

In form and content, Proba's *Cento* exhibits the lack of "inhibition about classical literature" characteristic of the early decades of the century, and especially of the 350s.[164] This 350s dating fits well with what we know about the poetess. Proba, aristocratic wife of the prominent Clodius Celsinus Adelphius, was probably converted to Christianity only after 353 and prior to 362. Her husband apparently tolerated his wife's new faith, and by the time of his death he, too, was converted.[165] Thus both Proba's poem and her life indicate the assimilation of pagan classical culture into a Christian world and evidence the beginnings of Christianity as a respectable aristocratic religion.

While the use of classical pagan imagery also continued in the visual arts, the religious meaning of this imagery does not seem noticeably revitalized. One thinks here of the many Dionysian, Muse-related, and seasonal sarcophagi from the period, completely sculpted but for the portraits of the deceased. These works appear publicly neutral, though they may have had personal religious significance. Classicizing tenden-

162. See, for example, A. Cameron, "Paganism and Literature in Late Fourth Century Rome," *Entretiens sur l'antiquité classique* 23 (1977): 1ff.

163. Proba *Cento*, l. 23, ed. Clark and Hatch, *Golden Bough, Oaken Cross*.

164. This argument for dating Proba's *Cento* is advanced by R. A. Markus, "Paganism, Christianity, and the Latin Classics in the Fourth Century," in *Latin Literature of the Fourth Century*, ed. J. W. Binns (London and Boston, 1974), p. 3; and by Clark and Hatch, *Golden Bough, Oaken Cross*, pp. 97–102. I am not convinced by the dating proposed by D. Shanzer, "The Anonymous *Carmen contra Paganos* and the Date and Identity of the Centonist Proba," *Revue des études augustiniennes* 32 (1986): 232–248.

165. For discussion, see Clark and Hatch, *Golden Bough, Oaken Cross*, pp. 97–102. Evidence for the conversion of Clodius Celsinus Adelphius is found in the *Cento* of Proba, ll. 599–604, ed. Clark and Hatch. Proba's own conversion after writing an earlier epic on the defeat of Magnentius probably occurred after 353; see the *Cento*, ll. 45–55; and Clark and Hatch, pp. 97–102.

cies in style or type often coincide with markedly pagan imagery in artifacts from this period, yet again, that is not reason enough to argue for
a revived or revitalized pagan religious significance: Christians could also
appreciate such works of art, as the image of Venus at her toilet on the
silver casket of the Christian bride Proiecta and the bacchic putti on the
Christian sarcophagus of Junius Bassus attest.[166]

I would suggest instead that the production of art and literature with
distinctly pagan motifs and the classicizing tendencies of this period resulted largely from the reassertion of aristocratic cultural traditions in the
calm following a divisive civil war. Constantius's visit in 357 may have
confirmed the viability of these traditions; he certainly appears to have
had pretensions to learning and was concerned with supporting literature and education.[167] But to speak of this flourishing of classical traditions as a pagan reaction is misleading, for it suggests a sharpening of
the lines between pagans and Christians. On the contrary, art and literature of the mid fourth century indicate rather the blurring of such
distinctions in Roman society and the assimilation of pagan classical
forms into a Christian framework.

Assimilation and accommodation, the dominant processes active in
350s Rome, were facilitated as well by the wide range of attitudes among
Christians toward contemporary pagans. While some Christians probably agreed with the hostile and evangelizing fervor of a Firmicus Maternus, others were undoubtedly more concerned with internal church
matters or affairs of the otherworld than with their pagan neighbors.
Interestingly, some see this decade as the time when asceticism, marked
by a turning away from the secular world, first appears among the
women of the Roman aristocracy.[168]

Many Christians probably felt that conversion did not mean they
had to give up their old ways and heritage entirely. Valentinus must have
been in this group, for presumably he appreciated the Codex-Calendar
of 354, with its balancing of pagan and Christian elements. These Christians felt no compunction about celebrating the pagan festivals and holidays as they always had, but they made sure to attend church services
as well.[169] Constantius's equilibrated appointments to the urban prefec-

---

166. Shelton, *The Esquiline Treasure*, pp. 63–68, includes a sensible discussion and
bibliography on classical revivals in late-antique art.

167. Ammianus Marcellinus 21.16.4; *C.Th.* 14.1.1.

168. *The Life of Melania the Younger*, trans. and commentary by E. A. Clark (New York,
1984), pp. 93–94.

169. See, for example, Augustine's diatribe against this practice in *Enarratio ad Psalmum* 88, *Sermo* 2.4 in *PL* 37, col. 1140. Cf. Augustine *De cat. rud.* 25.48.

ture evidence the same attitude: an open willingness to accommodate to the status quo, at least in Rome.

In sum, the mid fourth century was a period of accommodation and assimilation in Rome. Pagans and Christians coexisted more or less peacefully. This climate, fostered in part by the policies of Constantius II, greatly facilitated the incorporation of aristocratic pagan traditions into a Christian present. Christianity, too, was altered in the process, as can be seen in the emergence of a respectable aristocratic Christianity at this time. Among the elite strata of society especially, shared cultural values, class interests, and political considerations cut across religious categories and defused potential conflicts.

As the century progressed, it was perhaps inevitable that relations between pagans and Christians in Rome would become strained, particularly when later emperors revised Constantius's policies toward paganism.[170] Among scholars, the prevailing image of a last stand of the pagans of Rome in the last quarter of the century is a startling contrast to the image of Rome in the 350s advanced here. The questions are unavoidable: What happened to bring about the so-called "pagan reaction of the last Romans of Rome"? What put a halt to the forces for accommodation and assimilation that had been present in the first half of the century? And to what extent were the conflicts of the 380s and 390s, in fact, religiously motivated?

170. This far better known pagan reaction and revival in the last quarter of the fourth century provided the model for interpreting events in 350s Rome in terms of pagan-Christian conflict.

· VI ·

EPILOGUE: THE TURNING
OF THE TIDE

ANTIPAGAN LEGISLATION AND THE PAGAN
REACTIONS IN THE LATE FOURTH CENTURY

The tolerant atmosphere described at Rome in the 350s and reflected by the Codex-Calendar of 354 continued only for the next thirty years. A brief pagan revival under Constantius II's successor, Julian (361–363), was centered in the Greek East; thus, although it must have encouraged some Western pagans, this movement had little direct political impact in Rome.[1] Under Julian's successors, Jovian and Valentinian I, a policy of religious toleration prevailed. This thirty-year period saw a gradual undermining of paganism before the steady advance of Christianity, but it was not until the reigns of Gratian and the "most Christian of emperors," Theodosius, that official imperial policy concerning pagan cult changed markedly in the West; under these emperors the legal status of pagan cult was systematically attacked and the bond between pagan cult and the institutions that had traditionally supported it—the emperor and the state—ruptured. Hence, the antipagan laws of Gratian and Theodosius and the pagan response in the last two decades of the fourth century represent for the Latin West the turning of the tide.

In 382, Gratian, influenced by Bishop Ambrose of Milan (374–397)

---

1. Julian's revival of paganism has attracted a large body of scholarship: see in particular R. Browning, *The Emperor Julian* (London, 1976); and G. Bowersock, *Julian the Apostate* (London, 1978). The primary link between Julian's revival in the Greek East and the pagan reaction in the Latin West is the figure of Vettius Agorius Praetextatus, whose brand of paganism appears closest to Julian's. For his career, see *PLRE* 1:722–724.

and perhaps inspired by the activities of Theodosius in the Eastern empire, confiscated revenues earmarked for maintaining public sacrifices and ceremonies, diverted to the imperial treasury property willed by senators and Vestals to the upkeep of pagan ritual, and put an end to the exemption of pagan religious officials from compulsory public duties.[2] He also ordered the removal of the Altar of Victory from the Roman Senate, though he allowed her statue to remain.[3] These and certain other antipagan actions led in 382–384 to a protest by prominent Roman pagan senators. Symmachus, in his *Third State Paper*, requested the return of the Altar of Victory and of the status quo—namely, a return to the imperial policy of tolerance and benign neglect. His attempts were countered by Ambrose, whose persuasive powers proved compelling to Gratian and his successor, Valentinian II. Symmachus's petition was denied.

The antipagan legislation of Theodosius and the usurpation of Eugenius and Arbogast (392–394) constitute the second major episode of the pagan reaction.[4] Theodosius's harsh policies allegedly led Nicomachus Flavianus and other pagan aristocrats to revolt. Yet the rebellion of Eugenius and Arbogast, as recent scholars have argued, concerned not religious but dynastic recognition.[5] When Theodosius refused these men's claims to the Western throne, Eugenius, nominally a Christian, sought the support of Bishop Ambrose.[6] Only after Theodosius and Am-

---

2. Gratian's edict is not extant, but it is referred to in a code of A.D. 415, *C.Th.* 16.10.20.

3. Symmachus *Rel.* 3, ed. O. Seeck, in *MGH, Auctores Antiquissimi* 6.1 (Berlin, 1883); Ambrose *Ep.* 17–18. This controversy has been often discussed; for bibliography, see especially J. J. Sheridan, "The Altar of Victory: Paganism's Last Battle," *AC* 35 (1966): 186–206; B. Croke and J. Harries, *Religious Conflict in Fourth Century Rome: A Documentary Study* (Sydney, 1982), pp. 28–51; and, for the reedited texts, see R. Klein, *Der Streit um den Victoriaaltar* (Darmstadt, 1972).

4. J. J. O'Donnell, "The Demise of Paganism," *Traditio* 35 (1979): 43–88, cites (n. 1) recent scholarship on this much-discussed episode. I concur with O'Donnell that the most influential modern account of these events is H. Bloch, "A New Document of the Last Pagan Revival in the West, 393–4 A.D.," *HTR* 38 (1945): 199–244, which was revised and published (with plates) as "The Pagan Revival in the West at the End of the Fourth Century A.D.," in *The Conflict Between Paganism and Christianity in the Fourth Century*, ed. A. Momigliano (London, 1963), pp. 193–218.

5. See O'Donnell, "Demise of Paganism," pp. 43–88; J. J. O'Donnell "The Career of Virius Nicomachus Flavianus," *Phoenix* 32 (1978): 129–143; J. Matthews, *Western Aristocracies and Imperial Court* A.D. 364–425 (Oxford, 1975), pp. 183–252. For similar conclusions concerning literature, see A. Cameron, "Paganism and Literature in Late Fourth Century Rome," in *Christianisme et formes littéraires de l'antiquité tardive en Occident, Fondation Hardt, Entretiens sur l'antiquité classique*, no. 23, ed. M. Fuhrmann (Vandoeuvres, 1977), pp. 1–31.

6. For general discussion of this revolt, see *RAC* 6 (1966), s.v. "Eugenius," cols. 860–

brose refused to relent did Eugenius and Arbogast (though relying mostly on their Gallic armies for support) make some effort to win the approval of the pagan senatorial aristocracy. These attempts were limited, however, and did not come until after Eugenius had entered Italy and abandoned all hopes of a reconciliation with Theodosius. Earlier, Eugenius had turned down two requests by pagan senators for the return of the Altar of Victory. Now, in an attempt to win pagan favor, he agreed to this demand, and he also provided money from his own resources to prominent pagans, who might use it, it was understood, to finance pagan ceremonies.[7]

Moreover, the number of pagans involved in this revolt is not known, since no aristocrat other than Flavianus is named. The one inscription—recording the restoration of a temple of Hercules at Ostia—that is advanced as critical evidence for widespread pagan support of the revolt is problematic with regard to both its date and its pagan polemical intent: at the time, restoration of pagan buildings was not against imperial law.[8] After the usurpers' defeat at the Battle of Frigidus, only Flavianus appears to have chosen suicide over dishonor;[9] the other pagan senators, whoever they were and however many, accepted pardon and returned home in defeat. No evidence exists of any major repercussions against pagans or against Rome.

Thus, both late-fourth-century pagan political protests were quite limited in scope. The forces for toleration observed in the 350s served greatly to diminish the political reaction later in the century. In short, the dramatic struggle between the old and the new religion has been exaggerated; any pagan reaction that did occur took the form largely of isolated attempts to halt the processes of accommodation and assimilation so characteristic of earlier decades.

These reactionary episodes are, of course, noteworthy in that they register the negative response of pagan aristocrats to new imperial policy concerning the legal status of paganism. Moreover, both episodes revolve around defense of public state cult, the vitality of which is amply documented by the Codex-Calendar of 354. To focus on these reactions, however, is to create a misleading impression of the fourth century and

---

878; and Matthews, *Western Aristocracies*, pp. 238–258. Eugenius had earlier issued coins with Christian insignia.

7. Symmachus *Ep.* 57.6; and Paulinus of Milan *Vita Ambrosii* 26.

8. O'Donnell, "Demise of Paganism," pp. 137–139, argues convincingly for the limited support for Eugenius and (p. 140, n. 48) questions the interpretation of the Ostia inscription advanced by Bloch, "A New Document," pp. 199–244.

9. Rufinus *H.E.* 2.33 is the only contemporary source for Flavianus's suicide.

to underappreciate the historical forces that were working toward change. Far more important for understanding fourth-century Roman society is the blurring of distinctions between the pagan past and the Christian present that is observed so clearly in the Codex-Calendar of 354. Although some pagan aristocrats held to their views without bending, in the end accommodation facilitated the conversion to Christianity of the governing classes themselves—a process that was gaining real momentum in Rome in the 350s. Certainly some political conflict marked pagan-Christian relations in the last quarter of the century, but this conflict was far less severe than it might have been; the ability of pagans and Christians to share a common culture and, especially among senatorial aristocrats, a common set of assumptions and traditions helps to explain why political discord was relatively muffled at Rome and why, by the early 400s, the Roman aristocracy was predominantly Christian.

The new imperial policy established by Gratian and Theodosius reflected and implemented profound changes in Western religion and society as paganism lost its traditional institutional support. The results of these changes can be traced in the Roman calendar, of which we are indeed fortunate to possess two late-antique exempla: the Codex-Calendar of 354 and the calendar of Polemius Silvius of 448–449. These documents, one dated before and the other after the implementation of the new imperial policy, reveal much about the transformation of Roman society and religion in this critical period.[10]

THE CALENDAR OF 354 AND THE CALENDAR OF POLEMIUS SILVIUS: TRADITION AND INNOVATION

As we have seen, the Calendar of 354 records the traditional games, religious holidays, and imperial anniversaries actually celebrated in Rome. Pagan cult reigned virtually unchallenged in the mid fourth century, except for the offensive rite of animal sacrifice. In the second half of the century, this situation no longer held. The tide had turned. Christian emperors legislated against new aspects of pagan cult in an attempt to disassociate paganism from the culture and civic life of the empire. The very nature of the relationship between the state and paganism was

10. For the text of the calendar of Polemius Silvius, see Degrassi 1963, pp. 263–277; and Mommsen, *MGH* 1892, pp. 511–551. For discussion of Polemius and his calendar, see T. Mommsen, *Abhandlungen der K. sächsischen Gesellshaft der Wissenschaften 3* (1857): 231–277 (= *Gesammelte Schriften*, vol. 7 [Berlin, 1909], pp. 633–677); *RE* 21.1 (1951), s.v. "Polemius Silvius," cols. 1260–1263; and Stern 1953, pp. 32ff.

altered. Some of these antipagan sentiments were given expression in laws directed at the Roman calendar.

The Emperor Constantine initiated perhaps the most famous legal action relating to paganism in the Roman calendar when he established the Day of the Sun—*Dies Solis*—as a holiday.[11] This law reflects well Constantine's characteristic ambiguity concerning paganism: while Christians saw the day as devoted to their deity, pagans could observe it by honoring the pagan god Sol. According to Eusebius, Constantine also urged provincial governors to respect the days commemorating martyrs and duly to honor the festal seasons of the church, especially Easter.[12]

The first recorded change in the legal status of pagan holidays extant in the Theodosian Code is dated to 389.[13] The law in question ordered "all days to be court days" except for Harvest Holidays from 24 June to 1 August; Vintage Holidays from 23 August to 15 October; the New Year, 1 January; the *natales* of Rome and Constantinople; the holy days of Easter; Sundays; and the birthday and accession day of the emperor. Thus was removed the official status accorded to all the other traditional pagan holidays noted in both the Roman Calendar of 354 and the *Feriale Campanum* of 387, issued only two years before this law,[14] since by definition, a holiday was a day on which no civil or criminal court action could occur. Simultaneously, legal status was accorded to Christian holidays other than Sunday for the first time; these were now to be incorporated into the civic life of the state.

The 389 law is consistent with Gratian's actions aimed at disestablishing pagan cult; in its breadth, it prefigures Theodosius's sweeping law of 391 directed to the prefect of Rome, which banned all pagan sacrifices, both public and private, and prohibited access to the pagan temples.[15] It was not until 395, in the reigns of Theodosius's sons, Arcadius and Honorius, however, that the pagan holidays were explicitly removed from the calendar and abolished: "We call to remembrance that we formerly commanded by law [no longer extant] that the ceremonial days of pagan superstition should not be considered among the holidays."[16]

---

11. *C.Th.* 2.8.1 (A.D. 321), addressed to Helpidius, a vicar. In his translation, C. Pharr, *The Theodosian Code and Novels and the Sirmondian Constitutions* (Princeton, N.J., 1952), p. 44, n. 3 observes: "Constantine purposely identifies the pagan day for the worship of the Sun with the Lord's Day of the Christians."

12. Eusebius *Vita Constantini* 4.22–23.

13. *C.Th.* 2.8.19, Augg. Valentinian, Theodosius, and Arcadius to Albinus, prefect of Rome. The holy days of Easter are defined by this law as the seven days before and the seven after Easter.

14. *Feriale Campanum* (A.D. 387), in Degrassi 1963, pp. 282–283.

15. *C.Th.* 16.10.10.

16. *C.Th.* 2.8.22, addressed to Heraclianus, governor of Paphlagonia; trans. Pharr:

Neither these nor later laws regarding pagan festivals altered the legal status of *ludi* and *circenses*, since *ludi* were not, strictly speaking, *dies feriae* on which court actions were to be halted. On the contrary, the Theodosian Code attests that *ludi* and circus spectacles continued to be celebrated with imperial support into the fifth century.[17] Gladiatorial combat (ineffectively forbidden by Constantine as early as 325) continued at Rome, probably until 438—long after the Emperor Honorius had closed the gladiatorial schools in 399. Wild beast fighting and hunting, however, persisted until much later; the last we hear of *venationes* at Rome is in the critical account by Cassiodorus of 523.[18] Chariot racing and circuses survived at Rome well into the sixth century, with the last recorded races in the Circus Maximus being held under Totila in 549.[19]

The Theodosian Code records the attempt by Christian emperors to disassociate *ludi* and spectacles—so valuable in a popular political sense—from the pagan holidays that had originally occasioned them. By describing these celebrations as *voluptates*, as the Theodosian Code consistently does, Christian emperors could continue to support them as cultural and nonreligious events. The logic of this policy is expressed in a law of 399:

> Just as we have already abolished profane rites by a salutary law [no longer extant], so do we not allow the festal assemblies of citizens and the common pleasure of all to be abolished. Hence we decree that, according to ancient custom, amusements [*voluptates*] shall be furnished

---

"Sollemnes pagano(r)um superstitionis dies inter feriatos non haberi olim lege re-minis(c)imur imperasse." The previous law is not extant.

17. See, for example, *C.Th.* 16.10.17 (A.D. 399), to Apollodorus, proconsul of Africa; 15.5.3 (409); and 15.5.5 (425), which stipulates only that *ludi* not fall on Christian holidays. Cf. 2.8.23 (399) and 2.8.24 (400–405), which stipulate that games and circuses not be held on certain Christian holidays.

18. Although Constantine legislated against gladiatorial combats in A.D. 325 (*C.Th.* 15.12.1), the gladiatorial schools at Rome were not closed until 399 and the combats continued. Theodoret *H.E.* 5.26ff. tells of the intervention of the Eastern monk Telemachus in the games of Rome, which led to his being stoned to death by the angry crowd, dated to Honorius's reign (395–402). Prudentius *Contra Symm.* 2.1122ff. (402–403) urges Honorius to end the gladiatorial contests. For further discussion, see Geffcken 1978, p. 228; and for arguments that they were continued until 434–438, see G. Ville, "Les jeux de gladiateurs dans l'empire chrétien," *MEFR* 72 (1960): 273–335. The games are described by A. Cameron, *Porphyrius the Charioteer* (Oxford, 1973), pp. 228–232. Wild beast hunts continued as well; see Cassiodorus *Var.* 5.42; and Geffcken 1978, p. 228.

19. Procopius *Bell. Goth.* 7.37.4; see C. Petri, "Le sénat, le peuple chrétien, et les partis du cirque à Rome sous le pape Symmaque (495–514)," *MEFR* 78 (1966): 122–139. Circus games continued later in Byzantium, arguably until the twelfth century; see A. Cameron, *Circus Factions: Blues and Greens at Rome and Byzantium* (Oxford, 1976), pp. 297ff.

to the people, but without any sacrifice or any accursed superstition, and they shall be allowed to attend festal banquets whenever public vows so demand.[20]

Although Christian emperors chose to defend and define *ludi* as amusements, the people who attended these events did not necessarily experience them thus. Pagans and traditionalists likely continued to appreciate the religious intent of these games, even if their Christian contemporaries did not. As M. Beard remarks about interpretations of Vestal commemorations at Rome: "We need not always (and perhaps should never) accept the consciously formulated explanations of cult practices offered by contemporary observers or the actors themselves."[21]

The fourth-century imperial attempt to define *ludi* in nonreligious terms has a striking modern parallel that elucidates the difficulties inherent in legislating against festival celebrations. A case was brought before the Supreme Court concerning the seasonal display of a city-owned, life-sized nativity scene in Pawtucket, Rhode Island.[22] It was argued that this display violated the constitutional provision regarding separation of church and state. The Court majority appeared baffled that a celebration so—in its view—obviously benign, so completely "American" (scarcely different, the justices opined, from printing "In God We Trust" on currency), could have caused hard feelings, let alone a lawsuit. Substitute *Roman* for *American*, and one can see the emperors' argument, as revealed in the Theodosian Code.

But this 1984 view was held by only five of the nine justices. The dissenting opinion, stated by Justice Brennan, began from a different premise. The fact that "the Christmas holiday seems so familiar and agreeable is constitutionally irrelevant," he wrote; what matters is that the official display conveyed "the unique and exclusive benefit of public recognition and approval" of Christianity, while communicating to non-

20. *C.Th.* 16.10.17: "Ut profanos ritus iam salubri lege submovimus, ita festos conventus civium et communem omnium laetitiam non patimur submoveri. Unde absque ullo sacrificio atque ulla superstitione damnabili exhiberi populo voluptates secundum veterem consuetudinem, iniri etiam festa convivia, si quando exigunt publica vota, decernimus"; Emperors Arcadius and Honorius to Appollodorus, prefect of Africa (A.D. 399); trans. Pharr. This law is particularly interesting because it allows not only *ludi* and public vows as legal holidays but also "popular celebrations"—*festos conventus*—without sacrifice or pagan rituals. It should be recalled that these emperors also legislated against "Sollemnes pagano(rum) superstitionis dies" (*C.Th.* 2.8.22 [395]). This 399 law thus appears to clarify and reaffirm imperial support for popular celebrations. For the difficulty of applying this definition of *superstitio*, see pp. 205–209. For *voluptates* in legal usage, defined as "*delectatio*," see *Vocabularium Iurisprudentiae Romanae* (Berlin, 1894–1939), vol. 5, s.v. "Voluptas."

21. M. Beard, "The Sexual Status of Vestal Virgins," *JRS* 70 (1980): 26ff.

22. *New York Times*, 15 July 1984 (editorial).

Christians "the message that their views are not similarly worthy of public recognition nor entitled to public support."[23] Substitute *fourth-century
Christian* for *dissenting justices* in this case, and one can see the Christian
leaders' argument against the continuation of *ludi* and circus spectacles.[24] For the imperial laws of the late fourth and early fifth centuries
register the Christian opposition to these *ludi* as well. Beginning in 392,
in the reign of Theodosius, a series of laws legislated against just such
events, first on Sundays and then on other Christian holidays, namely,
the Paschal Days, Epiphany, and Christmas. A law of 400–405 explicitly
states that these restrictions were instituted "out of respect for religion."[25]

The attempts by Christian emperors to redefine the intrinsically religious nature of the Roman calendar as cultural, not cultic, and to outlaw
all pagan festivals were only partially and gradually successful. The pagan festivals and holidays, so unequivocally outlawed in 395, nevertheless continued to be celebrated—in some cases well into the fifth and
sixth centuries. Not only did the *Lupercalia*, for one, survive and continue
to be commemorated popularly at the capital, but its celebration in 495
was, a recent study claims, the "last official cult occasion to survive at
Rome."[26] In that year, the festival was vigorously opposed by Pope Gelasius, and its official cultic celebration was attacked. If the popular celebration of the *Lupercalia* continued after its last official cultic celebration
in 495, we do not know, but other popular holidays did outlast it, though
perhaps not with official recognition. A few are attested at Rome well
into the sixth century, such as the *Isidis navigium*, the *Natalis Martis*, and
the *Volcanalia* or *ludi Vulcanalici*.[27] Other popular pagan holidays are attested in the Latin West outside of Rome into the sixth century, including
the festival of Hercules in Spain,[28] and attempts to suppress pagan cele-

23. Ibid.
24. The Christian argument is fully articulated by Tertullian *De Spectaculis*. But see
too the famous homily against spectacles by John Chrysostom, *Contra ludos et theatra*, in
PG 56, pp. 263ff.; and Salvianus *De Gubernatione Dei* 6.129–130, *PL* 53, cols. 120–121.
25. *C.Th.* 2.8.24 (A.D. 400–405), trans. Pharr: "Religionis intuitu cavemus atque decernimus, ut (s)eptem diebus quadragesimae, septem paschalibus, quorum observationi-
bus et ieiuniis peccata purgantur, natalis etiam die et epifa(n)iae spectacula non edantur."
See also *C.Th.* 2.8.20, 21 (392), 2.8.23 (399), 2.8.25 (409).
26. A. W. J. Holleman, *Pope Gelasius I and the Lupercalia* (Amsterdam, 1974), pp. 1ff.
27. *Isidis navigium*, 5 March; see Degrassi 1963, p. 420, for citations into the sixth
century. *Natalis Martis*, 1 March, attested by Atto of Vercelli in the eighth century, *Sermo*
3, in *PL* 134, col. 836. *Volcanalia* or *ludi Vulcanalici*, 23 August; see Degrassi 1963, pp. 500–
501. The transformation of the pagan Roman calendar into a Christian one during the fifth
to tenth centuries is a topic that is yet to be studied adequately.
28. Latte 1960, pp. 371ff.

brations are known to have occasioned riots in Africa in the fourth and fifth centuries.[29]

At times it is difficult to determine exactly when a pagan festival ceased to be celebrated, for generally this happened gradually, in different localities and at different times. Many of the festivals, moreover, did not actually die out; rather, their traditional pagan meaning was transformed over time, with the commemoration of these holidays becoming a matter of popular custom, not of religious belief. So, for example, while the *Saturnalia*, perhaps the best known of the Roman holidays, noted on 17 December in the Calendar of 354, was originally intended to honor the god Saturn, Polemius Silvius records one of its distinctive rituals, the role reversal of master and slave, in his fifth-century calendar, and the holiday continued to be celebrated as a popular festival. Other customary aspects of this day, such as the exercise of good will and the exchange of presents, and even perhaps the wearing of paper hats, were continued within a Christian context: Christmas, celebrated in the Latin West on 25 December (in competition with the holiday in honor of Deus Sol Invictus), incorporated rites borrowed from the popular *Saturnalia*. Another example of a Roman festival transformed is provided by the Vintage Holidays. These were originally intended to offer thanks for the harvest to the pagan deities; the *Mammes vindemia*, for instance, noted on 5 September in the Calendar of 354, was devoted to Dionysius/Liber (see Chapter 3). In time, however, the religious significance of these holidays was overshadowed by more popular associations. Imperial decrees sanctioned their continued celebration.[30]

The pagan cultic meaning of a festival might be subsumed as well by imperial and civic connotations. Such, Alföldi argues, was the case with the *Isidis navigium*, a popular festival to Isis celebrated in March and associated with public vows on behalf of the emperor's well-being. Many of its rites—as, for example, the carrying of pictures of Isis on board her sacred ship—were retained in the Christian festival of the *Carnevale*, held in conjunction with Easter. At this festival, the ship or a representation of it was carried by the assembled celebrants.[31] Similarly, the New Year's

---

29. A. H. M. Jones, *The Late Roman Empire: A Social, Economic, and Administrative Survey (284–602)* (Oxford, 1964), p. 939.

30. For the *Saturnalia*, see Degrassi 1963, pp. 538–540. For Christmas, see *Encyclopedia of Religion and Ethics*, ed. J. Hastings (Edinburgh and New York, 1908–1926), s.v. "Christmas," 3:601–608, and "Christmas customs," pp. 608–610. For vintage holidays, see *C.Th.* 2.8.19.8; these included, for example, the *Mammes Vindemia*, 5 September in the Calendar of 354, and the *Vindemia*, 15 October in the *Menologia Rustica*; see Degrassi 1963, pp. 508, 521–522. For more general discussion, see Geffcken 1978, pp. 225ff.

31. A. Alföldi, *A Festival of Isis in Rome Under the Christian Emperors of the Fourth Century* (Budapest, 1937), pp. 46ff.

Day celebration on 1 January and the "natal days" of Rome and Constantinople became great civic events disassociated from their original cultic meaning.[32]

The fifth-century celebration of the *Lupercalia* suggests the difficulties imperial policymakers met in outlawing the "ceremonial days of pagan superstition."[33] This pagan holiday had from time immemorial been a purificatory rite and as such accepted as promoting fertility.[34] However accurate this learned view of the *Lupercalia* was, it was popularly obscured by the sensational rites of women being lashed to promote fertility. Thus in the third century, the holiday metamorphosed into a rite of punishment and public penance of women, and its fructifying intent changed from sexual to spiritual; public atonement and confession were now directed toward remission of sins and salvation. In the fourth century, after Constantine, the ritual of female flagellation "coarsened considerably."[35] By the end of the fifth century, in 494, Pope Gelasius I decried the rites of the *Lupercalia* as remnants of paganism: "diabolica figmenta."[36]

Opposition to Gelasius on this matter not only included the remaining pagan senators of Rome but was in fact led by the Christian senator Andromachus, who argues that the *Lupercalia* was merely an *imago* of the former pagan festival and that its continuance was important for the *Salus* of the Roman communality. He interpreted the acts of flagellation as *salutiferi*, by which he meant to convey the idea of individual purification from sin, a concept congenial to fifth-century Christian dogma and practice.[37] Andromachus argued for the *Lupercalia* as a Christian, but also as a patriotic Roman senator, and he is referred to as one of several Romans who believed that "the *Lupercalia* should be honored according to former custom."[38] At the heart of the controversy in 494 was the definition of the very nature of this holiday. Was it a pagan festival, as Pope Gelasius I viewed it and so banned it in accord with imperial law and Christian belief? Or was it a popular custom, celebrated, as Andromachus argued, as part of the great Roman aristocratic heritage?

32. M. Mesnil, *La fête des kalendes de janvier dans l'Empire Romain. Etude d'un rituel de nouvel an,* Collection Latomus, no. 115 (Brussels, 1970), pp. 53ff.

33. So the pagan holidays are referred to in, for example, *C.Th.* 2.8.22.

34. Holleman, *Pope Gelasius,* p. 11.

35. Ibid., pp. 11, 27–53, 153ff.

36. Gelasius I, *Lettre contre les Lupercales et dix-huit messes du sacramentaire léonien,* no. 8, ed. by G. Pomarès (Paris, 1959) = SC 65.

37. The notion of *salus* advanced by Andromachus can be disengaged from Gelasius's refutation. See ibid., nos. 17, 19, 24ʙ, 25ʙ, 26; and Holleman, *Pope Gelasius,* pp. 47–53.

38. Gelasius I, *Lettre,* p. 162: "Lupercalia secundum morem pristinum colenda constituunt." Pomarès cites this as part of the title of the letter in the *Collectio Avellana*; it was not Gelasius's title. See too Holleman, *Pope Gelasius,* pp. 47–53, 61ff.

The controversy over the *Lupercalia* indicates how problematic imperial policy concerning pagan holidays could be. These same difficulties are evidenced in the calendar of Polemius Silvius, written in Gaul in 448–449 and dedicated to the bishop of Lyons, Eucherius. In composing this avowedly Christian calendar, Polemius, considered one of the outstanding authors of his age,[39] probably used as a model the Codex-Calendar of 354, along with several other sources.[40] In the preface to his work he indicates that he has removed certain traditional calendric notations, including lunar letters, hebdomadals, nundinals, and references to the *dies aegyptiaci* (or unlucky days, as "the pagans foolishly called these days"), as well as pictures of the months, days, and astrological signs—even though none of these elements are to be considered evil, because "God has made all things good."[41]

Perhaps most fascinating is the revised calendar text, which Polemius himself compiled. Notable is his omission of many pagan festivals, such as the *Liberalici* (17 March), the *Iunonalia* (7 March), and the *Isidis navigium* (5 March). Some scholars have surmised that these popular festivals were intentionally eliminated because the Christian author objected to their pagan nomenclature.[42] If so, Polemius was inconsistent. For one thing, he does not omit the pagan names of the months. Moreover, he includes other pagan festivals, notably the *Carmentalia* (11 January), *Parentatio tumulorum* (13 February; listed as *Virgo Vestalis parentat* in the Calendar of 354), the *Lupercalia* (15 February), the *Quirinalia* (17 February), the *Terminalia* (23 February), the *Quinquatria* (19 March), the *Natalis urbis Romae* (21 April), and even the *Lavatio* (27 March), which, however, he apparently identifies with the Resurrection of Christ. He also includes the anniversary of the Muses (13 June), the only *natalis* of a pagan deity so

39. Polemius Silvius is so considered by the author of the Life of Hilarius, bishop of Arles (405–449), as observed by Mommsen, *MGH* 1892, p. 660; and Degrassi 1963, p. 263.

40. The only pagan festival in Polemius's calendar not recorded in the Calendar of 354 is the *Ancillarum Feriae*, on 7 July. Aside from the omission of imperial names from 19 August to 1 October and the mistaken 31 March notation *natalis Constantini* instead of the correct *Constantii*, Polemius's calendar is very similar to the Calendar of 354 in its historical information. Stern 1953, pp. 32ff., argues for Polemius's use of the Codex-Calendar of 354. Although this cannot be proven, nevertheless, Polemius must have derived the text of his calendar from earlier official calendars from Rome like the one in the Codex-Calendar of 354.

41. Degrassi 1963, p. 263, following Mommsen, *MGH* 1892, pp. 514–515, incorrectly states that Polemius has removed all elements pertaining to pagan superstition. But Polemius's prologue does not indicate this; rather, he says only that the names were omitted, "ut stulte gentiles locuntur nomina designari," and that "Deus universa bona constituit." Text in Mommsen, *MGH* 1892, p. 518.

42. Polemius Silvius's preface is so construed by Mommsen, *MGH* 1892, pp. 514–519; and by Degrassi 1963, pp. 263–277.

recognized. Polemius even provides some pagan celebrations with explanations of their ritual or origin—for example, the notation for 13 September: "Hoc die Romae in aede Minvervali . . . ex aere clipei figebantur"; for 17 December: "Feriae servorum" (i.e., the *Saturnalia*); for 13 February: "Parentatio tumulorum inc[ipit]"; and for 11 January: "Carmentalia de nomine matris Euandri."

It is not surprising that Polemius also includes the traditional notations for the great public games and circuses, such as the *ludi* to honor Apollo (6–13 July), for these were still legal celebrations. Some scholars consider it significant that he tends to omit the names of the pagan divinities to whom the *ludi* were dedicated, since these names were considered offensive to Christians.[43] Once more, however, Polemius is inconsistent: certain *ludi* retain their objectionable pagan nomenclature, as for example the (*ludi*) *Floria* on 27 April (= *ludi Florales* in the Calendar of 354) and the *circenses Fab[a]rici* on 1 June.[44]

The inclusion of some pagan festivals and *ludi* but not others raises the question of whether Polemius omitted only those festivals with names offensive to Christians. Yet the items included in both his calendar and the prologue suggest that he was more concerned with making his calendar comprehensible and, by implication, that he kept only what he considered useful or necessary. While antiquarian knowledge was certainly of interest to Polemius and cannot be ruled out in explaining the selection of pagan festivals and especially their explanations, the Christian festivals that he included are considered to reflect contemporary Gallic practice.[45] Thus, even if we do not know in detail how the pagan calendar in Gaul was Christianized, it is plausible that these pagan festivals too, along with the newer Christian holidays, were still commemorated in some way in that province.[46]

If we assume that the festivals Polemius recorded were still celebrated in Gaul and Rome, the results of the imperial policies directed at pagan holidays are apparent: fewer than half the pagan holidays and

43. See Degrassi 1963, pp. 263ff.; Mommsen, *MGH* 1892, pp. 513–514.

44. Certain scholars argue that Polemius was not aware of the paganism implied by these names. See Mommsen, *MGH* 1892, pp. 513–514; *RE*, s.v. "Polemius Silvius," cols. 1262–1263; and Degrassi 1963, p. 263.

45. See Mommsen, *MGH* 1892, pp. 518–519, for Polemius's preface; and pp. 520ff. for Polemius's antiquarianism, which appears in his historical and etymological notations.

46. The acts of the various church councils evidence the continuation of pagan festivals in Gaul and the difficulty of suppressing them. See, for example, the Acts of the Council of Aurelimensis in 541 (*MGH: Concilia Aevi Merovingici* 1.90). Cf. Augustine's complaints about pagan festivals in North Africa: *Ep.* 29.9; *Enarratio ad Psalmum* 88.14 = *CCL* 88 (Turnholt, Belg., 1977), p. 1294; and *De cat. rud.* 25.48 = *CCL* 46 (1969), p. 172.

some one hundred fewer days of *ludi* and *circenses* are recorded in the calendar of Polemius as compared with the Calendar of 354.[47] Of the surviving pagan holidays, many commemorate important moments in Roman history—or at least that is the aspect Polemius emphasizes. So, for example, the *Quirinalia*, on 17 February, is explained as "the day on which the fiction was invented that Romulus disappeared, though [in reality] he was killed by his own men; he was called Quirinus after the Sabine term for a spear, *curis*". The *Regifugium*, on 24 February, is identified as "when Tarquinius Superbus is said to have been expelled from the city [of Rome]."[48] Yet other pagan festivals, with explanations of their rituals, are also included, such as the *Lupercalia* on 15 February, which is elsewhere attested into the fifth century. One can also assume the continuing popularity of the *Parentatio tumulorum* (= *Virgo Vestalis parentat*) on 13 February (to which notation Polemius characteristically adds the information that "on that date Rome was freed from the siege of the Gauls") and the *Cara Cognatio* on 22 February.[49] Wherever possible, though, Polemius does maximize the festivals' historical elements and minimize their pagan cultic meaning.

Polemius was probably willing to include these traditionally pagan holidays in his Christian calendar because he viewed them as merely "cultural" manifestations and minimized or dismissed any "cultic" associations—thus following the precedent set by emperors who legislated against pagan holidays yet continued to support the *ludi* as traditional "amusements." Strikingly, Polemius's desire to preserve Roman culture is linked with a "well-educated" mind and a heightened awareness of the traditional and pagan elements in the Roman calendar (hence, perhaps, his omission of some of the pagan names of the *ludi*). At the same time, he has created an explicitly Christian calendar, beginning the calendar year in January because of the birth of Jesus Christ.[50]

47. We do not know to what degree Polemius's calendar for Gaul coincides with practices in fifth-century Rome, but he probably used the Codex-Calendar of 354 or some other calendar from Rome as a prototype. See note 40 above.

48. See Degrassi 1963, p. 265, for the *Quirinalia*: "Quo die Romulus, occisus a suis, Qui[rinus] ab hasta, quae a Sabinis curis vocatur, non apparuisse confictus est"; and ibid., for the *Regifugium*: "cum Tarquinius Superbus fertur ab Urbe expulsus."

49. For the *Lupercalia*, see Holleman, *Pope Gelasius*, pp. 1ff. For the *Parentatio tumulorum* (*Virgo Vestalis parentat* in the Calendar of 354), Polemius adds: "Quo die Roma liberata est de obsidione Gallorum"; see Degrassi 1963, pp. 408–409. For the *Cara Cognatio* (*Caristia* in the Calendar of 354), see ibid., p. 414, which also correctly notes that there is general agreement that the *Cara Cognatio* was transformed into the Christian *Cathedra Petri*. For fuller discussion of this transformation, see T. Klauser, *Die Kathedra im Totenkult der heidnischen und christlichen Antike* (Münster, 1927), pp. 152ff.; and Chapter 2 above, esp. notes 64–66.

50. Mommsen, *MGH* 1892, p. 519.

The calendar of Polemius Silvius is a fascinating example of the continuity of classical culture and Roman traditions into fifth-century Christian Gaul. Seen in this light, Polemius's inclusion of the *Natalis Musarum* becomes explicable, for the Muses represented to late-antique men like himself the Roman educational and cultural heritage in general, devoid of any cultic meaning.[51] Similarly, the production of a Roman calendar and the explanation and commemoration of the holidays recorded in it signified to Polemius and his contemporaries an important part of their classical Roman legacy, which should, they felt, be preserved and transmitted. Indeed, Polemius indicates that his impulse for producing the calendar was essentially didactic: "I had read the listing [i.e., calendar] which earlier men made by reckoners and annotated with difficult markings. I have changed the sense of things placed in it [my calendar] in order that it not be unintelligible to the less learned [*minus doctis*] because of its being so full [of detail]."[52] A recent study in fact contends that the "minus docti" designated by Polemius to receive this calendar were schoolchildren.[53]

In his emphasis on the didatic elements of the Roman calendar, Polemius calls to mind another important writer in the Latin West, whose floruit can now be dated to not earlier than ca. 430. Macrobius also wrote the *Saturnalia* allegedly to teach his son about the Roman past.[54] And in this work, the respected senator Praetextatus displays his erudition by delivering a lengthy discourse on the Roman calendar and its contents.[55]

To conclude, in 350s Rome it was the Christians' ability to share in the classical culture of the age that produced the emphatically traditional Calendar of 354 for its Christian aristocratic recipient. In the thirty years after its production, significant changes were wrought in pagan cult and culture. The tide turned. By the end of the fourth century, paganism was

51. For the "Cult of the Muses," see H. I. Marrou, "*Mousikòs Anér*. Etude sur les scènes de la vie intellectuelle figurant sur les monuments funéraires romains" (thesis, Université de Grenoble, 1937). For its visual aspects, see the section on "The Poet and the Muses" in *Age of Spirituality: Late Antique and Early Christian Art, 3d to 7th Century* (Catalogue of the Exhibition, Metropolitan Museum of Art), ed. K. Weitzmann (New York and Princeton, N.J., 1979), nos. 240–242 and G. M. A. Hanfmann, "The Continuity of Classical Art: Culture, Myth, and Faith," in *Age of Spirituality: A Symposium*, ed. K. Weitzmann (New York, 1980), pp. 75–100. It may well have become a school holiday, as E. Dulabahn, "Studies on the *Laterculus* of Polemius Silvius" (Ph.D. diss., Byrn Mawr College, 1986), p. 195, suggests, but without supporting evidence.

52. Mommsen, *MGH* 1892, p. 518: "Laterculum quem priores fecerunt cum difficilibus supputatoribus indiciis notatum legissem, ne minus doctis esset obscurior absolutione positarum in eo rerum significationem mutavi."

53. Dulabahn, "Studies on the *Laterculus*."

54. For Macrobius's *floruit* as no earlier than 430, see the convincing arguments of A. Cameron, "The Date and Identity of Macrobius," *JRS* 56 (1966): 25–38.

55. Macrobius *Sat.* 1.12–16 esp.

no longer the legal and public cult of the Roman state. Pagan reactions to imperial discriminatory measures failed to prevent the disestablishment of public cult. By 448–449, the forces for change had run their course: the majority of Roman aristocrats were Christian. But all was not lost. Roman culture, if not cult, survived, defended by Christians intent on preserving knowledge of the Roman past and its traditions. And so is explained the production of the expurgated and annotated calendar of Polemius Silvius, with its amalgam of traditional Roman festivals and Christian holidays, *ludi* without names and months without images.

Although I have focused on the changes wrought in the Roman calendar as seen in the calendar of Polemius Silvius compared with the Codex-Calendar of 354, I cannot conclude without noting the enduring importance of the Roman calendar and its traditions. Roman calendars continued to decorate the walls, not of pagan temples, but of Christian churches, including in medieval times S. Saba and SS. Quattro Coronati in Rome.[56] The annotation and production of texts about the Roman calendar likewise remained popular, as instanced by the annotated calendars of John the Lydian in the sixth century and of Bede in the seventh.[57] If the Roman Codex-Calendar of 354 looked back to its pagan past and reflected its fourth-century present, it also looked forward to the Christian times of subsequent centuries.

56. For these medieval wall calendars in Rome, see Magi 1972, pp. 41–42; A. Munoz, *Il restauro della Chiesa e del Chiostro dei SS. Quattro Coronati* (Rome, 1914), pp. 130ff., figs. 174–175; and for the no longer extant thirteenth-century calendar identifiable with S. Saba, figs. 176–177. In the fourth century, a calendar of the saints decorated the apse of S. Costanza in Rome: see H. Stern, "Les mosaïques de l'église de Sainte Constance à Rome," *Dumbarton Oaks Papers* 12 (1958): 159ff.

57. J. Lydus *De Mensibus* (6th century, only partly preserved), ed. R. Wunsch (Leipzig, 1948); Bede *De Temporibus* and *De Temporum Ratione*.

APPENDICES

APPENDIX I. THE MANUSCRIPTS AND THEIR TRADITION

This appendix provides a listing of all known manuscripts of the Codex-Calendar of 354, a reconstruction of the contents of the fourth-century original based on a collation of the manuscripts, and a detailed discussion of the most important manuscript copies.

MANUSCRIPTS

1. L. = Luxemburgensis. Ninth-century manuscript copy from fourth-century original. L. disappeared at Peiresc's death on 24 June 1637. Text and illustrations are described by Peiresc in a letter of 18 December 1620. Peiresc's letter is published by Mommsen, *MGH* 1892, pp. 17–29; by Strzygowski 1888, pp. 8–15; and by Stern 1953, pp. 14ff.

2. R. = Romanus, Rome, Bibliotheca Apostolica Vaticana. R1 = Barb. lat. 2154; R2 = Vat. lat. 9135. R1 was copied from L. in 1620; R2 was copied from R1 at the same time. Description of R. by Strzygowski 1888, pp. 7–20; by Stern 1953, pp. 14ff. Illustrated. (Figs. 1–23 from R1; Figs. 24–27 from R2.)

3. B. = Bruxellensis, Brussels, Bibliothèque Royale. MS. 7543–7549. B. was copied from L. between 1560 and 1571. Description of B. by Mommsen, *MGH* 1892, p. 29; by Gaspar and Lyna 1937.[1] Illustrated. (Figs. 44–52.)

4. V. = Vindobonensis, Vienna, Österreichische Nationalbibliothek. MS. 3416. V. was copied from L. ca. 1500–1510. Description of V. by Mommsen, *MGH* 1892, p. 31; by Hermann 1923.[2] Illustrated. (Figs. 29–35, 37–43.)

---

1. C. Gaspar and F. Lyna, *Les principaux manuscrits à peintures de la Bibliothèque Royale de Belgique,* vol. 1 (Paris, 1937), pp. 1–7, pls. 1–2.

2. J. H. Hermann, *Die illustrierten Handschriften und Inkunabel in Wien. Die frühmittelalterlichen Handschriften des Abendlandes,* vol. 1 (Leipzig, 1923), pp. 1–5. Stern 1953, p. 15,

5. S. G. = Sangallensis, St. Gallen, Bibliothèque du Convent. MS. 878. S. G. was copied from either the original fourth-century codex or a lost intermediary manuscript in Switzerland in the ninth century, according to Stern 1953, pp. 17ff. Description of S. G. by Mommsen, *MGH* 1982, pp. 32ff. Unillustrated.

6. Voss. = Vossianus, Leiden, Bibliothek der Rijksuniversiteit. Ms. Voss. lat. q. 79, fol. 93v. Voss. is a ninth-century manuscript copy of a sixth-century manuscript.[3] The page discussed here includes miniature illustrations set within a planisphere. Certain of these illustrations were copied from either the fourth-century Codex-Calendar of 354 or an intermediary copy. Description of Voss. by Thiele 1898, pp. 138–141; by Stern 1953, pp. 27–41; and by Köhler and Mütherich 1971.[4] Illustrated. (Figs. 53, 107.)

7. Ber. = Bernensis, Bern, Bibliothèque Municipale. MS. 108. Ber. was copied from L. in the tenth century for the bishop Werinhar de Strasbourg. Description of Ber. by Mommsen, *MGH* 1892, p. 30. Unillustrated.

8. A. = Ambiensis, Amiens, Bibliothèque Municipale. MS. 467. A. was copied from L. ca. 1608–1620.[5] Description of A. by Mommsen, *MGH* 1892, p. 30; and by Stern 1953, pp. 15ff.[6] Unillustrated.

9. Berl. = Berlinensis, Berlin, Staatsbibliothek Preussischer Kulturbesitz. Ms. lat. 61, fols. 231r–237r (new pagination). Berl. was copied from L. before

---

n. 1, dates V. to 1500–1510 and notes that Mommsen, *MGH* 1892, p. 31, had erroneously dated V. to 1480.

3. Voss. can be dated to the ninth century and prior to 842, according to C. L. Verkerk, "*Aratea*: A Review of the Literature Concerning Ms. Vossianus lat. q. 79 in Leiden University Library," *Journal of Medieval History* 6 (1980): 245–287. However, Voss. was created in the sixth century, according to Eastwood 1983, pp. 1–40.

4. G. Thiele, *Antike Himmelsbilder* (Berlin, 1898), pp. 138–141; W. Köhler and F. Mütherich, *Die karolingische Miniaturen*, vol. 4: *Die Hofschule Kaiser Lothars* (Berlin, 1971).

5. This is the dating advocated by Mommsen, *MGH* 1892, pp. 18, 30, which I believe is correct. Stern dates this copy to 1622–1628 and notes that it was copied for Renon de France, president of the tribunal of Malines. See note 6 below for further discussion.

6. Stern 1953, p. 15, differs from Mommsen, *MGH* 1892, pp. 18, 30, concerning A. on two points: its dating and numeration. Mommsen dates A. to 1608–1620, reasoning as follows: Peiresc had L. from 1620 until his death on 24 June 1637. Peiresc acknowledged that the president of Arras was the rightful owner of L. (Mommsen, *MGH* 1892, p. 18), but Peiresc did not return it to Arras nor did he let the manuscript out of his control (Stern 1953, pp. 37–40). The praescript to A., however, indicates that it was copied from L.: "ex cod. ms. antiquissimo d.n. de Francia praesidentis. in parlamento. Machliniensi" (*MGH* 1892, p. 18). Renon de France did not become president of the tribunal of Malines until 1622—two years after Peiresc received L. Thus Mommsen reasoned that this praescript, written in a hand different from that in A., was probably added after Renon de France became president in 1622 but that the copy itself had been executed before L. went to Peiresc, that is, before 1620, yet after the death of its previous owner, Christophorus d'Assonville Arrasiensis, ca. 1608. Mommsen's reasoning appears correct concerning the dating of A. His numeration of A. is not, however, its current one; A. is MS. 467—not 407.

1604, according to Stern. Description of Berl. by Mommsen, *MGH* 1892, pp. 30ff.; discussed by Stern 1953, p. 1A.[7] Illustrated. (Fig. 28.)

10. S. = fifteenth-century German manuscripts designated as a group by Stern 1953, pp. 21–27. These manuscripts contain certain illustrations copied from either the fourth-century codex or an intermediary copy.[8] These illustrations supply images missing from L., notably of the planets Jupiter and Venus and the four signs of the zodiac (the Ram = Ares; the Bull = Taurus; the Twins = Gemini; and the Crab = Cancer). The S. manuscripts include: (a) Vat. pal. lat. 1370, fols. 79–100. Rome, Bibliotheca Apostolica Vaticana. Dated to 1472 and copied in the region between Ulm and Nuremberg. Described by Stern 1953, p. 22. (Fig. 54 for fol. 98v.) (b) Ms. 266. Darmstadt, Stadtbibliothek. Fifteenth century. Described by Stern 1953, p. 21. (c) Ms. Cod. V2, G 81–83. Salzburg, Studienbibliothek. Fifteenth century. Described by Stern 1953, p. 22. (d) Manuscript now lost. Written in southern Germany (Swabia), dated to the second half of the fifteenth century. Described by A. Brown in *Archaeologia* 47 (1883): 337–360; noted by Stern 1953, p. 22.

11. T. = Tübingen, Universitätbibliothek. Ms. Md 2. T. was copied from L., the original or an intermediary. It is dated to 1404 or, according to Stern, to the third quarter of the fifteenth century, at Ulm. Described by Stern 1953, pp. 24–26. T. includes the illustrations of Jupiter and Venus (Figs. 55, 56) missing from all other manuscripts except S.[9]

RECONSTRUCTION OF THE ORDER AND CONTENTS OF THE CODEX-CALENDAR OF 354 ACCORDING TO THE MANUSCRIPTS

Sections[10]

I.   Dedication to Valentinus. R1 fol. 1; B. fol. 197; V. fol. 1.

II.   The Four City Tyches: images of the cities of Rome, Alexandria, Constantinople, and Trier. R1 fols. 2–5.

III.   Imperial Dedication. R1 fol. 6. List of *Natales Caesarum*. R1 fol. 7; B. fol. 198.

---

7. The historical evidence justifies Stern's date and source for Berl.; Stern 1953, p. 1A, erratum.

8. F. Saxl and E. Panofsky, "Classical Mythology in Medieval Art," *Metropolitan Museum Studies* 4 (1933): 247, first made this identification with the Codex-Calendar of 354.

9. Although all six of the manuscripts making up S. and T. show iconographic variations in their reproduction of the zodiac images, the inclusion of German translations of the Latin descriptions of the legends of the planets found in the Romanus copy indicates that these images were copied from the Codex-Calendar of 354. See Stern 1953, pp. 21–27, for further discussion.

10. Those sections in brackets and starred were probably not included in the original Codex-Calendar of 354.

IV.   The Seven Planets and Their Legends. R1 fols. 8–12. Legends only:
S.G. fols. 240v–241; B. fols. 198v–200v (missing Jupiter and Venus).

V.   *Effectus XII Signorum*. S.G. fol. 241.[11]

VI.   Calendar. Illustrations and Text of the Months.

Illustrations of February, March, August–December: R1 fols. 16–23; B. fols.
201–202; Berl. fols. 231–237.

Text of January, February, July–December: R2 fols. 232–239; B. fols. 203–
211.

Text of December: Ber. fol. 1r.

Text and illustrations for twelve months: V. fols. 2–15.

Illustrations (in miniature) for twelve months: Voss. fol. 93v.

Distichs of the months: S.G. fols. 301v–302; R1 fols. 16–23; R2 fols. 232–239;
Ber. fol. 1 (= verse 24).

[*Tetrastichs of the months: R1 fols. 16–23; R2 fols. 232–239.]

VII.   Portraits of the Consuls (Augustus Constantius and Caesar Gallus).
R1 fols. 13, 14.

VIII.   List of Consuls 508 B.C.–A.D. 354. V. fols. 25–38; Ber. fols. 2–13; B.
fols. 190r–191v.

IX.   Easter Cycle A.D. 312–358 with a continuation (albeit incorrect) to 410.
B. fols. 192r–193r; V. fols. 38v–40.

X.   List of Urban Prefects of Rome 254–354 (ending with Vitrasius Orfitus,
who entered office on 8 December 353). B. fols. 193v–195; V. fols. 40v–43v, 46v.

XI.   Depositions of the Bishops of Rome 255–352 (ending with the last deceased bishop, Iulius, d. 352). B. fol. 195; V. fol. 46; A. fol. 1.

XII.   Depositions of Martyrs. B. fol. 195v; V. fol. 44; A. fol. 1.

XIII.   List of Bishops of Rome (ending with Liberius, who entered office in
352). V. fols. 44v–45v, 65v–66; A. fols. 2–6v.

[*XIV.   Regions of the City of Rome. (*Notitia*). V. fols. 66v–69v. This *Notitia*
is dated 334–357.][12]

[*XV.   *World Chronicle* (*Liber Generationis*) from biblical creation until A.D.
334. V. fols. 55v–62v.]

XVI.   *Chronicle of the City of Rome* (*Chronica Urbis Romae*) from the kings of
Rome until the death of Licinius in A.D. 324. V. fols. 62–65v, 70; S.G. fol. 303.[13]

---

11. Mommsen, *MGH* 1892, p. 47, incorrectly reads *Effigies XII Signorum* for the correct
Effectus XII Signorum. As Stern 1953, pp. 60ff., noted, the *Effectus XII Signorum* has close
ties to a group of manuscripts that date from the thirteenth through the seventeenth centuries. However extended this tradition is, this page, in my view, was also included in the
original Codex-Calendar of 354.

12. Stern 1953, p. 16, incorrectly cites this section as part of B., fols. 195v, 196. G.
Bouchier, *De Doctrina Temporum Commentarius in Victorium Aquitanum* (Anvers, 1634), pp.
275–288, published an edition, copied from B., that did not include this section either.

13. Mommsen, *MGH* 1892, pp. 31–38, 203ff., lists as section XVII the Vienna Annals
(*Fasti Vindobonenses*), A.D. 390–573/575 (V., fols. 15–24, 47–53; S.G., fol. 303). This section

THE MANUSCRIPT COPIES

The Luxemburgensis Manuscript Copy

All of the illustrated manuscripts, except the miniatures in Voss., are based on the lost L. Fortunately, Peiresc's detailed description of L. survives in a letter of 18 December 1620, which he wrote to his friend Girolamo Aleandro the Younger. At the time, Aleandro was in the service of Maffeo Barberini, whose elevation to the papacy in 1623 (with the name of Urban VIII) explicates in part the survival of Peiresc's letter in the Bibliotheca Apostolica Vaticana.

According to Peiresc, L. began with the List of Consuls (section VIII), continued with the unillustrated sections (IX–XIII), and ended with the illustrated sections (I–VII). (This same order is preserved in B.) Mommsen reasoned that since the illustrated sections were preceded by a title page, these began the original manuscript.[14] In fact, two manuscripts, V. and Ber., preserve this presumed original order.

Peiresc's description of L. indicates that this manuscript was already damaged by the time he received it, sometime in December 1620.[15] Peiresc mentions only sections I–XIII in his letter, and specifies that certain folios were missing. The section for astrological signs, for instance, lacked both its title page and the representations of Jove and Venus; the Calendar proper was missing the text for the months March–June and the images for April–July. The R. and B. manuscripts reproduce L. in this diminished version (Figs. 1–27, 44–52). Fortunately, the Voss., the V., and the German manuscripts S. and T. of the fifteenth century were executed before L. lost these folios.

Peiresc's description of L. goes beyond a simple accounting of contents to include details of its execution, so critical in its reconstruction and dating. He records the colors of the inks used in the various sections, noting that the designs were executed in black ink on parchment and that the figures were drawn in only black ink.[16] Peiresc adds that the text of the Calendar; the Kalends, Ides, and names of the festivals celebrated on these days; and the astrological notations of the sun's movements in the various zodiac signs were written in red ink in majuscule lettering.[17] Peiresc also notes that in L. red ink was used in the unillustrated sections of the manuscript for every fourth year in the List of Consuls

---

is omitted from my listing, however, because it was not included in the original Codex-Calendar.

14. Mommsen, *MGH* 1892, pp. 36–38.

15. Stern 1953, p. 38.

16. Mommsen, *MGH* 1892, p. 23, n. 2.

17. Ibid., pp. 25–28. The Vienna manuscript reproduces this color scheme for the inks used in the text of the Calendar (section VI), as does R2. R2 includes the hebdomadal letters in red ink as well, a point not mentioned by Peiresc.

(section VIII), for the headings in the list of Easter dates (section IX), and for the headings in the Depositions of Bishops (section XI) and of Martyrs (section XII); in the illustrated section it was used for the dedicatory page inscription.[18]

The color scheme for L. is reproduced to a large degree in its manuscript copies. In V., only the dedicatory page does not follow Peiresc's description, since this was a later addition.[19] While R1 reproduces the colored ink scheme for the dedicatory page, unfortunately R1 lacks the other sections that Peiresc described as depicted in red.[20] R2 and V. follow Peiresc's color scheme for the Calendar text in every respect except the red ink for the hebdomadal lettering. Thus, Peiresc's description and the evidence provided by R. and V. indicate that red ink was used in L. for ornament in the chapter headings in the unillustrated sections, on the dedicatory page, and in the text of the Calendar itself. In fact, this use of color to highlight words and chapter headings coincides with the practice of Carolingian manuscript copyists in general.[21] And in the case of a calendar text, this color scheme is corroborated by ancient evidence, for red paint was often used to highlight black text in the Roman calendars painted or carved on the walls of houses and temples.[22] In sum, whereas the dearth of extant fourth-century manuscripts makes a comparison impossible, the evidence does indicate that the color scheme in L. was also probably that of the fourth-century original.

Just as a collation of manuscript copies allows one to reconstruct the inking scheme in L., it allows one to reconstruct the measurements of the lost manuscript as well. The height of the figures in V., 185–210mm, is so close to that of the figure in R. (180–200mm) that both seem to be based directly on L.[23] Moreover, these measures remain within the limits for codices as they are attested by the extant evidence and ancient sources.[24] It is therefore possible, and indeed probable, that the Carolingian copyist did reproduce approximately the size of the figures of his exemplar.

On the basis of the handwriting in L., and perhaps also on information we

---

18. Mommsen, *MGH* 1892, pp. 19–29.

19. For the problems concerning the dedicatory page, see my discussion of V., B., and notes 60–62 below.

20. In addition, R1 uses red ink for the names of the months in the *Natales Caesarum* and for the days of the week in the images of the planets, but Peiresc does not remark its usage here. Given his close attention to the inks, Peiresc has most likely merely failed to mention red ink in these sections of L.; we can assume, then, that the creator of R1 has reproduced these two folios accurately.

21. B. Bischoff, *Paläographie des römischen Altertums und des abendländischen Mittelalters* (Berlin, 1979), pp. 29–31.

22. For examples, see Degrassi 1963, pp. 1ff.

23. Stern 1953, p. 21. B. cannot be used for measurements, since arrangement of the illustrations was four to a page; nor can the Voss. miniatures.

24. E. G. Turner, *The Typology of the Early Codex*, ser. 18 (Philadelphia, 1977).

no longer have, Peiresc considered the manuscript an eighth- or ninth-century copy of a fourth-century original.[25] Peiresc's assessment of the date of the lost L. has been questioned. The illustrations in certain copies, particularly in R., are so similar to other works of Roman art from the fourth century that some scholars have argued that L. was not a Carolingian copy but, in fact, the fourth-century original. Others have posited a range of dates for L., from the sixth to the ninth century. Hence, a working hypothesis concerning the date of L. and its source is necessary for this study.

Since L. disappeared at Peiresc's death in 1637, the only way to verify his conclusion regarding the date of L. and its exemplar is through careful consideration of his description and his ability accurately to date manuscripts, as well as through close study of the copies of L., especially that which was executed under Peiresc's supervision, R. (Figs. 1–27). We can begin by noting that Peiresc's abilities in manuscript description and dating are still highly regarded; although he lived prior to Mabillon and to the scientific study of paleography, Peiresc's judgments on manuscripts still merit the respect of modern scholars who have used his assessments in studying other extant manuscript copies.[26]

M. Schapiro argued that the presence of Carolingian iconographic elements in copies of L. (especially R.) support Peiresc's conclusion that L. was a Carolingian copy of a fourth-century original. The base of the column in the representation of June in V. (Fig. 37), depicted in a characteristically medieval profile with a high scotia, is one such example.[27] But it was W. R. Köhler's analysis of the handwriting and certain letter forms in R.—in the listing of the *Natales Caesarum* (section III; Fig. 7) and in the planetary hours (section IV, upper halves only; Figs. 8–11)—as seventeenth-century imitations of Carolingian minuscule that provided the most convincing evidence for a ninth-century dating of the lost L. It seems unlikely that a seventeenth-century copyist would take such pains to introduce Carolingian writing while at the same time studiously reproducing late-antique imagery, especially since it was not the norm for copyists of that age to reproduce the handwriting of the exemplar.[28] Stern's analysis of the textual fragments of S. G. further support the conclusion that L. was a Carolingian copy and not the fourth-century original.[29]

Peiresc's assessment of L. as an intermediary copy and not the original Calendar is convincing. Nonetheless, his ninth-century dating has been questioned.

25. Mommsen, *MGH* 1892, pp. 19, 25–26. Peiresc describes L. as a manuscript "havuto ultimamente scritto già più di 7. o 800 anni al meno"; he notes that the handwriting of the distichs is "in carattero corsivo Romano, di 7. o 800 anni in circa," and that of the tables of the months "in carattere ordinario rotundo, di 7. o 800 anni in circa."

26. Stern 1953, pp. 350ff.; Eastwood 1983, p. 39.

27. M. Schapiro, "The Carolingian Copy of the Calendar of 354 A.D.," *The Art Bulletin* 22 (1940): 270–272.

28. Stern 1953, pp. 17–20; at p. 19, n. 4, he cites W. R. Köhler's analysis.

29. Stern 1953, pp. 17–20.

Recently, Eastwood has argued that L. should be dated as early as the sixth but no later than the ninth century, because (1) Peiresc's estimation of the hand-writing ranges from ca. 700–900 and (2) the imitation of Carolingian lettering in R. is not consistent, nor does it reflect precisely the lettering described by Peiresc.[30] On paleographic grounds, however, a date for L. prior to the ninth century is spurious. Admittedly, the seventeenth-century attempt in R. to imitate Carolingian minuscules may not be as consistent or skillful as one would like; but these traits should not be expected in manuscripts from the 1600s.[31] In any case, the writing is at least identifiable as an attempt at Carolingian minuscule. The characteristic *a* in the planetary hours, for instance, is a reasonable facsimile of a type found no earlier than the ninth century.[32] Such letters (the *s* is notable as well) make it highly unlikely that L. was copied before that century.

On the basis of iconographic and paleographic analyses, then, we can say that Peiresc's assessment of L. as a ninth- or eighth-century Carolingian manuscript copy stands firm. Moreover, the elements of fourth-century art and iconography that copies of L. (notably R.) so clearly preserve indicate that L.'s exemplar was probably the fourth-century original and not an intermediary manuscript.[33] The question arises, then, of how accurately L. copied the fourth-century original. Carolingian artists were eminently capable of reproducing forms of the late-antique period.[34] That our particular copy faithfully reproduced its original exemplar can be demonstrated by analysis of the individual copies of L., both in comparison with one another and in conjunction with fourth-century works of art.

The Romanus Manuscript Copies

Peiresc's excitement at the discovery of L. encouraged him to try to entice the famous engraver, Mellan, to produce a copy of it. Although such a copy was

30. Eastwood 1983, p. 39.

31. See note 45 below.

32. Eastwood 1983, p. 39, also suggested a ninth-century dating for this lettering.

33. See my discussion of fourth-century iconography preserved in R., and especially notes 49 and 50 below.

34. Schapiro, "The Carolingian Copy," pp. 270–272, notes another example of a late Roman secular manuscript reproduced in the Carolingian period, the *Notitia Dignitatum Imperii Romani*. See P. Berger, *The Insignia of the Notitia Dignitatum* (New York, 1981). There exist two ninth-century copies of a late-antique illustrated codex of the plays of Terence, which their editors have demonstrated to be faithful Carolingian copies; see further C. R. Morey and L. W. Jones, *The Miniatures of the Manuscripts of Terence*, 2 vols. (Princeton, N.J., 1931). For a general discussion of Carolingian copyists, see H. Swarzenski, "The Xanten Purple Leaf and the Carolingian Renaissance," *The Art Bulletin* 22 (1940): 1–23; and F. Mütherich, "Der karolingische Agrimensoren-Codex in Rom," *Aachener Kunstblätter* 45 (1974): 59–74.

made, it was executed not by Mellan but by another unknown engraver, who worked under Peiresc's careful supervision.[35] This manuscript (R1 = Barb. lat. 2154) was sent to Aleandro the Younger in Rome in December 1620, and is considered the most trustworthy of the copies of L. A reliable copy of R1, cited as R2 (= Vat. lat. 9135), is also preserved, but it is of inferior quality to R1 (Figs. 1 and 27).

R. was copied from L. after L. had lost several folios.[36] Consequently, R. contains the illustrations of only seven of the original twelve months: February, March, and August–December. Each month is placed within an ornate architectural frame and accompanied by verses.[37] The text for each month was written on the page opposite the illustration.

One additional illustration does exist, that for January (Fig. 16).[38] This, however, is a forgery. Peiresc mentioned to Aleandro that the folios missing from L. had been reconstructed by a certain Jean Gobille (or Sibille), a geographer, and he offered to send an example of one of these "forgeries" to Aleandro. The motivation for Gobille's act, at least in Peiresc's view, was financial. Indeed, the illustration for January in R. is stylistically quite different from the other months; moreover, comparison of the R. January with the same month in V. (Fig. 30) reveals that the R. image includes elements of dress and attributes absent from V. It therefore follows that this is the forgery alluded to by Peiresc.[39]

R1 is important for study of the Codex-Calendar, for it alone contains the illustrations of the cities (Figs. 2–5), the imperial dedication (Fig. 6), the illustrations of the two consuls of the year (Figs. 13–14), and the architectural decorations for the lists beginning with the *Natales Caesarum* (Fig. 7). In common with the other copies, R1 preserves the title page (Fig. 1), the depictions of the five planets (Figs. 8–12), the illustrated page of zodiac signs (Fig. 15) and the representations of seven months of the year (Figs. 17–23).

R1 is written in black ink, with red ink highlighting the names of the months in the *Natales Caesarum*, the days in the astrological sections, and the dedicatory inscription. The four illustrations of the cities and four of the five planets were

---

35. Stern 1953, pp. 352–354, suggests that Anne Rulman (1583–1639), a contemporary of Peiresc, was the engraver because of similarities in techniques noted in R1 and in his designs.

36. This loss can be dated to the period after V., 1500–1510, and before B., 1560–1571.

37. For the relationship between the verses and the text, see also Chapter 3.

38. One copy of January is included in R1; a second copy survives in R2.

39. For Peiresc's correspondence concerning January, see Mommsen, *MGH* 1892, p. 29. It appears that the verses were the source for the forgery. Peiresc notes: "Un certo Ioanne Sibille Geographo ha fatto un supplemento delle figure e inscrittioni che mancano già più di 30 anni, ma senza fondamento, di modo che non c'è niente che vaglia nè che risponda al vero, si comme per l'inscrittioni si guidica dall'editione dell'Hervartio, e per le figure dà versi antiqui stampati dal Pithaeo sotto'l titolo PICTURA MENSIUM, tanto conformi à queste medesime figure." Cf. Strzygowski 1888, pp. 17, 56–57; Stern 1953, p. 38, n. 5.

finished with sepia because, according to Peiresc, these designs were not yet ready for their envoy's departure in December 1620.[40]

R2 contains the same illustrations as R1, with the addition of the illustrated texts for October and November (Figs. 25, 26) and six unillustrated texts of the months (e.g. Fig. 24). Peiresc remarked in his letter that only two illustrated texts were ready to go with the envoy and were sent to Aleandro, but that the other months were similar.[41] These folios, complete with their architectural frames, provide important information for the reconstruction of L. and its fourth-century prototype. In them, the signs of the zodiac, the Kalends, Ides, and names of festivals, as well as the hebdomadals, are written in red ink, while the remaining lettering is in black.[42]

Two other manuscripts are worth mentioning here, for they, like R2, were copied from R1. While these manuscripts do not, unfortunately, add any new information to our knowledge of these illustrations, they do attest to the fidelity of the copying process and to the popularity of the Calendar's imagery in the Renaissance. The works in question are the illustrations of the months in the Codex Ashburnham 1061, now in the Bibliotheca Laurentiana in Florence; and the illustrations of the months in the Library of Windsor Castle, vol. 196: Designs of Cassiano del Pozzo, nos. 11363–11374, fols. 124–135.[43]

The illustrations and text in R1 are considered the most trustworthy copies of L. This fidelity is the result in no small part of Peiresc's care and personal involvement in the project, to which his letters to Aleandro attest, as do certain corrections in the text of R. Peiresc, of course, was experienced in such projects. Two pages of the Cotton Bible were copied under his supervision and faithfully reproduce the material, iconography, and style of the original, which survives.[44]

It is the presence of Carolingian elements of iconography and handwriting (the helmets of Roma and Trier, Figs. 2 and 5, for example) in R., however, that provides the most convincing evidence for its fidelity to L. The imitation of Carolingian letter forms alongside rustic capitals (corresponding to Peiresc's majuscule), as discussed above, is especially telling, since seventeenth-century copyists did not as a rule imitate Carolingian script.[45] In V., by contrast, one finds the

---

40. Mommsen, *MGH* 1892, pp. 19–28; Peiresc noted red ink for the dedicatory page of L. Although he did not mention red ink in these other sections, we can presume that its use in R. copies that in L. For the use of sepia, see Peiresc's testimony in Mommsen, *MGH* 1892, p. 29; and Stern 1953, p. 21.

41. Mommsen, *MGH* 1892, p. 29. It seems likely—but not certain—that the illustrated texts of October and November and the remaining unillustrated texts of the months in R2 were the pages sent by Peiresc, and not copies of R1.

42. This scheme coincides with the description in Peiresc except for the red ink for the hebdomadal lettering. See note 17 above.

43. Stern 1953, p. 20, believes that the designs in the Library of Windsor Castle were copied on R1. In a letter of 17 May 1629, however, Peiresc mentioned that he prepared these designs and sent them to the Chevalier del Pozzo; see Mommsen, *MGH* 1892, p. 12, n. 2. The designs themselves provide insufficient evidence to determine if they were copied from either L. or R. and, unfortunately, no new insights into the iconography of L. or R1.

44. Stern 1953, p. 351.

45. The general practice of Renaissance copyists was to translate their exemplar into

Gothic-humanistic script of the sixteenth century (see Fig. 31),[46] with no attempt made to reproduce the Carolingian handwriting. Admittedly, the copyist of R. is not consistent; he lapses into contemporary script elsewhere in the manuscript, and he does not try to imitate, for example, the two different scripts in the texts of the months (Figs. 25, 26) that Peiresc described.[47] In any case, even for Peiresc, the script of L. was of secondary importance relative to its iconography and text.[48]

The illustrations in R1 preserve iconographic and even stylistic elements observed in Roman art of the mid fourth century. Nordenfalk, for one, was particularly struck by the resemblance between the putti depicted in the Codex-Calendar and those on the contemporary sarcophagus of Junius Bassus.[49] And Stern observed the careful preservation of details of clothing, architecture, and figural representation in the Codex, which can be documented as originating in the fourth century. Thus, the depictions of *calliculae* or appliqués on the dress of the goddess Roma (Fig. 2) and the drapery of the consuls' togas (Figs. 13, 14), as much as the representation of August as a nude male drinking from a bowl (Fig. 19), are specific fourth-century iconographic details that were transmitted with care first from the archetype to L. and then to R.[50]

The Carolingian iconographic, stylistic, and handwriting elements in R. are so few that it has been suggested that in fact Peiresc's copy, R., corrected L.[51] If so, these corrections were not many, for if the copyist were to bother to correct the manuscript, why would he copy any of the Carolingian elements noted above? Moreover, nothing indicates that the creator of R. substantively altered the iconography or the text of L. That leaves only the style of L. for R.'s creator to have altered: if he in some way classicized L.'s style (and in a way we cannot now see), he nevertheless made R. with the greatest concern for preserving the integrity of L.'s iconography and text.

After examining the iconographic, architectural, ornamental, and figural composition of R., Stern concluded that it was a reliable copy in these regards and attested to a mid-fourth-century date for its archetype. My research on the Calendar illustrations and text in conjunction with study of late-antique art ver-

---

contemporary humanist script, which is precisely what the seventeenth-century copyist tends to do in R1; see A. Fairbank and B. Wolpe, *Renaissance Handwriting: An Anthology of Italic Scripts* (London, 1960), pp. 21–28. J. Stiennon, *Paléographie du Moyen Age* (Paris, 1973), pp. 25–56, notes: "A partir du XVI siècle, les recueils de spécimens gravés et publiés par les maitres d'écriture concernent à peu pres exclusivement des types d'écriture contemporains et ne font que rarement acception de modèles appartenant aux siècles révolus."

46. F. Mütherich, in a letter of 13 April 1984, relayed this assessment of the Vienna manuscript made by Prof. Bischoff.

47. See Mommsen, *MGH* 1892, pp. 19, 25–26.

48. Peiresc does not even include a complete description of the handwriting in the manuscript; see Mommsen, *MGH* 1892, pp. 19ff.

49. Nordenfalk 1936, pp. 1–36.

50. Stern 1953, pp. 131–133, for Roma; pp. 152–168 for consular images; pp. 258–263 for August.

51. Stern 1953, p. 354.

ifies Stern's conclusions. In discussing specific iconographic interpretations, of course, the need for corroborative evidence from fourth-century art and literature and other manuscript copies is obvious, even in R1. Nevertheless, the value and fidelity of this copy for the present study cannot be overemphasized.

The Vindobonensis Manuscript Copy

The Vindobonensis manuscript copy (Österreichische Nationalbibliothek, MS. 3416) reveals, in its style and in the history of its owner, Dr. Fuchsmagen, that it was copied in the region of Nuremberg ca. 1500–1510.[52] Analysis of the imagery leads me to attribute the designs of V. to the school of H. Vischer of Nuremberg, perhaps even to Peter Vischer himself, whose group was closely connected to the Nuremberg circle of A. Dürer.[53]

V. is extremely important for study of the illustrations of the Calendar of 354 because it was copied from L. before L. lost several folios.[54] Thus, only V. and Voss. contain the illustrations of all twelve months (V. fols. 2v–14r; Figs. 30–35, 37–43). In addition, V. includes an illustrated dedication page (Fig. 29) copied from a later edition,[55] as well as several unillustrated lists that were part of the original Codex-Calendar.[56] Some of these unillustrated lists are also found in R. and B.

The illustrations of the months in V. were executed with great concern for their visual appearance. The images are drawn in black and shaded with a brownish-gray ink. In the representations of January and February (Figs. 30, 32), red ink is used to illuminate the figures' faces and hands as well as certain details, such as the candle flames in January. These two months also demonstrate how V. reflects its provenance. The late Gothic forms of the objects depicted, such as the candelabra in January, the urn pouring water in February, and the snails at the base of the furniture in January and April ("a beloved motif of Peter Vischer") are characteristic of the style at Nuremberg at the beginning of the sixteenth century.[57]

Although V. reflects its provenance, the copyist was faithful to the iconog-

52. Stern 1953, p. 15, dates V. to this period because Dr. Fuchsmagen died in Vienna on 3 May 1510. For further discussion, see Mommsen, *MGH* 1892, pp. 31–32; Hermann, *Die Illustrierten Handschriften*, pp. 1–7.

53. According to Hermann, *Die Illustrierten Handschriften*, p. 3, folio 3 reads: "Johannis Fucsmagen doctoris"; Hermann attributes the designs to the school of H. Vischer of Nuremberg. An alternative view would attribute them to L. Cranach the Elder; see F. Winkler, "Die Bilder des Wiener Filocalus," *Jahrbuch der Königlichen Preussischen Kunstsammlungen* 57 (1938): 141–155. My analysis of April in Chapter 3 supports Hermann's attribution.

54. See note 36 above.

55. See the discussion of B. and notes 60–62 below.

56. In these sections the color scheme—black ink for text and red ink for titles—reproduces L. as described by Peiresc.

57. Hermann, *Die Illustrierten Handschriften*, pp. 2–5.

raphy and text of his exemplar. Compare, for example, V. with R1 and R2, B., and other manuscript copies from L. for the seven months preserved in these copies, and with the Voss. miniatures for the five remaining months. Differences in the style and shapes of objects represented are evident—for instance, the urn pouring water in February in R1 (Fig. 17) is different in shape from the late Gothic urn in V. (Fig. 32), as are the shapes of the jugs sunk into the ground for September in R1 (Fig. 20), V. (Fig. 40), and B. (Fig. 48). Particularly noticeable is the rendition of clothing and accessories. The feminine attire of February in V. is far more like that of a Viennese matron than of a Roman *matrona*; the rustic man depicted for the *Saturnalia* in December (Fig. 43) is bedecked with jewelry. Moreover, the copyist of V. tends to present the images as comprehensible objects: note the ermine cap on the head of the man who is sacrificing in January (Fig. 30), the sixteenth-century equivalent of a Roman *pileus*; or the basket lid on the floor in October (Fig. 41), the Viennese copyist's interpretation of a cord attached to the basket (as it is shown in R.). It must be noted, however, that all these differences are merely stylistic, not substantive.

The most obvious difference between V. and R. is V.'s tendency to omit attributes, especially when these represent objects unfamiliar to a Renaissance copyist, or were vague in L., as is suggested by their similarly uncertain rendition in R. For example, V. leaves out the jacket from the upper right corner of the illustration of August (Fig. 39) and the basket (of acorns?) from the upper right corner of October (Fig. 41), whereas these details are found in R1 (Figs. 19, 21). Moreover, V. does not reproduce the architectural framework, the verses, or the zodiac signs that in R. accompanied each month. Finally, in V. the copyist had a disconcerting tendency to move attributes and objects around on the page, such as the birds on a hook in December, which are to the left of the figure playing dice in V. but to his right in R.

To sum up, despite stylistic and formal (e.g., spatial) alterations in V., this copy, in comparison with R. and B., reveals itself to be trustworthy as regards the objects depicted and the iconography of the months. V. includes no details or attributes not attested in the other manuscript copies for the extant seven months or, generally, in Voss. for the remaining five (January, April, June–August) (see discussion of Voss. below). Corroborative evidence from other manuscript copies and from contemporary fourth-century art and archaeology confirms the basic veracity of V.'s iconography and text.

The Bruxellensis Manuscript Copy

Sometime after V. was produced (ca. 1500–1510), L. was damaged and lost several folios. The Bruxellensis (Bibliothèque Royale, MS. 7543–7549) was copied from L. in this reduced state, between 1560 and 1571.[58] B. preserves the illus-

---

58. In a praescript to B. it is noted that B. belonged to Jean Brenner of Nalbach, secretary of state and delegate to the provincial council of Luxemburg. Mommsen, *MGH*

trated dedication page (fol. 197; Fig. 44) and seven of the twelve months (Figs. 45–48; 50–52), which, however, the copyist has redistributed on the page.[59] Four months—February, March, August, and September—are now placed on one folio (fol. 201; see Fig. 49), and the other three—October–December—are on a second folio (fol. 202). In L., of course, each month was depicted on a single page opposite the text for that month. B. has also uniformly omitted the architectural framework for the months. Interestingly, B. does copy the tetrastichs as they appear in R.—that is, on the page opposite each month's text—but it leaves blank the pages where the illustrations should have been. The same procedure is followed for the texts of the *Natales Caesarum* (fol. 198) and of the Effects of the Planets (fols. 198v–200v), for these texts are disposed on the page as in R. but omitting the architectural frames and illustrations. Evidently, the primary intent of B. was to preserve L.'s text and information, not its imagery.

Despite these alterations, a comparison of R. and B. reveals that B. does faithfully reproduce the general iconography and the specific attributes for each month; only the birds are missing from the upper right corner of December in B. (Fig. 52). The details in B., however, tend to be more concrete than in R. For example, the toes on the foot of the February figure are well defined in B. but only lightly outlined in R1; and the basket with figs in the representation of September is boldly drawn in B. but rather loosely defined in R1. Yet while these two manuscripts display a noticeable difference in style, in content and iconography they seem true to their exemplar. The illustrations of the months in B. are particularly useful to us, for they corroborate further the veracity of R.

Only the dedicatory page (Fig. 44) in B. is problematic, for comparison of this copy with R1 reveals certain iconographic differences: a curtain is included in B., while the letter *s* from the monogram and a bullock from the neck of one putto are omitted. These same inconsistencies (plus an architectural backdrop) recur in Bucherius's well-known 1634 edition of the Codex-Calendar (Fig. 87),[60] which would seem to indicate that Bucherius based his edition on B.[61] The title

---

1892, p. 29, argues on the basis of fol. 212 that Brenner's son-in-law and guardian of the archives of Luxemburg, Remacle Huart, sent B. to Carol Langius ca. 1560, providing a *terminus post quem* for B. of 1560. However, to argue with Mommsen, fol. 212 does not indicate that Brenner actually sent B. at that time; the only secure date provided there is found in the indication that Brenner made a gift of L. to Christophe d'Assonville in the last years of Brenner's life. Brenner died in 1571 (Gaspar and Lyna, *Les principaux manuscrits*, p. 2). Hence, B. must predate 1571. Stern 1953, p. 37, incorrectly follows Strzygowski 1888, p. 5, and relates that Adrian Blanchard (another son-in-law of Brenner) gave L. to Christophe d'Assonville in 1580. In any case, it was Christophe d'Assonville's son-in-law, Renon de France, president of the council of Artois, who kept L. until it was passed to Peiresc in 1628.

59. Strzygowski 1888, pp. 23–24; Gaspar and Lyna, *Les principaux manuscrits*, pp. 3–4; Stern 1953, pp. 120–123.

60. Bouchier, *De Doctrina Temporum*, pp. 275–288.

61. Strzygowski 1888, pp. 23–24, remarks the title page as a later addition; cf. Mommsen, *MGH* 1892, p. 31, n. 1; Stern 1953, pp. 40, 120–123; and Gaspar and Lyna, *Les principaux manuscrits*, pp. 3–4.

page of V. (Fig. 29) reproduces the alterations found in Bucherius's version, including the backdrop. Moreover, only V. and Bucherius's edition depict the putti with covered genitalia; B. and R1 leave the putti in their nude state. Hence, there is little doubt that this page in V. was a later addition, based on Bucherius's publication.[62]

Comparison of the dedication page in R1 (Fig. 1) and B. (Fig. 44) indicates only one significant iconographic difference: the curtain in the background. Stern considers this curtain, found in B., V., and Bucherius's edition, a product of late-antique art.[63] Thus, if the curtain is authentic, as Stern argues, its omission from R1 is problematic. Three possible explanations suggest themselves: (1) The curtain was in L. and so was copied into B. but omitted from R1; (2) The curtain was not in L. and was added to B. by mistake; (3) B. was copied not from L. but from an intermediary manuscript, which had added this curtain. The third possibility seems unlikely; given the iconographic similarities between R. and B., B. probably was copied from L. And the overall veracity of R. leads me to doubt that the curtain would have been omitted from R1. The second possibility, then, seems the most convincing. The overall carelessness in execution and design of this page in B. tends to support this view; in addition to the omissions noted above, one can see that the dedicatory inscription was written and then scratched out twice on the page, as if the copyist could not work out the design, and that the *a* in *floreas* was squeezed into the inscription as an afterthought. Indeed, considering that B. concentrates more on the text than on the illustrations, it would seem unwise to trust its iconography over that of R1. Although certainty is impossible, the evidence strongly suggests that the curtain in the background of B. was a later addition.

The Miniatures of the Vossianus Manuscript

A single page (Fig. 53) in the Vossianus manuscript (Bibliothek der Rijksuniversiteit, Ms. Voss. lat. q. 79, fol. 93v) provides important evidence for the illustrations in the Codex-Calendar of 354. Because of the miniature format and the nature of the transmission of the manuscript, however, this evidence is limited to that which can be corroborated by other sources. Consequently, Voss. cannot be used with the same degree of reliability as the other copies of the Codex-Calendar. Nevertheless, it can be used for study of the images of the months; indeed, in this area it is especially helpful, since only Voss. and V. reproduce the full twelve-month cycle.

Voss. is a single-page illustration appended to a manuscript of the *Aratea*. It depicts a planisphere into which are inserted miniaturized representations of the months. Each month is depicted in its own medallion and placed in a circle between the signs of the zodiac, also in miniature. Since the zodiac signs were

---

62. Strzygowski 1888, pp. 23–24, remarks this point. Cf. Mommsen, *MGH* 1892, p. 31, n. 1; Stern 1953, pp. 120–123; Gaspar and Lyna, *Les principaux manuscrits*, pp. 3–4.
63. Stern 1953, pp. 120–123.

copied in a counterclockwise circle, beginning with Aquarius in January, while the twelve months proceed clockwise, the two cycles do not correspond on the page.[64] In the center of the circle is Terra, surrounded by the seven planets, which are identified by inscriptions and depicted in small medallions.

The configuration of the planets has allowed the original version of Voss. to be dated convincingly to 28 March 579.[65] The manuscript copy that we have, however, was made in the early ninth century, probably prior to 842.[66] Voss. has four noteworthy copies in addition—two in manuscript and two printed. A tenth-century manuscript copy from the Bibliothèque Municipale of Boulogne-sur-Mer (MS. 188, fol. 30r; Fig. 57) depicts a planisphere generally believed to have been copied from the same source as the planisphere in Voss.[67] Similarly, the zodiac circle in MS. 88 (fol. 11v) of the Bibliothèque Municipale of Bern (Fig. 58) is assumed to be derived from the Boulogne-sur-Mer manuscript.[68] Of the two printings of Voss., one was made by Grotius for his *Syntagma Arateorum* (Leiden, 1600), and one is a copy of that version made by Cellarius for *Harmonia Macrocosmica* (1708).[69]

The diverging directions of the zodiac and monthly cycles and the stylistic differences among the illustrations in Voss. point to a variety of iconographic sources. Voss. may well have been created as a mini-encyclopedia, with calendric information added to the predominantly astronomical data.[70] The importance of Voss. for this study, however, lies in the demonstrable connection between the illustrations in Voss. and those in the Codex-Calendar.

The Voss. illustrations fall into three categories: the zodiac cycle, the planets, and the months. The first group were probably not copied from the Codex-Calendar. The style of this cycle is quite different from that of the months and planets in Voss., which are certainly linked to the Codex-Calendar illustrations.[71] According to Stern, the Voss. zodiac circle is similar to that found in another Carolingian manuscript, the Utrecht Psalter; thus he posits a common model for these two manuscripts. Others, however, view the zodiac circle in Voss. and the Utrecht Psalter not as copies themselves, but as part of a still larger grouping of zodiac circles that preserve ancient artistic traditions still vibrant in the Carolingian period.[72] In any case, whatever the relationship of the Voss. zodiac to the Utrecht Psalter, it cannot be linked directly to that in the Codex-Calendar.

64. G. Thiele, *Antike Himmelsbilder*, pp. 138–141; Eastwood 1983, p. 33; Stern 1953, pp. 27–31.

65. Eastwood 1983, pp. 1–40.

66. C. L. Verkerk, "*Aratea*," pp. 279–281.

67. Ibid., p. 280. The Boulogne-sur-Mer mansucript is dated prior to 905 by Stern 1953, pp. 29–30; and to the end of the tenth century by Verkerk, who follows Byzanck's arguments.

68. Verkerk, "*Aratea*," pp. 267–270.

69. Eastwood 1983, nn. 7 and 8 and figs. 2 and 3.

70. Ibid., p. 32.

71. Thiele, *Antike Himmelsbilder*, p. 130; Stern 1953, pp. 27–31.

72. See, for example, Eastwood 1983, p. 34; S. Dufrenne, *Les illustrations du Psautier d'Utrecht. Sources et apport carolingien* (Paris, 1978), p. 70, n. 5.

The relationship between Voss. and the Codex-Calendar with regard to the illustrations of the planets is also open to question. Stern thought that the Voss. planets were copied from either the original fourth-century manuscript or a later copy, but one prior to 579.[73] He observed that two of the seven illustrations, Saturn and Mercury, faithfully reproduce the planetary images in R. This is true for the form and general movement of Mercury, as well as for his specific attributes—the caduceus, helmet, and mantle; however, the sack that Stern would see in Voss. and that corresponds to the one in R. is difficult to discern and, given its omission from Grotius's engraving (cf. Figs. 10, 53), may not even have been actually included.[74] Similarly, Saturn in Voss. is depicted with the same cloak, drapery, and gestures as in R1, but his head is not veiled and he holds a harpoon instead of a sickle (cf. Figs. 8, 53).[75] A third planet in Voss., Venus, can be tied to the iconography of the Codex-Calendar as evidenced by S. and T. (Figs. 54, 56). In all three of these copies, Venus is nude, with only a mantle covering her left shoulder; in her right hand she holds a flower.[76]

Saturn, Mercury, and Venus in Voss. may have been copied from the Codex-Calendar, but the designer of the manuscript clearly "proceeded with more liberty" in depicting the four remaining planets.[77] Although Mars, Sol, and Luna include some of the same attributes as are found in R., on the whole they, as well as Jupiter, diverge on too many details to be considered copies of the images in the Codex-Calendar.[78]

Most important for the present study in terms of establishing a connection between Voss. and the Codex-Calendar is the iconography of the months. According to Stern, only October in Voss. (Fig. 53) differs from that in R1 (Fig. 21), and then on one important point: the Voss. hunter does not wear a large floating cape, but a short tunic, hitched up around his hips.[79] The other eleven representations of the months in Voss. all reproduce the general iconography, movements, gestures, and attire of their monthly counterparts in the R., V., and B. manuscript copies. Although Voss. does omit many accompanying attributes of the months, Stern argues that this was the result in part of how the text was transmitted and in part of full-page codex illustrations being reproduced as miniatures.

73. Stern 1953, pp. 29–30.
74. For Grotius's engraving, see Eastwood 1983, fig. 2.
75. Stern 1953, pp. 29–30.
76. Ibid., pp. 27–28.
77. This liberty is acknowledged in ibid., p. 29.
78. Ibid., p. 30. Only one correction needs to be made to the otherwise excellent description by Stern of these planets. Sol seems to have two horses galloping to the left, not three, and they are not partly bovine. The illustration of Luna and Jupiter may be inspired by that in the main body of the *Aratea*; see Thiele, *Antike Himmelsbilder*, p. 137, fig. 58; Eastwood 1983, p. 35, n. 120; Stern 1953, p. 30. Mars alone is unlike any known representation of the god.
79. Stern 1953, p. 30. Only half of the medallion for October is preserved in Voss. The Boulogne-sur-Mer manuscript (Fig. 57) reproduces October with a short tunic, as does Grotius's engraving, *Syntagma Arateorum*, included in Eastwood 1983, fig. 2.

A brief comparison of Voss. (Fig. 53) with R. for the seven months extant in the latter manuscript bears out Stern's assessment.[80] I would add only that two months in Voss.—February and October—omit all accompanying attributes. February is a veiled figure wearing a long dress, turned to the right and holding a long rectangular object (= the duck in R.?). Thus, Voss. coincides with R. (Fig. 17) and V. (Fig. 32) for this month, although the Voss. February lacks the goose to the lower left of the figure, the urn spilling water and shells to the upper left, and the aquatic animal to the figure's right. Only half of the image of October survives in Voss., but the bottom half of the figure indicates that October is a hunter, as he is in R. (Fig. 21) and V. (Fig. 41). As noted above, October in Voss. wears a short tunic instead of the large cape found in R. and V. Like February, October in Voss. lacks his accompanying attributes, that is, the fruit basket and rabbit trap depicted in R. and V. March in Voss. is a single male, dressed in an animal skin, as he is in R. (Fig. 18). But here he stretches out his right hand to hold a lance, not to point to a bird in a window as in R.; his right hand holds an object of uncertain shape, perhaps the goat of R. August in Voss. is a nude male drinking out of a bowl, again as in R. (Fig. 19); in Voss., however, only the amphora is depicted beside him: the seasonal melons and jacket, shown in R., are missing. The Voss. September wears a loose mantle, and his left hand holds a basket, as in R. (Fig. 20); but September in Voss. holds in his right hand a long object of indistinct shape, which replaces the lizard of R. November is a male worshiper of Isis, depicted in Voss. with short hair, not bald as in R. (Fig. 22). In R. he is holding a sistrum in his right hand and a plate with cult objects in his left; in Voss. the sistrum looks more like a bird, and the plate is but vaguely outlined. All the other attributes of November depicted in R. are missing from Voss. December in Voss. is represented in a short tunic and holding a torch, yet again as he is in R. (Fig. 23). (Interestingly, in Voss. the flames from his torch extend outside the medallion.)[81] To the right of the figure in Voss. is a table with smoke; this replaces the table with dice in R.

The Voss. months of January, April, May, June, and July are extremely important for corroborating the corresponding depictions in the only other manuscript that preserves these months, V. In both Voss. and V. (Fig. 31), January is represented by a man dressed in a tunic or mantle that is partially draped over one arm; he performs a sacrifice before an altar or fire, depicted to his lower left. The Voss. illustration, however, has omitted the cap and cock which are his attributes in V. April in Voss. (Figs. 53, 107) and V. (Fig. 34) is depicted as a figure dancing with one arm raised overhead and body turned to the left. Here, though,

---

80. The following description of the images in Voss. is the result of my inspection of this manuscript. With the noted exceptions, I am in general agreement with the descriptions of the figures—zodiac, months, and planets—undertaken with painstaking care by Stern 1953, pp. 27–31; by Thiele, *Antike Himmelsbilder*, pp. 139ff.; and by Webster 1938, pp. 46–47.

81. The red basket in September and the lance in March in Voss. also extend outside the medallion design.

the altar with cult image and the candlestick shown in V. have been replaced in Voss. by four bands surrounded by what appear to be grapevines. To the lower right of the figure in Voss. are the remnants of dark lines, now impossible to read with certainty, though these may be the outlines of the musical instrument depicted in V. May in Voss. and V. (Fig. 35) is a man who sniffs a flower and carries a basket. But in Voss. he has short hair, not the flowing locks found in V.; and he holds a basket out of which protrude three round objects on sticks, not the fruit depicted in V. The Voss. May lacks all the accompanying attributes found in V. June in both Voss. and V. (Fig. 37) is represented by a man with his back turned toward the viewer. In Voss. he holds a long thin object, which may be the torch in V. Instead of a basket of fruits to his left, as in V., an amphora is shown to his right. Finally, July in Voss. and V. (Fig. 38) is a nude male standing in *contrapposto* holding a basket in his left hand; in Voss., however, the male holds a long, thin curved object in his right hand, which appears more like a sword or shepherd's crook than the purse depicted in V.

Comparison of Voss. (Fig. 53) with its Boulogne-sur-Mer manuscript copy (Fig. 57) for the illustrations of the months enables us to clarify some of the problematic iconography in the former. Yet there is a noticeable tendency in the Boulogne-sur-Mer version to omit attributes: only one month, August, has any accessory, and it looks more like a small pillow held to the head than the glass bowl out of which August drinks in Voss. Moreover, the illustrations in the Boulogne-sur-Mer manuscript tend to shift "from referential object, possible rituals, to types of persons."[82] Hence, the Boulogne-sur-Mer copy is of but limited aid for reading the iconography of Voss.

As the above summary shows, comparison with R. and V. for the extant illustrations of the months allows a rather circumscribed usefulness for Voss. Not only does Voss. omit certain attributes, but it also alters some attributes that were retained. March, for example, stretches out his right hand not to point to a bird in a window but to lean on a lance; September does not hold a lizard on a string, but a basket of fruit; and October holds a bird, not a rabbit.

These iconographic alterations raised doubts as to the link between Voss. and the Calendar of 354. Thiele was of the opinion that Voss. was not copied from the Codex-Calendar, or from any fourth-century manuscript;[83] he believed, rather, that Voss. was put together from separate elements, perhaps as late as the ninth century. In contrast, Nordenfalk argued that the miniatures in Voss. were copied directly from a classical source, though not from the Codex-Calendar of 354.[84] And Stern argued that the iconographic variations between Voss. and the Codex-Calendar resulted partly because Voss. was copied from a medieval copy rather than the fourth-century original. The mistaken direction of the zodiac cycle in Voss. indicated to Stern that the ninth-century copyist did not know

82. Eastwood 1983, p. 34.
83. Thiele, *Antike Himmelsbilder*, pp. 138–141, 144.
84. Nordenfalk 1936, pp. 23–30.

what he was transcribing; and the fact that the medallions for March and April are larger than those for the remaining months in his view confirmed that the months were a later addition by the ninth-century miniaturist.[85] Thus, Stern argued for a lively and wide-ranging tradition of calendar illustration continuing into the early Middle Ages and influenced by the Codex-Calendar of 354. This interpretation is indeed supported by the sixth-century dating of the images in Voss. and, more convincingly, by the iconographic connections between Voss. and the Codex, even though, for the same reasons, his argument for a ninth-century conflation of sources behind Voss. is far less convincing.

The results of this analysis of Voss. are important for our study of the Calendar of 354. First, the bulk of the iconographic evidence—the clear similarities and confluences in eleven of the twelve months—strongly indicates a link between Voss. and the illustrations of the months in the Codex-Calendar of 354 as these are preserved in its later copies, R1, V., and B. It must be reiterated, however, that, unlike these other copies, Voss. should not be considered a completely trustworthy reproduction of the months in the Calendar unless it is corroborated by other evidence, whether from other manuscript copies or from archaeological evidence. Second, the iconographic alterations in Voss. appear as either errors or conflations in transmission of a sixth-century manuscript via its ninth-century copy. Voss. may have been copied from the fourth-century original of the Codex-Calendar or from a later copy, produced after 354 but before 579. Whatever the date of this source, Voss. attests to the popularity of the Codex-Calendar of 354 in the sixth century. Thus one more link in the chain of transmission can be established.

85. Stern interprets the iconographic alterations in Voss. as a conflation of the sources behind Voss. By way of example, he cites the ninth-century poetry of Wandalbert de Prum, *De mensibus duodecim nominibus signis culturis aerisque qualitatibus*, as one possible source for the altered details of the months of April and October. See Stern 1953, p. 28, n. 3; p. 29.

APPENDIX II. COMPARABLE CALENDAR CYCLES FROM THE LATIN WEST

The following illustrated cycles of the months are relevant for discussion of the illustrations of the months in the Calendar of 354. The *locus classicus* for these cycles was the monograph by H. Stern, *Le calendrier du 354*, published in 1953. Since the appearance of this work, many new cycles or fragments of cycles have come to light. Stern published an updated catalogue, *Les calendriers romains illustrés*, in *ANRW* II 12.2 (1981): 431–475 (written in 1977). The other noteworthy catalogues cited here are Webster 1938; Levi 1941; Akerström-Hougen 1974; and Parrish 1984.

Reference will generally be to Stern 1981, for it is the most complete catalogue and provides the most recent bibliography. The number identifying each cycle indicates the number used in the present study. An asterisk (*) indicates cycles that have come to light since the appearance of Stern's 1953 study; a double asterisk (**) indicates cycles that have come to light since Stern 1981. The dates of the cycles are those generally accepted unless otherwise noted. The citations included for individual entries indicate where the cycle in question is most readily available or where it was first published and illustrated. The Figure numbers at the end of certain monument entries refer to illustrations in the present volume.

1.   *Altar of Gabii. Relief.* Dated: 1st–2d cent. by Stern 1981, pp. 434–435. First published by C. Ravaisson-Mollien, "Le bas-relief circulaire de Gabies," *Centenaire de la Société Nationale des Antiquaires de France* (Paris, 1804–1904) pp. 399–408.

2.   *Ostia. Frescoes.* Dated: 209–211 by Stern 1981, pp. 440–442; to 1st cent. A.D. by A. Piganiol, "Le calendrier d'Ostie," *Recherches sur les jeux romains* (Paris and Strasbourg, 1923), pp. 44–57; to the period of Septimius Severus by B. Andreae

in W. Helbig, *Führer durch die öffentlichen Sammlungen klassischer Altertümer in Rom,* 4th ed. (Tübingen, 1963), pp. 366ff., no. 467.

3. *Trier, Germany. Mosaic.** Dated: 2d–3d cent. by Stern 1981, p. 443; to early 3d cent. by K. Parlasca, *Die römischen Mosaiken in Deutschland* (Berlin, 1959), pp. 42–48. Figs. 93–97.

4. *Hellín, Spain. Mosaic.** Dated: 2d–3d cent. by Stern 1981, p. 442, and in "Mosaïque du Hellín (Albacète)," *Académie des Inscriptions et Belles-Lettres, Paris. Commission de la Fondation Piot. Monuments et mémoires* 54 (1966): 39–59. Figs. 102–106.

5. *Saint-Romain-en-Gaul (Rhône), France. Relief.* Dated: 2d–3d cent. by Stern 1981, pp. 445–449. First published by G. Lafaye, "Mosaïque de Saint-Romain-en-Gaul," *RA* 19, no. 1 (1892): 322–347.

6. *Door of Mars, Reims, France. Relief.* Dated: 2d–3d cent. by Stern 1981, pp. 449–453; to 2d cent. by G. Ch. Picard, "La 'Porte de Mars' à Reims," *Actes du 95e Congrès National des Sociétés Savantes* (Reims, 1970; Paris, 1974), pp. 59–73.

7. *Zliten, Tripolitania. Mosaic.** Dated: 2d–3d cent. by Stern 1981, p. 444. Stern 1953 included this mosaic but categorized it as only seasonal; he reclassified it as a cycle of the months in his later publication. Dated to the Flavian period by S. Aurigemma, *I mosaici di Zliten* (Rome and Milan, 1926), pp. 47ff.

8. *Tanis, Egypt. Painted glass plaque.* Dated: 2d–3d cent. by Stern 1981, p. 435. Described by W. M. Flinders Petrie, *Tanis I 1883/4* (London, 1885), pp. 48–49.

9. *El-Djem, Tunisia. Mosaic.** Dated: 2d–3d cent. by Stern 1981, pp. 435–440; and by L. Foucher, "Découvertes archéologiques à Thysdrus en 1961," *Notes et documents de l'Université de Tunis,* vol. 5 (Tunis, 1961), pp. 30–52. Figs. 59–70.

10. *Thina, Tunisia. Mosaic.** Dated: 2d–3d cent. by Stern 1981, p. 455. Described by M. Fendri, "Les thermes des mois à Thina. Rapport préliminaire de 1963," *Les cahiers de Tunisie* 12, nos. 45–46 (1964): 47ff.

11. *Sousse, Tunisia. Mosaic.** Dated: 2d–3d cent. by Stern 1981, pp. 454–455. Described by L. Foucher, "Note sur une mosaïque de Sousse: les mois de l'année," *Analecta archaeologica (Festschrift für Fritz Fremersdorf)* (Cologne, 1954), pp. 109–111.

12. *Boscéaz, Switzerland. Mosaic.* Dated: 3d cent. by Stern 1981, p. 453.

13. *S. Maria Maggiore, Rome. Fresco.** Dated: 4th cent. by Stern 1981, pp. 453–454; and by Magi 1972, pp. 1–103; to the 2d–3d cent. by M. R. Salzman, "New Evidence for the Dating of the Calendar at Santa Maria Maggiore in Rome," *TAPA* 111 (1981): 215–227. First published with illustrations by Magi 1972.

14. *Aquileia, Italy; now in Villa La Pietra, Florence, Italy. The Acton Mosaic.** Dated: 4th cent. by Stern 1981, p. 465. Stern 1953, p. 217, no. 10, published this mosaic, including the months of May, June, and September but dated it to the 5th–6th centuries and gave it a North African provenance. Stern 1981 attributed it to Aquileia and gave it a 4th-century date based on the information about its acquisition conveyed to him by its owner, M. H. Acton. The 1981 attribution appears correct. Figs. 98–100.

15.   *Ostia, Italy. Mosaic.* Dated: 4th cent. by Stern 1981, p. 462. Published by G. Becatti, *Mosaici e pavimenti marmorei* = *Scavi de Ostia,* vol. 4 (Rome, 1961), pt. 1, no. 438, pp. 235–241, and pt. 2, pl. CCII. Figs. 75–76.

16.   *Carthage, Tunisia. Mosaic.* Now at the British Museum. Dated: second half of 4th cent. by Stern 1981, pp. 464–465; and by Parrish 1984, no. 10. First published by A. W. Franks, "Recent Excavations at Carthage," *Archaeologia* 38, no. 1 (1860): 224ff. Figs. 71–74.

17.   *Carthage. Mosaic.* Not extant. Dated: late 4th–5th cent. by Stern 1981, pp. 466–469; and by Parrish 1984, no. 11. This mosaic survives in drawings published by R. Cagnat, "Une mosaïque de Carthage représentant les mois et les saisons," *Mémoires de la Société (Nationale) des Antiquaires de France* 57 (1896): 251–70. Fig. 88.

18.   *Catania, Sicily. Mosaic.* Dated: 4th cent. by Stern 1981, pp. 463–464. First published by G. Libertini, *Il Museo Biscari* (Rome and Milan, 1930), pp. 309ff., no. 1516. Fig. 101.

19.   *Rome and Leningrad. Mosaic.* Dated: 4th cent. by Stern 1981, p. 443. Only the months of May and June survive. Fig. 36 (May).

20.   *Carthage, Tunisia. Mosaic.* Not extant. Dated: 4th cent. by Stern 1953; 2d–3d cent. by Stern 1981, p. 444. N. Davis, *Carthage and Her Remains* (London, 1861), p. 200, describes the months of May and June: "May was a large boy with brick-red face, dressed in a short tunic bearing a basket of flowers. The execution was miserable. A little girl (?) of equal dimensions in deformity and bearing a basket of fruit personified June." There were originally five months. A second notice occurs in C.-E. Beulé, *Fouilles à Carthage* (Paris, 1861), p. 37.

21.   *Carthage, Tunisia. Dominus Julius Mosaic.*** Dated: 4th cent. by Parrish 1984, no. 9. Stern 1953, pp. 245, 251, and pl. 45.5, was familiar with this mosaic but did not consider it a representation of the months. It has been convincingly identified as including illustrations of the months by D. Parrish, "Two Mosaics from Roman Tunisia: An African Variation of the Season Theme," *AJA* 83 (1979): 279–283. Fig. 83.

22.   *Carthage, Tunisia. Mosaic.*** Dated: early 4th cent. by G. C. Picard, *La Carthage de St. Augustin* (Paris, 1965), p. 126; and by Parrish 1984, no. 13. Parrish and K. Dunbabin, *The Mosaics of Roman North Africa* (Oxford, 1978) pp. 144–145, 254, both identified this mosaic as a sacred calendar with illustrations of feasts. Fig. 92.

23.   *Sabratha, Libya. Fresco.*** Dated: 2d cent. by G. Caputo and F. Ghedini, *Il tempio d'Ercole di Sabratha,* Monografie di Archéologia Libica, no. 19 (Rome, 1984).

24.   *Fraga, Spain. Mosaic.*** Dated: second half of 4th cent., identified as a cycle of the months from a Roman villa, by Dimas Fernández Galiano, "El calendario romano de Fraga," *Boletín del Seminario de Estudios de Arte y Arqueologia,* vol. 52 (Valladolid, Spain, 1986), pp. 163–196; and again in *Mosaicos romanos del Convento Cesaraugustano* (Zaragoza, Spain, 1987), pp. 73–85. Nonetheless, its fragmentary state makes its identification as a cycle of the months questionable.

25. *Rome. Monumental Solarium and Calendar.*** Dated: Augustan Age, re-constructed in the Domitianic period, according to its excavator, E. Büchner, *Die Sonnenuhr des Augustus* (Rome, 1982). Although not technically an illustrated cycle of the months, this monumental bronze lettered calendar deserves notation in any discussion of calendar cycles.

26. *Pompeii, Italy. Fresco.*** Dated: before A.D. 79. Not noted by Stern 1981. Painted medallions accompanying a wall calendar according to W. Helbig, *Wandgemälde der von Vesuv verschütteten Städte Campaniens*, vol. 2 (Leipzig, 1868), p. 202, no. 1020; and to C. R. Long, *The Twelve Gods in Greek and Roman Art*, EPRO 107 (Leiden, 1987), pp. 32–33.

In addition to the cycles from the Latin West, several cycles of the months from the Greek East have come to light since Stern 1953:

27. *Thebes, Greece. Mosaic.** Dated: *terminus ante quem* of 9th–10th cents., by Akerström-Hougen 1974, p. 121. It includes the months of February, April, May, and July.

28. *Argos, Greece. Mosaic.** Dated: 6th cent. by Stern 1953, who knew only the months of January and February (pl. 32.1). The remaining ten months were published in 1957; full publication and study by Akerström-Hougen 1974. Figs. 89–91.

29. *Beirut, Lebanon. Mosaic.** Dated: 450–550 by its excavator, M. Chéhab, as reported by Akerström-Hougen 1974, p. 126, fig. 82.1. Includes months of April and October.

APPENDIX III. LATIN POETRY OF THE MONTHS

The following is a concise list with dates of the Latin poetry of the months. Numbers refer to the *Anthologia Latina*, vols. 1.1 and 1.2, ed. A. Riese (Leipzig, 1894–1906).

1.　117. *Laus omnium mensium.* Dated: ca. 530 by Courtney 1988, pp. 33–57; dated before 524–534 in *Anth. Lat.* 1.1:132 and by Stern 1981, p. 469.

2.　394. *Versus de numero singulorum dierum* or *Dira patet.* Dated: contemporary with or later than *Anth. Lat.* 395 by Courtney 1988, p. 35; not datable according to Stern 1981, p. 469, and *Anth. Lat.* 1.1:132–133.

3.　395. *Tetrastichon authenticon de singulis mensibus.* Dated: post-Orientius, i.e., mid 5th cent., by Courtney 1988, pp. 35–36 (because of the form *olli,* line 11); but dated to the 4th cent. by Stern 1981, p. 469; and to the Augustan Age by Baehrens 1882, p. 204; cf. *Anth. Lat.* 1.1:309ff. These verses were added to the Calendar of 354 after its original publication.

4.　490a. *Officia duodecim mensium.* Dated: Carolingian period (755–877) by H. Stern, "Poésies et représentations carolingiennes et byzantines des mois," *RA* 45 (1955): 143ff.; dated to mid 5th cent. (i.e., contemporary with nos. 394, 395) by Courtney 1988, p. 36.

5.　665. Distichs may have been included in the Calendar of 354. Mistakenly entitled *Monosticha de mensibus* by Riese; should be *Disticha de mensibus*. Dated: Augustan Age by Baehrens 1882, p. 204. These verses were given a secure *terminus post quem* in the mid 1st cent. by A. E. Housman, "Disticha de Mensibus," *CQ* 26 (1932): 130, on the basis of the shortening of the final *o* in *concedo,* line 23.

6.　874a. *Ad Trasimundum comitem Capuae de mensibus.* Dated: 496–523 by Stern 1981, p. 469; and by Courtney 1988, p. 37. This poem is firmly identified with the Thrasimund of Dracontius, the Vandal king of North Africa, who ruled 496–523.

7. 639. *Monosticha de mensibus* = Ausonius *Ecloga* 9, ed. S. Prete (Leipzig, 1978). Dated: 4th cent. because of its secure authorship.

8. *Disticha de mensibus* = Ausonius *Ecloga* 10, ed. S. Prete (Leipzig, 1978). Dated: 4th cent. because of its secure authorship.

The following three poems deal with the astrological signs and the seasons and are included by Stern 1981, pp. 469–470, in his discussion of the poetry of the months.

9. 640. *In quo mense quod signum sit ad cursum solis* = Vat. Reg. 435. Dated: 4th cent. because attributed to Ausonius in *Anth. Lat.* 1.2:106–107; not datable according to Stern 1981, p. 469.

10. 642. Dated: 1st cent. B.C. because of its attribution to Quintus Cicero in *Anth. Lat.* 1.2:108–109; not datable according to Stern 1981, p. 469.

11. 864. *De quattuor anni tempestatibus.* Dated: Not datable according to *Anth. Lat.* 1.2:315; and Stern 1981, p. 469. Author anonymous.

The following three poems are in Greek, but they are included as important comparable poetry of the months. References are to the *Anthologia Palatina*, Book 9, ed. P. Waltz and G. Soury, vol. 8 (Paris, 1974).

12. *A. P.* 9.383. Egyptian provenance. Not dated.

13. *A. P.* 9.384. Not dated.

14. *A. P.* 9.580. Dated: after 500 by Stern 1953, pp. 228–229, 284–286; and to 500–542 by Courtney 1988, p. 38. Discussed by Stern, "A propos des poésies des mois de l'Anthologie Palatine," *REG* 65 (1952): 374–384.

APPENDIX IV. THE TEXT OF THE DISTICHS (*ANTHOLOGIA LATINA* 665) IN THE CALENDAR OF 354

The text of the distichs (*Anthologia Latina,* vol. 1.2, ed. A. Riese [Leipzig, 1906], no. 665) that I use in my discussion of the Calendar of 354 is derived largely from the S.G. manuscript, which is badly damaged. Variations of S.G. that are preserved in R1 and R2 and in Ber. (line 24) are noted where relevant. Stern 1953, pp. 359–360, also published the distichs; unfortunately, he was not aware of the important paper by A. E. Housman, "Disticha de Mensibus," *CQ* 26 (1932): 129–136. Thus Stern's text does not benefit from Housman's many excellent emendations and solutions.

Citation of emendations is by the name of the scholar who first proposed it. Professor Richard Tarrant's emendations were conveyed to me in private correspondence. Editions of *Anth. Lat.* 665 (and of 395) relevant to this discussion were published by:

Baehrens = E. Baehrens, *Poetae Latini minores* (Leipzig, 1882), pp. 210ff.

Binder = G. Binder, *Der Kalender des Filocalus oder der Chronograph vom Jahre 354* (Meisenheim/Glan, 1970–1971).

Courtney = E. Courtney, "The Roman Months in Art and Literature," *Museum Helveticum* 45 (1988): 33–57.

Housman = A. E. Housman, "Disticha de Mensibus," *CQ* 26 (1932): 129–136.

Riese = A. Riese, *Anthologia Latina,* vol. 1.2 (Leipzig, 1906), no. 665.

Schenkl = H. Schenkl, "Zu den lateinischen Monatsgedichten," *Festschrift für O. Benndorf zum 60. Geburtstag* (Vienna, 1898), pp. 29–36.

Shackleton Bailey = D. R. Shackleton Bailey, *Latin Anthology* (Stuttgart, 1982).

Stern = H. Stern, *Le Calendrier de 354* (1953), pp. 359–360.

ANTHOLOGIA LATINA 665

January

1. *Primus*, Iane, tibi sacratur †ut omnia† mensis
2.   undique cui semper cuncta videre licet.

  1. *primus* Schenkl: *primis* S.G.
     ut omnia S.G.: *et omnia* Schenkl: *nomine* Riese: *sacratus it ordine* Housman.
     R1, the false copy by Jean Gobille, cites: *Janus adest bifrons primusque ingreditur*
annum (Two-faced Janus is here and is the first to begin the year).

February

3. Umbrarum est alter, quo mense putatur honore
4.   pervia terra dato Manibus esse vagis.

March

5. Condita Mavortis magno sub nomine Roma
6.   non habet *errorem*: Romulus auctor erit.

  5. *nomine* S.G.: *numine* Schenkl, Riese: *Mavortis magno sub nomine tempora condi*
Housman, Courtney.
    6. *errorem* Schenkl: *errore* S.G.
     Romulus S.G.: *Martius* Baehrens.

April

7. *Caesareae* Veneris *mensis*, quo floribus arva
8.   prompta virent, avibus *quo* sonat omne nemus.

  7. *Caesareae* (or *Caesaris et*) *Veneris mensis* Schenkl: †*Caesarem ut*† S.G.: *At sacer est*
Veneri mensis Baehrens: *cesset ver* Courtney.
    8. *prompta* S.G.: *compta* Riese.
     quo Riese: *quod* S.G.

May

9. Hos sequitur *laetus* toto iam corpore Maius
10.   Mercurio et Maia quem tribuisse *Iovem*.

  9. *laetus* Riese: *laicus* S.G.
  10. *Maia* S.G.: *Maiae* Riese.
     Iove⟨m⟩ Housman: *Iove* S.G., R1: *iuvat* Baehrens: ⟨*fama sato*⟩ *Maia . . . Iovem*
Housman.

June

11. Iunius ipse sui causam tibi nominis edit
12.   praegravida attollens fertilitate sata.

July

13. *Quam* bene, Quintilis, *mutasti* nomen! *honori*
14.   *Caesareo, Iuli*, te pia causa dedit.

13. *Quam* Riese: *Nam* S.G.
    mutasti Riese: *mutati* S.G.
    honori Riese: *honore* S.G.
14. *Caesareo* Riese: *Iuli* Mommsen, Housman: *Caesare qui Iulio* S.G.

August

15. Tu quoque, Sextilis, venerabilis omnibus annis,
16.   Numinis Augusti nomen †in anno venis†.

16. †in anno venis† S.G.: *nomine notus eris* Riese: *nomina magna geris* Baehrens: *adepte venis* Housman: *nomen adepte, veni* Tarrant.

September

17. *Tempora maturis* September vincta racemis
18.   velate; ⟨e⟩ numero nosceris ipse tuo.

17. *tempora maturis* Haupt, Housman: *temporis autumni* S.G.: *temporibus autumnis* R1.
    September R.: *Septimber* S.G.
    vincta S.G.: *vineta* R.
18. *velate* ⟨e⟩ Haupt, Housman: *velate iam* S.G.

October

19. Octobri laetus portat vindemitor uvas,
20.   omnis ager Bacchi munere, voce sonat.

20. *munere, voce sonat* S.G.: *munera dives ovat* Riese.

November

21. Frondibus amissis repetunt sua frigora mensem,
22.   cum iuga Centaurus celsa retorquet eques.

22. *retorque[t]*, with *eques* omitted R.: *torquet* S.G.

December

23. Argumenta tibi mensis concedo *Decembris*
24.   †quae sis quam vis . . . †

23. *Decembris* Housman: *December* S.G.: *tuis festis* Baehrens, Riese: *concludo* Riese.
24.   *quae sis quam vis* R. and Ber.: *Quis quemvis* Riese: *Quale sis quemvis* Baehrens: *Quae † . . . † quamvis annum † . . . † claudere possis* Stern: *qui squamis annum claudere piscis [amas]* Housman: *quae sis quam vis annum claudere possis* Courtney. Missing from S.G. No conjecture or later manuscript resolves the text satisfactorily.

APPENDIX V. DATING THE
CODEX-CALENDAR OF 354

The only evidence for dating the original compilation and publication of the Codex-Calendar of 354 is to be found in its manuscripts and contents. But this evidence is indeed complicated: so knowledgeable a scholar as T. Mommsen had difficulty reconciling the pagan elements in the Codex with its mid-fourth-century date and thus changed his opinion on this issue several times. In the end he settled on 354, the date suggested by Peiresc in 1620.[1] On the basis of Mommsen's 354 dating, scholars identified the consular portraits as the two consuls of the year, the Emperor Constantius and his Caesar Gallus (Figs. 13, 14).[2] Nevertheless, certain historians in the first half of this century remained uncomfortable with this dating and wanted to attribute the Codex-Calendar to the pagan revival under Julian, i.e., 355/360–360/363; consequently, they identified the consular portraits as Julian and Constantius II.[3]

Stern returned to the question of the dating of the Codex-Calendar in his 1953 study, arguing convincingly for a 354 date.[4] There can be little doubt that the Codex was published in the reign of the Emperor Constantius: in the list of the *Natales Caesarum*, this emperor is called *D(ominus) N(oster)*; moreover, the notation *N(atalis) Constantii* for 7 August and 8 November does not include the epithet *Divi*, which would denote a deified (i.e., deceased) ruler, thereby signi-

---

1. Mommsen 1850a, p. 571, first dated the Codex-Calendar to 340–350. In *CIL* 1863, p. 332, he redated it to the spring of 354, arguing that it was intended for use in 355; the images of Gallus and Constantius were to be reidentified as Julian and Constantius. In *MGH* 1892, pp. 9ff., and *CIL* 1893, p. 254, Mommsen abandoned this hypothesis and suggested that the Codex-Calendar had been composed for use in 354; see Peiresc, in *MGH* 1892, p. 28.

2. See, for example, Strzygowski 1888, pp. 97ff.

3. See, for example, G. Volgraff, "De Figura Mensis Januarii e Codice Luxemburgensi Deperdito exscripta," *Mnemosyne* 59 (1931): 401.

4. Stern 1953, pp. 42–45.

fying that Constantius was still very much alive, whereas on 27 February and 25 July Constantine is designated as *Divus*. Further analysis of the Codex-Calendar led Stern to date it to the period under Constantius as Augustus, but after the assassination of his brother Constans—so between 18 January 350 and Constantius's death on 3 November 361. No mention is made of Constans or Constantine II in the list of *Natales Caesarum*, or in the actual text of the Calendar; and only one imperial portrait heads the list of *Natales Caesarum*, signifying that a sole Augustus was in control of the empire. Given the political situation at Rome—Magnentius and his supporters had control over the city from January 350 to September 352—Stern was able to narrow the Calendar's publication date further to September 352–3 November 361.

The unillustrated sections (VIII–XVI) allow us to ascertain the precise date of the Codex-Calendar's compilation. The list below will be of use for our discussion here:[5]

Sections

VIII.	List of Consuls, 245–354
IX.	Easter Cycle, 312–358 (predicted)
X.	List of Urban Prefects of Rome, 254–354
XI.	Depositions of the Bishops of Rome, 255–352
XII.	Depositions of Martyrs
XIII.	List of Bishops of Rome (from Peter to 352)
[*XIV.	Regions of the City of Rome (*Notitia*) (dated 334–357)]
[*XV.	*World Chronicle* (*Liber Generationis*) (from the biblical Creation to A.D. 334)]
XVI.	*Chronicle of the City of Rome* (*Chronica Urbis Romae*) (from the kings to the death of Licinius in A.D. 324)

Several of these unillustrated lists reveal different phases of composition. The list of Depositions of Bishops, for example, reveals two phases of composition: the first, from 255, ends with the death of Pope Sylvester, 31 December 335 or 1 January 336; the second, from 336–352 and ending with the deaths of Popes Marius (7 October 336) and Julius (12 April 352), was added later. Indeed, the unillustrated lists as a whole represent at least three phases of composition—334, 336 and 354—indicating that the information included in the Codex-Calendar was drawn from a wide variety of sources. Considered together, though, these lists reveal 354 as the last stage of composition: the List of Consuls (section VIII) records the consuls for 354; the List of Urban Prefects (section X) records as its last entry the name Vitrasius Orfitus, who entered office on 8 December 353; and the List of Bishops (section XI) records the name of the Caesar Gallus under the entry for Bishop Liberius, for Gallus was Caesar from 352 to November 354. This last point is important, for it coincides with the plural *Augusti* found in the dedication in section III. Obviously Gallus, who was Caesar when Constantius

---

5. Those sections in brackets and starred were probably not included in the original Codex-Calendar of 354. See the discussion in Chapter 2.

was Augustus, had not yet died or news of his death had not yet reached Rome. Based on this date and on the presence of Vitrasius Orfitus's name as urban prefect in section X, Stern concluded that the Codex-Calendar appeared sometime after 8 December 353 but before or soon after November 354, when Gallus was removed from office and executed.

One problem remains with dating the Codex-Calendar to 354 and to the reign of Constantius, and that concerns the plural imperial dedication, *Salvis Augustis.* A 354 date would mean that this inscription refers to both the Caesar Gallus and the Augustus Constantius with the same title—Augustus. Given Ammianus's well-known portrait of Constantius as a paranoid ruler jealous of his position, however, as well as the very real difference between the two titles (Caesar and Augustus) in the fourth century, the omission of this distinction in the dedication is perplexing.

Mommsen, who first noted this problem for the 354 dating, later became convinced by the weight of the internal evidence that the Codex-Calendar had to be so dated; he therefore suggested that in unofficial documents, such as the Calendar, both Caesar and Augustus could be addressed as Augustus. But neither he nor Stern has provided evidence to support this suggestion.[6] And without further proof, Mommsen's argument is unconvincing, especially given the careful, elaborate, and personalized execution of the page and its obvious derivation from official imperial sources. The acclamation *Salvis Augustis* is a formulaic wish for imperial well-being found on altars and monuments; often it is joined with the name of the donor, though in the Codex-Calendar it is the recipient who is so named.[7]

One could argue that the plural dedication reflects an earlier stage of composition when several Augusti were in power, as was the case in 337–350. But this alternative is not satisfactory either, for if the page and its dedication were prepared earlier, would the designer be so careless as to leave the plural *Augusti* unchanged in this otherwise personalized and carefully considered design for Valentinus? Again the lack of parallel examples for this usage presents a stumbling block.

The solution for the plural dedication lies finally in the formula's derivation and its accompanying illustration on coins and medallions issued under Constantius. The Codex-Calendar's representation of Victory inscribing a large shield recurs on several contemporary pieces, most importantly on a contemporary medallion of Constantius as Augustus and Gallus as Caesar dated September 352–Winter 354.[8]

A large number of these bronze medallions were produced in the first years

6. Mommsen 1850, pp. 571ff.; Mommsen, *CIL* 1863, p. 332; Stern 1953, p. 43.

7. Cf. *CIL* 6.180 = *ILS* 3703, where the inscription carefully distinguishes between Augustus and Caesar.

8. *RIC* 8, p. 294, no. 421, with a Victory inscribing a shield, which she rests on her left knee; and see ibid., "Index, Type/Legend," s.v. "Victory stg.," pp. 587–588, for variations in iconographic details of a Victory inscribing a shield.

of Magnentius's reign, to honor Constantius as well as Magnentius himself by means of the plural *Augusti*.[9] The survival and reuse of dies from the reign of Magnentius for the medallions of Constantius accounts for the strange medley of styles and treatment on Constantius's medallions. "Two such dies, Victoria Aug. Nostri and Virtus Aug. Nostri, for example, are Magnentian reverses with the legends recut. Victoria Augg., if it should be confirmed, will be the simple re-use of old dies from the reign of Magnentius."[10] Although we have a good example of a medallion with the plural dedication—Victoria Augg.—that is close in date to the Codex-Calendar, it also, unfortunately, requires confirmation.[11] The other contemporary medallions with legends Victoria Augustorum, Virtus Augustorum, and Virtus Augg. described by Kent in *Roman Imperial Coinage* (vol. 8) are similarly in need of confirmation. The gold coins from the years when Constantius was sole Augustus and Julian or Gallus was Caesar do, however, confirm the plural usage, Augusti.[12]

The simplified legend with *Augusti* on 350s coins and medallions to commemorate the reign of Constantius as sole Augustus is explicable given the reuse of dies and the spatial constraints on coins. Moreover, just as the iconography (Victory inscribing a shield) on the dedicatory page of the Codex-Calendar points to an offical, numismatic source, so too does its inscription. The plural *Augusti* in the Codex thus becomes clear, and we need not hesitate in dating the Codex-Calendar to the year A.D. 354.

9. Ibid., pp. 290–292, nos. 406–418, with legends "Victoria" or "Virtus Augustorum," as in nos. 406–410 (abbreviated as "Victoria Augg."); and nos. 411–412, "Victoria Augg."

10. Ibid., p. 246.

11. For the medallion inscribed "Victoria Augg.," dated to the period 26 September 352–Winter 354, see ibid., p. 294, n. 427.

12. For a Constantinian coin with Gallus, see ibid., p. 270, no. 231, with the legend "Victoria Augustorum"; and for coins with Julian, see pp. 221–222, nos. 240–241, also with the legend "Victoria Augustorum."

APPENDIX VI. CONSULAR DATING AS A CRITERION FOR SOURCE ANALYSIS OF THE CODEX-CALENDAR OF 354

Comparison of consular dating in certain sections of the Codex-Calendar of 354 may shed new light on the sources and circumstances of its production. We can begin with the consular notations for the turbulent years 351–354. The List of Consuls (section VIII) deletes the names of the usurpers Magnentius and Decentius and records 351 as "post Sergio et Nigriniano," 352 as "Constancio V et Constantio iun.(ior)," 353 as "Constancio VI et Constantio II," and 354 as "Constantio VII et Constantio III."[1] The Easter Cycle (section IX) and the List of Bishops of Rome (section XIII) also include corrected consular notations for these years; the List of Urban Prefects (section X), however, does not.

Three hypothetical solutions may be invoked to explain this potentially significant variation in consular dating: (1) the List of Urban Prefects was completed by September 353 and so was not corrected (whereas the other lists of consuls, bishops, and Easter dates, since they were not yet finished, could easily accommodate changes); (2) the List of Urban Prefects was derived from a different source from that used for the List of Consuls and perhaps from that used for the Christian sections (IX and XIII); or (3) the Christian sections used the List of Consuls for their calculations (which would explain the affinities in consular notations between these lists) but were derived from the same source as the List of Urban Prefects.

The first hypothesis appears unlikely, because the List of Urban Prefects was completed up to and including the prefect for 354; thus, it was apparently still

---

1. For the text, see Mommsen, *MGH* 1892, p. 61; see also pp. 50–61 for the List of Consuls; and pp. 39–195 for the text of the Codex–Calendar of 354.

being worked on in December 353. The third hypothesis also seems improbable, since the List of Bishops records the usurpers who do not appear in the List of Consuls; hence, not all the Christian sections depended on the consular list. But since the Easter Cycle does not record the usurpers, it does not agree with the List of Urban Prefects either, suggesting that all the Christian sections were not derived from the same source as the List of Urban Prefects.

The second hypothesis, then, appears the most probable; it is also supported by other consular notations. The names of two other notorious usurpers of the fourth century, Maxentius and Romulus, are included for 308, 309, 310, and 312 in the List of Urban Prefects, but not in the List of Consuls. These usurpers are also omitted from the Easter Cycle and the List of Bishops of Rome.[2] The latter list does, however, note 308 as being "the times of Maxentius" and records both sets of consuls for 311, namely, those officially recognized ("Maximiano VIII solo"), as in the corrected List of Consuls, and those who were appointed for that year by the usurper ("Volusiano et Rufino"), as in the List of Urban Prefects.[3] The *Chronicle of the City of Rome* (section XVI), which ends in 324, also includes the usurper Maxentius for 308–310 and 312.[4]

To summarize, the List of Consuls agrees with the consular notations found in the Christian Easter Cycle and in the List of Bishops for the years 308–312 and 351–353, although the List of Bishops also notes the consuls appointed by the usurper Maxentius. None of these three sections, however—the List of Consuls, the Easter Cycle, or the List of Bishops—coincides fully with the consular notations in the List of Urban Prefects. Only the *Chronicle of Rome* agrees with this last list. Thus, it appears that the Easter Cycle and the List of Consuls derive from another source than that used for the List of Urban Prefects.[5] The List of Bishops of Rome recorded both the official and the unofficial consular notations for 308 and 311, but only the official view for 354; this section probably also has a different source from that used for the urban prefects.

If this analysis is correct, then the documents themselves suggest that the source for the List of Urban Prefects and that for the List of Consuls and the Easter Cycle, and perhaps for the List of Bishops of Rome as well, was not the same. Can we get closer to the source for these unexpurgated, unofficial consular notations in the List of Urban Prefects?

Two opinions have been expressed on this subject. Mommsen and Stern suggest that the List of Urban Prefects was copied from the registers of the archives of the Roman bishops.[6] The principal arguments in support of this thesis

2. The Easter Cycle (section IX) records for 312 "Constantino II et Licinio II."

3. The List of Bishops of Rome in Mommsen, *MGH* 1892, p. 76, notes that the Bishop Marcellus: "fuit temporibus Maxenti."

4. Mommsen, *MGH* 1892, p. 148.

5. A tie between sections VIII and IX is likely, since the Easter Cycle (IX) was probably calculated using the List of Consuls (VIII).

6. Mommsen, *MGH* 1892, p. 65; Stern 1953, p. 114.

are that (a) the List of Urban Prefects is followed by the Christian lists of the Depositions of Bishops and Martyrs (sections XI and XII) and of Bishops of Rome and (b) the first of these (section XI) covers the same time period, 254–353, as the List of Urban Prefects. The second view is that of De Rossi and Chastagnol, who argue that all four of these lists probably derive from the prefectural archives.[7] De Rossi, for one, conjectured that from the mid third century the church had to register with the urban prefect in Rome; Chastagnol continued this argument, stating that even if Mommsen's position was correct, the Roman church had copied its lists of prefects from the prefectural archives in the first place.

Chastagnol may be correct, insofar as the church probably began its historical recordkeeping only in the mid third century and did, most likely, have to copy its list from the archives of the urban prefect.[8] But the inclusion of usurpers as consuls in the fourth-century List of Urban Prefects, their exclusion from the Easter Cycle, and their sporadic notation in the List of Bishops of Rome prove problematic for Chastagnol's view. If the prefectural archives were the direct source for our list of prefects, it seems unlikely that the notations on the usurpers would have been retained, especially since the List of Consuls was corrected; leaving the usurpers' names suggests a remarkable lack of tact and a great degree of independence, both of which conflict with what is known about this office in the fourth century.[9]

Rather, what appears most probable is that the List of Urban Prefects was not derived directly from any official source, whether imperial or urban prefectural, since it clearly reflects the "unofficial" view of recent Roman consular history. Perhaps it was derived from church archives; if so, the church may have used the archives of the urban prefecture for its own purposes sometime earlier in the third century, but not in 354. An equally likely source would be a list circulated by booksellers in Rome.[10]

Thus, the consular formulas suggest that although the List of Urban Prefects may once have begun in the archives of the urban prefect, by the fourth century it was apparently derived from some other unofficial source. Further support for this view comes from the *Chronicle of the City of Rome*, whose sources are indisputably unofficial and which reflects the same version of recent Roman consular history as does the List of Urban Prefects. Moreover, given that the Christian Easter Cycle and List of Bishops of Rome did utilize the corrected and official consular dating, different sources for these two sections and for the List of Urban

7. G. B. De Rossi, *La Roma sotteranea cristiana* (Rome, 1864–1877), 2:vi; and Chastagnol 1960, p. 1, n. 2.

8. See Chapter 2, notes 53 and 54.

9. Chastagnol 1960, esp. pp. 385–388. Ammianus Marcellinus 14.6.1 calls the office of urban prefect a *delata dignitas*.

10. This kind of unofficial source—booksellers in Constantinople—was suggested for the later fourth-century and early fifth-century Greek consular annals as well; see Chapter 2, note 36.

Prefects must have been used—providing yet more support for the second hypothesis.

We cannot be certain of the sources of the annexed sections in the Codex-Calendar. I hope that analysis of the consular dating in these sections has shed some new light on the subject, however tentative the conclusions may be. Regardless how obscure the sources, the accuracy of the information conveyed by these lists remains clear.

APPENDIX VII. A FOURTH-CENTURY VARIANT MYTH

Servius *Ad Aen.* 3.279 records a Roman myth that pertains to the illustration of April in the Calendar of 354 (see Chapter 3). Festus, 326 Müller ed. (436 Lindsay ed.), relates a similar story of an old mime, whose singing in the midst of an attack by enemy archers saved the state—as the origin of the stock saying "Salva res (est dum cantat) senex" reflects. Festus's account has been correlated with the *ludi Apollinares* celebrated in 211 b.c. and interrupted by Hannibal's advance on Rome, as told by Livy (26.10.2–8 and 26.23.3) and discussed by A. Otto.[1] Servius *Ad Aen.* 8.110 relates this same account as the origin of the proverb "Salva res est, saltat senex." Although the accounts in Festus, Livy, and Servius (8.110) may all refer to the events of 211 b.c. (which occurred several years before the arrival of the Magna Mater in Rome, the proposed subject of the illustration of April), there is no evidence to identify Servius's *Ad Aen.* 3.279 with the *ludi Apollinares.* On the contrary, Servius distinctly refers to *ludi* in honor of the Mother of the Gods and makes no mention of an enemy attack with arrows; even the proverb is different from that explained by Festus and by Servius in *Ad Aen.* 8.110.

Clearly, the accounts in Festus and Servius 3.279 are variants of the same mythical motif, as is the account related by Ammianus Marcellinus, 23.5.3. The original version of this theme matters little to my argument concerning the illustration of April in the Calendar of 354. What does matter is that Servius used the variant with an elderly mime in connection with the festival of the Magna Mater, and it is this festival that is illustrated in the fourth-century Calendar.

One final note: Ovid *Fasti* 3.38 specifies a *canus sacerdos* at the installation of

---

1. A. Otto, *Sprichwörter und sprichwörtlichen Redensarten der Römer* (Leipzig, 1890), pp. 317–318.

the Magna Mater in Rome. Does this refer to the myth? And does it perhaps elucidate the depiction of an elderly male figure in the illustration of April in the Calendar of 354?[2]

2. I would like to thank Professor Alan Cameron for bringing to my attention the issues raised by the passage of Servius concerning Roman etymology and legend.

General Index

In this Index, as throughout this study, the terms "the Calendar" and "the Calendar of 354" refer to the Calendar section of the Codex-Calendar of 354.

Index of Illustrated Subjects

Compositor: J. Jarrett Engineering, Inc.
      Text: 10/13 Palatino
   Display: Palatino
   Printer: Malloy Lithographing, Inc.
    Binder: Malloy Lithographing, Inc.